THE
HAMLYN
DICTIONARY
of
TWENTIETH CENTURY HISTORY

THE
HAMLYN
DICTIONARY
of
TWENTIETH
CENTURY HISTORY

John Buchanan Brown

HAMLYN

First published 1989 by
The Hamlyn Publishing Group Limited
Michelin House, 81 Fulham Road
London SW3 6RB

ISBN 0 600 56518 1

Typeset by J&L Composition Ltd, Filey, North Yorkshire

Printed in Great Britain by
William Collins and Sons

INTRODUCTION

Limitations of space confine this dictionary to a range of entries covering political history but necessarily excluding technical, scientific and medical advances during the twentieth century and, as regrettably, its cultural and artistic developments. Nevertheless, the dictionary provides a comprehensive survey of the people, places and events that have shaped the development of the world during our fascinating but turbulent era and should prove an absorbing guide for both the student and the interested general reader.

The period covered is from 1900 to 1988, updated where possible to the time of going to press (May 1989).

Among the sources consulted, particular acknowledgement should be made to *The Annual Register*, *The Chronicle of the 20th Century*, *The International Dictionary of 20th Century Biography* (Edward Vernoff & Rima Shore), *The New Columbia Encyclopedia*, *The Penguin Dictionary of Twentieth Century History* (Alan Palmer) and *Le Petit Robert 2 (Dictionnaire universel de noms propres)*, their information being updated from *The Independent*.

ABBREVIATIONS

AFL	American Federation of Labor
AFPFL	Anti-Fascist People's Freedom League
ANC	African National Congress
ANZUS	Australia, New Zealand and the United States
APRA	Popular American Revolutionary Alliance
BEF	British Expeditionary Force
BENELUX	Belgium, the Netherlands and Luxembourg
CDU	Christian Democratic Union
CIA	Central Intelligence Agency
CIGS	Chief of the Imperial General Staff
C-in-C	Commander in Chief
CIO	Congress of Industrial Organizations
COMECON	Council for Mutual Economic Assistance
CPP	Convention People's Party
EC	European Community
ECSC	European Coal and Steel Community
EEC	European Economic Community
EFTA	European Free Trade Association
ELF	Eritrean Liberation Front
EOKA	Revolutionary Organization of Cypriot Struggle
ETA	Basque Homeland and Liberty
EURATOM	European Atomic Energy Community
FAO	Food and Agriculture Organization
FFI	French Forces of the Interior
FFL	Free French Forces
FLN	National Liberation Front
FLQ	Quebec Liberation Front
FMLN	Farabundo Martí National Liberation Front
FNLA	National Front for the Liberation of Angola
FRELIMO	Mozambique Liberation Front

GATT	General Agreement on Tariffs and Trade
GDR	German Democratic Republic
GFR	German Federal Republic
ILO	International Labour Organization
IMF	International Monetary Fund
INLA	Irish National Liberation Army
IRA	Irish Republican Army
IWW	Industrial Workers of the World
KGB	Committee of State Security
MP	Member of Parliament
MPLA	Popular Movement for the Liberation of Angola
NASA	National Aeronautics and Space Administration
NATO	North Atlantic Treaty Organization
NEP	New Economic Policy
NHS	National Health Service
NKVD	People's Committee for Home Affairs
NRA	National Resistance Army
NTT	Nippon Telephone and Telegraph
OAPEC	Organization of Arab Petroleum Exporting Countries
OAS	Organization of American States
OAS	Secret Army Organization
OAU	Organization of African Unity
OEEC	Organization for European Economic Co-operation
OPEC	Organization of Petroleum Exporting Countries
OSS	Office of Strategic Services
PASOK	Panhellenic Socialist Movement
PLO	Palestine Liberation Organization
PNI	Indonesian Nationalist Party
PNP	People's National Party
PPP	People's Progressive Party
PRI	Institutional Revolutionary Party
RAF	Royal Air Force
RFC	Royal Flying Corps
RSA	Republic of South Africa
SA	Sturmabteilungen (Brown Shirts)
SALT	Strategic Arms Limitation Treaty

Abbreviations

SDLP	Social Democratic and Labour Party
SEATO	South East Asia Treaty Organization
SHAPE	Supreme Headquarters Allied Powers in Europe
SOE	Special Operations Executive
SPLA	Sudan People's Liberation Army
START	Strategic Arms Reduction Talks
SWAPO	South West Africa People's Organization
TGWU	Transport and General Workers Union
TUC	Trades Union Congress
UAP	United Australia Party
UAR	United Arab Republic
UDI	Unilateral Declaration of Independence
UN	United Nations
UNESCO	United Nations Educational Scientific and Cultural Organization
UNICEF	United Nations International Children's Emergency Fund
UNIP	United National Independence Party
UNITA	National Union for the Total Independence of Angola
USAAF	United States Army Air Force
USSR	Union of Soviet Socialist Republics
ZANU	Zimbabwe African National Union
ZAPU	Zimbabwe African People's Union
WHO	World Health Organization

A

Abd el-Krim, Muhammad ben (c1882–1963), Moroccan nationalist. He led a rising of Rif tribes and defeated the Spanish (1921) but was defeated (1926) by Franco-Spanish forces. He escaped from exile (1947) to Cairo.

Abdication crisis see **Edward VIII**

Abdul Hamid II (1842–1918), sultan of Turkey (1876–1909). He crushed the reformist Young Turk Movement and ruled absolutely. He encouraged Pan-Islamic movements and was responsible for the Armenian Massacres. In 1908 his attempt to counter the Young Turk Revolution failed and he was deposed. His employment of German instructors in the army and concessions to German business interests (Berlin-Baghdad Railway) drew Turkey to the side of the Central Powers in World War I.

Abdul Rahman, Tunku (1903–   ), Malaysian political leader. He was co-founder (1945) of the Malay National Organization (president, 1952–55). Strongly anti-Communist during the Emergency, he became chief minister (1955) and then first prime minister of the independent Federation of Malaya. In 1963 his proposed Federation of Malaysia was approved. He came out of political retirement (1970–88) to oppose Dr Mahathir Mohamad.

Abdullah Ibn Hussein (1882–1951), emir of Transjordan (1921–46) and king of Jordan (1946–51). The third son of Hussein Ibn Ali, king of Hejaz, he joined T. E. Lawrence during World War I. Following Ibn Saud's conquest of the Hejaz (1921), he was created emir of Transjordan by the British. In 1948, having joined the Arab-Israeli war, he annexed East Jerusalem and the West Bank. He was assassinated in Jerusalem in 1951.

Abyssinia see **Ethiopia**

Acheson, Dean Gooderham (1893–1971), US secretary of state (1949–53). He countered Soviet expansionism by economic aid and by regional defence pacts (NATO, ANZUS). His attempt to disassociate the United States from the Chiang Kai-shek regime and apparent breaches of security in his own department (see **Hiss, Alger**) forced his resignation. He remained a foreign policy spokesman for the Democrats and influenced the Kennedy administration (1961–63).

Aden see under **Yemen**

Adenauer, Konrad (1876–1967), German statesman. An influential member of the Catholic Centre Party in imperial Germany, he was mayor of Cologne during 1917–33. Chancellor of the German Federal Republic (1949–63), he also acted as foreign minister (1951–55) to negotiate a peace treaty with the western allies (1952) and recognition of West German sovereignty by the USSR (1955). He ensured German integration into a European framework by membership of NATO (1955) and of the EEC. To allow his Christian Democrats (CDU) to remain in a governing coalition with the Free Democrats in the wake of the *Der Spiegel* Affair, he himself resigned (1963). *Der Alte* – 'the Old Man' – restored German democracy and was a major European statesman in the immediate postwar period.

Afghanistan A republic of central Asia. Throughout the 19th century the focus of rivalry between the Russian and British empires, Afghanistan remained neutral in World War I and finally asserted its independence from British control in the Treaty of Rawalpindi (1921), which concluded the Third Afghan War (1919). The Emir Ammanallah declared himself king (1923), but his attempts to westernize his country caused resentment and he was deposed by his cousin, Nadir Shah. The latter (assassinated in 1933) was succeeded by his son, Muhammad Zahir Shah, who ruled until overthrown by an army coup in 1973. Muhammad Daud Khan (prime minister, 1953–63) became president of a republic but was overthrown and killed in a Soviet-backed coup and replaced by Hafizullah Amin. He, in turn, was killed by the KGB when Soviet forces invaded Afghanistan in December 1979 to buttress a communist takeover and set up Babrak Karmal in his place. Uncoordinated attacks by the mujahedin – supplied from camps in Iran and Pakistan and financed by the United States, Saudi Arabia and the Persian Gulf states – were met by ruthless air and ground attacks which devastated the country, killed thousands of non-combatants and forced some five million to take refuge in Iran and Pakistan, but failed to crush resistance. By 1988 the Soviet invaders had conceded defeat and, having suffered some 15,000 casualties, withdrew their forces by 15 February 1989. Despite their efforts to reach an accommodation with the mujahedin, they left the government of Dr Najibullah – who had replaced Karmal in 1986 – to face the onslaught of a deeply divided guerrilla force.

African National Congress A South African political movement founded in 1912 to promote the welfare of the black community, which united with the Indian community (1926) to work for a racially integrated nation. Under the presidency (1952–67) of Chief Luthuli it fought apartheid by non-violent means but, faced with ever more repressive government measures (the Congress itself was declared illegal in 1961), its military arm, Umkhonto we Sizwe ('The Sword of the Nation') was formed by Nelson Mandela to undertake acts of sabotage and reprisal. The ANC maintains offices throughout the world to enlist support and to organize pressure upon the South African government with the aim of ending apartheid and ultimately of introducing black majority rule.

Agadir Incident An attempt by Germany to challenge French interests in Morocco. On 1 July 1911 the German government sent the gunboat *Panther* to the Moroccan port of Agadir on the Atlantic coast in protest against the French military occupation of Fez and Meknes. The threat of a European war was averted when in November the French prime minister, Joseph Caillaux, ceded French territory in Africa to Germany in exchange for French freedom of action in Morocco.

Albania A republic on the Adriatic coast of Europe. Formerly part of the Ottoman Empire, it proclaimed its independence during the Balkan War of 1912, but in 1913 was forced by the great powers to cede territory to Serbia, Montenegro and Greece. A battleground during World War I, its independence was recognized in 1920. In 1922 Ahmed Zogu became prime minister. Driven out by a revolution in 1924, he returned in the following year as president and in 1928 declared himself king (as King Zog). In 1939 Mussolini invaded and absorbed the country. During World War II Britain supplied arms to the communist resistance led by Enver Hoxha who, in collaboration with Marshal Tito, liberated the country (1944) and took power in 1946. A policy of collaboration with Yugoslavia was followed until Tito's break with Stalin (1948), after which Albania pursued a strongly pro-Soviet Stalinist line. With the reconciliation of the Soviet Union and Yugoslavia (1961), Hoxha turned for assistance to China and Albania became unique as a European Maoist state. Chinese aid was abruptly ended in 1978 and, until his death in 1985, Hoxha isolated Albania under a repressive and anachronistically Stalinist regime. Since his death there have been some signs of relaxation.

Alexander, Harold Rupert Leofric George (1891–1969, Earl Alexander of Tunis), British soldier. He served on Western Front in World War I, commanded an operational brigade in India (1934–38), and the 1st Division BEF in France (1939–40). In 1942 he was sent to secure the retreat of British forces from Burma and in the same year replaced Auchinleck as C-in-C Middle East. With Montgomery as commander of the 8th Army, he drove the Axis forces from North Africa and subsequently commanded the Allied armies which invaded Sicily and

Italy and had entered Austria by the end of World War II. Earl Alexander was governor-general of Canada (1946–52) and served as minister of defence (1952–54).

Alfonso XIII (1886–1941), king of Spain (1902–31). From the begining of his reign there were anarchist outrages, accompanied by labour unrest and pressure for Catalan autonomy. Spain remained neutral in World War I, but royal prestige suffered from the defeats inflicted by Abd el-Krim. Having supported the right-wing policies of Primo de Rivera, when the latter fell from power Alfonso retired into exile (1931) without formally renouncing the throne.

Algeciras Conference A meeting of European powers held during January-March 1906. It reaffirmed Morocco's territorial integrity and also the rights of all nations to enjoy unrestricted commercial access, but granted the French and Spanish governments the power to police their respective zones.

Algeria A republic of North Africa. Occupied by France between 1830–37 and claimed as French territory in 1848, Algeria was heavily colonized throughout the 19th century. In 1900 it was granted a degree of autonomy but all political power and the benefits of agricultural and industrial development remained with the settlers. Islamic nationalism was slow to develop – the aim of the Muslim élites was assimilation with France – but obstruction by the French, the fall of France (1940) and the Allied landings (1942) encouraged ideas of independence. Despite promised reforms, there were uprisings in 1945 by the Muslim population which were savagely repressed. Militants from various independence movements set up a revolutionary committee and launched an insurrection in November 1954. Most nationalist groups rallied to the FLN which by 1956 controlled large areas of the countryside and had established urban guerrillas in the cities. Efforts to negotiate a ceasefire in an increasingly brutal war were thwarted when Ben Bella and four other FLN leaders were interned after their airliner was intercepted and diverted to Algiers. When French government policy inclined towards peace, the settlers rose in revolt and brought down the Fourth Republic (1958). De Gaulle returned to power, initially appearing to support the settlers' call for a 'French' Algeria, but in 1959 pronounced for self-determination and opened negotiations at Evian. A ceasefire with the FLN (1960) ran counter to French army opinion that military victory was in their grasp. Consequently in April 1960 a group of generals, led by Raoul Salan, attempted an unsuccessful coup. Nothing, however, could prevent the creation of an independent republic and, after referenda in

France (April 1962) and in Algeria (July 1962), independence was achieved.

Ben Bella was released and elected president (1963). He was supplanted (1965) by Colonel Houari Boumédienne who followed a generally hard line in his dealings with the West (expropriation of European interests, strongly anti-Israeli stance, support of terrorist organizations and backing for the Polisario Front) and created a repressive, single-party state. His government was faced with immense problems – the mass exodus of Europeans with their technical and administrative expertise and 10% or 1 million of the population killed in the war – but met the challenge and, thanks to the discovery of oil and natural gas in the Sahara, achieved a great measure of recovery. In 1978 Boumédienne died. His successor, Chadli Bendjedid, adopted a more conciliatory attitude towards the west and a less repressive internal policy. However, the country was beset by economic problems – a population explosion, high unemployment among the young and falling world prices for oil and natural gas – made worse by restrictions by France on the numbers of migrant workers it admitted. Resentment at a corrective austerity programme and discontent with the ruling FLN erupted into riots during 1988. When order had been restored, a referendum approved the president's plan to reform the constitution, but he faced opposition from Islamic fundamentalists and left-wingers alike to his policy of liberalizing economic and political structures.

Ali Khan, Liaquat   see Liaquat Ali Khan

Allenby, Edmund Henry Hynman   (1861–1936, Viscount Allenby), British soldier. He served in South Africa before and during the Boer War, and commanded the Cavalry Division BEF (1914) and the 3rd Army (1915–17) in France. After his transfer to Palestine (1917), his campaign, employing deception, air power, motorized forces and cavalry, and combining regular forces with T.E. Lawrence's Arab irregulars, defeated the Turks at Gaza, captured Jerusalem (9 December 1917), cleared Syria and took Damascus. His final victory at Megiddo (September 1918) forced the Turks to conclude an armistice at Mudros (30 October 1918). Created viscount in 1919, he served as high commissioner for Egypt and the Sudan (1919–25).

Allende Gossens, Dr Salvador   (1908–73), president of Chile 1970–73. Co-founder of the Chilean Socialist Party (1933), he was minister of health (1939–42) and president of the senate (1965–69). After three unsuccessful bids for the presidency, in 1970 he was elected by a narrow plurality and with communist support. His programme of nationalization and land reform attempted to give Chile a socialist economy, but brought inflation, stagnation and industrial unrest. Chile became the victim of US-Soviet intrigue until the military under General Pinochet and with the backing of the CIA staged the coup in which Allende met his death (1973).

Alliance for Progress An inter-American programme of economic assistance advanced by the United States at a conference at Punte del Este, Uruguay, in August 1961 mainly as a counterpoise to Cuban influence in Latin-America. The scheme was administered through the OAS and was used as an instrument of policy by Presidents Kennedy and Johnson.

Alto-Adige see **Trentino-Alto-Adige**

American Federation of Labor An organization of craft unions formed in 1886. It was strictly non-political and, under such leaders as Gompers and Meany, its more radical members tended to break away from time to time. In 1955 it merged with the Congress of Industrial Organizations to form the AFL-CIO.

Amin, Idi (*c*1925–), Ugandan political leader. As C-in-C of the Uganda army in 1971 he led a coup which overthrew Milton Obote. The expulsion of the Asian community (1972) reduced the country to economic chaos in which he ruled through terror, his victims including the archbishop of Uganda (1977), and hastened its disintegration. There were armed clashes with Kenyan and Tanzanian troops and in 1979 an invasion of Ugandan exiles with Tanzanian support overthrew Amin. He escaped to Libya.

Amnesty International see under **human rights**

Amritsar Massacre An incident in which an Indian crowd was fired on by British soldiers. In 1919 there were widespread disturbances in India when the Rowlatt Act was passed retaining wartime emergency powers to combat Gandhi's Civil Disobedience Campaign. In April 1919 General Reginald Dyer ordered troops in the Punjab city of Amritsar to open fire when rioters refused to disperse: 379 demonstrators were killed and some thousand wounded.

Andropov, Yuri Vladimirovich (1914–84), Soviet statesman. As ambassador to Hungary (1954–57) he played an integral role in suppressing the Hungarian Uprising (1956). Promoted to head the KGB in 1967, he succeeded Leonid Brezhnev as head of state on the latter's death. Mikhail Gorbachov was his protégé.

Anglo-French Agreement The convention of 1904, known as the 'Entente Cordiale', which ostensibly settled points at issue between the two countries in the Pacific and in Africa. The agreement had a far wider significance, however, drawing Britain and France together to meet the threat of German expansion.

Anglo-German Naval Agreement An accord (1935) by which Britain unilaterally agreed to relax the provisions of the Treaty of Versailles to allow Nazi Germany to build up its naval forces to 35% of those of the United Kingdom. The French felt a sense of betrayal and this appeasement further weakened Anglo-French unity.

Anglo-Russian Agreement A convention of 1907 which fixed the respective spheres of influence where the two Empires were in collision in Persia [Iran], Afghanistan and Tibet. As in the case of the Anglo-French Agreement three years before, this was less a settlement of disputes than a drawing together in the face of the perceived threat of German expansion.

Anglo-Soviet Trade Agreement (1921) see **Arcos Raid**

Angola A republic of southwest Africa. From the 15th century the Portuguese established coastal settlements, but the interior was not colonized until the late 19th century. In 1961 three separate nationalist organizations rose in revolt against Portuguese rule. After bitter fighting and the overthrow of Dr Caetano's regime in Portugal (1974) the new government granted Angolan independence (1975). The elections called for under the statute of independence were never held. Instead there was a struggle for power between the FNLA, which had originally operated out of Zaïre, the Zambia-based and Soviet-backed MPLA, and Jonas Savimbi's UNITA. In the event the MPLA, with Soviet tanks and Cuban troops successfully occupied most of the country and established a government. (A South African incursion aimed at nipping the new regime in the bud was hastily evacuated when the United States withdrew its support.) UNITA fought on, backed by South African regular units. These made repeated incursions from Namibia against SWAPO guerrillas based in Southern Angola. UNITA achieved a considerable degree of success with the help of South African heavy artillery and aircraft, but became a pawn in east-west politics. In December 1988 agreement was reached in New York for Cuban troops to withdraw in return for South African co-operation in implementing Namibian independence. Since neither side appeared ready completely to abandon its Angolan protégés, despite an MPLA offer of an amnesty (January 1989), there seemed no end to the civil war.

Anschluss The union of Austria with Germany. The integration of Austria in a Greater Germany had been the wish of the German-speaking majority in Austria after the fall of the Hapsburgs in 1918. The union was prohibited by the Treaty of Versailles, but the desire remained and grew in strength after Hitler (himself an Austrian) became German chancellor in 1933. Union came in 1938 when Hitler forced the Austrian chancellor, Kurt von Schuschnigg, to resign. His Nazi replacement, Artur Seyss-Inquart, invited the German army to invade, the Anschluss being confirmed by a plebiscite (10 April).

Antarctica The South Polar landmass which became the focus for scientific co-operation during the International Geophysical Year (1957–58). In 1959 the 22 signatories of the Antarctic Treaty pledged co-operation for scientific purposes and banned nuclear explosions and the dumping of radioactive waste there from 1961 to 1989, without prejudice to their often conflicting claims to sovereignty. In 1988 a minerals convention, laying down safeguards for potential exploitation, was opened for signature.

Anti-Comintern Pact An agreement concluded by Germany, Italy and Japan in 1936 which pledged its signatories to combat the Communist International. It led in 1940 to the inclusion of Japan within the original Rome-Berlin Axis.

Antonescu, Ion (1882–1946), Romanian soldier and dictator. He served in World War I and was appointed chief of staff (1933). His Iron Guard connections led to his dismissal and brief imprisonment, but King Carol recalled him as minister of defence (1938) and prime minister (1940). Having forced Carol to abdicate, Antonescu ruled in the name of Carol's son, Michael, supporting Hitler and committing the Romanian army to the Russian campaign. The German defeat enabled Michael to turn the tables. Antonescu was overthrown (1944), imprisoned and executed as a war criminal (1946).

ANZUS A mutual defence pact (1951) between Australia, New Zealand and the United States which was part of the US regional security policy for the Pacific. Similar treaties had been signed with the Philippines and were about to be signed with Japan. It is indicative of the greater independence of Commonwealth countries after World War II.

Apartheid A system of racial segregation and white South African dominance institutionalized by Daniel Malan and his successors following the 1948 electoral victory of the Nationalist Party. Non-whites were disenfranchised, forbidden to strike and oppressively controlled by Pass Laws, and their children's education was strictly segregated (1953). Mixed marriages were banned. The Group Areas Acts (1950–68), which designated specific areas for the races, caused great hardship by the uprooting of whole communities. Under the Bantu Self-Government Act

(1959) seven black African states were to be created as 'homelands'. Opposition was muzzled by the blanket provisions of the Suppression of Communism Act (1950) but has continued to grow within South Africa and enjoys worldwide support in the form of UN resolutions, boycotts of South African goods, economic sanctions, the outlawing of South Africans from international sport and the withdrawal of multinational companies from the Republic. In consequence there has been some relaxation of apartheid – pass laws were modified, the right to form trade unions and take strike action was granted, Asians and Coloureds (mixed race) were given limited political rights (1984) and mixed marriages became legal (1985). However this predictably caused a backlash among Afrikaaner extremists and failed to satisfy black aspirations for majority rule. See also **Transkei**.

Apollo missions see **space flight**

Arab League A confederation of Arab states, which following discussions held in Alexandria in 1944, was formally inaugurated in Cairo on 22 March 1945. Its original members (Egypt [expelled 1977], Iraq, Lebanon, Saudi Arabia, Syria, Transjordan [Jordan], Yemen, and a Palestinian representative) were joined by Libya (1951), Sudan (1956), Tunisia and Morocco (1958), Kuwait (1961), Algeria (1962), Yemen PDR (1968) and the United Arab Emirates (1971). It has been most effectively concerned with economic and cultural co-operation among Arab states. Its original role as mouthpiece for Palestinian rights has been largely taken over by the PLO.

Arafat, Yasir (1929–), president of the self-declared state of Palestine. Born in Gaza, he served in the Egyptian army during the Suez campaign. He joined the Al Fatah group within the PLO (c1957), becoming head of its military arm (1965) and PLO chairman (1969). Despite expulsion from Jordan (1971), Lebanon (1982) and Syria (1983), and factional struggles inspired by the ambitions of different Arab states to control it, Arafat remained head of the PLO. By renouncing terrorism and accepting the right of Israel to exist (1988), he swung world opinion against the continued denial of Palestinian rights.

Arcos Raid The search by police in 1927 of the premises of the official Soviet trade mission established in London under the Anglo-Soviet Trade Agreement (1921). In May 1927 the police were authorized to enter and search their offices for evidence of Soviet involvement in the General Strike. The British government then annulled the trade agreement, claiming that the Soviet trade mission had been involved in anti-British activities.

Argentina A South American republic which proclaimed its independence from Spain in 1810, only to fall into an anarchy of provincial rivalries. Military dictatorship in the 1880s and European immigration and investment (especially British) helped to create a prosperous economy. Political power rested with the landowners and the army, notwithstanding the emergence of the reformist radical presidents, Hipolito Irigoyen (1916–22 and 1928–30), and Roberto M. Ortiz (1938–42). The interests of the urban working class were ignored until Juan Perón came to power in a coup (1944) and was elected president with their support (1946). His regime suppressed political opposition and abrogated the 1853 constitution to enable Perón to be re-elected (1949). The death (1952) of his wife Eva, who was widely popular with the workers, began his decline, accentuated by growing economic crises and a breach with the Roman Catholic Church over the legalization of divorce (1955), and he fell from power in 1957. His supporters and left-wing movements unsettled the civilian governments of Presidents Frondizi (1958–62) and Illia (1963–66) and the military regimes with which they were interspersed. In 1973 Perón returned, but he was a dying man and in 1974 he was succeeded by his widow Isabel. She failed to control inflation, worsening economic conditions and the activities of left-wing guerrillas and was ousted by an army coup. From 1976 to 1981 Generals Videla and Viola attempted to solve the economic problem and to defeat the guerrillas. In the first they failed; in the second they succeeded – but only at the cost of grave violations of human rights. During the 'dirty war' thousands of men and women were abducted by the armed forces, tortured and done to death. In 1982 General Leopoldo Galtieri came to power and, to divert attention from the austerities of his solutions to Argentina's economic problems, invaded the Falkland Islands. The Argentine defeat led to the immediate replacement of Galtieri (later tried and imprisoned) and subsequently to the election (December 1983) of a civilian president, Raoul Alfonsin. He had to quell army revolts (1987 and 1988) in protest at his policy of bringing to justice the worst offenders in the 'dirty war' and, in January 1989, an apparent resurgence of left-wing violence. In the 1989 election he was defeated by the Peronist candidate.

arms control see **disarmament**

Armenian Massacres The mass murder during 1894–96 of the Christian minority in Armenia by the Ottoman Sultan, Abdul Hamid II, posing as the defender of Islam. In 1915–16 even more brutal massacres of the Armenians were conducted by the Turkish Army when nearly two million men, women and children were deported to Syria, about 600,000 being slaughtered or dying during the journey.

Armstrong, Neil (1930–), US astronaut, the first man to set foot on the moon. He served in Korea, joined the US space programme and made his moon landing in *Apollo 11* on 21 July 1969.

Arnold, Henry Harley (1886–1950), US Air Force officer. He graduated from West Point (1907) and was associated with the development of military aviation from 1911, becoming chief of the Air Corps (1938) and deputy chief of Staff Air (1940). During 1941–45 he was the presiding genius of US air power as chief of the United States Army Air Force (USAAF).

Asquith, Herbert Henry (1852–1928, Earl of Oxford and Asquith), British statesman. A barrister and a Liberal MP (1886–1918 and 1920–24), he was home secretary (1892–95) and then chancellor of the exchequer (1905–08) under Campbell-Bannerman, whom he succeeded as prime minister. While introducing wide social reforms, including pensions (1908) and unemployment insurance (1911), he faced the constitutional crisis of the 'People's Budget' of 1909 – resolved by the Parliament Act (1911) – and the threat of civil war in Ireland following the introduction of the Home Rule Bill (1912) and the suffragette agitation (see **women's rights**). In 1915 he re-formed the government as a coalition with the Conservatives, with whom Lloyd George plotted and unseated him (1916). He remained leader of the Liberal Party until 1926.

Assad, Hafez (1930–), Syrian political leader. He joined the Ba'ath Party (1955), was commissioned as a pilot (1955), rising through plots and coups to command the air force (1963). After internal Ba'athist struggles he emerged as minister of defence (1966) and, following a successful coup, as president (1970). He ruthlessly maintained himself in power, crushing a revolt by the Muslim Brotherhood (1982) in which most of the city of Hama was destroyed and thousands of its inhabitants killed.

Atlantic Charter The declaration issued after the meeting between Churchill and Roosevelt off Newfoundland in August 1941 and later endorsed by the USSR and the 14 other nations at war with the Axis Powers. The United States (still at peace) supported publicly the war aims of the Allies – no territorial aggrandizement, self-determination and the disarmament of the aggressor nations in the event of an Allied victory.

atom bomb see **Manhattan Project**

Attlee, Clement Richard (1883–1967, Earl Attlee), British statesman, under whom the Welfare State was created. A barrister, he lived as a social worker in the East End of London before serving throughout

World War I. Mayor of Stepney (1919–20) and MP (1922–55), he was a junior minister in Ramsay MacDonald's Labour government (1930–31) but refused to join the National Government of 1931. Elected leader of the Labour Party (1935), during the Spanish Civil War he warmly supported the Republic, encouraging volunteers to join the International Brigades. In 1940 he joined Churchill's government as Lord Privy Seal and was appointed deputy prime minister and dominions secretary (1942). After his party's landslide victory in 1945, as prime minister he initiated a stream of legislation which transformed the economy, introduced the National Health Service and brought independence to India and Pakistan. Returned to power with a majority of five (1950), he was defeated when he went to the country again in 1951. In 1955 he was succeeded by Hugh Gaitskell as Labour leader.

Auchinleck, Sir Claude John Eyre (1884–1981), British soldier. Commissioned in the Indian army (1904), he served in World War I and in 1940 commanded the British forces sent to Norway. In 1941 he was appointed C-in-C India, but in the same year exchanged commands with the C-in-C Middle East, Wavell. In November 1941 he cleared the Axis forces from Cyrenaica, but Rommel's counter-attack drove the 8th Army back to the Egyptian frontier. Auchinleck took personal command and halted the German offensive at the first Battle of El Alamein. He never enjoyed the confidence of Churchill and, having built up his forces to resume the offensive, was replaced in August 1942 by General Alexander. In 1943 he was appointed C-in-C India and in 1947 efficiently and tactfully divided the old Indian Army between the new states of India and Pakistan.

Auriol, Vincent (1884–1966), French statesman. A lawyer and socialist, he was finance minister in Léon Blum's Popular Front government (1936) and minister of justice in Camille Chautemps' cabinet (1937). He rallied to de Gaulle in London (1943) and after the liberation of France presided over the two assemblies. As first president of the Fourth Republic (1947–54), he used his moderating influence to help keep the balance between the extremes of Communism and Gaullism.

Australia Independent Commonwealth nation in the southern hemisphere. First used as a penal settlement, by the end of the 19th century it comprised six self-governing colonies which agreed to a federal constitution embodied in the Australian Commonwealth Act (1900) and effective from 1 January 1901. In 1911 the Northern Territories joined the federation. Early federal governments set a pattern for liberal social legislation with votes for women (1902), old-age pensions (1909) and maternity benefits (1912), but rigidly enforced a 'White Australia' policy on immigration. Australian units served in the Boer War and in World War I, the prime minister, William Hughes, was committed to the Allied cause in which Australians won an unrivalled reputation for gallantry on the Western Front, in Palestine and especially at Gallipoli. The flourishing Australian economy, based on agriculture (grain and wool) and mining, shared the world-wide slump in the 1930s, to the point at which unemployment reached 25% of the working population, but had recovered by the outbreak of World War II. In 1939 Robert Menzies succeeded to the leadership of the United Australia (later Liberal) Party and to the premiership on the death of Joseph Lyons. His commitment to the Allied war effort made him neglect domestic politics and in 1941 his party was defeated and the Labour government of John Curtin succeeded. In December 1941 Japan entered the war and brought a radical change to Australian orientations. Having faced the threat of Japanese attack and bearing the brunt of the Allied counter-offensive in the southwest Pacific, postwar Australia emerged as a world power and, more specifically, as a Pacific power, its interests more closely aligned with those of the United States. Australian troops fought in Korea, in 1951 the country joined the ANZUS pact and in 1966 sent troops to Vietnam. Large-scale immigration from southern Europe (Italy, Greece, Yugoslavia) tended to weaken the British connection and the focus of Australian trade shifted following the adhesion of Britain to the EEC and the economic expansion of Japan. This was recognized by the Australia Bill (1986) which severed the last constitutional ties between Australia and Britain, although – despite a strong movement in favour of a republic – the link with the crown was still preserved.

Austria A republic of central Europe. It came into existence on 12 November 1918 with the socialist Karl Renner as head of a provisional government and subsequently the country's first chancellor (1919–20). Pan-German sentiment sought unification with republican Germany, but this was forbidden under the Versailles Treaty. Austria, badly hit by the depression, was bitterly divided between the right-wing rural voter and the left-wing urban, and especially Viennese, industrial worker, and private armies formed by extremists on both sides clashed. The chancellor, Engelbert Dollfuss, a Christian Democrat, created a corporate state against which the left rose in rebellion (1934). They were suppressed by the army, but Dollfuss was assassinated during an unsuccessful coup by the Austrian Nazis, whose party he had suppressed (1933). His successor, Kurt Schuschnigg, came under increasing pressure from Hitler who, in 1938 forced upon him the Anschluss by which the Austria was absorbed into a greater Germany.

Following the German defeat in 1945, Austria was occupied by the four Allies who divided the country into separate zones. Although they recognized Austrian independence, their disagreements delayed signature of the Austrian State Treaty, ending the occupation, until 1955. In the meantime a provisional government had been formed under Karl Renner who was elected first president of the new republic in December 1945. Successive governments worked to build up domestic prosperity and to employ Austrian neutralism in the field of international mediation – Vienna becoming an important international conference centre – until the election to the presidency of Kurt Waldheim (1986) reopened a past which Austrians had endeavoured to bury for good.

Austria-Hungary   A monarchy of central Europe comprising the empire of Austria, the kingdom of Hungary and various dependent territories, established in 1867. German and Magyar were the official languages; there were separate parliaments, but a unified foreign policy. However, minorities within both halves of the so-called Dual Monarchy continued to undermine the old multinational Hapsburg Empire. To counter pan-Slavism Austria-Hungary risked war to annex Bosnia-Hercegovina (1908) and, after the murder of the Archduke Franz Ferdinand at Sarajevo, its ultimatum to Serbia precipitated World War I. This proved fatal to the Dual Monarchy. On the death of Franz Josef (1916), his successor Charles I approached the Allies, but his peace moves were rebuffed (1917). In October 1918 Charles issued a federal constitution, but both Hungary and Czechoslovakia declared their independence and after signature of an armistice (11 November 1918) he abdicated and went into exile in Switzerland.

Austrian State Treaty   The agreement (signed in 1955) which ended military occupation by the four signatories (France, Britain, the United States and the USSR) and restored full sovereignty to the Austrian Republic. The country was pledged to neutrality and to the payment of heavy reparations to the Soviet Union.

Awami League   A moderate socialist political party formed in Pakistan in 1949 in opposition to the Muslim League. In 1953, as the Awami People's League under the leadership of Sheikh Mujibur Rahman, it demanded greater autonomy for East Pakistan and became the ruling political party when the latter gained its independence in 1971 as Bangladesh.

Axis powers   The term used to designate the coalition led by Germany,

Italy, Japan and their allies in World War II, taking its name from the Rome-Berlin 'Axis' of the 1936 alliance between Nazi Germany and Fascist Italy.

Ayub Khan, Muhammad (1907–74), Pakistani soldier and statesman. Commissioned in the Indian Army (1928), he served in the Burma campaign (1942–45) and after independence was C-in-C East Pakistan (Bangladesh) before becoming C-in-C of the Pakistan army (1951). He proclaimed martial law and assumed presidential powers in 1958 (confirmed by referendum, 1960), introducing electoral changes, land reform and economic development. Although he defeated Jinnah's daughter Fatimah in an election for president (1965), his prestige was irremediably damaged by the defeat of Pakistan by India and after widespread unrest – especially in East Pakistan – he resigned power to General Yaha Khan.

Azaña y Diaz, Manuel (1880–1940), Spanish political leader. Minister of war and later prime minister (1931–33) in President Zamora's first republican government, he pursued a strongly socialist and anticlerical policy in the reform of education and a purge of the officer corps. He was compelled to resign in 1933 over the forcible suppression of anarchist agitation, but was elected president in 1936, with the support of the Popular Front. A mere figurehead, he fled to France on the fall of the republic (1939) and died in exile.

Azikiwe, Benjamin Nnamdi (1904–), Nigerian statesman. A newspaper owner who from 1937 engaged in nationalist politics (leading a general strike in 1945), he became prime minister of Eastern Nigeria (1954–59). He was governor-general (1960) and first president of the Republic of Nigeria (1963–66), but was ousted by a military coup and retired from public life.

B

Ba'ath Socialist Party A pan-Arab political movement founded in Syria (1952), it became the ruling party in both Syria and Iraq. There was bitter factionalism within the Syrian party and deep division between it and the party in Iraq, while its secularism exposed it to the hostility of Islamic fundamentalists such as the Muslim Brotherhood.

Badoglio, Pietro (1871–1956), Italian soldier. Chief-of-staff (1919–21, 1925–28, and 1936–40) and governor of Libya (1928–33), he commanded the Italian forces in Ethiopia (1935–36). Dismissed by Mussolini in 1940 because of his opposition, he was recalled by King Victor Emmanuel to negotiate the Italian armistice (1943).

Baghdad Pact see **Central Treaty Organization**

Baldwin, Stanley (1867–1947, Earl Baldwin of Bewdley), British statesman. A Conservative MP from 1908, he became president of the Board of Trade (1921) and chancellor of the exchequer (1922–23). He succeeded Bonar Law as prime minister in 1923, subsequently holding office during 1924–29 and 1935–37. He broke the General Strike, ably handled the crisis of Edward VIII's abdication, but showed reluctance to rearm in the face of Hitler's aggressive policies.

Balewa, Alhaji Sir Abubakar Tafawa (1912–66), Nigerian statesman. A Hausa, he was chief minister in the pre-independence Legislative Council (1957) and became first prime minister of independent Nigeria (1960), but fell victim to tribal rivalry, being assassinated in a coup led by Ibo officers.

Balfour, Arthur James (1848–1930, Earl Balfour), British statesman. A Conservative MP (1874–1905, 1906–22), he succeeded his uncle Lord Salisbury as prime minister in 1902. The Conservatives' split over Tariff Reform lost them the 1906 election, but Balfour remained their leader until 1911. During World War I he was foreign secretary (1916–19) and played an important part in the postwar settlement.

Balfour Declaration The pledge made by the British foreign secretary, Arthur Balfour, on 2 November 1917, that Britain would support a Jewish national home in Palestine provided that the rights of the non-Jewish communities there were safeguarded and that Jewish rights and status in other countries were not compromised.

Balkan Entente see **Balkan Pact**

Balkan League The alliance formed in 1912 by Serbia and Bulgaria (later joined by Greece and Montenegro) to plan military action against the Turks and divide their European territories in the event of victory.

Balkan Pact 1 A non-aggression treaty guaranteeing existing frontiers signed in 1934 by Yugoslavia, Romania, Greece and Turkey who set up a permanent council which held regular meetings, until the 'Little Entente' crumbled in 1940 in the face of German aggression. Bulgaria was invited but declined to join, since it did not accept the existing frontiers of Macedonia. 2 A pact providing for mutual assistance in the event of an attack on any one party signed by Yugoslavia, Turkey and Greece in 1954. The Cyprus problem and Graeco-Turkish tensions soon made it a dead letter.

Balkan Wars The two military conflicts in southeastern Europe in 1912–13. In the first, short war (1912) the Balkan League drove the Turks from their European possessions and confirmed the independence of Albania. The second (1913) began when the victors disputed the spoils and the Bulgarians attacked the Serbs and the Greeks. With Turkish and Romanian help Bulgaria was defeated, ceding territory to Turkey and Romania and losing Thrace and Macedonia to Serbia and Greece.

Baltic republics The name given to Estonia, Latvia and Lithuania collectively.

Banda, Dr Hastings Kamuzu (c1905–), president of Malawi. A qualified doctor, he returned to Nyasaland (1958) to lead the Malawi National Congress in opposition to the Central African Federation and suffered arrest and imprisonment. He was appointed prime minister in 1963 when self-government was granted. On achieving independence in 1964 Nyasaland took the name of Malawi and Dr Banda was elected its first president in 1966, making himself president for life in 1971. An autocrat who repressed all opposition to his rule, he remained essentially a pragmatist in foreign relations, while at home he developed the agricultural prosperity of the peasant communities from which he himself came.

Bandaranaike, Sirimavo (1916–), Sri Lankan political leader. She succeeded her husband, S.W.R.D. Bandaranaike (1959), and led the Sri Lanka Freedom Party to electoral victory, becoming the world's first woman prime minister (1960–65). She returned to power (1970) and continued her husband's socialist policies. In 1972 she introduced a new constitution and renamed Ceylon the Republic of Sri Lanka, but her pro-Sinhalese policy alienated the Tamil minority and her high-handed methods brought electoral defeat (1977). In 1980 she was disenfranchised and deprived of her parliamentary seat for electoral irregularities, but returned to run unsuccessfully for president in 1988.

Bandaranaike, Solomon West Ridgeway Dias (1899–1959), Sri Lankan political leader. A barrister and leader of the Ceylon National Congress, after his country achieved independence he became minister of health (1948–51). He founded and led the Sri Lanka Freedom Party to victory in 1956. As prime minister he pursued policies which were neutralist and socialist and favoured the Sinhalese at the expense of the Tamils. He was assassinated by a Buddhist monk (1959).

Bandung Conference A meeting of states in Indonesia in 1955 organized by President Sukarno. Its aim was to establish an area of peace in Asia and Africa by drawing together nations in a non-alignment and neutralism in the Cold War and in opposition to colonial oppression.

Bangladesh A republic of southern Asia. After Indian independence (1947) East Bengal became East Pakistan. In 1970 popular discontent at the fact that the province with over half the population and providing two-thirds of the state's foreign income should fail to receive its due share from a government seated in West Pakistan gave the Awami People's League a landslide victory. The president of Pakistan, Yaha Khan, met demands for autonomy by postponing opening the assembly. The League called a general strike, refused to pay taxes and declared Bangladesh independent. Yaha Khan imprisoned the League's leader, Mujibur Rahman, and sent in the army. The brutal civil war which left one million Bangladeshi dead and sent a further ten million as refugees to India ended only when Indian forces defeated the Pakistani army. In January 1972 Sheikh Mujibur Rahman was released, being confirmed in power by the 1973 elections, but his incompetence, tyranny and corruption brought his overthrow and murder in a 1975 army coup, the leader of which was himself assassinated in November of that year. After a period of civilian rule Major-General Zia Rahman became president in 1977. He made cautious attempts to return to parliamentary government, but was assassinated by mutinous troops in 1981, his successor being overthrown by an army coup in 1982. This brought to power General Mohammed Hossain Ershad who as president held the country together despite natural disasters (the cyclone of 1985 and the disastrous floods of 1988) and the endemic problems of inflation, a population explosion and political unrest.

Bao-Dai (regnal name of Nguyen Vinh Thuy, 1913–), emperor of Annam 1925–45. He ruled Annam as a French protectorate, proclaiming its independence (1945). When the Republic of Vietnam was formed he became its head of state (1949), but after the French defeat and partition of the country, he was ousted by his prime minister, Ngo Dinh Diem, and went into exile.

Baring, Evelyn (1841–1917, 1st Earl of Cromer), British administrator. As British agent in Egypt (1883–1907) he was virtually the country's ruler, reforming finances, administration, communications and agriculture, and establishing the Anglo-Egyptian government of the Sudan.

Baruch, Bernard Manes (1870–1965), US financier and presidential adviser. Chairman of the War Industries Board (1918–19) in World War I, during World War II he acted as special adviser to James F. Byrnes. He was also the personal friend and adviser of Sir Winston Churchill.

Barzani, Mustafa al- (1903–79), Kurdish leader. He commanded the armed forces of the Kurdish republic (1945) until driven into exile by Iraqi troops. He returned (1958) and led an uprising in support of autonomy (1961), but was finally defeated by Saddam Hussein and died in exile in the United States.

Basic Treaty, The An agreement negotiated by Chancellor Willy Brandt as part of his *Ostpolitik* in 1972. It regulates relations between the German Federal Republic and the German Democratic Republic.

Batista y Zalvidar, Fulgencio (1901–73), Cuban political leader. He took part in the military coups of 1933. President Grau San Martín promoted him chief of staff and he became the effective ruler of the country, with his own three-year plan of social and economic reform. In 1940 he was elected president. Prior to the 1952 elections, in which he was a candidate, he took power in a coup, confirming his presidency by fraudulent elections (1954). The armed rising led by Fidel Castro against his oppressive and corrupt regime eventually drove him out of the country (1959).

Batlle y Ordóñez, José (1856–1929), Uruguayan statesman. As president of Uruguay (1903–07 and 1911–15), he ended anarchy and civil war (1904), introduced programmes of political and social reform, played a key role in framing the 1917 constitution and was a major influence in political life.

Battenberg see **Mountbatten**

Bay of Pigs incident see under **Cuba**

Beatty, David (1871–1936, Earl Beatty), British naval officer. He commanded the battle cruiser squadron at the Helgoland Bight (1914), Dogger Bank (1915) and Jutland (1916), succeeding Jellicoe in command of the grand fleet (1916).

Beck, Ludwig (1880–1944), German soldier. He served on the German general staff in World War I, becoming its effective chief by 1933. In 1938 he resigned in protest against the planned invasion of Czechoslovakia and his opposition to Hitler cost him his life after the failure of the July Conspiracy in 1944.

Begin, Menachem (1913–), Israeli political leader. He made his way to Palestine in 1942 where he joined Irgun Zvai Leumi. Elected to the Israeli parliament (1948), he held ministerial office (1967–70). He was leader of the Likud Party from 1970 and became prime minister after the 1977 elections. He continued the policy of massive retaliation against the Palestine Liberation Organization. In 1979 he accepted President Sadat's initiative. Peace with Egypt enabled Israel to launch a full-scale invasion of Lebanon in 1982. However, apparent Israeli connivance at the massacres of Palestinian refugees led to Begin's resignation and retirement in 1983.

Belgian Congo see under **Zaïre**

Belgium A constitutional monarchy of northwestern Europe. Industrial and colonial expansion during the 19th century was accompanied by industrial unrest and the rise of socialist parties. In both world wars Germany, despite guarantees of neutrality, invaded and occupied Belgium. The part played by King Leopold III during World War II aroused controversy as did the grant of independence to the Belgian Congo (Zaïre), but the most serious domestic issue was that of language and the bitter divisions between French- and Flemish-speakers. This was in part resolved by the 1971 constitution dividing the country into three semi-autonomous regions. Despite such internal divisions Belgium has consistently worked towards European unity. Its capital, Brussels, houses the headquarters of the EEC, NATO and SHAPE.

Belgrade Conference see **Helsinki Agreement**

Belize A republic of Central America and a member of the Commonwealth (formerly British Honduras). Settlements by British loggers were established in the 17th century, resisting all efforts to dislodge them by Spain which in 1798 recognized the British colony. Guatemala has constantly laid claim to Belize and a British force was brought in to protect the new republic in 1981.

Ben Bella, Muhammad Ahmed (1916–), Algerian political leader. He led a terrorist group within the Algerian nationalist movement (1947). Imprisoned by the French, he escaped to Cairo and helped to found the FLN which he directed from 1952 to 1956 when he was again captured by the French. Released under the Evian Agreements, he became prime minister (1962) and president (1963) of an independent Algeria, but was overthrown by Colonel Boumédienne and kept under house arrest (1965–79). On his release he went into exile.

Benelux The economic association of Belgium, the Netherlands and Luxembourg which progressed from a customs union (1 January 1948) to an agreement (signed in 1958 and effective from 1960) for the free movement of workers, capital and services within the three countries.

Beneš, Edvard (1884–1948), Czechoslovak statesman. During World War I he and Tomáš Masaryk persuaded the Allies to grant Czech independence in a postwar settlement. He served as foreign minister (1918–35), as representative at the Paris Conference and architect of the Little Entente (see **Balkan Pacts**). He succeeded Masaryk as president in 1935, resigning in 1938 after the Munich Agreement to become president of the Czech government in exile (1940). Confirmed in office in the free elections held in 1946, he retired after the communist coup in 1948 and died soon afterwards.

Ben-Gurion, David (1886–1973), Israeli statesman. Having emigrated to Palestine in 1906, he served with the British in World War I. He became an active socialist as secretary-general of Histadrut (1921) and then of Mapai (1930). He was subsequently chairman of the Jewish Agency (1935–48) and one of the founders of Haganah. Prime minister of Israel (1948–53, 1955–63), he remained active in politics and in 1965 led the faction of Mapai which was critical of the policies of Golda Meir.

Bennett, Richard Bedford (1870–1947, Viscount Bennett), Canadian statesman, was prime minister (1930–35). A champion of Imperial Preference, his was the moving spirit at the Ottawa Conference (1932) over which he presided. However, his centralizing policies and the effects of the Depression led to his defeat by Mackenzie King's Liberals in 1935. Bennett remained leader of the opposition until he retired in 1938.

Beria, Lavrenti Pavlovich (1899–1953), Soviet commissar and security chief. Stalin promoted him from first secretary of the Georgian Communist Party to head of the NKVD (1938), commissar and later minister for internal affairs (1942). After Stalin's death (1953) he became first deputy premier, but his colleagues, who feared him and suspected that he had hastened Stalin's death with a view to succeeding him, caused Beria to be rapidly tried and executed in December 1953.

Berlin airlift The transport of supplies organized during June 1948–September 1949 by the western allies in order to bring fuel and food into their occupation zones of Berlin in a successful effort to break the Soviet land blockade of the city.

Berlin–Baghdad Railway In line with the increasingly important role German commercial and government interests were playing in Ottoman Turkey, in 1899 a German consortium was granted the concession to build a railway from the Bosphorus to the Persian Gulf. This aroused fears of German encroachment and led Russia and Britain to settle their differences in the Anglo-Russian Agreement (1907).

Berlin Wall The fortified barrier separating West Berlin from East Berlin and East Germany. The Communist authorities sealed the border between the German Federal and Democratic Republics after the workers' uprising in East Berlin in 1953 and the flight of thousands of Germans to the west. A wall was built in Berlin between the two zones in 1961 when other measures to stem the flow of refugees proved ineffective.

Betancourt, Romulo (1908–81), Venezuelan statesman. The founder of the Democratic Action Party, Betancourt came to power in 1945 in a military coup. He instituted social and economic reforms and obtained for Venezuela 50% of oil company profits. Forced into exile after the military coup of 1948, he returned as president (1958–64).

Bethmann-Hollweg, Theobald von (1856–1921), German statesman, became chancellor in succession to von Bülow (1909). His domestic reforms were liberal, but Kaiser Wilhelm II and the German general staff nullified his efforts to preserve European peace. During World War I his powers were gradually reduced and he was forced to resign in 1917.

Bevan, Aneurin (1897-1960), British politician. The spokesman for the south Wales miners in the General Strike (1926), as MP for Ebbw Vale (1929-60) he became an outstanding orator. As minister of health (1945-51) he was responsible for the introduction of the National Health Service. He resigned (April 1951) three months after becoming minister of labour in protest at the imposition of charges in the health service. He led the Bevanite faction of the Labour party in opposition to Hugh Gaitskell (1951-57), becoming deputy leader of the party (1959).

Beveridge, William Henry (1879-1963, 1st Baron), British civil servant and economist. The report which he prepared for the government in 1942, *Social Insurance and Allied Services*, 'the Beveridge Report', provided the basis of the Labour party's postwar social legislation – the National Health Service, planned public spending, control of private investment and full employment.

Bevin, Ernest (1881-1951), British statesman and trade union leader. In 1911 he became secretary of the Dockers' Union and spent ten years amalgamating it with some 50 smaller unions to form the TGWU, of which he became general secretary (1921). A leading member of the General Council of the TUC (1925-40), he was an outstanding minister of labour in World War II. As foreign secretary in the Labour government (1948-51), he resisted the USSR as strongly as he had resisted the Communists in the trade unions. He ensured prompt acceptance of the Marshall Plan and helped create NATO (1949), but avoided closer involvement with Europe because of his strong feeling for the Commonwealth. He initiated the Colombo Plan, and his resistance to Jewish claims in Palestine earned him hostility both at home and in the United States. He remained foreign secretary until within five weeks of his death.

Bhutto, Zulfikar Ali (1928-79), Pakistani political leader. A barrister, he held various office under Muhammad Ayub Khan and as foreign minister (1963-66) sought Chinese help against India. His People's Party won a majority of seats in West Pakistan and in 1971 Bhutto became Pakistan's first non-military president. In 1973 his new constitution transferred executive authority to the prime minister from the president, and Bhutto resigned the latter office in order to become prime minister, but allegations of vote-rigging in the 1977 elections caused widespread rioting and army intervention. Bhutto was deposed, arrested for conspiracy to murder (1977), tried and condemned to death (1978), and hanged on 4 April 1979.

His daughter, **Benazir Bhutto**, imprisoned and exiled after his execution, returned in 1986 to lead the Pakistan People's Party against the regime and to win the 1988 elections after Mohammad Zia's death. In November 1988 she became the first woman prime minister of a Muslim country.

Biafra A secessionist republic formed from the predominately Ibo Eastern Region of Nigeria. Following the massacre of Ibo traders in the Hausa Northern Region in September 1966, on 30 May 1967 the governor of the Eastern Region, Colonel Ojukwu, declared the independence of the so-called Republic of Biafra. In July the president of Nigeria, General Gowon, sent in the army to reabsorb the Eastern Region into the Federation of Nigeria. The rebellion ended on 15 January 1970 after over one million Ibos had died of disease and starvation.

Bidault, Georges (1899-1983), French political leader. A resistance leader in World War II, he was prime minister (1949-50) and several times foreign minister. He welcomed de Gaulle's return to power, but broke with the general over his policy in Algeria. He joined the OAS (1962) and, it was claimed, directed it from his exile in Brazil.

Black and Tans   A special force recruited in 1920 to asssist the Royal Irish Constabulary during the time of unrest in Ireland and so-called from their green-black caps and khaki uniforms. They were brutal and indisciplined and as disliked and despised by the police and army as they were hated by the country at large.

Black Hand   A secret society active in the Serbian army (1911) and aiming to liberate Serbs under Austro-Hungarian and Turkish rule. It was able to influence Serbian policy during the Balkan Wars and trained and despatched the terrorists who murdered the Archduke Franz Ferdinand at Sarajevo (1914). The Serbian authorities suppressed the movement and executed its leaders (1917) on charges of plotting the murder of the Prince Regent.

Black September   A Palestinian terrorist group formed by Abu Nidal and named after the suppression of the PLO by the Jordanians in 1970. It was responsible for assassinations, hijackings and bomb outrages, the most notorious being the murders of 11 Israeli athletes at the Munich Olympic Games (1972).

Bloody Sunday 1   The clash between police and demonstrators in Trafalgar Square on 13 November 1887. Two people were killed when Life Guards cleared the square. **2** The incident which provoked the Russian Revolution of 1905 when, on 22 January 1905, troops opened fire on a peaceful procession making its way to the Winter Palace in St Petersburg (Leningrad) with a petition to the tsar. Over a hundred people were killed. **3** The events of 30 January 1970 when troops opened fire on Nationalist demonstrators in Londonderry: 13 people were killed.

Blucher, Vasily Konstantinovich   (1889-1937), Soviet soldier. He joined the Bolsheviks (1916) and rose to high command in the Red Army. On his return from acting as military adviser to the Kuomintang he was made C-in-C of far eastern forces. Promoted marshal in 1936, he fell victim to Stalin's Great Purge. He was rehabilitated in 1956.

Blum, Léon   (1872-1950), French statesman. A cabinet secretary during World War I, he drew up the French Socialist Party programme (1919) and as head of that party led the Popular Front government (1936-38). Despite its social reforms it failed to satisfy its radical supporters who were bitterly disappointed by its failure to intervene in the Civil War in Spain. Arraigned by the Vichy régime at Riom, he was deported by the Germans to Buchenwald. He survived to become prime minister (1946-47) and to help draw up the constitution of the Fourth Republic.

Bock, Fedor von   (1880-1945), German soldier. He led the German armies in the occupation of Austria (1938), and the invasions of Poland

(1939) and France (1940), but failed to take Moscow (1941). He was finally dismissed for his failure at Stalingrad (1942).

Boer War The culmination of long years of hostility between Boers and British settlers in South Africa. The Boers were initially successful, defeating British forces and laying siege to the garrisons at Mafeking and Ladysmith (1899). British reinforcements defeated them in the field. Their capital, Pretoria, was captured on 5 June 1900 and their president, Paulus Kruger, fled. There followed an increasingly bitter guerrilla war between British mobile columns and Boer commandos until peace was concluded by the Treaty of Veereeniging in May 1902.

Bokassa, Jean Bedel (1921-), African military leader. Appointed C-in-C (1960) of the forces of the newly created Central African Republic, he overthrew the civilian government (1966) and ruled with increasingly capricious and repressive absolutism, crowning himself emperor (1977). His brutality embarrassed the French government which, in 1979, in his absence, backed a coup which reinstated the former president David Dacko. Sentenced to death in absentia (1980), in 1988 Bokassa returned from exile in France to stand trial. His death sentence was commuted to life imprisonment.

Bolivia A republic of South America. In 1903 it was forced to cede the Acre River region to Brazil after years of fighting, and the Chaco area to Paraguay after the Chaco War (1932-35). In a country constantly bedevilled by army coups, it was only the high price of Bolivian tin and wolfram during World War II which enabled a civilian government to embark upon an effective programme of social and economic reform. The fall in world prices halted this programme and reintroduced a period of political instability characterized by military coups, abortive guerrilla movements (see **Guevara, Ernesto [Che]**), and by the increasing influence of the cocaine barons.

Bolsheviks (Russian *bolsheviki*, 'the majority'), The name adopted by Lenin's radical faction of the Russian Social Democrat Workers' Party when they obtained a temporary majority on the party's executive (1903). In 1912 the Bolsheviks established a separate Central Committee, thus effectively cutting themselves off from the Social Democrats, and directed the Revolution of October 1917. Until 1952 'Bolshevik' formed part of the official name of the Soviet Communist Party.

Borden, Sir Robert Laird (1854-1937), Canadian statesman. As prime minister (1911-20) he organized the Canadian war effort in World War I, when nearly 500,000 volunteers served overseas, and succeeded in making the self-governing dominions of the Commonwealth equal partners with Britain in foreign affairs.

Borneo see **Indonesia, Malaysia**

Bose, Subhas Chandra (1897–1945), Indian nationalist and leader of the left wing of the Indian National Congress. Imprisoned for his Axis sympathies in World War II, he escaped to Germany (1941). He later joined the Japanese to establish an Indian provisional government in Singapore and recruit Indian volunteers to fight for them in Burma. Escaping the Japanese collapse, he was killed in an air crash in Taiwan.

Bosnia-Hercegovina A region in southeastern Europe and a Turkish province, placed under Austro-Hungarian administration after the Russo-Turkish War (1877–78). Anticipating Turkish demands for its return after the Young Turk Revolution, the Austrians annexed the region (1908). This provoked Serbian nationalists, whose assassination of the Archduke Franz Ferdinand precipitated World War I. Under the Treaty of Neuilly it became part of the kingdom of Yugoslavia and during World War II was incorporated into the puppet state of Croatia. Its rugged country was the scene of bitter fighting between Axis forces and their Croat auxiliaries, and Tito's partisans.

Botha, Louis (1862–1919), South African soldier and statesman. An able Boer military commander who, after the Boer War, worked for reconciliation. As leader of the Unionist Party, he became the first prime minister of the new dominion in 1910. During World War I he suppressed a Boer revolt (1915) and commanded the forces which conquered German South West Africa (Namibia).

Botha, Pieter Willem (1916–), South African Nationalist politician. He was minister of defence, and prime minister 1978–89. Events forced him to ease apartheid, with the consequent formation (1982) of the white extremist Conservative Party which made gains in both national elections (1987) and municipal elections (1988). He relinquished party leadership after a stroke, but retained the presidency (1989).

Boumédienne, Houari (1925–78), Algerian political leader. He joined the FLN (1954), becoming its chief of staff (1960). Minister of defence under Ben Bella, he supplanted him in a coup (1965) and held power as president, prime minister and chairman of the Revolutionary Council. He instituted single-party rule and a socialist economy. His foreign policy, equally revolutionary, included support for the Polisario Front, the PLO and similar movements.

Bourassa, Henri (1868–1952), Canadian politician. Founder of the Quebec Nationalist Party, a forerunner of the separatist movement, he stood for isolationism, opposing Canadian participation in the Boer War and in World War I.

Bourguiba, Habib ibn Ali (1902–), Tunisian statesman. Imprisoned by the French authorities (1934–36, 1938–42) for his nationalist policies, on his return from exile in Cairo (1949) he was again imprisoned for advocating Tunisian independence. When this was granted (1956), he became prime minister. In 1957 the powers of the hereditary ruler, the dey, were abolished and Bourguiba was elected president, remaining in office until 1987, when his senility forced members of his ruling party to remove him.

Boxer Rising An outbreak of violence in China in 1900, covertly supported by the Chinese authorities, and fomented by the secret Society of the Harmonious Fists. It was directed against European business, missionary and political influences in China and resulted in the siege of the foreign legation quarter in Peking. A six-nation expeditionary force repressed the uprising by methods which intensified hatred of Europeans and swelled support for the Chinese nationalist, Sun Yat-sen.

Bradley, Omar Nelson (1893–1981), US soldier. He served in World War I, and in World War II commanded the US 2nd Corps in Tunisia and Sicily (1943), the 1st Army in the Normandy landings (June 1944), and the 12th Army Group from August 1944 to the end of the war. As chairman of the Joint Chiefs of Staff (1948–53), he helped to build up NATO and advised against MacArthur's attempt to extend the Korean War.

Braga, Teofilo (1843–1924), Portuguese politician. An ardent anti-clerical and republican, he headed the provisional government of 1910–11 and was elected president in 1915.

Brandeis, Louis Dembitz (1856–1941), US lawyer. Having formulated the Democrats' economic and social policy (1912), he was appointed by President Wilson as a justice of the Supreme Court, where he was to support Roosevelt's New Deal legislation.

Brandt, Willy (Herbert Ernest Karl Frahm, 1913–), West German statesman. A Social Democrat, he fled to Norway when the Nazis came to power (1933) and took Norwegian citizenship and the name of Brandt. As mayor of West Berlin (1957–66), as foreign minister in Kiesinger's coalition government (1966–69) and as chancellor (1969–74), he pursued a policy of détente which brought non-aggression pacts with the Soviet Union and Poland (1971) and the Basic Treaty (1972) with East Germany. Forced out of German political life in 1974 by a spy scandal, he became an advocate for massive aid to the Third World. He was awarded the Nobel Peace Prize in 1971.

Bratislava Conference The meeting in August 1968 between Alexander

Dubček and Warsaw Pact representatives led by Leonid Brezhnev, who agreed that the Czechs might pursue their own domestic policy provided they remained within the pact. Soviet troops invaded Czechoslovakia (21 August) and suppressed the reformist movement.

Brazil A South American state, which became a republic under a federal constitution in 1891. In the late 19th century Brazil experienced a rubber boom which ended shortly before World War I, when the country became largely dependent upon its coffee exports. The collapse of commodity prices in the Depression brought poverty and unrest and Getulio Vargas took power in an army coup. Under his 'Estado Novo' (1930–45), a form of the corporate state, there was a successful programme of industrialization. This led to improvements in the health, education and welfare of the industrial and urban worker, but the peasants were largely neglected. During 1945–64 attempts were made to achieve a greater measure of democracy, but they foundered on acute inflation, and economic difficulties caused in part by the extravagant schemes of President Kubitschek, who transferred the capital to the new city of Brasilia (1960). His successor, President Goulart, was overthrown by an army coup in 1964. Since then the presidency has been held by a succession of army officers, none capable of controlling high inflation, mounting foreign debt, rural and urban pauperization, and a massive destruction of the environment. In 1988 the left-wing Workers' Party emerged victorious in the municipal elections, raising doubts about the army's attitude to the presidential elections, due in November 1989, the first free elections to be held since 1964.

Brazzaville Declaration The statement issued by General de Gaulle in 1944 which formalized the postwar Union Française, under which French citizenship was granted throughout the colonial empire, the individual colonies having their representatives in the French National Assembly and their own semi-autonomous local assemblies.

Brest-Litovsk, Treaty of The peace treaty signed by Lenin with the Central Powers in March 1918, under which he surrendered large areas of imperial Russia. The German defeat subsequently annulled this humiliating treaty.

Bretton Woods Conference The UN monetary and financial conference, called on the initiative of President Roosevelt in July 1944, which agreed to the establishment of the International Monetary Fund and the World Bank.

Brezhnev, Leonid Ilych (1906–82), Soviet statesman. He served in World War II as a political commissar and, backed by Khrushchev, became first secretary of the Communist Party in July 1964. He used the post to oust Khrushchev (October 1964) and to assume full power. His rule was characterized by formulation of the 'Brezhnev doctrine' – the Soviet right to intervene in another socialist state to preserve socialism – used to justify the invasion of Czechoslovakia in 1968, and by a system of corruption, inefficiency and repression for which he has been made the scapegoat by Gorbachov.

Briand, Aristide (1862–1932), French statesman. He held ministerial office over 20 times and was 11 times prime minister. As foreign minister he was dedicated to European peace and reconciliation (Locarno and Kellog-Briand pacts) and active in the League of Nations, and in 1930 made proposals for a United States of Europe. He was awarded the Nobel Peace Prize in 1926.

Britain see **United Kingdom**

British Commonwealth see **Commonwealth**

British Guiana see **Guyana**

British Honduras see **Belize**

British North Borneo see **Malaysia**

Bruce, Stanley Melbourne (1883–1967, Viscount Bruce), Australian statesman. He served in World War I, entered politics as a supporter of Hughes' Nationalists and became prime minister (1923–29). After his defeat in a general election, he resigned the party leadership and became foreign affairs spokesman. He was principal Australian delegate to the Ottawa Conference (1932) and to the League of Nations. As Australian high commissioner in London (1933–45) he was Australia's representative on Churchill's war cabinet.

Bruning, Heinrich (1885–1970), German statesman. As leader of the Catholic Centre Party and a fiscal expert, he was appointed chancellor by President Hindenburg in 1930 in an effort to restore financial order and to counter the rise of Hitler. In 1932 he was replaced by von Papen. He escaped from Germany in 1934 and settled in the United States, lecturing at Harvard (1937–52). In 1951 he returned to West Germany, to a professorship at Cologne University.

Brusilov, Alexei Alexeievich (1853–1926), Russian soldier. He served in the Russo-Turkish (1877) and Russo-Japanese (1904–05) Wars. In World War I he commanded the 8th Army in Galicia (1914–15) and on the southwestern front where his offensive broke the Austrians (June 1916) and was halted (August) only by lack of munitions. C-in-C under the provisional government, he later held posts in the Red Army.

Brussels, Treaty of A defensive alliance (signed in March 1948 and valid for 50 years) between the United Kingdom, France, Belgium, the Netherlands and Luxembourg, which foreshadowed NATO. In 1955 West Germany and Italy became formal associates.

Bryan, William Jennings (1860–1925), US Democratic politician. Three times nominated as unsuccessful presidential candidate (1896, 1900 and 1908), he helped to secure the nomination for Woodrow Wilson in 1912, whom he served as secretary of state. Best known for his attacks on the gold standard, Bryan was an ardent supporter of social reform, women's suffrage, prohibition and religious fundamentalism.

Bucharest, Treaty of The agreement (1913) which ended the second Balkan War, with cessions of territory by Bulgaria to Greece, Montenegro, Romania and Serbia.

Bulgaria A republic of eastern Europe. An autonomous principality under Ferdinand III after the the Russo-Turkish War (1878), it became an independent kingdom (1908). Hopes of territorial aggrandizment were disappointed in the Balkan Wars (1912–13). In 1915 Bulgaria joined the Central Powers, but was defeated, and paid reparations and lost territory under the Treaty of Neuilly. The Agrarian Party held power during 1919–23 but when its leader, Stambolisky, was overthrown and murdered the country relapsed in political anarchy and the economic hardships of the Depression. In 1935 the king, Boris III, established his personal dictatorship, siding with the Axis powers during World War II but, because of the strength of pro-Russian feeling, he never declared war on the Soviet Union. He adopted an independent line, dying in mysterious circumstances after a visit to Hitler in 1943. In 1944 the country was liberated by the Red Army and, after a short period of coalition rule, the Communists seized power in 1946 and declared a republic. The political opposition under Petrov was eliminated by the Communist leader, Dimitrov, who imposed a repressive one-party state, nationalizing industry and collectivizing agriculture. His successor and brother-in-law, Vulko Chervenko, initiated a series of Stalinist purges, but fell from power (1956) during the Khrushchev era. Todor Zhivkov, first secretary of the Bulgarian Communist Party, succeeded him and closely followed all the twists and turns of Soviet policy.

Bülow, Prince Bernhard von (1849–1929), German statesman. A favourite of Kaiser Wilhelm II, he became foreign minister in 1897 and chancellor in 1900. His aggressive foreign policies (Agadir Incident) isolated Germany. He lost the Kaiser's favour and was dismissed in 1909.

Burma A republic of southeast Asia. Absorbed into Britain's Indian empire (1885), Burma received limited local government in 1923 and in

1937 a separate legislature and a responsible cabinet. After Japanese occupation in World War II (1941–45), Burmese resistance forces (the Anti-Fascist People's Freedom League) under Aung San headed the independence movement. In 1948 the country became an independent republic, but suffered from revolts by non-Burmese hill tribesmen and from the presence of Chinese Nationalist troops. The AFPFL won the 1951–52 elections but its plans to socialize the country were thwarted by lack of trained personnel and by a fall in the price of rice (the major export) after the Korean War. In 1962 the army C-in-C, General We Nin, seized power and gradually isolated Burma. There was continuous war with tribal guerrillas and an economic paralysis under his Burma Socialist Programme party. Despite his savage suppression of all dissent, in 1988 a popular uprising against We Nin initially appeared successful. He was forced to retire, but a military junta under General Saw Muaung took control and, although promising elections in 1989, repressed most hopes of democracy.

Burns, John (1858–1943), British trade unionist and politician. He led the London Dock Strike (1889), and was elected independent socialist MP (1892), but quarrelled with Keir Hardie and joined the Liberals, serving as president of the Local Government Board (1905–14) and then of the Board of Trade. A pacifist, he resigned on the outbreak of World War I. He was the first manual worker to become a British cabinet minister and a privy councillor.

Bush, George Herbert Walker (1924–), US statesman. He served in the US navy in World War II, was a Republican representative (1967–71), and US ambassador to the United Nations (1971–72). He held office as chairman of the Republican National Committee (1972–73) at the time of Watergate. Director of the CIA (1976–77), he was vice president under Reagan throughout his term of office, succeeding him in 1989 as 41st president of the United States.

Bustamente, Sir William Alexander (1884–1977), Jamaican statesman. Taken to Spain as a child, he returned to Jamaica in 1932 and became a militant trade unionist, founding the Jamaica Labour Party (1943). He assumed office as chief minister (1953–55) and after independence as prime minister (1962–65). He opposed the West Indian Federation. In 1965 he was forced to retire because of ill-health.

Butler, Richard Austen (1902–82, Lord Butler), British statesman. An MP (1929–65), he held minor government posts (1932–40). In 1941 Churchill appointed him minister of education and his Education Act of 1944 set the pattern of state education for the next generation. He was chancellor of the exchequer (1951–55), home secretary (1957–62) and foreign secretary (1963–65). Although he was made deputy prime minister (1962–65), the highest office eluded him. He was, however, profoundly influential in British politics, persuading the Conservatives to accept an evolving welfare state.

Byrnes, James Francis (1879–1972), US administrator. Byrnes was the budgetary expert of Roosevelt's New Deal, and director of Economic Stabilization (1942) and of War Mobilization (1943). In 1945 Truman appointed him secretary of state, a post which he held until 1947. His initially conciliatory attitude towards the Soviet Union subsequently hardened.

C

Caetano, Dr Marcello (1906–), Portuguese politician. A close associate of Dr Salazar, he held a number of government posts – minister for the colonies (1944–47), deputy premier (1955–58) – and succeeded him as prime minister (1968). He introduced some social and economic reforms, but was overthrown by a military coup in 1974.

Cairo Conference A meeting between Churchill, Roosevelt and Chiang Kai-shek in November 1943 to define Allied war aims in the Far East – primarily the unconditional surrender of Japan and the restoration of all Japanese conquests since 1894.

Callaghan, Leonard James (1912– , Earl Callaghan), British statesman. He served in the Royal Navy in World War II, and was a Labour MP (1945–80). He held minor government posts (1947–51) and stood unsuccessfully (1963) for leadership of the Labour Party. Chancellor of the exchequer (1964–67), home secretary (1967–70) and foreign secretary (1974–76) under Harold Wilson, he succeeded him as leader of the Labour Party (1976–80) and as prime minister (1976–79).

Calles, Plutarco Elías (1877–1945), Mexican political leader. An associate of Carranza and Obregón, he succeeded the latter as president (1924–28) and wielded real power until 1934. He founded the National Revolutionary Party (renamed the Institutional Revolutionary Party in 1946), but his revolutionary fervour diminished in proportion to his increasing power and his wealth as a landowner and financier. He smashed both Communist and non-Communist trade unions, persecuted the Church and raised his own private army. Cardenas' election as president put an end to his influence.

Cambodia see **Kampuchea**

Cambon, Paul (1843–1924), French diplomat. As ambassador to London (1898–1920) he was immensely influential in promoting good relations between France and Britain (Anglo-French Agreement, 1904) and the triple alliance of Britain, France and Russia.

Camp David Talks Discussions held in 1978 under the auspices of President Carter and on the initiative of President Sadat, who together worked out the main terms of the peace treaty between Israel and Egypt. Signed in Washington (26 March 1979), this restored normal diplomatic relations, creating demilitarized zones between the two countries and providing for Israel's phased withdrawal from Sinai.

Campaign for Nuclear Disarmament An organization formed in 1958 which advocated nuclear disarmament by Britain. It enjoyed widespread support for some years but later lost momentum. However, it received a fresh impetus in the early 1980s at a time of increased international tension. See also **disarmament**.

Campbell-Bannerman, Sir Henry (1836–1908), British statesman. A Liberal MP (1868–1908), he held office under Gladstone and Rosebery and in 1899 was elected leader of his party. In 1905 he became prime minister and, as an opponent of the Boer War, worked for reconciliation in South Africa, in addition to pursuing a programme of progressive land reform and trade union legislation.

Canada An independent member of the Commonwealth in North America, with a two-chamber federal parliament. The 19th century saw large-scale immigration and the development of agriculture and mining, as well as the exploitation of timber, and in the second half of the 20th century there was vast industrial expansion. Suspicion that US interests were being favoured brought down Sir Wilfred Laurier's Liberal government in 1911 after 15 years in power. The Liberals returned to power (1921–30), but under the stresses of the Depression were succeeded by the Conservatives (1930–35). There followed a long period of Liberal rule under Mackenzie King (1935–48), St Laurent (1948–57), Pearson (1963–68) and Trudeau (1968–84), with a brief Conservative interlude (1957–63 and 1979–80). The major problem faced by the Trudeau administrations was that of separatism in the French-Canadian province of Quebec which erupted into terrorist violence in the 1970s. The federation was preserved, the French language was granted official parity with English but, more important, by his policy of 'patriation' Trudeau sought to create a separate Canadian identity. This was effected by transferring the sovereignty of the 1867 constitution from Britain to Canada on 17 April 1982. Nonetheless, in the 1984 elections, the Liberals dropped to third place, Brian Mulroney's Conservatives gained power with the largest majority in Canadian history and retained it in the 1988 elections on a programme of closer economic ties with the United States.

Canaris, Wilhelm (1887–1945), German admiral. Appointed head of military intelligence (1935), he used his position to oppose Hitler. He came under suspicion, was dismissed in 1944 and executed after the failure of the July Conspiracy.

Cárdenas, Lázaro (1895–1970), Mexican statesman. He was elected president (1934) with the backing of Calles, whose power he then broke, sending him into exile and destroying his corrupt system with a programme of land redistribution to the peasants and nationalization of foreign-owned enterprises.

Caribbean Federation   see **West Indies Federation**

Carmona, Antonio Oscar de Fragoso   (1869–1951), Portuguese soldier and statesman. A minister in the 1926 military government, he overthrew the coup leader General Gomes da Costa (1926) and as president (1928–51), acted as head of state in Salazar's corporatist regime.

Carson, Edward Henry   (1854–1935, Baron Carson), Irish lawyer and politician. A Unionist MP (1892–1921), he was solicitor-general during 1900–06. In 1910 he organized the Ulster Volunteers to resist Home Rule, raising a private army of 80,000 men which forced the Liberal government of the day to exclude Ulster from its provisions. He served briefly as attorney-general in Asquith's wartime coalition before joining the intrigue which made Lloyd George prime minister (1916). A formidable advocate, noted for his cross-examination of Oscar Wilde (1895), after his retirement from politics he sat as a lord of appeal (1921–29).

Carter, James Earl [Jimmy]   (1924–), 39th President of the United States. Democrat Governor of Georgia (1971), in 1976 he defeated Gerald Ford for a presidency which was marked by the success of the Camp David talks and by the SALT II disarmament negotiations. However, US-Soviet relations deteriorated following the invasion of Afghanistan (1979), while Carter's failure to secure the release of the US embassy hostages in Tehran ensured his defeat in 1980 by Ronald Reagan.

Casablanca Conference   The meeting between Churchill and Roosevelt in January 1943 which agreed plans for the invasion of Sicily and Italy, for the bombing campaign against Germany, for the unconditional surrender of the Axis Powers and for the transfer of British forces to the Far East after the surrender of Germany.

Casement, Sir Roger David   (1864–1916), Irish patriot. As a British consular official he exposed the brutalities of the rubber trade in the Congo (1904) and in Brazil (1910), and was knighted for his services (1911). After his retirement in 1911 he devoted himself to Irish nationalism and in 1916 he was arrested shortly after landing from a German U-boat on a mission to prevent the Easter Rising. Found guilty of treason, he was hanged.

Castro, Fidel   (1927–), Cuban Communist leader. As a young lawyer and vocal opponent of the Batista regime, he organized his 26 July Movement in Mexico, returned to Cuba and began guerrilla operations (1956). Disguising his political affiliations, he gained the sympathy of the United States and the support of liberal opinion to overthrow Batista in January 1959. In 1961 the Americans withdrew support when Castro aligned himself with the USSR and China. He now declared himself as a Marxist-Leninist, executed or imprisoned his political opponents and established a programme of expropriation, nationalization and collectivization. After the CIA-backed invasion attempt by Cuban exiles at the Bay of Pigs (April 1961) had been repelled with humiliating ease, Castro precipitated the Missile Crisis and actively supported revolution in Latin America. The United States responded with an economic blockade. Castro was able to obtain sufficient Soviet aid to maintain a basic standard of living at the cost of providing the USSR with the military manpower for its adventures in Angola and Ethiopia. An autocrat, Castro remained unenthusiastic about perestroika.

Ceauşescu, Nicolae (1918–), Romanian political leader. A revolutionary from an early age, while in prison he met Gheorghiu-Dej, the future Romanian Communist leader who was to advance his career in the Communist government (1947). From 1957 he was Gheorghiu-Dej's deputy and succeeded as general secretary on the latter's death in 1965. In 1967, having eliminated internal opposition, he took the office of president and head of state. His regime became characterized by a massive personality cult, corruption, inefficiency and nepotism at home and a foreign policy independent enough to engage the sympathy of the West without inviting Soviet intervention. This sympathy was lost by his megalomania and gross infringements of human rights.

Central African Federation see **Rhodesia and Nyasaland, Federation of**

Central Powers A term originally applied to the three powers of the Triple Alliance of 1882 (Germany, Italy and Austria-Hungary) but, when Italy first remained neutral and then joined the Allies in World War I, it was used to describe Germany, Austria-Hungary and their allies, Turkey and Bulgaria.

Central Treaty Organization A mutual security organization established in 1955 by Britain, Turkey, Iraq and Pakistan, and at first known as the Middle East Treaty Organization. The new name was adopted when Iraq left the organization in 1959, and the headquarters were moved from Baghdad to Ankara. Iran became a member but withdrew when the Islamic Republic was proclaimed.

Centre Party In imperial Germany the party founded in 1871 to represent the views of Roman Catholics and politically midway between the socialists and the nationalists. In 1917 its leader Erzberger carried a resolution in favour of peace negotiations. Influential under the Weimar Republic – Bruning and von Papen belonged to it – it was dissolved by Hitler in 1933.

Ceylon see **Sri Lanka**

Chaco Dispute The conflict over the sub-Andean area claimed by both Bolivia and Paraguay from 1879. Suggestions that it contained oil deposits led to armed clashes (1927) and, when arbitration had been rejected (1929) and further talks had failed (1931), war broke out. After Bolivia had suffered a series of defeats (1932–35), peace negotiations awarded the bulk of the territory to Paraguay, with access for Bolivian trade via the Paraguay River to the sea.

Chad A republic of north Africa. As a French colony it formed the most northerly portion of French Equatorial Africa and was the first to join de Gaulle in 1940. France granted autonomy in 1958 and independence in 1960 under President Tombalbaye, who came from the non-Muslim south. In 1975 he was overthrown and assassinated in a Libyan-backed coup by the northerner, Goukouni Oueddi, who in his turn was ousted by Hissene Habré (1982). In the ensuing civil war France and the United States supported Habre. Goukouni fell out with his Libyan supporters when Habré's offensive (1987) regained most of the country except for the mineral-rich Aozou Strip. This remained in Libyan hands until its ownership should be settled by arbitration.

Chamberlain, Joseph (1836–1914), British politician. A radical Lord Mayor of Birmingham (1875), where he had made his fortune, in 1877 he entered parliament as a Liberal but rallied to the Conservatives in opposition to Home Rule (1886), serving as colonial secretary (1895–1903) under Salisbury and Balfour. He combined social reform at home with fervent imperialism abroad. His Tariff Reform campaign to end free trade in favour of Imperial Preference (1903–06) split the Conservative Party.

Chamberlain, Sir (Joseph) Austen (1863–1937), British statesman. The eldest son of Joseph and half-brother of Neville Chamberlain, he was a conservative MP (1892–1937). He held office before World War I, was member of the war cabinet and became an influential figure in postwar Conservative and National governments, especially as foreign secretary (1924–29), when he was largely responsible for the Locarno Treaty (1925).

Chamberlain, Neville (1869–1940), British statesman. After a career in business and local government, he sat as Conservative MP (1918–40) and was a competent minister of health (1923, 1924–29) and an orthodox chancellor of the exchequer (1923–24, 1931–37). In 1937 he succeeded Baldwin as prime minister and was forced to grapple with international crises while lacking any experience of foreign affairs. His policy of appeasement towards Germany culminated in the Munich Agreements. Occupation of Czechoslovakia revealed the nature of German ambition, but efforts to contain it by a Franco-British alliance with the USSR were thwarted by the Nazi-Soviet Pact (1939). The guarantees given to Poland led to the outbreak of World War II, but Chamberlain was by now a sick man. His apparently lax prosecution of the war combined with the failure of the Anglo-French expedition to Norway (April 1940) to bring his defeat in Parliament and resignation. Churchill retained him in his cabinet until his death.

Chambers, Whittaker see **Hiss, Alger**

Chanak Crisis The crisis in relations between Britain and Turkey in 1922. Following the defeat of the Greeks at Smyrna, Turkey planned to reoccupy European territories granted to the Greeks under the Treaty of Sèvres. Lloyd George wished to block this move by force if necessary, but the local British commander reached a compromise with the Turks, subsequently upheld by the Treaty of Lausanne. The crisis brought down Lloyd George whose actions had precipitated the risk of war between Britain and Turkey.

Chang Tso-lin (1873–1928), Chinese warlord. Appointed inspector general of Manchuria (1918), he attempted to control the Peking government by occupying the Peking-Tiensin area (1926). Driven out by Chiang Kai-shek (1928), he died when the Japanese planted a bomb on his train.

Ch'en Yi (1901–72), Chinese soldier and statesman. After the collapse of the Kuomintang–Communist alliance (1927), he joined the 4th Red Army, proving an outstanding military commander. An early supporter of Mao Tse-tung, he became mayor of Shanghai (1949) and in 1958 succeeded Chou En-lai as foreign minister. Severely criticized in the Cultural Revolution, he was eclipsed when Chou became prime minister in 1967.

Chiang Ch'ing (c1913–), Chinese Communist leader and actress who married Mao Tse-tung as his second wife (1939). She remained in the background until the Cultural Revolution, but thereafter wielded increasing political power. Arrested after Mao's death (1976), she was tried as one of the Gang of Four and given a suspended death sentence (1981).

Chiang Kai-shek (1887–1975), Chinese soldier and statesman. After

military training in Japan he returned to China to take part in the 1911
Revolution and to serve as military aide to Sun Yat-sen's Canton regime
(1917). After the death in 1925 of Sun Yat-sen (whose sister-in-law,
Soong Mei-ling, he married in 1927) he became leader of the Kuomintang
and, having defeated Chang Tso-lin, its chairman and C-in-C (June
1928). Although the warlords had been suppressed, there were army
mutinies in 1930, 1933 and 1936, and intermittent clashes with the
Communists from 1927. Further problems were caused by the Japanese
seizure of Manchuria (1931), and in 1936 Chiang Kai-shek was
kidnapped in the Sian Incident. In 1937 the Japanese invasion forced him
to withdraw to southwest China where, from his capital Chungking he
organized resistance throughout World War II. He gained great prestige
in the West and, as the Chinese leader, attended the Cairo Conference
(1943). In 1947 civil war with the Communists broke out and, by 1950,
the Kuomintang had been driven from the mainland and had taken
refuge on Taiwan. Here Chiang Kai-shek established an American-
backed military regime which he led until his death.

Chifley, Joseph Benedict (1885–1951), Australian statesman. A railway-
man and trade unionist, he was minister of defence (1929–31) and, as
Curtin's finance minister (1941–45), was responsible for the Australian
Labor Party's postwar planning and for social insurance schemes. He
took office as prime minister in 1945, but was defeated in 1949 by
Menzies on the issue of communist infiltration of key trade unions.

Chile A republic of South America. It gained a dominant position in the
area by its victory over Bolivia and Peru in the War of the Pacific (1879–
83) and by its economic development (nitrate and copper) and industrialization in the 1900s. A long period of stability enabled parliamentary
government to emerge and power struggles were between the executive
(president) and legislative (congress) branches of government, with the
army remaining neutral. From 1891 the legislature was in control, until
the constitution of 1925 awarded greater powers to the presidency.
Economic hardships had been caused by the collapse of the nitrate
industry after World War I and initially successful efforts to restore
prosperity were defeated by the Depression. Despite attempts at social
and economic reform by President Alessandri (1920–24 and 1932–38), a
Popular Front government came to power in 1938. Labour problems and
chronic inflation plagued the efforts of successive administrations and,
although Eduardo Frei and his Christian Democrats brought in measures
of land reform after 1964 and assumed control of American-owned
mining companies, they failed to satisfy the grievances of the workers.

The Marxist, Salvador Allende was elected president in 1970. By adopting an 'open road to socialism' and by expropriating American interests he antagonized the United States, and the CIA backed an army coup which toppled Allende (who died in the uprising) and placed General Pinochet in power (1973). His measures to restore economic and social stability succeeded at the cost of grave violations of human rights. In 1988 some political exiles were allowed to return prior to a national referendum to determine whether General Pinochet was to be the sole candidate in the 1990 presidential elections. In a free vote 55% replied 'no' and this was seen as the first step in bringing his increasingly unpopular rule to an end.

China A republic of southeast Asia. The 19th-century decline of the Manchu Empire was accelerated by military defeat in the Sino-Japanese war (1894–95). In a vain effort to eliminate foreign influence and restore the prestige of the dynasty, the Empress T'zu Hsi encouraged the Boxer Uprising (1900). In 1911 Sun Yat-sen's revolutionary movement expelled the Manchus and established a republic of which he was the first president. In 1912 he resigned in favour of Yuan Shi-kai, the army commander, retaining a power base in Canton, so that on the death of Yuan (1916) the country was split between the north (devastated by contending warlords) and the south (controlled by Sun Yat-sen's Kuomintang). The Paris Conference, ignoring Chinese wishes, assigned to Japan the former German concessions which Japan had occupied during World War I, uniting patriotic feeling in the May Fourth Movement and leading indirectly to the founding of the Chinese Communist Party (1921). After Sun's death in 1925 his successor, Chiang Kai-shek, in alliance with the Communists, advanced north and defeated the warlords. Chiang then turned on the Communists, forcing their leader, Mao Tse-tung, to go on the Long March to establish a secure base at Yenan (1934). Civil war was ended by the Sian Incident (1936) and Chiang now made common cause with Mao against the Japanese, who had seized Manchuria (1931). In 1937 the Japanese invaded China and occupied most of the country, the Communists continuing the struggle in the northwest and Chiang's Nationalists in the southwest, the latter receiving considerable aid when the United States entered the war (1941). After the Japanese defeat, the uneasy truce between Nationalists and Communists was broken in 1947 and the Nationalist armies, thoroughly demoralized by Kuomintang corruption, were isolated by guerrilla warfare (1947–48) and then defeated in set-piece battles (1948–49), the survivors taking refuge in Taiwan (1950). The Communist regime proclaimed the Chinese People's Republic on 1 October 1949, eliminated all opposition and attempted to root out religion. Until 1956 China was closely allied with the USSR which supplied economic aid and technical assistance. This was abruptly withdrawn when Mao denounced Khrushchev's revisionism and in an effort to make good this loss he took the disastrous Great Leap Forward and, on its failure, initiated the Cultural Revolution. Mao dominated China until his death (1976). Meantime Chinese foreign policy reflected in addition to anti-revisionism an anti-imperialism manifest in support for North Korea and Vietnam and in not entirely disinterested aid to the Third World. Its further objectives were to re-establish China's traditional borders, infringed by 'unequal' 19th-century treaties. In pursuit of this Tibet was occupied (1950) and a border war with India fought (1962), and it was a cause of heightened tension in the ideological dispute with the USSR. Here border clashes occurred but they never progressed beyond this level, perhaps because China had exploded an atom bomb in 1964 and a hydrogen bomb in 1967. The threat of Soviet aggression drew Chou En-lai, to work for an accommodation with the United States. Aid to African countries ensured their support at the United Nations to which China was admitted when the United States withdrew its veto in 1971. In 1972 President Nixon visited Peking and this process of detente was continued after Mao's death (1976) by Zhoa Zlyang (prime minister, 1980) and Hu Yaobang (party chairman, 1981). Together with the veteran party secretary, Deng Xiao-ping, they sought to attract western aid and investment and to liberalize the economy. An attempt to introduce a market economy into a single-party state was not a success, but their foreign policy brought agreement with the United Kingdom to return Hong Kong to Chinese sovereignty in 1997 and a possible rapprochement with the USSR, formalized by Gorbachov's state visit (May 1989). This coincided with massive demonstrations against the government.

China lobby see **Soong Mei-ling**

Chou En-lai (1898–1976), Chinese statesman. From a Mandarin family, he studied at university in Japan (1917–19) and in Europe (1920–22), where he met Ho Chi Minh. A founder member of the Chinese Communist Party, he returned to China to work with the Kuomintang, then in alliance with the Communists, escaping execution when Chiang Kai-shek broke with the Communists. He joined Mao Tse-tung (1931) as political adviser sharing the Long March, helped negotiate the release of Chiang Kai-shek (Sian Incident, 1936) and was chief Communist liaison officer with the Kuomintang (1936–46). As prime minister (1949–74) and foreign minister (1949–58) under the People's Republic, he played a distinguished role at the Geneva and Bandung Conferences (1954 and 1958) and in the rapprochement with the United States (1972). He would have seemed the natural successor to Mao Tse-tung, but predeceased him.

Christlich-Democratische Union (Christian Democrats) A German political party founded by Konrad Adenauer and Ludwig Erhard after World War II. Right of centre and in some respects the heir of the prewar Catholic Centre Party, it was deliberately non-denominational and the party of German economic and democratic regeneration.

Churchill, Sir Winston Leonard Spencer (1874–1965), British statesman. The son of Lord Randolph Churchill, he was commissioned in the 4th Hussars (1894), saw service in India and the Sudan (1898), and was a reporter in Cuba (1895) and during the Boer War. Elected a Conservative MP (1900), he switched to the Liberals over Free Trade (1904) and sat as a Liberal (1906–22). As president of the board of trade (1908–10) and home secretary (1910–11) he gave effect to Asquith's social reforms, but was criticized over the Tonypandy Riots. As 1st lord of the admiralty (1911–15) he expanded the Royal Navy and had it at war stations six days before war was actually declared, but resigned after the failure of the Dardanelles campaign and fought as a battalion commander on the western front. He served in Lloyd George's wartime and postwar coalitions as minister of munitions (1917–18), minister of war and air (1919–20) and as colonial secretary (1921–22), losing his seat in the 1922 election. In 1924 he was elected as 'constitutional anti-socialist', rejoining the Conservative Party in 1925 and remaining an MP until his retirement in 1964. He was chancellor of the exchequer under Baldwin (1924–29), but became alienated from the party leadership through its encouragement of Indian independence, its failure to rearm in the face of German resurgence and its appeasement of Hitler. In World War II he was recalled by Neville Chamberlain as 1st lord of the admiralty (1939), succeeding him as prime minister in May 1940. Any criticism of his conduct of the war must be tempered by the realization of the inspiration which he provided for the British people as a whole. Defeated in the 1945 election, he became leader of the opposition and began his monumental *History of the Second World War* (1948–53). In 1946 he made his famous speech at Fulton, Missouri, warning the United States against Soviet imperialism and coining the phrase 'iron curtain'. In 1951 and again in 1955, he led the Conservatives to electoral victory, but resigned the premiership after the second return to power on grounds of age and health.

Chu Teh (1886–1976), Chinese soldier. An officer of the Chinese imperial army, a follower of Sun Yat-sen (1911) and a warlord (1916–20), he went to Europe, met Chou En-lai and joined the Chinese Communist Party (1922). After his return (1925) he led an unsuccessful rising against Chiang Kai-shek (1927) and then joined Mao Tse-tung (1931). The remnants of his troops formed the nucleus of the Red Guards whom he led during the Long March (1934–35), and these in turn became the cadres of the Red Armies he raised, trained and led, first against the Japanese and then to victory against the Nationalists (1947–49). As C-in-C of the army under the people's republic, he was promoted marshal (1955) and became deputy chairman of the people's republic (1954–59), but was dismissed (1959) and eclipsed during the Cultural Revolution.

Ciano, Galeazzo (1903–44), Italian politician and diplomat. He joined the Fascists and took part in the March on Rome (1922). Entering the diplomatic service (1930), he married a daughter of Mussolini, who appointed him minister of press and propaganda (1934) and of foreign affairs (1936). Although he had helped to form the Axis and signed the Pact of Steel (1939), he opposed Italy's entry into the war, and attempted (from 1942) to obtain Mussolini's resignation and a separate peace with the Allies. He was in consequence executed for treason by order of his father-in-law.

Clark, Mark Wayne (1896–1984), US soldier. He served in France in World War I. He became chief of staff of ground forces (1942), and as Eisenhower's deputy made secret contacts with the French before the Allied landings in North Africa. He subsequently commanded the US 5th Army in North Africa and Italy (1943–44). Allied commander in Italy (1945), he later headed the US occupation forces in Austria. He was supreme commander of the UN forces in Korea (1952–53) and C-in-C US Forces Far East before his retirement in 1954.

Clemenceau, Georges Benjamin (1841–1929), French statesman. A radical who retired to the United States during the Second Empire, he returned to France on the fall of Napoleon III (1870) and became an increasingly left-wing radical deputy (1871–93). Involved in the Panama scandal, he did not return to political life until 1902. As minister of the interior (1906) and later as prime minister he pushed through anti-clerical legislation, strengthened the Franco-British alliance and weathered the first Moroccan crisis, but his harsh suppression of a miners' strike alienated the socialists and brought down his government (1909). He ceaselessly warned against Germany's aggressive intentions and during the war was a constant critic of French policy. In 1917 he was recalled by President Poincaré as prime minister and restored French confidence both by his repression of defeatism and by the appointment of Foch as supreme commander of the Allied forces.

Collins, Michael (1890–1922), Irish patriot and political leader. Imprisoned for his part in the Easter Rising (1916), he led the IRA during the civil war, but agreed on pragmatic grounds to the treaty establishing the Irish Free State (1921). He was assassinated by republican extremists.

Colombia A republic of South America. The 19th century was a period of increasingly bitter political conflict, culminating in civil war (1899–1902) which cost the lives of some 100,000 Colombians, and so weakened the country that the United States was able to detach the province of Panama and allow the building of the canal. However, between 1904 and 1946, under successive Conservative and Liberal governments, political stability and considerable economic advances were achieved. Political rivalry then led to widespread violence and invited military intervention (1953–58). Since then, despite political conflict, murderous warfare between drug traffickers and the activities of four guerrilla movements, the civilian government has been able to keep down inflation and attain some economic growth.

Colombo Plan A plan for economic co-operation, established at Colombo in 1951, following a meeting of Commonwealth foreign ministers the previous year. Under the plan the developed members of the Commonwealth (Australia, Canada, New Zealand and the United Kingdom) make available funds and technical assistance to aid less-developed members in south and southeast Asia. At the suggestion of Menzies, the Australian prime minister, the United States became the major contributor to the plan – extended frequently beyond its original seven-year period – and its beneficiaries include other than Commonwealth countries.

COMECON The Council for Mutual Economic Assistance set up by Stalin in 1949 as a counter to the Marshall Plan, its original members being the Soviet Union and its eastern European satellites. Cuba joined in 1972 and Vietnam in 1978.

Cominform The Communist Information Bureau formed in 1947 after the Warsaw meeting of Soviet, eastern European and Italian and French Communist Party leaders, to co-ordinate activities throughout Europe. Their first major decision was to move their headquarters from Belgrade, expel Yugoslavia from the bureau and denounce Tito (1948). Khrushchev formally dissolved the bureau in 1956 as a goodwill gesture towards Tito and the West.

Comintern   The Communist International or Third International founded by Lenin in 1919, with Zinoviev as president to anticipate any revival of the Second (Socialist) International under non-Communist leadership and to keep control of international communism securely in Russian hands. It was dissolved in 1943 by Stalin as a gesture of friendship to his Western allies. See also **Anti-Comintern Pact**.

Common Market   see **European Community**

Commonwealth, The   An informal association which evolved from the interwar British Commonwealth and Empire of self-governing Dominions and colonies owing allegiance to the British crown. Since gaining complete independence these countries have maintained the British connection by virtue of the fact that Queen Elizabeth is head of the Commonwealth. In the tradition of the interwar imperial conferences, heads of Commonwealth countries meet at about 18-monthly intervals, while a secretariat, established in 1965, exists to further continuing political, economic and cultural co-operation.

Communist parties   The success of the Bolshevik October Revolution (1917) enabled Lenin to split the socialist movement by founding the Third International and creating a nominally international Communist Party, which was in fact subservient ideologically and politically to the USSR. Except in France and Italy after World War II, the direct political influence of the party in Western Europe and North America has been slight, but its covert role within other socialist movements in furthering the aims of Soviet policy has been considerable. The revelations of Stalin's crimes (1956), the Hungarian Uprising (1956) and the invasion of Czechoslovakia (1968) have discouraged 'fellow-travellers' and produced within the western parties a Euro-Communism more independent of the USSR. In eastern Europe Communist parties have been the agents of Soviet imperialism: in Latin America Cuba, Nicaragua (and more briefly, Chile) have come under Communist control, while the party has been influential in Mexico and has activated guerrilla movements elsewhere. In Islamic countries – and especially since the Iranian Revolution and the Soviet invasion of Afghanistan – it has been eclipsed by religious fundamentalism. As a secular religion Communism has had its heretics (Trotsky) and its Great Schism (Mao Tse-tung), but both in the USSR, in eastern Europe and even in China, the failure of the system has brought demands for liberal reforms. The party is now faced with the problem of retaining power while making enough concessions to political pluralism to avoid revolution.

concentration camps   Centres for the detention of political prisoners, racial minority groups and others. Towards the end of the Boer War, to prevent their giving food and information to the Boer commandos, civilians were concentrated into camps where poor administration and lack of sanitation caused much hardship. The name was later applied to the camps established in Nazi Germany and the USSR, where a deliberate policy of extermination was practised, using forced labour on starvation rations as a means of eliminating political opponents and those who were believed to be the natural enemies of the state. The most notorious camps were in Nazi Germany, where millions were murdered or died of disease or hunger.

Conference of the Ambassadors see **London, Treaty of**

Congo, Belgian see **Zaïre**

Congress Party The Indian National Congress, founded in 1885 as an educational movement, which became the political arm of Indian and, more specifically, of Hindu nationalism. Its early leaders included the extremist Tilak but, from 1915, under M.K. Gandhi, it adopted a non-violent policy of civil disobedience. Following the implementation of the India Act (1935), the party formed the governments of six provinces, but was banned when it refused co-operation during World War II. In India, after partition (1947), when Pandit Nehru was prime minister (1947–64) it gained a monopoly of political power and retained this position until the contest for leadership between Indira Gandhi and Morarji Desai eventually split the party (1969). These divisions, revelations of corruption and Mrs Gandhi's dictatorial methods led to the party's defeat in 1977. Reorganized, it returned to power in 1980 against stiff and continuing opposition.

Conrad, Franz (1852–1925, Graf von Hotzendorf), Austro-Hungarian field marshal. As chief of staff, he led his country's armies in World War 1 until 1917, when he was demoted to a command on the Italian front for his opposition to the Emperor Charles's peace initiative.

Conservative Party In Great Britain during the 19th century it was the old Tory Party revitalized by Peel and Disraeli. Its inability to initiate social reform and its divisions over tariff reform led to its defeat by the Liberals (1905) and it did not become the party of government until 1922. During the interwar period Conservatives accepted earlier Liberal social legislation and its consequent institutional change, just as Conservative governments from 1951 accepted most, if not all, the changes effected by the Labour governments (1945–51). The advent to the leadership of Margaret Thatcher (1975) and her successive governments (1979 onwards) with their monetarism and their rigid application of a market economy have given the party a strong flavour of 19th century liberalism.

Coolidge, Calvin   (1872–1933), 30th president of the United States (1923–29). A republican governor of Massacchussets (1919–21), he was Harding's vice-president, succeeding to the presidency upon the latter's death (1923). He himself was untouched by his predecessor's scandals, but his laissez-faire economic policy and encouragement of big business provoked the Wall Street crash seven months after he left office.

Corfu   An island in the Ionian Sea off the west coast of Greece and Albania, it was under a British protectorate from 1815 until its cession to Greece in 1864. It was notable in the 20th century for (1) *The Corfu Pact* (1917) concluded between leaders of the Serbs and the Southern Slavs when the Serbian government in exile was located here, which set the parameters of the postwar kingdom of Yugoslavia. (2) *The Corfu Incident* (1923) when Mussolini bombarded and occupied the island in retaliation for the shooting of an Italian general and four of his staff while demarcating the Graeco-Albanian frontier. The Italians withdrew under League of Nations pressure.

Coty, René   (1882–1962), French statesman. From 1946 he led the Independents, held ministerial office and was elected president of the Fourth Republic in succession to Vincent Auriol. In the crisis of 1958 he supported General de Gaulle and resigned on the creation of the Fifth Republic.

Country Party   An Australian political party representing agricultural interests. It has frequently held the balance of power and formed coalition governments with the Nationalists, exercising an influence out of all proportion to its size.

Couve de Murville, Maurice   (1907–   ), French diplomat and statesman. As de Gaulle's foreign secretary (1958–68) he successfully excluded the United Kingdom from the European Community and took France out of NATO. He was briefly prime minister in 1968.

Cripps, Sir Richard Stafford   (1889–1952), British statesman. Solicitor general in the first Labour government, he resigned when the National government was formed in 1931. He became the spokesman for the left wing of the Labour Party and was expelled in 1939 for advocating a Popular Front with the Communists. During World War II he served as ambassador in Moscow (1940–42), leader of the House of Commons and member of the war cabinet. His failure to secure agreement on Indian independence (1946) made partition inevitable. As chancellor of the exchequer (1947–50), he initiated a policy of austerity which enabled

Britain to overcome postwar economic crises and preserve full employment and the welfare state.

Croatia A constituent republic of Yugoslavia. In the 19th century, under the Dual Monarchy, it was a semi-autonomous region of the kingdom of Hungary. During World War I Croat nationalist politicians reached agreement with the Serbs on the formation of a kingdom of Yugoslavia, of which Croatia became a part in 1919 after the fall of the Dual Monarchy. But the Croats resented Serb hegemony and their fascist Ustase movement was responsible for the murder of Alexander II (1934). After the German invasion (1941) Ante Pavelic set up an independent state under Axis patronage, fighting a merciless war against Tito's partisans. Croat exiles have continued to express their hatred of the Communist regime in sporadic outbreaks of terrorism since the end of World War II.

Cromer, Lord see **Baring, Evelyn**

Cuba A republic in the Caribbean. A former Spanish colony, after the Spanish-American War of 1898 Cuba became an American protectorate (1899–1902). The 1901 constitution granted independence but allowed the United States the right of intervention. Thus Cuba exchanged Spanish colonial for American economic domination under more or less corrupt presidents, culminating in Batista. Yet when Batista was himself overthrown by Fidel Castro's successful guerrilla campaign (1959), Cuba was to pass from American to Soviet domination. The early promise of liberal reforms vanished in the apparatus of the Communist state, nationalization of commerce and industry, collectivization of the land, suppression of the media, and imprisonment of political opponents. Thousands fled into exile and from their numbers the CIA recruited an invasion force which landed at the Bay of Pits in 1961 and was dispersed by Castro with humiliating ease. In 1962 the USSR provoked the Missile Crisis by building launching sites in Cuba. President Kennedy declared a naval blockade and, faced by the threat of retaliation against the USSR, Khrushchev agreed to dismantle the sites and recall the vessels carrying the missiles. Cuba's open espousal of revolutionary movements caused all Latin American countries except Mexico to break off economic and diplomatic relations during the 1960s, these ties only being gradually restored some ten years later. Economically dependent upon the USSR, Cuba provided surrogate forces for Communist interventions in Angola and Ethiopia. The regime had yet to feel the full effects of Gorbachov's reforming policies.

Cultural Revolution The destructive revolutionary movement initiated by

Mao Tse-tung in 1965 to prevent a liberalization of the regime in China. His cult was encouraged and Red Guards conducted a campaign of violence and denunciation against the supposed supporters of the head of state, Liu Shao-chi, in all walks of life, but especially academics and intellectuals. The revolution became so destructive that in 1968 Mao was compelled to call in the army to restore order.

Cunningham, Andrew Browne (1883–1963, Viscount Cunningham), British admiral. As C-in-C of the Mediterranean Fleet (from 1939), he defeated the Italian navy at Taranto (1943) and kept the Mediterranean open to Allied shipping throughout the North African campaigns.

Curragh Incident A near-mutiny among army officers in Ireland in 1914. Fearing that troops might be sent from the Curragh Camp near Dublin to Ulster to enforce Home Rule, the officer commanding the 3rd Cavalry Brigade and 57 of his officers declared that they would rather be dismissed than obey the order. Assured that they would not be required to do so, they withdrew their threat of resignation. This breach of the code of non-interference in political matters by officers of the armed forces aroused considerable bitterness among professional soldiers on the eve of World War I.

Curtin, John (1885–1945), Australian statesman. A trade unionist and federal MP (1928–31, 1934–45), he became leader of the Labor Party in 1935 and prime minister in 1941. He collaborated closely with the United States in the defence of Australia, but from 1943 sought increasing British participation to balance US influence. He died in office shortly before the end of the war in the Far East.

Curzon, George Nathaniel (1859–1925, Marquis of Kedleston), British statesman. A Conservative MP (1886–98), he served as undersecretary of state for India (1891–92) and for foreign affairs (1895–98). As viceroy of India (1898–1905), he introduced administrative and economic reform, but his partition of Bengal (1905) angered Hindu opinion. When the government declined to support him in a quarrel with the C-in-C, Lord Kitchener, he resigned. He held office in Asquith's coalition government (1915) and under Lloyd George (1916–19). He was foreign secretary (1919–24), but his ambitions of becoming prime minister were thwarted when Baldwin was chosen Conservative leader.

Curzon Line The line of demarcation proposed in 1920 by the British foreign secretary, Lord Curzon, between the new Polish state and the USSR. It was not accepted by the Poles – who were granted more extensive territories – but served, more or less, as the border between the Soviets and the Nazis after the German conquest of Poland in 1939 and remained the border in the postwar settlement.

Cyprus An island republic in the Mediterranean. In 1878 Turkey ceded the administration – but not the sovereignty – of the island to Britain. Formally annexed (1914), in 1925 Cyprus became a crown colony, but 80% of the population was Greek and the growing movement for union (enosis) with Greece culminated in riots in 1931. Temporarily suppressed, the movement broke out into violence in 1955 after solutions proposed by Britain (1948) and Greece (1951 and 1953) had proved unacceptable. Led by Colonel Grivas, and with the support of Archbishop Makarios, EOKA extremists waged a guerrilla war. Under a compromise settlement (Zurich and London, 1959), Cyprus became an independent republic within the Commonwealth in August 1960, jointly guaranteed by Britain, Greece and Turkey. Intercommunal tensions almost brought about war between Greece and Turkey, and in 1964 a UN peace-keeping force was sent to the island. By 1970 the Turks had withdrawn to their own enclaves and set up their own unofficial parliament. In the cause of enosis former EOKA members, backed by some Greek officers of the Cyprus national guard, first attempted to assassinate Makarios and then in 1974, with the backing of the Greek government, mounted a coup which overthrew him. The Turks promptly invaded the island to protect their minority, occupying some 40% of the north and effectively partitioning it. In 1983, the Turkish Cypriot leader, Rauf Denktash unilaterally declared this area an independent republic. In 1975 Makarios returned and, until his death in 1977, worked towards a federal solution, a process continued by his successors, Denktash and President Vassiliou, in talks under UN auspices (1988).

Czechoslovakia. A republic in central Europe. It came into existence in November 1918 after the defeat of Austria-Hungary in World War I. Its independence was formally recognized by the Treaty of St Germain (1919) and its boundaries by the Treaty of Trianon (1920). It included minorities which resented Czech dominance of the prosperous and democratic new state. The president (Masaryk) and the foreign minister (Beneš) looked to the Little Entente and to France to protect the country's territorial integrity. In the event, the republic was to break up when Hitler's claims to the Sudetenland were satisfied by France and Britain under the Munich Agreement (1938), which also ceded Ruthenia to Hungary and established Slovak autonomy under Tiso's puppet regime. Finally, Germany annexed the remaining territories of Bohemia and Moravia in March 1939, declaring them a German protectorate. During World War II Beneš established a government in exile in London (1940), Czech units fought on the Allied side and a Czech force led by

General Svoboda accompanied the Red Army which, jointly with the Americans, liberated the country in 1945. Under the postwar settlement the pre-1938 borders were re-established (with the exception of Ruthenia, ceded to the USSR, and the acquisition of a small enclave from Hungary). In free elections the Communist Party under Klement Gottwald gained a third of the seats, but Beneš was elected president. In 1947 Soviet pressure prevented Czechoslovakia from receiving aid under the Marshall Plan. In 1948, after a Communist coup, the non-Communist foreign minister, Jan Masaryk, died in mysterious circumstances and a Stalinist regime was installed. All opposition was suppressed – whether non-Communist or from rivals within the party – and a series of political trials culminated in the execution of Rudolf Slansky (1952). Gottwald (d. 1953) was succeeded by Novotny who continued the regime until in 1968 Slovak resentment of Czech dominance and the continuing economic crisis led to the appointment of Alexander Dubček as prime minister (January) and the replacement of Novotny by General Svoboda as president (March). There followed the so-called 'Prague Spring' when Dubček's programme of reform would have ensured a considerable measure of economic and political freedom had not the USSR crushed the movement by sending its troops to Prague in August, demoting (1969) and then expelling Dubček from the party (1970). Soviet intervention caused widespread protests at the time and these continued despite government repression. Their focus was the Charter 77 Group, formed after the Helsinki Agreements, which was persecuted in the face of international criticism, and the newly introduced policy of perestroika in the USSR.

D

Daladier, Edouard (1884–1970), French statesman. A Radical-Socialist deputy (1919–40), he held ministerial office from 1924, was briefly prime minister (1933, 1934). Supporting the Popular Front, he was minister of defence in Léon Blum's first cabinet and succeeded him as prime minister (1938–40). Having signed the Munich Agreement (1938), he tried to prepare France for war. As foreign minister in Paul Reynaud's government he was arrested by the Vichy authorities (1940) and was one of the defendants who made a farce of the Riom Trials. Deported to Germany (1943–45), he was a Radical deputy in the Fourth Republic (1946–58).

Dalai Lama (1935–   ), the spiritual and temporal ruler of Tibet. Installed as 14th Dalai Lama (1940), he assumed full powers of spiritual leadership in 1950 when the Chinese invaded Tibet. In 1959 the Tibetan people rose in revolt against Chinese oppression and the Dalai Lama fled to India. Since then he has attempted to rouse world opinion to the plight of his people and to negotiate with the Chinese authorities for a modus vivendi in Tibet.

Dalton, Edward Hugh John Neale (1887–1962), British statesman. Entering Parliament in 1924, he was Labour undersecretary of state for foreign affairs (1929–31), later holding office as minister of economic warfare (1940–42) and president of the board of trade (1942–45) in Churchill's war cabinet. Appointed chancellor of the exchequer in Attlee's government (1945), he was forced to resign for indiscreetly revealing in advance his 1947 budget proposals. He remained active in politics until 1957.

D'Annunzio, Gabriele (1863–1938), Italian poet and patriot. An ardent nationalist, he used a literary reputation to promote his views and to support Italy's entry into World War I, in which he served gallantly as a pilot. In 1919 he led a private army which seized Fiume (claimed by Yugoslavia at the Paris peace conference), and held it until ejected in 1921 by naval forces. In 1922 D'Annunzio welcomed Mussolini's March on Rome but thereafter lived in retirement.

Darlan, François (1881–1942), French admiral and statesman. C-in-C of the French fleet at the outbreak of World War II, he joined the Vichy government in 1940 as minister of marine (June) and, after Laval's resignation (December), became vice premier, interior and foreign minister and Pétain's heir-designate, posts which he was forced to resign when, on Hitler's insistence, Laval was reinstated. At the time of the Allied landings in North Africa he was in Algiers and ordered French forces not to oppose the invasion. Appointed high commissioner by the Americans as a counterpoise to de Gaulle, he was assassinated.

Dawes Plan The scheme evolved by a committee chaired by the American banker, Charles Gates Dawes (1865–1951), for payment of reparations by Germany. It came into effect in 1924 but was superseded by the Young Plan in 1929, when it became apparent that the scale of repayment was more than the German economy could bear.

Dayan, Moshe (1915–81), Israeli soldier and statesman. Born in Palestine, he joined Haganah and during World War II served with Wingate's Jewish Auxilliaries in Syria against the Vichy French. He commanded a battalion in the Arab-Israeli War (1948) and as chief of staff planned the Sinai Campaign (1956). He was Ben Gurion's minister of agriculture (1959–65) and minister of defence in the Six Day War (1967). In 1974 he resigned as minister of defence, being generally blamed for the near-defeat Israel suffered in the Yom Kippur War (1973), but returned as Begin's foreign minister (1977–79).

Deakin, Alfred (1856–1919), Australian statesman. A Liberal and an advocate of Australian federation, he was the second prime minister of the Commonwealth of Australia (1903–04), returning to office in 1905–08 and in 1909–10. Responsible for introducing old-age pensions and sickness benefits, he was an enthusiastic advocate of imperial preference.

Debs, Eugene Victor (1855–1926), American socialist and trade union organizer. He helped to found the Industrial Workers of the World (1905) and, in 1898, the Social Democratic Party (renamed the Socialist Party in 1901), standing as its presidential candidate in 1900, 1908, 1912 and 1920. He suffered imprisonment both for his union activities (1894) and for his pacificism in World War I.

De Gasperi, Alcide (1881–1954), Italian statesman. He represented the Trentino region first in the Austrian parliament (1911) and then in the Italian one (1921–24). Imprisoned for his anti-fascist activities, after World War II he led the Christian Democratic Party – the successor to Don Sturzo's Popular Party of which he had been secretary–general – and served as premier and foreign minister to ensure a republican and parliamentary regime in postwar Italy. With Monnet, Schuman and Adenauer he was one of the proponents of European co-operation.

Delcassé, Théophile (1852–1923), French statesman. The architect, with

Cambon, of the Entente Cordiale, as French foreign minister (1898–1905) he worked to resolve colonial differences with Britain and to build up an alliance between Britain, France and Russia in the face of an aggressive Germany.

Democratic Party One of the two main political parties in the United States. Originally drawing its strength from recent immigrants and the rural poor of the west, it was overshadowed after the Civil War and only twice broke the Republican monopoly of the presidency before Woodrow Wilson's election in 1912. The immediate postwar mood of isolationism saw a return to Republican presidents and not until the Depression did the Democrats regain the White House. Roosevelt was elected in 1932 (and re-elected in 1936, 1940 and 1944) and his New Deal policy made it the party of the middle-class intellectual, of organized labour and of the southern states, dedicated to reform and to programmes of government industrial aid and welfare schemes. Truman retained the presidency for the Democrats in 1948, but Stevenson lost in 1952 and 1956 to Eisenhower. Kennedy (1960) and Johnson (1964) achieved substantial measures of reform during their presidencies, but a Republican, Nixon, was returned in 1968 and 1972. In 1976 the Democrat, Jimmy Carter, was elected less on his own merits than on the weakness of his opponent, Gerald Ford, and the effects of the Watergate scandal. Subsequently, Democratic presidential candidates were defeated by Reagan (1980 and 1984) and by Bush (1988). This decline has been largely due to loss of traditional support, since working class and middle America prefers the image of the enterprise culture projected by the Republicans to the left-wing welfare image with which the Democrats have been associated. However, the party has continued to control Congress – and thus to modify or hamper a president's legislative programme – when there has been a Republican in the White House.

Deng Xiao-ping (1902–), Chinese political leader. A veteran Communist, appointed vice premier (1952) and secretary-general of the party (1956), he held senior posts until the Cultural Revolution, when he was removed from office as 'number two capitalist roader' only to be reinstated in 1973. In 1976, after an inter-party struggle, he was once again demoted, only to be restored to positions of even greater power after the 11th Party Congress (1977). From then on he was the effective ruler of China, and even after his retirement Deng continued to exert considerable influence.

Denikin, Anton Ivanovich (1872–1947), Russian soldier. Deputy chief of staff (1917), he then served the Provisional Government as a field commander and after the October Revolution fought the Bolsheviks in

southern Russia and the Caucasus until March 1920. He escaped and
lived in exile in France and the United States.

Depression, The The industrial and agricultural slump which affected
the whole world during 1928–34 and was precipitated by the 1929 Wall
Street stock market crash. In the financial panic which followed there
were bank failures across the United States, while the failure of the
Austrian Credit Anstalt had a knock-on effect throughout central and
eastern Europe. Shortage of capital limited output and reduced con-
sumption worldwide, affecting both industrialized and non-industrialized
nations. The demand for raw materials, goods and services was
restricted, bringing widespread and extreme levels of unemployment and
bankruptcy. This failure of existing institutions encouraged revolutionary
movements to seek their abolition. The effects of the Depression were
alleviated in the United States by the New Deal, while in Europe
rearmament tended to stimulate the economy.

Derby Scheme The scheme initiated by the minister for war, the Earl of
Derby, in 1915 to stimulate voluntary enlistment in the British forces. Its
failure led to the introduction of conscription in 1916.

Desai, Morarji Ranchhodji (1896–), Indian statesman. A notably efficient
minister in the post-independence Bombay state government, he was
elected to the national parliament (1957) and served as finance minister
(1958–63). In 1966 he was defeated for leadership of the Congress Party
by Indira Gandhi, but served as her finance minister until his dismissal in
1969. He joined the opposition Congress Party and later formed the
Janata Party, becoming an ineffective prime minister (1977–79).

De Valera, Eamon (1882–1975), Irish statesman. His US citizenship (he
was born in New York) gained him a reprieve from the death sentence for
taking part in the Easter Rising (1916) as commandant of the Dublin
brigade of the Irish Volunteers. Released under an amnesty, he resumed
his political and military activities as Sinn Fein MP and as president of
the Irish Volunteers (1917–21). President of Sinn Fein (1917–26) and of
the 'Irish Republic' (1919–22), he took part in the Civil War (1922–23)
and was imprisoned (1923–24). From 1926 he led the Fianna Fail party
in opposition to the 1921 treaty. As prime minister (1932–48), he secured
complete Irish independence (1937) and maintained Irish neutrality
during World War II. He was again prime minister (1951–54, 1957–59),
and president from 1959 until he retired from office in 1973.

Diaz, Armando (1861–1928), Italian soldier. Appointed C-in-C (1917), he
defeated the Austro-Hungarian armies at Vittorio-Veneto (1918). He was
minister of war (1922–24) under Mussolini.

Díaz, Porfirio (1830–1915), Mexican soldier and dictator. Having served with Juárez against the Emperor Maximilian, he was subsequently defeated by him in the contest for the presidency. In 1871 he rose in revolt, only to be driven into exile. Returning in 1876 he seized power, encouraging foreign capital to exploit the Mexican economy to his profit, and to that of foreign investors and a wealthy minority of his own supporters. In 1911 Díaz was overthrown by Madero.

Diefenbaker, John George (1895–1979), Canadian statesman. As leader of the Progressive Conservatives (1956) he formed the minority government (1957) which ended 22 years of Liberal rule. Confirmed in power (1958), he followed a policy of Commonwealth co-operation, but lost seats in the 1962 election on a defence policy judged too pro-American and resigned (1963), leading the opposition until his retirement (1967).

Diem, Ngo Dinh (1901–63), South Vietnamese political leader. Involved in nationalist politics before and during World War II, he was forced by the French to seek exile in the United States. He returned in 1954, with US support, to head an anti-Communist government and in 1956 to oust Bao Dai as head of state. His nepotism and anti-Buddhist policy alienated his people and his US backers. In 1963 a military coup mounted with the connivance of the CIA overthrew Diem. He and other members of his family were killed.

Dimitrov, Georgi (1882–1949), Bulgarian Communist leader. He directed Communist activities in Bulgaria from 1917 until the failure of an uprising in 1923. Escaping to Russia he became a Comintern agent. Arrested in Berlin in 1933 and accused of complicity in the Reichstag Fire, he conducted a brilliant defence which brought his acquital and deportation to the USSR, where he became secretary of the Comintern (1934–43). In 1944 he returned to Bulgaria with the Red Army, overthrew the monarchy (1946) and became prime minister of a ruthlessly repressive Communist state. His initiative in promoting an association of Balkan Communist states lost him favour with Stalin. Summoned to Moscow to recant, he died under medical treatment there in 1949.

disarmament Organized efforts to outlaw war began in the mid-19th century and in the Hague Conferences (1899, 1907) there developed an institution, the Hague Tribunal (see under **International Court of Justice**), through which international disputes could be settled by arb tration rather than by force. Between the wars, concern that the threat of war might be increased by the scale of armaments led to such unavailing efforts as the Locarno Treaty and the naval conferences in

London and Washington. Since World War II nuclear weapons have proved an incomparably greater threat, but mutual mistrust between the superpowers has made progress disappointingly slow. Following the Geneva Conference between the United States and the USSR, a test ban treaty was signed in Moscow (1963) and, under the aegis of the UN Disarmament Commission (formed 1954), a non-proliferation treaty (1968). In 1969 the United States and the USSR began Strategic Arms Limitation Talks (SALT 1), which brought agreement (1972). However SALT 2 (begun in 1974) failed when the US Senate refused to ratify the treaty signed by Carter and Brezhnev in 1979. In 1982 President Reagan initiated the Strategic Arms Reduction Talks (START) which brought agreement (1987) to abolish Soviet and American medium-range nuclear missiles. This success offered hope for conventional arms reductions in Europe, where talks have been held in Vienna since 1981 without any real progress being made. Meanwhile a fresh problem of arms control has arisen with the use of chemical weapons in the Iran-Iraq conflict.

Djilas, Milovan (1911–), Yugoslav Communist dissident. He joined the Communist Party (1929) and was imprisoned (1933–36). A successful partisan commander (1941–44) and envoy in Moscow (1944–45), he became an intimate of Tito and member of the Yugoslav ruling circle (1945–53), but was expelled from the party and dismissed from his government posts (1954) and given a suspended prison sentence in 1955 for 'hostile propaganda'. This amounted to articles in the official press critical of abuses. He was imprisoned (1956–61) for his support of the Hungarian Uprising and again (1962–66) for publishing *The New Class*, a stinging criticism of the oligarchic tendencies of Communist parties in power.

Doenitz, Karl (1891–1980), German naval officer. A specialist in submarine warfare, he rebuilt the U-boat fleet (1935–39) and commanded it during World War II, succeeding Admiral Raeder as C-in-C of the German navy (1943). As Hitler's successor, Doenitz authorized Germany's unconditional surrender (1945) and was tried and sentenced to ten years' imprisonment (1946–56) by the Nuremberg Tribunal.

Dollfuss, Engelbert (1892–1934), Austrian political leader. He joined the Christian Social Party and, as a result of his success in combating the effects of the Depression as minister of agriculture (1931), he was appointed chancellor in 1932. He met the threat of incorporation into Germany by banning the Austrian Nazi Party, but was forced to rely upon the support of von Starhemberg with his Heimwehr against the left.

Doriot, Jacques

He proclaimed the corporate state in May 1934 after the crushing of the socialist opposition in February by the Heimwehr and the army. His position remained insecure and he was murdered in an abortive Nazi coup in July 1934.

Doriot, Jacques (1898–1945), French fascist sympathizer. Expelled from the Communist Party (1934) for advocating a Popular Front, in 1936 he founded the fascist Parti Populaire Français. He became a collaborator (1940), raising recruits to fight with the German army on the Russian front. Having fled to Germany on the fall of Vichy (1944), he was reported killed in an air raid.

Douglas, William Orville (1898–1980), US jurist. A liberal and supporter of the New Deal, he was appointed to the Supreme Court by Roosevelt. His decisions consistently supported civil rights, conservation and civil liberties, particularly the rights of free speech.

Douglas-Home, Alexander Frederick (1903– , Baron Home of the Hirsel), British statesman. Conservative MP (1931–45, 1950–51 and 1963–74), he was parliamentary private secretary to Chamberlain (1937–39), minister of state for Scotland (1951–55), Commonwealth minister (1955–60) and foreign secretary (1960–63). He succeeded Macmillan as prime minister when the latter resigned in 1963. Despite the effects of the Profumo Scandal Douglas-Home was only narrowly defeated in the 1964 election. In 1965 he was replaced as Conservative leader by Edward Heath, in whose cabinet he served as foreign secretary (1970–74).

Dowding, Hugh Caswall Tremenheere (1882–1970, 1st Baron), British air chief marshal. He served with distinction in France in World War I and as air officer commanding in Palestine and Transjordan in the interwar years. In 1936 he was appointed C-in-C Fighter Command, defeating the German air force in the Battle of Britain. He retired in 1942.

Dreyfus, Alfred (1859–1935), French army officer. He was sentenced to life imprisonment for espionage on the slenderest evidence (1894), an injustice that it took 12 years to put right. In the process French society became so bitterly divided that the effects were felt up to and during World War I and even in the politics which produced the Vichy regime in World War II.

Dubček, Alexander (1921–), Czechoslovak Communist leader. A member of the Slovak Communist underground in World War II, he became first secretary of the Slovak Communist Party (1958), replacing Novotny as first secretary of the Czechoslovak Communist Party (1960). He was about to introduce a programme of reform ('socialism with a human face') when, despite assurances given to the contrary, Soviet and

Warsaw Pact forces invaded Czechoslovakia in August 1968. Dubček was dismissed as first secretary (1969) and expelled from the party (1970). The ideals of his 'Prague Spring' took a new significance in Gorbachov's perestroika policy and Dubček emerged once more to express them in a speech at Bologna University in November 1988.

Dulles, John Foster (1888–1969), US statesman and diplomat. He helped draft the UN Charter (1945), and served as US delegate in 1946, 1947 and 1950. After being appointed secretary of state (1953) by President Eisenhower, his main concern was to build up a system of alliances against potential Soviet aggression (NATO and SEATO), promising 'massive retaliation' against any attack and formulating the 'Eisenhower Doctrine' of military and economic aid to friendly nations in the Middle East. He was personally antagonistic to Eden, and the Suez Crisis (1956) strained Anglo-American relations. In 1958 he sent US troops into Lebanon. He died shortly after resigning office.

Duma The Russian parliament created by Tsar Nicholas II in response to the demands of the 1905 Revolution. All four Dumas (1905, 1907, 1907–12 and 1912–17) found themselves more or less in conflict with the tsar and hampered in their ability to effect more than a few of the necessary reforms. After the tsar's abdication (1917), a committee of the Duma authorized Prince Lvov to form the Provisional Government.

Dumbarton Oaks Conference The meetings held near Washington, DC, in August 1944 between the United States, the United Kingdom, the USSR and China from which tentative proposals emerged for the formation of the United Nations.

Dutch East Indies see **Indonesia**

Duvalier, François (1907–71), Haitian president. A country doctor and sometime minister of health, he came to power in an army coup in 1957 and until his death ruled Haiti with increasing corruption and despotism, instilling fear through voodoo and his notorious Tonton Macoutes. 'Papa Doc's' son, Jean Claude Duvalier (1951–), succeeded him and ruled as president for life until forced to flee the country after riots in 1986.

E

East Germany   see **German Democratic Republic**

Easter Rising   The armed rebellion (24–29 April 1916) led by Patrick Pearse and James Connolly who seized the post office and other buildings in Dublin and proclaimed an independent republic. The rising was crushed, Pearse, Connolly and 12 other leaders were executed and De Valera was reprieved.

Ebert, Friedrich   (1871–1925), German statesman. Leader of the Social Democrat Party (1913), he backed the imperial German war effort and in 1918 co-operated with Prince Maximilian of Baden, succeeding him as chancellor. In 1919 he was elected president, suppressing the Spartakists (1919) and defeating the Kapp Putsch (1920). He accepted the Versailles Treaty and promulgated the constitution of the Weimar Republic. See also **Germany**.

Eden, Robert Anthony   (1897–1977, Earl of Avon), British statesman and diplomat. A soldier in World War I, he became a Conservative MP in 1923. An influential supporter of the League of Nations, he replaced Hoare as foreign secretary (1935) when the provisions of the Hoare-Laval Pact were revealed, resigning in 1938 in protest against Chamberlain's policy of appeasement. He was Churchill's foreign secretary (1940–45 and 1951–55), succeeding him as prime minister in 1955 although in failing health. He responded to Nasser's nationalization of the Suez Canal by colluding with the French and Israelis in an attack on Suez. With the failure of the operation, Eden's health collapsed. He resigned in 1957 and retired from public life.

Edward VII   (1841–1910), king of Great Britain (1901–10), was the eldest son of Queen Victoria. His familiarity with French society facilitated the Anglo-French Agreement (1904), while the well-known mutual anti-pathy between him and Kaiser Wilhelm II strengthened German suspicions of British policy.

Edward VIII   (1894–1972), king of Great Britain and Northern Ireland. A popular Prince of Wales, he showed a selfish disregard for the duties of a constitutional monarch, which became apparent on his accession in January 1936. In the 'Abdication crisis', the king preferred to renounce his throne rather than give up his mistress, Mrs Wallis Simpson, an

American divorcee. On 11 December he abdicated, left the country and in 1937 married Mrs Simpson. During World War II he served as governor of the Bahamas (1940–45). He lived thereafter in France. He was created Duke of Windsor at the time of his abdication.

Egypt A republic of northeast Africa. Nominally part of the Ottoman Empire (see **Turkey**) until 1914, in practice it had been ruled by independent governors (khedives) whose indebtedness to European financiers led to increasing intervention by Britain and France. On the outbreak of World War I Britain declared a protectorate and Egypt became the base of operations in the Palestine campaign. The British presence aroused strong nationalist feelings (see **Wafd**), which were unsatisfied by the acknowledgement of Egyptian independence under King Fuad in 1922. Eventually in 1936 it was agreed gradually to withdraw British garrisons to the Canal Zone. Their departure was postponed by the outbreak of World War II. In the postwar era the Egyptian army became the focus of nationalism. Defeat in the Arab-Israeli War (1948), the continued British presence in the Canal Zone and the corruptions of King Farouk's regime provoked a group of junior officers under General Neguib, who took power in 1952. Neguib was deposed in 1954 by Colonel Nasser. In 1956, following the evacuation of British troops, Anglo-American financial support for the building of the Aswan dam was withheld. Nasser promptly nationalized the Suez Canal and then won a diplomatic victory when he forced the withdrawal of the Anglo-French invasion force. Egypt now turned to the USSR to finance the building of the Aswan dam and to equip and train the Egyptian army Egypt itself played a leading role in the Arab world, being linked with Syria during 1958–61 as the United Arab Republic. Sadat became president after the sudden death of Nasser in 1970 and in 1972 reversed his policy by expelling Soviet military advisers and taking complete control of all military bases. Defeat in the Six Day War (1967) and, despite intial success, in the Yom Kippur War (1973), made Egypt turn to diplomacy rather than military action. In consequence relations with more militant Arab states became strained and in 1977 there were frontier incidents with Libya. However, Egypt secured the reopening of the Suez Canal (1975) and, following the Camp David Talks, the withdrawal of Israeli forces from Sinai. Peaceful settlements with Israel aroused the hostility of Arab fundamentalists who assassinated President Sadat in 1981. His successor, President Mubarak, continued his predecessor's policy, faced with the severe problems of a population growing faster than the economy which can sustain it and an Islamic fundamentalism which fed on the discontents and fanned disorders. Under such pressure it was natural that Egypt should risk Israeli displeasure by recognizing the Palestinian proclamation of an independent state in November 1988.

Eighteenth Amendment   see under **Prohibition**

Einaudi, Luigi   (1874–1961), Italian statesman. Professor of economics, Turin University (1900–43) and an anti-fascist, he escaped to Switzerland. Governor of the Bank of Italy (1945–48) and De Gasperi's minister of finance (1947), he introduced measures which successfully combated inflation. He was president of Italy (1948–55).

Eire   see **Ireland**

Eisenhower, Dwight David   (1890–1969), US soldier and 34th president of the United States. He graduated from West Point (1919), was chief of operations (1942), and commanded US forces in the North African landings (1942) and the Allied armies in the conquest of Tunisia. After directing the invasions of Sicily and Italy, in 1943 he was appointed supreme commander, Allied Expeditionary Force, and directed the planning and execution of the invasion of France in June 1944 and the operations which led to the surrender of German armies in the West in May 1945. General of the army (1944), commander of US occupation forces in Germany (1945) and chief of US army staff (1945–48), in 1948 he became president of Columbia University, taking leave of absence (1950–52) to organize NATO forces as supreme commander Allied powers in Europe. In 1952 he won the Republican nomination and then the presidency. As president – the first soldier since Grant – he played the role of supreme commander delegating to his vice-president, Richard Nixon, responsibility for party politics, to his secretary of state, Dulles, the conduct of foreign affairs and to Sherman Adams financial and economic strategy, intervening only when absolutely necessary, as in the Macarthy Investigations or at Little Rock at home. In foreign affairs this allowed Dulles to pursue a vigorous policy of Soviet containment while Eisenhower himself could keep more friendly contact on a personal basis with Soviet leaders. After supporting Nixon's unsuccessful bid for the presidency in 1960, Eisenhower retired from public life.

Eisenhower Doctrine   see under **Dulles, John Foster**

Elizabeth II   (1926–   ), Queen of Great Britain and Northern Ireland, head of the Commonwealth, who succeeded her father, George VI, on 8 February 1952. She adapted the constitutional monarchy to the changing conditions of the 20th century, shedding much of the formality surrounding royalty while preserving the office as a focus of national patriotism. It is, however, as head of the Commonwealth, that she has renewed the monarchy as a means of linking together the very diverse nations which once comprised the British Empire.

Elliot-Murray-Kynynmund, Gilbert John   (1845–1914, 4th Earl of Minto), British statesman. Having held office as governor-general of Canada (1898–1904), as viceroy of India (1905–10) he prepared with the secretary of state for India, John Morley (1838–1923), the reforms in 1909 which set India on the path to self-government.

El Salvador   A republic of Central America. It achieved separate identity, although subject to outside interference from Guatemala and Nicaragua, during the 19th century. Political instability during the 20th century produced a series of military dictators, the longest-running being General Martinez (1931–44). Externally there was growing tension with Guatemala caused by the influx from El Salvador of landless peasants and this erupted into outright war in 1969 following violent clashes at an international football match between their respective teams. El Salvador withdrew its forces after the OAS imposed a truce. Throughout the 1970s there was growing unrest and acts of terrorism and in 1979 a full-scale guerrilla war began. The reaction of the right and of the army was the murder of their political opponents, including Archbishop Romero, who was assassinated in 1980 while celebrating mass. The fall of Somoza in neighbouring Nicaragua had alarmed the US government. Military aid was increased, but the activities of the right-wing death squads was curbed and support given to the moderate liberalism of José Napoleon Duarte (1926–). He was defeated by the right-wing extremist Roberto d'Aubuisson in the 1982 elections and resigned the presidency, returning to power in 1984. The Marxist Farabundo Martí National Liberation Front (FMLN) remained a constant threat and, although its activities were restrained after the peace pact signed by Central American leaders in 1987, disturbances increased again towards the end of 1988 as a result of the terminal illness of President Duarte and in response to the renewed activities of right-wing death squads in the run-up to the 1989 presidential elections. These returned the right-wing Arena candidate, Alfredo Cristiani.

Enosis   The agitation of Greek communities under alien rule for political integration with the mother-country. Such a campaign was conducted by Venizelos in Crete in the early years of the 20th century, but is most obviously associated with Cyprus. Here it fuelled riots in 1931 and inspired Colonel Grivas' guerrilla war against the British, and led to the temporary ousting of Archbishop Makarios in 1974 and the Turkish invasion and partition of the island.

Entente Cordiale

Entente Cordiale see **Anglo-French Agreement**

Enver Pasha (1881–1922), Turkish soldier. A leader of the Young Turk Revolution (1908), he commanded forces against the Italians in Libya (1911) and in the Balkan Wars, and his influence as minister of war (1914) brought Turkey into World War I on the side of the Central Powers. During the war he commanded in the Caucasus and, after the October Revolution and the Turkish armistice, became involved in Russian Civil War and was killed by Soviet troops.

EOKA (Ethniki Organosis Kyprion Agoniston) The name borne by Colonel Grivas' nationalist guerrillas in Cyprus.

Erhard, Ludwig (1897–1977), German statesman. Professor of economics at Munich University (1945–49), he was closely involved in industrial reconstruction in Bavaria. Elected to the Bundestag, he was appointed minister of economic affairs by Chancellor Adenauer (1949). His currency reforms and his espousal of free enterprise fuelled the postwar 'economic miracle', for which he has been given the credit. Appointed deputy chancellor (1957), he succeeded Adenauer as chancellor (1963–66).

Eritrea A country in northeast Africa on the southern Red Sea Coast. A former Italian colony, it was used as a base for the successful Italian invasion of Ethiopia (1935–36). Liberated by British forces in World War II, it was administered by Britain as a UN trust territory until 1952. Differing in race, religion and language from the Ethiopians, the inhabitants disputed the claims of Ethiopia to the territory and the UN general assembly made the area an autonomous federal region within the then Ethiopian Empire. In 1962 Ethiopia absorbed Eritrea and the Eritrean Liberation Front was formed and began a guerrilla war for the region's independence. Despite Soviet and Cuban support, Ethiopia failed to subdue the ELF which controlled a substantial part of the region.

Estonia A constituent republic of the Soviet Union. Ruled as a province of the Russian Empire, Estonia underwent a nationalist revival towards the end of the 19th century and suffered severe reprisals after the failure of the 1905 Revolution. Independence was granted by the provisional government after the abdication of the tsar (1917), but the October Revolution imposed a Bolshevik regime on the capital Tallinn. Estonia was subsequently occupied by the Germans, independence being proclaimed once more, in 1918, after the German defeat and recognized by the USSR in the Treaty of Tartu (1920). Following a period of political instability, Estonia came under the authoritarian rule of Constantin Pats

(1934–39). The more democratic 1938 constitution was short-lived: under the secret clauses of the Nazi-Soviet Pact, Estonia was annexed by the USSR in 1940 and reoccupied after World War II. Despite deportations and Russification, Estonian nationalism remained a strong force and Estonians became the most outspoken advocates of autonomy under Gorbachov's policy of perestroika. In 1988 the Popular Front (under the leadership of the local Communist party) demonstrated for greater independence and the Estonian parliament voted in favour of the republic's right to exclusive possession of national assets and the freedom to veto laws passed in Moscow. Estonians opposed the draft amendment to the Soviet constitution allowing Moscow to veto legislation by the constituent republics which was deemed to infringe the Soviet constitution.

Ethiopia A republic in east Africa. During the 19th century it preserved its independence under an imperial family which claimed descent from Solomon and the Queen of Sheba. The emperor Menelik was in turn succeeded (1) by his grandson (1913, deposed in 1916); (2) his daughter, and on her death in 1930 by his grand-nephew, Haile Selassie. In 1936 the Italian conquest drove the emperor into exile. He returned in 1941, when British forces liberated the country during World War II, survived a coup attempt in 1960, but was deposed (1974) when a reformist government was overthrown in a military coup. In 1977 the coup leader, Brigadier Terefi Benti, was removed from power by a group of Marxist officers led by Colonel Mengistu. The Marxist regime inherited civil war in Eritrea and was almost immediately engaged in war with the Somali Republic, which invaded the Ogaden in support of the Somali Liberation Front. With Russian and Cuban aid, the Somalis were cleared out of the region and this same help was employed against the Eritreans and (from 1979) against rebels in the northern province of Tigré. The regime also had to meet a series of famines from 1980 onwards. These were exacerbated by a misguided policy of collectivization, but ameliorated by a massive programme of aid from the west. In 1987 Colonel Mengistu became president, with a nominally civilian government elected from a single-party list under the 1986 constitution.

Europe, Council of A body set up in 1949 and operating in a consultative capacity through a committeee of ministers and the European Assembly, meeting three times a year at Strasbourg. It remains independent of the European Community. In 1955 the council set up a commission and court of human rights to hear complaints brought against member governments either by their own citizens or by other member governments.

European Atomic Energy Community (EURATOM) and European Coal and Steel Community see under **European Community**

European Community The body created in July 1967 through the integration of the executives of the three extant European Communities.

(1) *European Atomic Energy Community*, established by the Treaty of Rome (1957), to encourage co-operation among member states in nuclear research and the peaceful uses of nuclear energy.

(2) *European Coal and Steel Community* (ECSC), the first of the communities. Stemming from the Schuman Plan (1950), it came into being in 1952 when France, the German Federal Republic, Italy and the Benelux countries created a common market for coal and steel, which has since been joined by other Community members.

(3) *European Economic Community* (EEC). Paul Henri Spaak's proposals for closer economic co-operation between ECSC states by means of free trade and free movement of labour and capital were embodied in the Treaty of Rome (March 1957) and the Common Market came into being on 1 January 1958. Members had the right to veto the applications by other European states to join the community (a provision that the socialist Spaak had inserted to block the membership of such right-wing regimes as Spain and Portugal) and this was used by France against Britain in 1963 and 1967. With the retirement of General de Gaulle (1969) Denmark, the Republic of Ireland and Britain became members (1973). Norway withdrew when a referendum showed that the majority of the population opposed joining. In 1981 Greece joined the EEC, in 1985 Spain and Portugal became members and subsequently Turkey made approaches for membership. The community comprises a council of ministers and an elected European parliament, a European court of justice and a European investment bank set up to finance projects in the Third World as well as in the community. The whole is managed by a Brussels-based civil service headed by commissioners serving for a limited term and chosen in turn from member countries. The tendency of the community was towards closer co-operation, with economies to be fully integrated in 1992, but the ultimate aim of common taxation rates and a common currency seemed likely to provoke a crisis of nationality.

European Economic Community see under **European Community**

European Defence Community An abortive plan for integrated armed forces proposed by the French prime minister, René Pleven, in 1950 as a means of reconciling French public opinion to possible German rearmament. In fact the same end was achieved in 1955 when West Germany became a member of NATO.

European Free Trade Association (EFTA)   An association which came into being in May 1960, following an agreement reached in Stockholm in November 1959 between Austria, Denmark, Norway, Portugal, Sweden, Switzerland and Britain to promote trade and economic co-operation between them as a measure of economic protection against the European Economic Community. In 1972 Denmark and Britain left EFTA and in 1975 the remaining members together with Iceland (joined 1970) signed an agreement with the EEC providing for free trade in industrial products.

Evatt, Herbert Vere   (1894–1965), Australian lawyer and statesman. A high court justice (1931–40), he entered the federal parliament (1941) and served as attorney-general and as minister of external affairs (1941–49) in Curtin's and in Chifley's Labor governments. As Australian delegate to the San Francisco Conference (1945), he successfully tabled no less than 26 amendments, limiting the powers of the UN security council and enhancing those of the general assembly. He led the Labor opposition to the Menzies government, defeating its attempt to proscribe the Australian Communist Party. He retired from politics to serve as chief justice of New South Wales (1960–62).

Evian Agreements   The discussions between the French government and Algerian nationalists, held in March 1962 at Evian, which resulted in a cease-fire in the Algerian War, linked with recognition of Algerian independence, and set out terms for a referendum on Algerian self-determination.

F

Falange A Spanish political party founded by José Antonio Primo de Rivera, who gave a specifically Spanish and traditionalist bias to its basic fascist tenets. Falange militia supported the Nationalists during the Spanish Civil War and the party was merged by Franco with the Carlists to form the sole legal political party. It remained almost entirely under his control and after his death its influence largely disappeared.

Falkland Islands A British colony in the South Atlantic. British sovereignty was constantly disputed by both Chile and Argentina, and in 1946 Argentina took its claim to the United Nations but without avail. During 1946–82 there were sporadic demonstrations in Argentina in support of the claim and some minor incidents in the waters around the islands. In 1982 the coincidence of abortive negotiations between Britain and Argentina over sovereignty, the withdrawal of British naval units from the South Atlantic and unrest at home led the Argentine president, General Galtieri, to launch an invasion, first of South Georgia (19 March) and then of the Falklands themselves (2 April). Attempts at mediation by the United States and Peru proved unavailing. A British task force recaptured South Georgia on 25 April and landed on the Falklands (21 May), retaking the islands and forcing the Argentine surrender (14 June). The failure of the Argentine invasion led to the fall, trial and imprisonment of General Galtieri, but this brought no solution to the crisis. In Argentina itself, revenge for the country's defeat became a nationalist rallying cry. Britain meanwhile fortified the islands, while showing readiness to discuss any arrangement for their future which did not involve loss of sovereignty.

Fanfani, Amintore (1908–), Italian statesman. Prime minister (1958, 1954–59 and 1960–63, when he included in his cabinet the moderate socialist, Nenni), he subsequently served as foreign minister (1965 and 1966–68), prime minister again (1982–83) and president of the Italian senate (1968–73, 1973–76).

Farouk (1920–65), king of Egypt. He succeeded his father, King Fuad, in 1936. During World War II his court was a hotbed of Axis intrigue and the British imposed (1942) as prime minister Nahas Pasha, from the Wafd party, with which the king had been in constant conflict. The corruption of the court circle and defeat in the Arab-Israeli War (1948) led to his overthrow by a military coup (1952), his abdication and exile.

fascism A revolutionary ideology formulated in Italy by Mussolini in the aftermath of World War I. Although characterized as right wing, it shared with revolutionary socialism a contempt for liberal institutions, for capitalism and and for middle-class morality, appealing to nationalist and patriotic ideals rather than to internationalism. Fascism demanded the subordination of the individual to the state, that state being a corporate entity in which group rather than individual interests were to be represented and in which each class had its responsibilities and duties. Although itself a violent revolutionary party, fascism was accepted by many since it offered its violence as a counter-force to revolutionary socialism, protecting capitalism – which it then controlled for its own ends – appealing to patriotism and posing as a guardian of morality. Fascism was strictly speaking an Italian phenomenon: similar conditions created a similar movement in Germany – nazism. In Spain the falange drew its inspiration from fascism and Salazar's regime in Portugal was modelled on its idea of the corporate state. In South America various military dictators adopted the trappings of fascism, but the Peronist movement most closely revealed its working-class origins.

Fawcett, Dame Millicent Garrett (1847–1929), campaigner for women's rights. A pioneer in achieving higher education for women and president of the National Union of Women's Suffrage Societies (1897–1918), she deplored the militancy of Emmeline Pankhurst.

Feisal I (1885–1933), king of Iraq. The third son of Hussein, emir and king of Hejaz, he escaped from the Turkish army in 1916 to join Lawrence and lead the Arab revolt. In 1920 he proclaimed himself king of Syria and Palestine, but was ousted by the French, the mandatory power in Syria. With British backing and following a referendum he was proclaimed king of Iraq (1921). His grandson, Feisal II (1935–58), succeeeded on the death of his father in 1939 and was murdered in 1958 when the monarchy was overthrown by Brigadier Kassem.

Feisal, Ibn Abdul-Aziz al Saud (1905–75), king of Saudi Arabia. A son of Ibn Saud whom he helped to create Saudi Arabia, he became prime minister and minister of foreign affairs (1958–61 and 1961–64) to his brother King Saud. He came to the throne following his brother's enforced abdication (1964), instituting energetic reforms. As an ardent anti-Communist and anti-Zionist he achieved a dominant position in the Arab world. He was assassinated by a nephew in 1975.

Ferdinand (1861–1948), king of Bulgaria. He was chosen prince of

Bulgaria in 1887 but, because of Russian opposition, was not recognized as such by the European powers until 1897. In 1908 he took advantage of the Young Turk Revolution to proclaim his country's complete independence from Turkey, with himself as king. To recoup the losses of the second Balkan War (1913), Ferdinand brought Bulgaria into World War I on the side of the Central Powers in 1916. After initial success against Serbia, the Bulgarian armies were defeated in 1918 and Ferdinand was forced to abdicate in favour of his son Boris III.

Figueres Ferrer, José (1906–   ), Costa Rican statesman. In 1948 he led a revolution to ensure that the newly elected president Ulate took power. As provisional president (1948–49) he laid the foundations of national stability by abolishing the army and nationalizing financial and communications services. As president (1953–58 and 1970–74) he instituted educational and social reform and undertook a wide-ranging programme of public works.

Finland A republic of Scandinavia. A Russian grand duchy during the 19th century, Finnish nationalism was roused by a deliberate policy of Russification, relaxed after the 1905 Revolution, only to be more severely imposed (1910–16). The October Revolution gave the Finns the opportunity to proclaim their independence. In the ensuing civil war the Bolsheviks were expelled by Marshal Mannerheim and a republic proclaimed (1919) and recognized by the USSR (Treaty of Tartu, 1920). The new state defeated threats from both left and right. The Communist party was suppressed in 1923 and the extreme right-wing party, the Lapua Movement, suffered the same fate in 1932 after an abortive coup. Finnish governments followed a policy of consolidation at home and neutrality abroad. However, despite a non-aggression pact signed between the two countries in 1932, shortly after the outbreak of World War II, the USSR launched an attack on Finland and by sheer weight of numbers crushed Finnish resistance in March 1940. Under the ensuing peace treaty the USSR annexed 11 % of Finland's agricultural and industrial resources. To regain their lost territories the Finns allied themselves with the Germans in their attack on the USSR in 1941, but by skilful diplomacy managed to keep such a degree of independence as to be able to sign a separate armistice with the Soviets in 1944. Peace terms included further loss of territory in northern Finland and very heavy reparations paid to the Soviet Union. In return Finland has enjoyed a unique relationship with its powerful neighbour. Its Social Democratic governments have, in return for the strictest neutrality and the avoidance any act which might be deemed provocative, been allowed freedom and independence, including associate membership of EFTA (1961) and free trade in industrial goods with the European Community (1974). This position allowed Helsinki to be chosen as the site for the 1975 conference on human rights.

Fisher, John Arbuthnot (1841–1920, Baron Fisher), British admiral. As first sea lord (1904–09) he reorganized the Royal Navy to meet the German threat to British naval supremacy with a programme of naval rearmament. As C-in-C Mediterranean (1899–1902) he had already revolutionized tactics and training and his influence upon his service would have been greater had he been able to work with others. In 1910 he resigned after a quarrel with a fellow admiral and, although he was recalled by Churchill as first sea lord in 1914, relations were strained and Fisher resigned in 1915 because of his disagreement with the Dardanelles campaign.

Foch, Ferdinand (1851–1921), French soldier and marshal of France. In 1914, having halted the German advance through Lorraine, he then led the 9th Army in the victory of the Marne. By 1917 he had become chief of general staff in succession to Pétain and was then sent to rally the Italians after their rout at Caporetto and to help establish the supreme allied war council. Appointed supreme allied commander on the western front in the crisis of March 1918, he halted the German offensive on the Somme, counterattacked and defeated Ludendorff in the second Battle of the Marne (July) and launched the general offensive (August) which led to the German defeat. Foch signed the armistice which ended World War I (11 November 1918).

Food and Agriculture Organization (FAO) A specialized agency of the United Nations founded in 1945. In collaboration with the World Bank (since 1945) and the World Health Organization (since 1948) it has worked to achieve higher standards of nutrition world-wide by encouraging the exchange of information between governments, providing investment and expert advice and administering a world food programme for the Third World.

Ford, Gerald Rudolf (1913–   ), 38th president of the United States. Born Leslie Lynch King Jr, he took his stepfather's name when his mother remarried after her divorce. A lawyer who served in the US navy in World War II, he sat as Republican in the House of Representatives (1948–73) and served as house minority leader (1965–73). In 1973 Nixon chose him to replace Vice-President Agnew when the latter was forced to resign over allegations of financial malpractice, and in 1974 he replaced the president when Nixon was forced out of office by the Watergate scandal. He was thus the only man in US history to have held the presidency and the vice-presidency by appointment and not by election. As president he was overshadowed by his secretary of state, Kissinger, and, having won the Republican nomination in the 1976 presidential election, was defeated by Jimmy Carter.

Formosa see **Taiwan**

Fourteen Points The declaration made on 8 January 1918 by President Wilson to the US Congress outlining his aims for a peace settlement once victory had been gained in World War I. They comprised 14 points, the first five being general – open treaties between nations, the freedom of the seas, the removal of trade barriers, the reduction of armaments and the adjustment of colonial claims to take into account the wishes and interests of the inhabitants. Eight points, relating to specific matters of European sovereignty and territorial integrity, pledged the creation of a Polish state, the division of Austria-Hungary in conformity with its nationalities and the revision of Italy's frontiers on the same principle. The 14th point envisaged the creation of what was to become the League of Nations. The Fourteen Points became a very valuable propaganda instrument, but they were considerably diluted at the Paris Conference. They first enunciated the principle of self-determination – of considerable significance after World War II – but in practice denied it when a territorially denuded Austria was forbidden union with Germany immediately after World War I.

France A republic of northwestern Europe. During the 20th century it has been governed by four regimes.

(1) *The Third Republic.* This came into being in 1870 after the Franco-Prussian War and the fall of the Second Empire. In its early years, there was always the possibility of the restoration of the monarchy, but republicanism gradually became the dominant strain. Internally, the Dreyfus affair saw the eclipse of the traditionalist right and the contest for political power before World War I lay between Radicals and Socialists whose anticlerical policy brought about the separation of church and state (1905). Abroad, the late 19th century had seen the rapid development of a French empire in Africa and Indo-China and a successful attempt to build alliances in Europe. Italy was to be detached from the Triple Alliance, agreement was reached with Russia, but above all Britain was turned from its traditional alignment with Germany to alliance with France (1904). Clemenceau led France to victory in World War I, but at the cost of heavy casualties and of a weariness which betrayed itself in political instability – there were no less than 44

governments under 20 different prime ministers between 1918 and 1940. Disillusion with their failure to solve national problems and the international crisis of the Depression fostered extremism in both right and left, imperilling public order, as in the 1934 Stavisky riots. In foreign affairs the disaccord between the wartime allies was to prove fatal, specifically the failure of the British to support France over the Rhineland (1936) or to back French commitments to the integrity of Czechoslovakia. Daladier, who had succeeded Blum's and Chautemps' Popular Front governments, signed the Munich Agreement and took France into World War II. French demoralization and the comprehensive defeat of its armed forces brought about the collapse of the republic (1940).

(2) *The Vichy regime.* One of the last acts of the Third Republic had been to recall the hero of World War I, Marshal Pétain, as prime minister when the seat of government was moved to Bordeaux (17 June 1940). Pétain now signed an armistice with the Germans, under the terms of which the northern half of the country became occupied territory, and established at Vichy, in the unoccupied zone, the seat of government of the so-called 'French State'. Leading members of the old regime were arraigned in the Riom Trials for their responsibility for the fall of France. The British naval bombardment of the French fleet at Mers el-Kebir provided patriotic Frenchmen with an excuse for standing aloof from Britain's war. Hitler's invasion of the USSR and the emergence of a Communist resistance led the extreme right to frightful atrocities against their countrymen. The French State was, however, a charade, and whether Laval or Darlan exercised executive authority under Pétain, the power was always in German hands. Vichy's shadowy authority all but vanished in 1942 when the Germans occupied the whole of France in the wake of the Allied landings in North Africa, and collapsed in 1944.

(3) *The Provisional Government.* On 18 June 1940 de Gaulle made his appeal to the French people to fight on with Britain. A few French colonies rallied to the Free French, others were to be wrested from the Vichy regime and an underground resistance was built up in metropolitan France. All these movements were directed from London by de Gaulle, to whom the Americans gave lukewarm support. Accordingly, after the North African landings, the United States first recognized Darlan and, after his assassination, set up General Giraud as his successor. Finally, the rival organizations were fused (1943) under de Gaulle in a committee with the task of directing the Free French war effort in co-ordination with the different political and other groupings

within the Resistance, in order to collaborate with the Allied invasion. On 3 June 1944 the Committee of National Liberation became the Provisional Government and resumed its seat in Paris after the liberation of the city (25 August 1944). For the remainder of the war and in its immediate aftermath (the 1945 elections having confirmed de Gaulle as head of state) the Provisional Government had to meet the problems of purging collaborators, of repairing the physical, economic and psychological damage of the war and of agreeing upon a new constitution.

(4) *The Fourth Republic.* De Gaulle had envisaged a constitution giving greater executive authority to the president, but was disappointed in his hopes and resigned (1946). The Fourth Republic came into being early in 1947 with Vincent Auriol as first president and with a constitution too closely modelled upon that of the Third Republic, with which it was to share the same chronic instability. Despite this, and thanks to the aid given under the Marshall Plan, the French economy gradually recovered and France played an important role, through Robert Schuman and Jean Monnet, in laying the foundations of what became the European Community. Overseas it was faced by the problems of decolonization. While the transition to the semi-autonomy of the Union Française under the Brazzaville Declaration was relatively smooth, in Indo-China and in Algeria nationalist movements sought independence through armed struggle. The Indo-China War (1946–54) ended with the defeat at Dien Bien-Phu, the Geneva Agreements which gave the region independence and the fall of Mendès-France's government. The new prime minister, Guy Mollet, adopted a hard line on Algeria, but was brought down by the financial crisis which followed the failure of the Suez operation. The situation in Algeria became more serious and, when the settlers rose in revolt in May 1958, the president, René Coty, called in General de Gaulle.

(5) *The Fifth Republic.* De Gaulle's new constitution gave the president far wider executive powers and, having been elected in December 1958 (and re-elected in 1965) with comfortable majorities in the National Assembly, he implemented his policies through his prime ministers, Debré (1959–62), Pompidou (1962–68) and Couve de Murville (1968–69). Algeria was granted its independence (and the right-wing reaction repressed) and a policy was followed which aimed to restore confidence at home and give France a dominant role in Europe. Although former colonies in Africa were granted independence, the French government remained more influential than Britain in its former colonies. In Europe France asserted its independence by withdrawing from NATO (1966)

and developing an independent nuclear deterrent (1959–66), and its position in Europe by blocking the entry of Britain to the European Community. In 1968 increasing social tensions erupted in student riots in May. The government weathered the storm but, failing to gain acceptance in a referendum for planned reforms of the Senate, de Gaulle resigned in 1969 and withdrew from public life. He was succeeded as president by Georges Pompidou and, despite strong left-wing criticism of the regime, on his death in 1974 the socialist candidate, François Mitterand, was defeated by Valéry Giscard d'Estaing. In 1981 the tables were turned with the election of Mitterand and a socialist government. In the 1986 elections the socialists lost their majority and there was a period of 'co-habitation' between a socialist president and right-wing prime ministers, but in the 1988 elections Mitterand was re-elected president and a socialist government under Michel Rocard came to power.

Franchet d'Esperey, Louis Félix Marie François (1856–1942), French soldier and marshal of France. He served in Indo-China, Algeria and during the Boxer Rising in China (1900). He commanded the 5th Army in the Battle of the Marne (1914), and the eastern (1916) and northern (1917) army groups on the western front. In 1918 he was appointed C-in-C Salonika where he transformed a stalemate into a brilliant offensive campaign which knocked Bulgaria out of the war.

Franco y Bahamonde, Francisco (1892–1975), Spanish soldier and head of state. He served in Morocco (1910–27) with great distinction against Abd el-Krim, was appointed chief of general staff, suppressing the strike of miners in the Asturias (1934), but was relegated to the governorship of the Canary Islands (1936). In July 1936 he joined the Nationalist military revolt, flew to Morocco and led an expeditionary force to Spain. In October he became head of the Nationalist government and in the following year merged all its political parties into the Falange. With German and Italian help, he defeated the Russian-backed Republicans, ruthlessly suppressed all opposition and established a corporate state. During World War II he skilfully avoided entering the war on the side of the Axis and, despite the enmity of the European left, his anti-Communist stance gave him US support in exchange for bases in Spain. In 1947 he declared Spain a monarchy, with himself as regent, and in 1969 nominated Prince Juan Carlos as his successor. Despite mounting criticism of his regime from all quarters – the left, the Falange (excluded from real power) and the Basques – and the murder by Basque terrorists in 1973 of his vice-president, Admiral Carrero Blanco, he passed his powers on to the prince three weeks before his death.

Franz Ferdinand   (1863–1914), Austrian archduke and next in succession to his great uncle, Franz Josef. He roused the opposition of ruling circles by his support of universal suffrage and the creation of a third, Slav, monarchy under Croatian leadership. It was this that motivated his murder by the Serbian patriot, Gavrilo Princip, at Sarajevo on 28 June 1914, precipitating World War I.

Franz Josef   (1830–1916), emperor of Austria (1848–1916) and king of Hungary (1867–1916). His reign, one of the longest of any European sovereign, was the concerted and painstaking effort of an autocrat to hold together a crumbling multi-racial empire in the face of revolutionary movements, Italian irridentism, Magyar nationalism, Pan-Slavism and Prussian aggression. In 1859 the French helped to eject the Austrians from Lombardy. In 1866 Prussia crushed Austria in the Austro-Prussian War and assumed leadership of Germany. Magyar aspirations were, however, satisfied by the creation of the dual monarchy of Austria-Hungary in 1867. Personal tragedy haunted him: his wife, the Empress Elizabeth, was murdered; his son, the Archduke Rudolf, committed suicide at Mayerling; his brother, Maximilian, was shot by a Mexican firing squad when his empire collapsed; and his heir, the archduke Franz Ferdinand, was assassinated at Sarajevo, precipitating the world war which was to destroy Austria-Hungary.

Fraser, John Malcolm   (1930–   ), Australian statesman. He held office in the Liberal governments of Harold Holt and John Gorton. Becoming party leader in 1975, he succeeded Whitlam as caretaker prime minister, and was confirmed in office in the elections of 1975, 1977 and 1980, but was defeated by Bob Hawke in 1983.

Fraser, Peter   (1884–1950), New Zealand statesman. Active in Labour politics in London before emigrating to New Zealand in 1910, he became deputy leader of the New Zealand Labour Party (1933). He entered the cabinet in 1935 and in 1940 succeeded Michael Joseph Savage as prime minister. A staunch, but independent ally in World War II, he helped determine UN Trusteeship as chairman of the trusteeship committee at the San Francisco Conference (1945), while at home he initiated important social and welfare legislation.

Frelimo   see under **Mozambique**

French, John Denton Pinkstone   (1852–1925, Earl of Ypres), British soldier. He served in the Sudan (1884–85) and in the Boer War (1899–1902). Appointed chief of the imperial general staff (1912) and promoted to field marshal (1913), he commanded the BEF in France (1914). His failure as a field commander led to his transfer in 1915 to the command of home forces. He was lord lieutenant of Ireland (1918–21).

Front de Libération du Québec (FLQ). A Quebec separatist organization which during the 1970s used terrorist methods – including the kidnapping of a British official and the murder of the Canadian minister of labour – to achieve its ends.

Frunze, Mikhail Vasilyevich (1885–1925), Soviet general. Sentenced to exile in Siberia as a revolutionary (1914), he escaped to join the October Revolution and to lead the red armies which defeated Kolchak in Siberia and Wrangel in the Caucasus and the Crimea, and established Soviet control in Turkestan. As people's commissar for the army and navy (1924–25), he reorganized the Soviet armed forces. The Soviet military academy is named after him.

Fuad I (1868–1936), sultan (1917) and king (1923–36) of Egypt. As the Pasha Ahmed, Fuad founded the University of Cairo (1906). He succeeded his brother Hussein in 1917 and was proclaimed king in 1923. His reign witnessed a prolonged struggle between the crown and the Wafd, during which the 1923 constitution was abrogated (1928). In 1935 prolonged agitation brought about the restoration of the 1923 constitution. He was succeeded by his son, Farouk.

G

Gaddafi, Muammar al-   see **Qaddafi, Muammar al-**

Gagarin, Yuri Alekseyevich   (1934–68), Soviet cosmonaut. On 12 April 1961 he was the first man to be launched by rocket into orbital flight. His vehicle, *Vostok*, made one earth orbit under ground control. Gagarin was later killed test-flying an aircraft.

Gaitskell, Hugh Todd Naylor   (1906–63), British statesman. An economist and civil servant in World War II, he was elected Labour MP (1945). He quickly made his mark, being appointed minister of fuel and power (1949) and succeeding Cripps as chancellor of the exchequer in 1950. His introduction of National Health Service charges angered the left wing of his party, but in 1955 he was elected leader in succession to Attlee. Although he defeated an attempt by Harold Wilson to replace him as leader at the party conference in 1961, Gaitskell could not persuade the left to abandon unilateral nuclear disarmament or nationalization. However, he continued to fight for a less doctrinaire approach and his efforts to broaden the appeal of the party contributed to the Labour victory in 1964.

Gamelin, Maurice Gustave   (1872–1958), French soldier. He served on Joffre's staff (1902–11), then as his chief of staff (1914), and later as a divisional commander in World War I. He suppressed the Druze Rebellion in Syria (1925–27) and was appointed chief of the national defence staff (1938). Made C-in-C allied forces (1939), after the German breakthrough (1940), he was relieved of his command and replaced by Weygand. He was one of the defendants at the Riom Trials and was deported to Germany (1943).

Gandhi, Indira   (1917–84), Indian stateswoman. Pandit Nehru's daughter, she was imprisoned for political activities during World War II and acted as her father's aide during his period as prime minister (1947–64). A minister (1964–66) in the government of Lal Bahadur Shastri, she was elected leader of the Congress Party after his death. On 24 January 1966 she became prime minister. Her rival, Desai, led a faction against the official Congress Party, but was defeated in the 1969 and 1971 elections. Charged by her opponents with electoral corruption, she was found guilty and banned from public office for six years (1975). While her appeal was pending Mrs Gandhi invoked emergency powers to imprison her prominent opponents, to ban most political parties and to force measures through parliament giving her quasi-dictatorial powers. Resentment brought the country to the verge of civil war but tensions lessened with the electoral victory of Desai's party, the Janata Alliance. Mrs Gandhi resigned on 22 March 1977. Re-elected in January 1980, her government was faced by increasing violence from Sikh separatists in the Punjab. The Indian army responded by storming the Sikh Golden Temple at Amritsar. The prime minister was held responsible for this sacrilege and assassinated by her own Sikh guards in October 1984. She was succeeded by her son, Rajiv Gandhi (1944–).

Gandhi, Mohandas Karamchand (1869–1948), Indian political and spiritual leader. He studied law at Ahmedabad and qualified as a barrister in London. After practising without success in Bombay, he emigrated to South Africa (1893), where he served as a stretcher bearer in the Boer War. He led the Indian community (1907–14) with some success against the Transvaal government's discriminatory laws, perfecting the strategy of passive resistance (*satyagraha*). In 1915 he returned to India to found an *ashram* (religious retreat), but his status was such that he became the leader of the Congress Party in the 1920s. His civil disobedience campaigns attempted to maintain non-violent ideals, but he abandoned them when they led to violence and attempted to curb the terrorism of more militant Indian nationalism. Although imprisoned in 1922, 1930, 1933 and 1942 for his anti-British activities, he was held in genuine respect and attended the Round Table Conference (1931). Having worked for Indian independence from 1942, he played a crucial part in the discussions which preceded independence and partition. Gandhi's religious philosophy evolved from Hinduism, but his concern for the untouchables and his regard for Muslim rights all outraged orthodox opinion and he was murdered by a Hindu fanatic on 30 January 1948.

Gang of Four The leaders of the radical group of Chinese communists opposed to Deng Xiao Ping – Jiang Qinq, Zhang Chungquia, Wang Hongwen and Yao Wenyuan – denounced by Hua Kuofeng in 1976 and tried and condemned in 1980.

Gaulle, Charles André Joseph Marie de (1890–1970), French soldier and statesman. He served with distinction in World War I until taken prisoner in 1916. In the interwar years he fought with the Poles against the Red Army (1920), served as an instructor, held staff appointments, commanded an infantry battalion, joined the French general staff in the Lebanon and published the theories of mechanized warfare which were anathema to the high command. During World War II he commanded the 4th Armoured Division against the German panzers in May 1940 and was then appointed under-secretary of national defence by Reynaud (June). He opposed Pétain's and Weygand's decision to seek an armistice, escaped to London, issued his appeal to the French people (18 June 1940) to continue the war and attempted to rally the French colonies. From London he directed the Free French Forces in the field and co-ordinated the work of the Resistance in France itself. His independence alienated the United States which tried and failed to relegate him to a subordinate role on the Committee of National Liberation formed in 1943 after the North African landings, although it was to exclude the French from the Yalta and Potsdam conferences. After the liberation de Gaulle was elected president of the Provisional Government (1945), but when the constitution he proposed for the Fourth Republic was rejected, he retired (1946). The next twelve years were spent in writing his war memoirs and in building a following which achieved some success in local and national elections but remained an opposition party. In 1958 the 13 May uprising in Algiers brought about his recall. On 1 June he was empowered to act as head of state for six months, with special powers for Algeria. In September a referendum approved the constitution of the Fifth Republic, under which the president was given effective executive powers and allowed to appeal directly to the people through referenda, and in December de Gaulle was duly elected its first president. From then until his retirement in 1969 he exercised power through a succession of prime ministers, his policy being to restore French national prestige and to exert French influence in Europe and throughout the world. In all this de Gaulle was largely successful, particularly in restoring French self-respect after the traumas of defeat and occupation and the losing of colonial wars in Indo-China and Algeria. However, politial opposition from the left developed during the 1960s, with the growth of economic problems and these erupted into the student strikes and industrial unrest of May 1968. Although de Gaulle weathered the immediate crisis, when in 1969 his proposals for constitutional reform were rejected, he retired from political life. As a soldier, statesman and writer, de Gaulle was a giant among pygmies.

Gaza Strip   An area of some 100 square miles on the Mediterranean coast on the southern borders of Israel round the town of Gaza. Originally part of Palestine, it was administered by Egypt (1948–56), occupied by Israel during the Sinai campaign (1956), then administered by the United Nations (1957–67) and briefly by a mixed Arab force (1967). After the

July War it was ruled by Israel as occupied territory. Its inhabitants are mainly Arab refugees from what is now Israel, housed in refugee camps and providing the Israelis with a pool of cheap labour. From December 1967 onwards it was a main centre of the *intifada* (uprising) against Israeli occupation and suffered severely from Israeli efforts to suppress this.

Gdansk   A town in Poland which was until 1919 as Danzig the capital of the German province of West Prussia. It was then designated a free city under a League of Nations commissioner, with the aim of providing Poland with access to the sea prior to the development of the port of Gdynia. In 1935 the Nazis won a majority of seats in the city assembly and in 1939 the refusal of the Poles to accede to demands for its return to Germany was one of the excuses for the German invasion. Liberated by the Red Army in 1945, the city was incorporated into Poland in the postwar settlement. In 1970 its Lenin Shipyards were the centre of strike action which was suppressed by force and in 1980 the same shipyards were the birthplace of the free trade union Solidarity.

General Agreement on Tariffs and Trade (GATT)   A specialized UN agency established in 1948 to further international trade by reducing tariffs and eliminating discrimination in international commerce.

General Strike   The strike was called by the British Trade Union Congress in 1926 when, following the Samuel Report on the coalmining industry, owners attempted to cut wages and lengthen hours of work. The strike involved miners, transport workers, printers and workers in heavy industry and lasted nine days. Baldwin's government recruited volunteers to keep essential services running and mobilized the armed forces to distribute food. The TUC called off the strike in the face of these measures, but the miners remained on strike until August. In 1927 the Trades Disputes Act (repealed by the Labour government in 1946) made general strikes illegal.

Geneva   The capital of the Swiss canton of that name has become neutral ground in international politics where opposing interests have been able to meet. It is the headquarters of the International Red Cross, the League of Nations held its sessions there (1920–46) and among other international bodies with their headquarters at Geneva are the International Labour Organization and the World Health Organization.

Geneva conferences   For the conferences held between the wars and after World War II concerning arms reduction see under **disarmament**. Other important conferences include

(1) *May–July 1954*. This was devoted to settling the Korean and Indo-China Wars. Nothing was achieved in the first case, but the second

liquidated French colonial holdings in southeast Asia and brought into being the independent states of North and South Vietnam, Laos and Kampuchea.

(2) *July 1955*. The summit meeting between Eisenhower, Khrushchev, Eden and the French prime minister, Edgar Faure, designed to ease the tensions of the cold war.

(3) *December 1973*. An abortive conference, under UN auspices, which failed to reach any peaceful settlement in the Middle East.

(4) *October–November 1976*. An attempt to reach a settlement on Rhodesia (see under **Zimbabwe**).

Geneva conventions The agreements adopted (but not always ratified) by many countries on the treatment of wounded combatants in time of war. The convention of 1906 banned cruel methods of war. The convention of 1929 dealt with prisoners of war and civilians in occupied territories. Previous provisions were amended and enlarged in 1949 in the light of World War II experience.

Genoa Conference see under **Rapallo, Treaties of**

George V (1865–1936), king of Great Britain (1910–36), was the second son of Edward VII. He showed restraint and observance of the constitutional proprieties over the Parliament Act (1911), in the Irish crisis (1913–14), in the selection of Baldwin as prime minister (1923) and in the formation of a National Government (1931). These qualities and his devotion to duty (and that of his consort, Queen Mary) served to strengthen the monarchy.

George VI (1895–1952), king of Great Britain and Northern Ireland (1936–52), was the second son of George V. He served in the Royal Navy and saw action at the Battle of Jutland (1916). As Duke of York he was closely associated with youth welfare in the interwar years. In 1936 he succeeded to the throne on the abdication of his brother, Edward VIII. He restored the prestige of the monarchy through the family life enjoyed with his consort, Queen Elizabeth, and their daughters, and through their identification with their people in World War II.

German Democratic Republic (East Germany) A republic of central Europe. It came into being in October 1949 and comprised the former Soviet occupation zone of Germany. The first president was the veteran communist, Wilhelm Pieck, but the real power was exercised by Walther Ulbricht as first deputy prime minister and secretary of the Socialist Unity Party. This, the sole political party, exercised rigid control and imposed an orthodox socialist economic regime, provoking the 17 June 1953 rising, which was suppressed by the Red Army. Mass migration to the west ensued and the communist authorities responded by closing the frontier with the German Federal Republic and eventually building the Berlin Wall. On Pieck's death in 1960 the presidency was replaced by a council of state, of which Ulbricht remained chairman until his retirement in 1971, when he was succeeded by Honecker. The German Democratic Republic played a major role in Comecon and in the Warsaw Pact and, although the rigid Stalinism of Ulbricht was to a slight degree relaxed and the Protestant church became the mouthpiece of muted criticism by peace and ecological movements, it remained initially impervious to Gorbachov's reformist efforts.

German Federal Republic (West Germany)   A republic of central Europe: created in 1949 from the American, British and French occupation zones of Germany. Marshall Aid assisted the 'economic miracle' by which the Federal Republic became economically the strongest state in western Europe, fully integrated into the European Community and NATO. In the postwar period a stable government and economy were established by successive chancellors Adenauer and Erhard, while Brandt established better relations with the Soviet bloc and in particular with the German Democratic Republic, a policy maintained by his' successor, Schmidt. This policy, initiated in 1972, culminated in the state visit by the East German leader, Honecker, to the Federal Republic in September 1987. From 1987 the response of the federal foreign minister, Hans Dietrich Genser, to Gorbachov's reforms roused fears of German neutralism among the republic's NATO allies.

Germany   A country of central Europe. During the 20th century it was governed by the following regimes.

(1) *German Empire.* Proclaimed (1871), after the defeat of France, when the king of Prussia became the Emperor Wilhelm I. Conscious of its military power, its technological superiority, its advanced educational and welfare systems and its leadership in so many cultural spheres, Germany entered the 20th century in an expansionist and aggressive mood, without a strong government to curb the impetuosity of the kaiser, Wilhelm II. Britain was alarmed by the creation of a German high seas fleet by Tirpitz which directly challenged the Royal Navy. French fears were roused by German activities in Morocco (the Agadir Incident), while Russia was concerned at German support for Austrian expansion into the Balkans and, specifically, by the annexation of Bosnia-Hercegovina (1908). The scene was therefore set for World War I, a conflict involving the Central Powers (Germany, Austria-Hungary and their lesser allies) and the Entente (France, Britain, Russia and their

allies). The year 1917 marked the peak of the Central Powers' achievement, with Russia knocked out of the war and the submarine campaign causing considerable hardship to the Allies. However, by the end of 1918 they had been comprehensively defeated and Germany was forced to seek an armistice. The kaiser abdicated and a provisional government was set up under Prince Maximilian of Baden. The constituent assembly elected Ebert as president and on 9 November 1919 proclaimed a republic.

(2) *Weimar Republic*. The new regime faced attacks from both left and right – from the Spartakists and from the organizers of the Kapp Putsch. It weathered these storms, the unemployment and inflation caused by defeat and the burden of reparations stipulated under the Treaty of Versailles (eased by the Dawes Plan), only to fall victim to the Depression which followed the Wall Street Crash of 1929. Hitler's Nazi Party increased its strength from 12 to 109 seats in the 1930 elections and in 1932 became the largest single party with 230 seats. On 30 January 1933 Hindenburg appointed Hitler chancellor and on 23 March the new chancellor initiated legislation to suspend the Weimar Republic and initiate the Third Reich.

(3) *Third Reich*. Hitler had come to power by appealing to a national sense of humiliation over the Treaty of Versailles, to fear of communism and to a revulsion against the established parties over their inability to solve the problems of the economy. The Nazi Party became the sole legal political party, having itself been purged in the Night of the Long Knives, while the Communist Party was outlawed after the Reichstag fire and its members, along with trade union leaders and other opponents, placed in concentration camps. German society was totally subordinated to the Nazi Party and Hitler combined the offices of president and chancellor in his own person after the death of Hindenburg in 1934, declaring himself Führer or leader of the German people. A viciously anti-semitic policy was instituted in the Nuremberg Laws and culminated in the annihilation of much of European Jewry in the Holocaust of World War II. Unemployment was eliminated by a series of massive public works and by large-scale rearmament in defiance of the Versailles Treaty, itself negated by the Anglo-German Naval Treaty (1935) and by the remilitarization of the Rhineland (1936). In 1938 the Anschluss incorporated Austria into a Greater Germany and in the same year, following the Munich Agreement, a similar fate befell the Sudetenland, the rest of Czechoslovakia being dismembered and declared German protectorates in 1939. In August 1939 the Nazi-Soviet

Pact paved the way for the German invasion of Poland in September and the outbreak of World War II. In April 1940 German forces invaded and occupied Denmark and Norway and in May conquered the Low Countries and France. The projected invasion of Britain was foiled by defeat in the Battle of Britain and in 1941 Hitler turned to the east. Before launching his attack on Russia in June, German forces invaded and occupied Yugoslavia and Greece. By 1942 the tide of German success in Russia had been turned. Thereafter as the Red Army rolled inexorably westward Anglo-American forces cleared North Africa (1942), and invaded Italy (1943) and France (1944). By 1945 the Third Reich had collapsed. On 30 April Hitler committed suicide and on 8 May the Germans agreed to unconditional surrender. Germany ceased to exist and became divided into four occupation zones from which emerged the two postwar German states. See **German Democratic Republic, German Federal Republic.**

Ghana A republic of West Africa. In 1874 Britain established the Gold Coast colony, incorporating the Northern Territory in 1897. After World War I part of the German colony of Togoland was administered under mandate from the Gold Coast. In March 1946 Africans were granted a majority in the assembly under a new constitution, but would be satisfied with nothing short of independence. This was granted in 1957, following victories in the 1954 and 1956 elections by the Convention People's Party led by Kwame Nkruma. In 1960 Nkruma declared the country a republic (under the name of Ghana) and made himself president for life. His increasingly dictatorial rule and the country's economic ills led to army intervention in 1966 and the installation of a democratic government. In 1972 an army coup placed a supreme military council in power, but this was overthrown by another army faction in 1978. In 1979 junior officers of the Armed Forces Revolutionary Council, led by Flight Lieutenant Jerry Rawlings, purged their senior officers, four of whom were executed together with many racketeers. A new civilian government was installed and Rawlings withdrew from political life only to re-emerge in 1982 to conduct a fresh purge of corrupt officials.

Gheorghiu-Dej, Georghe (1901-65), Romanian political leader. A leading figure in the Romanian Communist Party, he was elected its general secretary (1945), consolidating his position by his ultra-Stalinism and anti-Titoist activities. In 1952 he increased his power by a purge of his opponents and in 1961 was elected president, ruling both state and party until his death. Once in complete control he adopted a line of policy far more independent of the USSR and also attempted to build up

Romania's industrial base – policies followed by his successor Ceausescu.

Giap, Vo Nguyen (1912-   ), Vietnamese Communist soldier. He joined the Communist Party (1933), escaped to China (1939) and helped Ho Chi Minh organize his guerrillas first against the Japanese (1942-45) and then against the French and US forces (1946-75). He was the victor at Dien Bien Phu (1954). When his forces entered Saigon the Socialist Republic of Vietnam was proclaimed. In 1976 General Giap was appointed a deputy premier and minister of defence, holding the latter post until his retirement from active politics in 1982.

Gibraltar   A British crown colony near the southern extremity of Spain. It was captured from Spain (1704) and confirmed as a British possession by the Treaty of Utrecht (1713). Having besieged it unsuccessfully three times during the 18th century, Spain renounced all claims to Gibraltar in the first Treaty of Versailles (1783). Up to the end of World War II Gibraltar was an important base and naval dockyard. Spain made fresh demands for the return of Gibraltar in 1939 and resumed them after World War II, taking its cause to the United Nations in 1963. Self-government was introduced into the colony in 1964 and, after a referendum in 1967 had confirmed the inhabitants' determination to remain British subjects, this was extended in 1969. In retaliation the Spanish authorities introduced a land blockade of the colony which was lifted for pedestrians only in 1982 and for traffic in 1985.

Gierek, Edward (1913-   ), Polish Communist leader. He worked as a miner in France and Belgium and joined the French and Belgian Communist parties (1931 and 1937 respectively). Returning to Poland 1948, he succeeded Gomulka as first secretary of the Polish United Workers' Party in 1970 in the aftermath of industrial unrest, holding office until forced to resign in similar circumstances in 1980.

Giolitti, Giovanni (1842-1928), Italian statesman. He entered parliament (1882), serving as finance minister (1889-90) before becoming prime minister for the first time (1892-93). Between 1900 and 1914 he dominated Italian politics and was three times prime minister (1903-05, 1906-09 and 1911-14). A Liberal, he introduced progressive social and industrial legislation, including universal male suffrage (1912) and, although he favoured the conquest of Libya (1911), he opposed Italy's entry into World War I. As prime minister again (1920) he had hoped to contain fascism in the 1921 elections, but instead enabled Mussolini to gain a parliamentary foothold. Following the murder of Matteottti (1924) he became an active anti-fascist.

Giraud, Henri (1879-1949), French soldier. He served in World War I, was captured by the Germans in 1940, but in 1942 escaped and, after the North Africa landings and the assassination of Darlan, became commander of the French forces in North Africa. Although defeated in the ensuing power struggle with de Gaulle, Giraud was responsible for forming the Free French Forces which fought in Tunisia, liberated Corsica and joined the invasion of Italy.

Giscard d'Estaing, Valery (1926-), French statesman. As minister of finance and economic affairs (1962-66) he introduced measures to reduce inflation (1963) but was dismissed by de Gaulle in 1966. Recalled in 1969 to his old post by Pompidou, he served in his and Messmer's cabinets until 1972. In 1974 he was elected president, but his term of office was marked by scandals and in particular his association with Bokassa and he was defeated by Mitterand when he stood for re-election in 1981.

Glenn, John Herschel, Jr (1921-), US cosmonaut. The first American – and the third man – to be launched into space flight, he made three earth orbits on 20 February 1962. He entered politics on retirement from the space programme and was elected a senator (1974), but failed to secure the Democratic presidential nomination (1984).

Glubb, John Bagot (1897-1986), British soldier. He served in World War I and with the administration in Iraq (1926-30), transferring to Transjordan where he became the adviser and close personal friend of King Abdullah and commander of the Arab Legion. He was forced to resign after the Arab-Israeli War (1956).

Goa A city and district on the west coast of India. Occupied by the Portuguese in 1510, it was forcibly annexed by India in 1962.

Goebbels, Josef Paul (1897-1945), German Nazi leader. He joined the Nazi Party and was put in charge of its political propaganda (1929), being appointed minister of enlightenment and propaganda when Hitler came to power (1933), holding the post until 1945. A gifted orator, he was one of the first to rouse mass support for a regime by harnessing the media to play upon crowd psychology. He was, with Rosenberg, the theorist of Nazism. In 1944 he was appointed Reich Commissioner for total mobilization, maintaining civilian morale until the very end when, having poisoned his wife and six children, he committed suicide in Berlin.

Goerdeler, Karl Friedrich (1884-1945), German public servant. Lord mayor of Leipzig (1930-37) and price commissioner (1931-32 and 1934-35), while in office he consistently opposed Nazi measures. After resigning he organized the opposition to Hitler which culminated in the July Conspiracy. He was arrested in August 1944 and executed the following February.

Goering, Hermann Wilhelm (1893-1946), German Nazi leader. A World War I air ace, he joined the Nazi Party (1922) and was wounded in the Munich Putsch. In 1928 he was elected to the Reichstag, becoming its president in 1932. He eased Hitler's path to power and was rewarded appropriately by becoming prime minister and interior minister of Prussia, where he established the Gestapo. As air minister (1935) he built up the Luftwaffe and in 1937 supplanted Schacht as minister of economy, dictating until 1943 the pattern of German industry. He reached the peak of his power in 1940 when he was created Reichs-marschall. His prestige suffered with the failure of the Luftwaffe to defend Germany from air attack and his health was undermined by his drug addiction. He offered a brilliant defence during his trial at Nuremberg and committed suicide to avoid execution.

Gold Coast see **Ghana**

gold standard The system whereby the exchange rate of national currencies is based upon the price of gold and under which, prior to World War I, most European and North American banks were pledged to exchange their notes for gold. Since it prevents a state from manipulating its currency, it was abandoned during the 1920s and 1930s.

Gomez, Juan Vicente (1857–1935), Venezuelan dictator. A guerrilla leader (1899), he became president (1908), exercising supreme power until his death in 1935. A virtually illiterate peasant of mixed Indian and white parentage, he established a police state which crushed all opposition through imprisonment and torture. He placed the country on a sound economic basis and raised the general standard of living, but made himself immensely wealthy.

Gompers, Samuel (1850–1924), US trade unionist. He emigrated to the United States (1863) and in 1881 helped to found what became the American Federation of Labor, of which he was first and only president (except in 1895) until his death. His rejection of socialism and con-centration upon obtaining higher wages, shorter hours and greater freedom for his members set its mark upon US trade unionism and distinguished it from European models.

Gomulka, Wladyslaw (1905–82), Polish Communist leader. A trade unionist in Galicia, he was secretary-general (1943–49) of the Polish Workers' Party which he helped to found. Imprisoned in 1951 for alleged complicity with Tito, he was released in 1955 and after, the anti-Soviet riots in Poznan (1956), he became party first secretary. While retaining defence links with the USSR, he tried to give Polish socialism a more human face, reversing collectivization of agriculture, curbing the powers of the secret police and (1957–58) introducing a measure of political reform. Many of his more liberal measures were reversed in 1962–63 in the face of growing unrest and Gomułka himself was forced to resign in favour of Edward Gierek in December 1970 following riots in the Baltic ports.

Gorbachov, Mikhail (1931–), Soviet leader. After graduating from Moscow University he rose through the Communist Party hierarchy to become a non-voting member of the Politburo (1979) and full member (1980). He gained power as Andropov's protégé, but was not elected first secretary of the party until after the death of Chernenko in 1985. As ruler of a superpower with what is in many respects a Third World economy, his short- and medium-term objectives were to reform the Soviet economy, preferably with western capital and expertise. To gain the confidence of the west and also to correct economic imbalance, Soviet military expenditure was to be curbed by withdrawal from Afghanistan (1988–89), by an agreement with the United States to eliminate medium-range nuclear missiles and by discussions on the possiblities of reducing ground forces both in Europe and on the Chinese border. At home a campaign of reconstruction ('perestroika') and openness ('glasnost') was intended to provide the neccessary structure and spirit of enterprise to carry out economic reforms. The new constitution agreed by the 1988 party congress, the relaxation of party control and the revelation of Stalin's crimes and Brezhnev's corruptions had an unsettling effect, unleashing ethnic strife and leading to calls for virtual independence from the Baltic republics.

Goremykin, Ivan Longinovich (1839–1917), Russian politician. Minister of the interior (1895–99) and prime minister (1906 and 1914–16), he proved an incompetent reactionary whose encouragement of Rasputin seriously damaged the imperial family. He was lynched after the October Revolution (1917).

Gorton, John Grey (1911–), Australian statesman. He entered politics after service in the air force in World War II and held cabinet posts in the governments of Robert Menzies and Harold Holt. After Holt's death, he was chosen to succeed him as Liberal leader and prime minister, but was ousted from both positions in 1971 following a dispute with leading members of his party.

Gottwald, Klement (1896–1953), Czechoslovak Communist leader. A founder-member of the Czechoslovak Communist Party (1921), he became secretary-general (1929). During the 1930s he was the Comintern's representative in his country and, after the Munich Agreements (1938), escaped to Moscow, returning with the Red Army in 1945, to head the coalition government which came to power after the 1946 elections. The prospects of electoral defeat prompted him to mount the 1948 coup, after which he succeeded Beneš as president and imposed a repressive Stalinist regime. He made the Czech economy totally subservient to that of the USSR and organized secret police, concentration camps, political trials and the purge and execution of close associates such as Rudolf Slansky.

Gramsci, Antonio (1891–1937), Italian Communist leader and Marxist theoretician. As leader of the Italian Communist Party (1923) and a member of the Italian parliament (1924), he attempted to fight fascism in alliance with the socialists. Arrested and imprisoned in 1926, he continued to elaborate a Marxist philosophy which, since his death in prison, has strongly influenced European left-wing thought.

Graziani, Rodolfo (1882–1955), Italian soldier. He served in World War I and in Libya (1921–33) and was governor of Eritrea (1935). He led the conquest of Ethiopia (for which he was promoted marshal and ennobled, 1936), but as C-in-C in Libya in World War II, was routed by Wavell (1940–41) and resigned his command. In 1945 he was appointed minister of defence in Mussolini's Republic of Salo, for which he was tried, convicted and briefly imprisoned in 1950. He was later active in neo-fascist politics.

Great Britain see **United Kingdom**

Great Leap Forward Chinese slogan used to describe the crash programme of communist social engineering based upon the ill-conceived people's communes, so disastrously put into effect during 1958–62.

Greece A republic of southwest Europe. During the 19th century a newly independent Greece gradually acquired more territory. In the early 20th century, after the Balkan Wars (1912–13), southeast Macedonia and western Thrace were incorporated and in 1913 Crete became part of the Hellenic kingdom. During World War I the king, Constantine I, wished to remain neutral in opposition to his prime minister, Venizelos, whom he dismissed. The Allies forced the king to abdicate, Venizelos returned to office and Greece entered the war. In 1921 the Allies encouraged Greece to invade Asia Minor where it was routed by Mustafa Kemal Atatürk. Under the Treaty of Lausanne (1923) Greece not only lost the Turkish territories awarded under the peace settlement but had to accept a population exchange under which Greek communities were repatriated in exchange for Bulgarian and Turkish groups. The national humiliation forced the new king, George II, to abdicate and a republic was proclaimed (1924). Until a disputed referendum restored the monarchy in 1935, Greece suffered from the economic hardships and from endemic political instability. George II allowed his prime minister, General Metaxas to establish a virtual dictatorship (1936–40). In October 1940 Mussolini launched an unsuccessful invasion of Greece, but when the Germans determined to pacify the Balkans as a prelude to their invasion of the USSR, the Greek army was defeated, together with a small British expeditionary force, and the country came under German occupation in 1941. There was sustained resistance to the Germans from rival royalist and communist guerrilla bands. When Athens was liberated by the Allies in October 1944 the communists attempted a coup, foiled by British intervention on the side of the government of the regent, Archbishop Damaskinos. In 1946, following the plebiscite under which George II (1890–1947) was for a second time restored to the throne, a civil war broke out, lasting until 1949 when the breach between Stalin and Tito deprived communist insurgents of refuge and support in Yugoslavia. The Greek army had been led by Marshal Papagos, who now resigned to become prime minister (1950) under the new king Paul (1901–64). In a policy to be followed by his successor Karamanlis, he strove to build up the Greek economy with US aid and to integrate Greece with the western allies through membership (1951) of NATO. The Greek government also endeavoured to strengthen its ties with its neighbours by the treaty of alliance (1954) with Turkey and Yugoslavia, although problems over Cyprus and the Aegean were to cause friction with both Britain and Turkey. The liberal Centre Union came to power in 1964 and its leader, George Papandreou, became prime minister, but tension grew between the premier and the royalists, Colonel Grivas alleging a left-wing military conspiracy to bring the premier's son Andreas Papandreou to power. In April 1967 right-wing elements in the army seized power and initiated the so-called 'Colonels' regime'. In December King Constantine II went into exile after failing to regain power and Colonel Papadopoulos became prime minister, abolishing the monarchy and declaring a republic in 1973. Papadopoulos and his fellow-colonels instituted a repressive regime, but public dissatisfaction with loss of freedom and a stagnating economy came to a head in 1974 when the coup in Cyprus – backed by the colonels – led to Turkish invasion and partition of the island. The army moved to head off a revolution. Papadopoulos and other leading members of his regime were arrested, tried and sentenced to long periods of imprisonment (1975). Karamanlis became prime minister when his New Democracy Party won the 1974 elections. Greece remained a republic – the restoration of the monarchy was rejected by a referendum held at the end of 1974 – and moved to closer integration with western Europe, becoming a member of the European Community on 1 January 1981. The 1981 elections returned Andreas Papandreou's Panhellenic Socialist Movement to power on an anti-American platform. It was re-elected in 1985.

Grenada A country in the West Indies and a member of the Commonwealth, which was granted independence in 1974. In 1979 its prime minister, Sir Eric Gairy, while absent at the United Nations was overthrown in a coup led by Maurice Bishop. Bishop instituted a left-wing dictatorship and, with Cuban help, began to enlarge the local airport. This provided the pretext for US forces to invade the island in October 1983, after Bishop had himself been deposed and executed by government colleagues.

Grey, Edward (1862–1933, Viscount Grey) British statesman. A Liberal MP (1885–1916) and foreign secretary (1905–16), he continued the Conservative policy of strengthening the Anglo-French Agreement and concluded a similar treaty with Russia (1907). Believing in international arbitration, he employed it to end the Balkan Wars, but as strongly defended Britain's obligation to come to the help of Belgium in 1914. During World War I his diplomatic skill helped to detach Italy from the Triple Alliance through the secret Treaty of London (1915). He received a peerage in 1916 and was president of the League of Nations Union from 1918 until his death.

Griffith, Arthur (1872–1922), Irish statesman. A founder of Sinn Fein (1905), he took no part in the Easter Rising but was imprisoned several times by the British during 1916–18. Elected to parliament in 1918, he joined the other Sinn Fein members in forming the Dail Eireann of which he was vice president. He led the delegation which negotiated the treaty establishing the Irish Free State (1922), becoming its first president when De Valera rejected its provisions. He died suddenly at the outbreak of the civil war.

Grivas, Georgios Theodoros (1898–1974), Greek Cypriot soldier. He served in the Greek army during World War II, led a guerrilla band during the German occupation and fought in the civil war. He returned to Cyprus where he formed the terrorist organisation, EOKA, which fought the British (1955–59). A proponent of enosis he disapproved of Cypriot independence within the Commonwealth, but accepted command of the Cypriot national guard. He was recalled to Greece in 1967 after his men committed atrocities against the Turkish community. He returned to Cyprus secretly in 1971 to organize a coup against Makarios, but died in hiding before it was mounted.

Gromyko, Andrei Andreyevich (1909–), Soviet statesman. He joined the Communist Party (1931), entering the diplomatic service (1939) and holding appointments as Soviet ambassador to the United States (1943–46), head of the Soviet delegation to the Dumbarton Oaks Conference, permanent delegate to the United Nations (1946–48) and ambassador to the United Kingdom (1952–53). As Soviet foreign minister 1957–85, he played a leading role in the formulation of his country's policy. In July 1985 he became president, being succeeded in 1988 by Gorbachov.

Gronchi, Giovanni (1887–1978), Italian statesman. An MP (1919–24), until forced out of political life as an opponent of fascism, he was leader of the resistance to Mussolini (1942) and one of the founders of the postwar Christian Democrat Party. He was successively speaker of the Chamber of Deputies (1948–55) and president of the republic (1955–62).

Group Areas Acts see **apartheid**

Guatemala A republic of Central America. From the mid-19th century the country was governed by a series of military juntas and more or less right-wing dictatorships, culminating in that of General Ubico (1931–44). He was succeeded, after Guatemala's first free elections, by President Arevalo whose policy of social and agrarian reform was continued and accentuated by his socialist successor, Colonel Arbenz (1950). When Arbenz expropriated the American United Fruit Company, a coup instigated by the CIA placed a military regime in power, and different military factions continued, with a civilian interlude (1966–70), to excercise power and to engage in an increasingly 'dirty war' with left-wing guerrillas and their sympathizers. In 1986 a civilian government took over, but despite talks with representatives of the guerrillas the conflict continued.

Guderian, Heinz (1888–1954), German soldier. He served as an infantry officer and on the general staff in World War I and under von Seeckt in the postwar period. He developed the theory of armoured warfare which he put decisively into practice in World War II in Poland (1939) and France (1940). In June 1941 he led the 2nd Panzer Army in the invasion of Russia, but was dismissed in December when his troops failed to capture Moscow. In 1943 he was reinstated as inspector general of armoured troops and became Chief of Staff in 1944 after the July Conspiracy.

Guevara, Ernesto [Che] (1928–67), South American revolutionary. An Argentinian by birth, he trained as a doctor in Buenos Aires, took part in anti-Peronist agitation (1952) and then fled to Bolivia where he worked in a leper colony. In 1953 he moved to Guatemala, escaping to Mexico when

Arbenz was overthrown. He joined Fidel Castro in his invasion of Cuba, becoming one of his most able guerrilla commanders. Following the overthrow of Batista (1959), he was placed in charge of the economy but, never an orthodox communist, he left Cuba in 1965 to foster revolution elsewhere and was captured and executed by the army when leading a guerrilla force in Bolivia.

Guyana A republic of South America. Formerly British Guiana, it gained independence in 1966. The independence movement had been led by Cheddi Jagan's People's Progressive Party (PPP) which won elections in 1951, 1953 and 1957 and 1961. However, on the grounds of Jagan's overt communist sympathies, Britain encouraged the split on racial lines between Jagan's mainly Indian supporters and the black community, led by Forbes Burnham (1923–85), who formed the breakaway People's National Congress and won the 1964 elections. In 1980 Burnham exchanged the office of prime minister for that of executive president of the newly constituted socialist republic. Political opposition was suppressed, and the country suffered from economic stagnation and ever lower standards of living.

H

Haganah A force raised by Jewish settlers to protect themselves during the Arab rising (1936) in Palestine, and which became the military arm of the Jewish Agency and the nucleus of the Israeli army. It was separate from such terrorist groups as the Stern Gang and Irgun Zvai Leumi.

Hague Conferences see under **disarmament**

Hague Tribunal see under **International Court of Justice**

Haig, Douglas (1861–1928, Earl Haig), British field marshal. He served in the Sudan (1898) and in the Boer War (1899–1902). He commanded the 1st Corps (1914) and succeeded French in command of the British Expeditionary Force (1915). His conduct of British operations on the western front in World War I has been subject to extremes of criticism and of adulation, but in the final analysis, in 1918 his counter-offensive proved decisive in the German defeat. Haig devoted his later years to ex-servicemen's welfare as president of the British Legion.

Haile Selassie I (regnal name of Ras Tafari Makonnen, 1892–1975), emperor of Ethiopia. The grandnephew and favourite of the emperor Menelik II, he deposed Menelik's grandson and successor (1916) when the latter apostatized to Islam, setting Menelik's daughter on the throne, acting as her regent (1917) and succeeding on her death in 1930. His policy of modernization and reform – slavery was officially abolished in 1924 – was interrupted by the Italian conquest which drove him into exile (1936). British forces restored the emperor (1941) but, despite a policy of political and social reform and strong support for Pan-Africanism, there was an unsuccessful attempt to dethrone him in 1960. The emperor's autocratic rule and isolation from his people led to a successful coup in 1974, triggered by a famine. He was imprisoned but allowed to return to his palace to die.

Haiti A republic forming the western half of the Caribbean island of Hispaniola. In the later 19th century the country was ruled by a succession of presidents and dictators. Law and order broke down completely in 1915: the United States landed marines and governed until 1930, maintaining fiscal control until 1947. By 1950 Haiti was a dictatorship, to which Dr François Duvalier succeeded in 1957, ruling with increasing brutality and corruption until his death in 1971. In 1986 a popular uprising drove out Duvalier's son and successor, Jean Claude, but any hopes of the introduction of a more democratic government were dashed when the presidential elections of 1987 were cancelled because of violence and the reins of power remained in the hands of the army.

Haldane, Richard Burdon (1856–1928, Viscount Haldane), British statesman and philosopher. A Liberal MP (1885–1911), he served as war minister (1905–12), his judicious series of army reforms creating a general staff (1906) and the territorial army (1907) and ensuring that in 1914 Britain was fully prepared for a continental war. He was lord chancellor (1912–15), returning to this office in 1924 under Ramsay MacDonald.

Halifax, Lord see **Wood, Edward Frederick Lindley**

Hammarskjöld, Dag (1905–61), secretary general of the United Nations (1953–61), succeeding Trygve Lie. He won great respect for his impartiality, but his handling of the Congo crisis (see under **Zaïre**) incurred the wrath of Khrushchev who tried to limit his powers. Hammarskjöld was killed when his aircraft crashed on the Zambian frontier while he was engaged in a peace-seeking mission in the Congo (1961).

Hardie, James Keir (1856–1915), British socialist, miner and trade unionist. He founded the Scottish Parliamentary Labour Party (1888) and was an Independent Socialist MP (1892–95) and, subsequently, an Independent Labour Party MP (1900–15). He led the establishment of the Labour Representative Committee (1900) and as chairman of the Parliamentary Labour Party (1906) helped to ensure that the British labour movement secured its own parliamentary representation.

Harding, Warren Gamaliel (1865–1923), 29th president of the United States. As a senator he showed little but the gift for oratory, but was adopted as a compromise Republican presidential candidate in 1920. He won handsomely on a programme of protectionism and isolationism, rejecting membership of the League of Nations. Agreeably incompetent, he favoured big business, and allowed unacceptable levels of corruption among his entourage (see **Teapot Dome Scandal**). His sudden death precluded the possibility of his impeachment. He was succeeded by his vice-president, Coolidge.

Harriman, William Averell (1891–1986), US diplomat and administrator. As a personal friend he advised Roosevelt in the National Recovery Administration (1934–35) and in the Department of Commerce (1937–40). In 1941 the president appointed him chief overseas administrator of lend-lease, ambassador to Moscow (1943–46) and to London (1946). He was Truman's secretary of commerce (1946–48), was involved in the Marshall Plan and was director of the Mutual Security Agency (1951–53). He was governor of New York (1955–59). Harriman failed to secure the Democratic presidential nomination in 1956, but held high office in the State Department and served as roving ambassador for Presidents Kennedy and Johnson, acting as chief US negotiator of the Nuclear Test Ban Treaty (1963) and the president's personal representative at the Vietnam peace talks (1968–69) in Paris.

Harris, Sir Arthur Travers (1892–1984), British air chief marshal. He served in World War I and was appointed C-in-C Bomber Command (1942) in World War II. His policy of saturation night bombing, so costly in the lives of his aircrew, was widely approved at the time, but has since been criticized on both military and moral grounds.

Hassan II (1929–), king of Morocco. He succeeded his father (1961) and initiated a programme of reforms. He reassumed emergency powers (1965) following internal unrest and a border war with Algeria (1963–64). In 1972 he devolved some powers on a Moroccan parliament. He survived several assassination attempts, but his proclamation of Moroccan sovereignty over the former Spanish Sahara (1975) won him popularity despite the war with the Polisario Front.

Heath, Edward Richard George (1916–), British statesman. He served in World War II, becoming a Conservative MP in 1950. As chief whip (1955–59) he helped to hold his party together over the Suez crisis. As lord privy seal under Macmillan he led the negotiations (1961–63) for entry into the European Community which were blocked by de Gaulle. He became the first elected leader of the Conservative Party and prime minister following the Conservative victory in the 1970 election. His major achievement was Britain's entry into the European Community (1973), but his administration was faced by the grave economic problems caused by the increase in oil prices and by conflict with the trade unions. An attempt to reform trade union law and to impose an incomes policy brought the miners' strike which reduced British industry to a three-day week (1974). Calling an election on the issue of the strike, Heath received insufficient support to form a government and lost the subsequent election. In 1975 he was defeated by Margaret Thatcher in a new election for the Conservative Party leadership.

Heinemann, Gustav (1899–1976), German political leader. In 1952 he left the Christian Democrat party, which he had helped to found, to head a splinter group advocating a disarmed, unified and neutral Germany. In 1957 he joined the Social Democrats and was a reforming minister of justice in Kiesinger's coalition government (1966–69). He was president of the German Federal Republic (1969–74).

Helsinki Agreements The agreements reached at the conference of 33 European nations, together with the United States and Canada, held between 30 July and 1 August 1975. They were the culmination of a series of meetings which took place at Geneva between September 1973 and July 1975 to discuss matters of security, economic and technical co-operation, and human rights.

Henlein, Konrad (1898–1945), German politician. As leader of the German party in the Sudetenland of Czechoslovakia, he paved the way for Hitler's seizure of the area (1938) and was nominated Gauleiter as his reward.

Herriot, Edouard (1872–1957), French statesman. President of the Radical Party (1919–57), mayor of Lyon (1905–41 and 1945–57), he was a member of the Senate (1912–19) and of the Chamber of Deputies (1919–40). He was three times prime minister (1924–25, 1926 and 1932), leading a coalition of the French left. As president of the Chamber of Deputies, in 1940 he called upon the French to rally to Marshal Pétain, but soon became an opponent of the Vichy regime. He was placed under house arrest (1942) and deported to Germany (1944). In the Fourth Republic he was the respected and well-loved president of the National Assembly (1947–54).

Hertzog, James Barry Munnick (1866–1942), South African political leader. He fought against the British during the Boer War, but became minister of justice (1910–12) in the first cabinet of the Union of South Africa. A strong Afrikaaner who favoured neutrality during World War I, he broke with Louis Botha to form the National Party. As prime minister of coalition governments with Labour (1924–29) and Smuts' United Party (1933–39), he shared neither the republicanism nor the apartheid views of younger members of his party, but his reluctance to enter World War II led to his retirement.

Hercegovina see under **Bosnia-Hercegovina**

Hess, Rudolf (1894–1987), German Nazi leader. After war service he became Hitler's political secretary, joining his Putsch (1923), and sharing his imprisonment. He was appointed Deputy Führer (1933). In 1941 he flew an aircraft from Germany and parachuted into Scotland with offers of a negotiated peace. He was imprisoned, tried at Nuremberg and served a life sentence in Spandau gaol (Berlin), where he committed suicide in suspicious circumstances.

Heuss, Theodor (1884–1963), German political leader. After World War

II he founded the Free Democrat Party and was the first President of the German Federal Republic (1949–59).

Himmler, Heinrich (1900–45), German Nazi leader. He took part in the Munich Putsch (1923) and in 1929 was appointed head of the newly formed SS. In 1933 he took charge of the Munich police and then of the Bavarian political police. Having carried through the Night of the Long Knives (1934), Himmler was appointed chief of German police and head of the Gestapo (founded by Goering in 1933). Completely loyal to Hitler, he used these various forces to terrorize political opposition in Germany itself, to crush resistance movements in the occupied countries during World War II and, above all, to destroy European Jewry in the Holocaust. In 1943 he was appointed minister of the interior and crushed the July Conspiracy (1944). In April 1945 he attempted to negotiate secretly a German surrender and was expelled from the Nazi Party by Hitler. He was arrested shortly after the end of the war by British troops as he tried to make his escape, and committed suicide.

Hindenburg, Paul von Beneckendorff und von (1847–1934), German field marshal and president. He retired from military service in 1911, having fought in the Austro-Prussian (1866) and Franco-Prussian wars (1870–71). In 1914 he was recalled to command in East Prussia where, thanks to his chief of staff, Ludendorff, he defeated the Russians at the battles of Tannenberg and the Masurian Lakes (1914). Placed in supreme command of the eastern front and victorious in Poland and Lithuania (1915), he was appointed chief of the high command of the German general staff. Given control not simply of all German forces, but of those of Austria-Hungary as well and with Ludendorff as his quartermaster-general, he mobilized the entire German economy for total war and exercised the political power to dismiss the chancellor, Bethmann-Hollweg (1917), and the foreign minister, von Kuhlmann (1918), for defeatism. After the failure of the German offensive in 1918, Hindenburg sought an armistice, took the oath of allegiance to the Weimar Republic and on the death of Ebert in 1925 was elected president. Re-elected in 1932, he was too senile and without the constitutional powers to oppose Hitler, whom he appointed chancellor in 1933.

Hirohito (1901–89), emperor of Japan. Created regent in 1921, he succeeded his father in 1926 and as god-emperor presided over his country's annexation of Manchuria, invasion of China, attack on Pearl Harbor and occupation of much of southeast Asia. Following the destruction of Hiroshima and Nagasaki by atomic bombs (1945), he ordered the imperial forces to surrender. Allied fears of Japanese social disintegration saved him from the fate of so many of his ministers – trial and execution as war criminals – and although he was forced to renounce his divinity (1946) he retained his imperial rank, title and prestige.

Hiss, Alger (1904–), US diplomat. Having denied charges made by an ex-communist, Whitaker Chambers, that he had passed secret documents to the USSR, Hiss was indicted for perjury since the statute of limitations prevented a prosecution for espionage. The jury at his first trial (1949) failed to agree but he was found guilty at his second trial (1950) and sentenced to five years' imprisonment.

Hitler, Adolf (1889–1945), German Nazi dictator. Born in Upper Austria, he settled in Munich in 1913 and during World War I served in the Bavarian infantry and was decorated for gallantry. After Germany's defeat Hitler returned to Munich, joined the small group of ex-servicemen who had formed the German Workers' Party (1919). He renamed it (1920) the National Socialist German Workers' (or Nazi) Party, reorganizing it (1921) as a paramilitary force which in 1923 attempted a Putsch against the Bavarian state government. Although it failed and Hitler was tried and imprisoned, it made his name known throughout Germany. While in prison Hitler formulated his political programme in *Mein Kampf* and on his release built up his party's organization. In the more normal conditions following the success of the Dawes Plan (1924) Nazism had little appeal, but after the Wall Street Crash (1929) and the Depression he could appeal to the workers with his strident anti-semitism, blaming their woes on an international conspiracy of Jewish financiers, while to the middle classes, the industrialists and the upper classes his violent anticommunism promised protection against red revolution. He challenged Hindenburg for the presidency in 1932 and, although he was beaten, the Nazis became the largest party in the Reichstag. With widespread street violence between Nazi and Communist gangs, in 1933 Hindenburg was forced to appoint Hitler chancellor. Once in power Hitler proceeded to eliminate both rivals within his own party in the Night of the Long Knives and the political opposition, and to impose his will upon a disarmed and disunited Europe (see under **Germany:** *Third Reich*). A series of bloodless victories was followed by the invasion of Poland and the outbreak of World War II. Hitler had always trusted to his 'intuition' and it had served him well both politically and militarily until 1942 when his sense of infallibility betrayed him at Stalingrad. Thereafter his personal conduct of the war became ever more disastrous until, on 30 April 1945, he committed suicide in his Berlin bunker shortly after marrying his mistress Eva Braun.

Hoare, Samuel John Gurney (1880–1959, Viscount Templewood), British statesman. A Conservative MP (1910), he was secretary of state for air (1922–24, 1924–29 and 1930). As secretary of state for India (1931–35), he was responsible for the Government of India Act (1935) which gave a measure of home rule to India. The public outcry over the Hoare-Laval Pact forced his resignation as foreign secretary (1935), but he returned as home secretary (1936–39). During World War II he served as ambassador in Madrid (1940–44).

Hoare-Laval Pact (1935) The secret treaty between the British and French governments which, having denounced the Italian invasion of Ethiopia, proposed a settlement which partitioned the country between the contending parties. So strong was the outcry at this appeasement of aggression that Hoare and the French prime minister, Pierre Laval, were forced to resign.

Ho Chi Minh (Nguyen Tat Thanh, 1890–1969), Vietnamese Communist leader. He left Vietnam for Europe (1911) and the United States, settling in France towards the end of World War I and becoming a founder-member of the French Communist Party (1921). After studies in Moscow (1922–25), he was sent as an agent to the far east, helping to found the Communist Party of Indo-China while in Canton (1925–27) and later working for the Comintern in Moscow and China. Returning to Indo-China in 1940, he staged an abortive uprising in Saigon and Hanoi and then, after escaping to China, formed an independence movement, the Viet Minh, which began guerrilla operations against the Japanese (1942). After the Japanese surrender Ho Chi Minh proclaimed the independent Republic of Vietnam. Agreement about remaining within the French Union broke down and in the war which ensued (1946–54), the French were defeated. The subsequent Geneva agreements tacitly recognized Ho Chi Min's presidency of North Vietnam, but he claimed authority over the south as well. Thereafter, while instituting a rigid system of industrialization and collectivization in the North, Ho Chi Minh tried to subvert the regime in South Vietnam through Viet Cong guerrillas and the active intervention of his own Viet Minh. He died before his schemes came to fruition.

Holocaust The name given to the systematic attempt by the Nazis to wipe out European Jews by isolating them in ghettos or rounding them up and interning them and then transporting them to extermination camps in Germany and Poland. There they were either gassed and cremated immediately or reserved for that fate when no longer able to undertake slave labour on starvation rations. Some six million men, women, and children were done to death in this way.

Holt, Harold Edgar   (1908–67), Australian statesman. A close associate of Robert Menzies, he held office in his Liberal governments (1949–66) and succeeded him as prime minister on his retirement in 1966. He caused controversy by increasing the numbers of Australian troops supporting the United States forces in Vietnam. He was accidentally drowned in 1967.

Holyoake, Sir Keith Jacka   (1904–83), New Zealand statesman. A farmer and a Nationalist politician, he became deputy party leader (1947) and served as deputy prime minister and minister of agriculture (1949–57). He deputized for the prime minister, Sir Sidney Holland (1893–1961), when the latter was taken ill in 1957, becoming prime minister (1960–72). He was firmly committed to a multiracial Commonwealth and closely co-operated with Australia economically after the blow to New Zealand agriculture caused by Britain's entry into the European Community. He supported SEATO and the US involvement in Vietnam. He was governor-general (1977–80).

Home, Lord   see **Douglas-Home, Alexander Frederick**

Home Rule   A movement to restore an Irish parliament to Dublin which gained strength towards the end of the 19th century as a focus for Irish grievances. The Liberal prime minister, Gladstone, introduced two home rule bills but both were defeated. In 1912 Asquith introduced a home rule bill which brought Ireland to the brink of civil war. Protestant Ulster, under such leaders as Carson, prepared to offer armed resistance and matters became so critical by 1914 as to affect army loyalty (see **Curragh Incident**). The outbreak of World War I caused the implementation of legislation to be postponed and, in the event, southern Ireland became a self-governing dominion, the Irish Free State, under the 1921 treaty.

Honduras, British   see **Belize**

Honecker, Erich   (1912–   ), German Communist leader. Imprisoned for ten years by the Nazis, after World War II he joined Ulbricht's Socialist Unity Party in the German Democratic Republic, rising through the party ranks to succeed him as leader in 1971. Honecker had been responsible for security and he retained a repressive regime, loyally supporting the Soviet line. However, relations with the German Federal Republic gradually eased and in 1987 Honecker was the first East German head of state to make an official visit to that country.

Hong Kong   British crown colony comprising the island of that name and an enclave (New Territories) on the estuary of the Pearl River in southeast China. The island itself had been a British possession since

1841 and the New Territories were granted under a 99-year lease in 1898. During World War II the colony was occupied by the Japanese and after the war developed into a major financial and industrial centre, its own problems of overcrowding exacerbated by a flood of refugees from the communist regimes in China and Vietnam. After the expiry of the lease on the New Territories in 1997 when the whole colony would pass under Chinese control, the Sino-British agreement of 1984 promised that capitalism would be preserved. Locally, however, fears were expressed on this score since the development of truly representative local government appeared to have been stunted, it was believed, at the behest of the Chinese government.

Hoover, Herbert Clark (1874–1964), 31st President of the United States. A mining engineer, he directed relief operations in Europe during and after World War I and served as secretary of commerce (1921–29) under Harding and Coolidge. In 1928 he won the presidential election as a Republican, but was immediately faced by the Wall Street Crash (1929) – blamed on his acceptance as secretary for commerce of unrestrained stock market speculation – and then by the Depression. His belief in the corrective power of market forces prevented him from giving more than token federal assistance to the economy and he was easily defeated by Roosevelt with his plans for a New Deal in the 1932 elections.

Horthy de Nagybanya, Miklos (1869–1957), Hungarian regent. He distinguished himself in World War I and was promoted C-in-C of the Austro-Hungarian Navy (1918). Minister of war in the counter-revolutionary government (1919), after the expulsion of Béla Kun he was named regent of Hungary (1920). In 1921 he opposed two attempts to restore the last Hapsburg emperor, Charles I, and gradually acquired dictatorial powers. His attempt to remain neutral in World War II was unavailing but, realizing that the defeat of Germany was imminent, in 1944 he sent a mission to Moscow to negotiate a separate peace. Horthy was promptly arrested by the Germans. He gave evidence at the Nuremberg trials and spent the rest of his life in exile in Portugal.

Hotzendorf, Franz Conrad, Graf von, see under **Conrad**

Hoxha, Enver (1908–86), Albanian Communist leader. As a student in the 1930s he joined the French Communist Party. He returned to Albania in 1936 and in 1941 formed a communist resistance movement which moved into the vacuum left by the German retreat (1944). (For his subsequent career, see under **Albania**.)

Hua Kuo-feng (1912–), Chinese statesman. He served in the communist 8th Route Army and was appointed deputy governor of Hunan

(1950). Despite criticism during the Cultural Revolution he was elected to the party central committee (1969) and to the politburo (1973). He succeeded Chou En-lai as prime minister (1975) and, on the death of Mao Tse-tung (1976), won the battle for control of the party. As chairman of the central committee he suppressed the Gang of Four, but in 1980 was succeeded as prime minister by Zhao Ziyang and in 1981 as party chairman by Hu Yaobang.

Huerta, Victoriano (1854–1916), Mexican political leader. He served under Porfirio Díaz and, reluctantly appointed to the command of Mexican federal forces by Madero, staged a successful coup (1913) in which Madero was shot 'attempting to escape'. US opinion was outraged and President Wilson declared an arms embargo. Huerta responded by imprisoning US citizens. There was a clash on the Arizona border and US marines were landed at Vera Cruz. Driven from power, Huerta fled to Europe (1914) and in 1916 died of alcoholic poisoning in the United States.

Hughes, William Morris (1864–1952), Australian statesman. He emigrated to Australia (1884) and was elected to the first federal parliament (1901), remaining a member for the rest of his life. Minister for external affairs in the 1904 Labour government and attorney general (1908–09, 1910–13 and 1914–21), in 1915 he succeeded Andrew Fisher as prime minister, but broke with the Labor Party (1916) on the conscription issue, heading a coalition government (1916–23). Overseas he was the stalwart imperial statesman; at home he was less highly regarded. In 1931 he founded the United Australia Party and held office in various governments until 1941. Always a controversial figure, he was a strong supporter of the 'white Australia' policy on immigration.

Hull, Cordell (1871–1955), US statesman, lawyer and judge. As a Democratic congressman (1907–21 and 1923–31) he promoted important tax legislation. He subsequently became a senator (1931–33). In 1933 Roosevelt appointed him his secretary of state. He worked to remove trade barriers by reciprocal agreements, fostered 'good neighbour' policy in Latin America and pressed for aid to the Allies after the outbreak of World War II. He was largely responsible for the creation of the United Nations, for which he was awarded the Nobel peace prize in 1945.

human rights On 10 December 1948 the Universal Declaration of Human Rights was presented to the General Assembly of the United Nations at the Palais de Chaillot, Paris. Composed at the instigation of Eleanor Roosevelt, it included amongst its 30 articles freedom of thought, expression and assembly; freedom from discrimination, from illegal detention and from torture; and freedom to have a home, employment, health and education. Rights were defined in covenants and these covenants ratified by a growing number of states. Codes of conduct were laid down and complaints procedures agreed, but as yet there has been little effective implementation of these proposals. Although Article 5 explicitly forbids the use of torture, some 40 countries are known routinely to employ it. In the west the emphasis has been most strongly upon abuses of political, intellectual and religious freedom, a prominent role being played by Amnesty International, which fights for the rights of prisoners of conscience worldwide and without ideological discrimination. The Helsinki Agreements led to the creation in the USSR of a group led by Andrei Sakharov to monitor the agreements and in Czechoslovakia the Charter 77 Group was formed to undertake a similar programme.

Hungary   A republic of Central Europe. Hungary became independent with the defeat of the Central Powers and the proclamation of a republic in October 1918. Karyoli's liberal regime was soon overthrown by Béla Kun's socialist revolution of March 1919. Backed by the Allies, counter-revolutionary forces supported by Romanian and Czechoslovak troops overthrew Kun and on 1 March 1920 Admiral Horthy was proclaimed regent of Hungary. The Treaty of Trianon deprived Hungary of two-thirds of its territory and it was resentment at this that drove it to side with Hitler. Hungary was rewarded at the expense of Czechoslovakia, after the Munich Agreement (1938), and of Yugoslavia and Romania in 1940–41. Horthy was anxious to preserve Hungarian neutrality, but the Germans deliberately fabricated an incident (the bombing of Kassa blamed on the USSR) to draw Hungary into the war. Failing to make a separate peace with the Soviets, Hungary was invaded and occupied by the Red Army in 1944–45. Free elections in 1945 gave a large majority to the Smallholders Party, but control of the secret police enabled the communists to arrest leading politicians, force the prime minister from office and declare a people's republic in 1949. With Matyas Rákosi as premier, a Stalinist regime was established. Hostility to his measures forced Rákosi temporarily from power and, between 1953 and 1955, Imre Nagy took his place. Rákosi was finally removed from power in 1956 by the uprising of workers and students. Nagy returned as prime minister, with János Kádar as party secretary, and Soviet troops began to withdraw. However, Nagy's reform programme alarmed the USSR and Kadar deserted the revolution. Soviet forces invaded and crushed all resistance, Nagy and other leaders being abducted to the USSR and subsequently executed. A period of repression was gradually eased as

Kadar sought to introduce some of the reforms initiated during the uprising. By 1968 there was considerable decentralization of economic planning and from 1987 the one-party system was modified to the extent of allowing electors to chose from two candidates from that party. By 1989 Hungary had become the first Soviet bloc country to set a timetable for multi-party elections.

Husak, Gustav (1913–), Czechoslovak political leader. He joined the Communist party (1933) and during World War II was one of the leaders of the Slovak uprising against the Germans. Arrested during Gottwald's purges and imprisoned (1951–60), he was rehabilitated (1963). In 1968 he was one of the architects of the 'Prague spring', but changed sides after the Soviet invasion. In 1969 he displaced Dubček as party secretary and in 1975 became president of an increasingly anachronistic and repressive regime.

Hussein, Saddam (1937–), Iraqi political leader. A student activist in the Ba'ath Party, he was wounded in an attempt on the life of General Kassem (1959). He escaped to Egypt, returning after Kassem's fall (1963). Imprisoned (1964–66), he escaped and reorganized the Ba'ath Party, being the power behind the 1968 coup and the real leader of the government of which he became president (1979). He now instituted a purge of his rivals and (1980) of the Iraqi Shi'ite community as a prelude to his invasion of Iran. Although the war (1980–88) brought great suffering, he won considerable prestige by forcing Iran to agree to a truce. He continued the process of crushing Kurdish resistance, apparently using chemical weapons.

Hussein Ibn Ali (1856–1931), sherif of Mecca and king of Hejaz. He supported the Arab Revolt in World War I on the British assurance that all Arab lands not under French control would be liberated. He refused to sign the Treaty of Versailles and received no British help when he was attacked by Ibn Saud and driven from his kingdom in 1924. He lived in exile in Cyprus (1924–30) and died in Amman, the capital of his son Abdullah, the emir of Transjordan. Another son, Feisal, became king of Iraq.

Hussein Ibn Talal (1935– , Hussein I), king of Jordan (1953–). In 1967 he joined the Arab-Israeli war and as a result lost control of East Jerusalem and the West Bank territories. In 1970 the PLO staged an uprising in Jordan which the king suppressed with the aid of loyal Bedouin troops of the Arab Legion and expelled the Palestinians. Following the Sadat initiative, both Egypt and Jordan became the focus of US attempts to secure a Middle East settlement. As the former ruler of the West Bank, Hussein was cast by the Israelis as the Palestinian spokesman, a role he renounced in 1988, during the *intifada* (uprising). He continued to maintain a delicate balance between moderate prowestern interests, Israeli intransigence over the Palestinian problem and the interests of the Arab world.

I

Ibn Saud (c1888–1953), king of Saudi Arabia. In 1902 he succeeded his father as emir of Najd, organized a revolt against the Turks and conquered the province of Al Hasa (1913). As leader of the ultra-orthodox Wahabi sect, Ibn Saud was the rival of Hussein Ibn Ali, sherif of Mecca, and took no part in the Arab Revolt (1916), but drove Hussein from the Hejaz (1924), which he incorporated into his own kingdom of Saudi Arabia, proclaimed in 1926. In 1933 he concluded an agreement with an American company to exploit Saudi-Arabian oil resources, which were to provide an enormous revenue for his successors. During World War II he remained neutral, but favoured the Allies and, although an anti-Zionist, took only a small part in the war of 1948. He ruled his country as an absolute sovereign in strict accordance with Islamic law.

Ikeda, Hayato (1899–1965), Japanese statesman. A treasury official (1925–48), he was elected as a Liberal-Democrat (1949), becoming finance minister (1949–52 and 1956–57) and international trade and industry minister (1959–60), in which post he promoted the growth of Japanese industry to a dominant position in the postwar world. In 1960 he succeeded Nobusuke Kishi as prime minister, retiring in 1964, shortly before his death from cancer.

Imperial Conferences see under **Commonwealth, The**

imperial preference The doctrine which considered the British Empire as a single economic unit, its dominions and colonies enjoying mutually advantageous trading terms and protection from foreign competition by tariff walls. The concept was inspired by Joseph Chamberlain's Tariff Reform League but, because it ran counter to the then dogma of free trade, it was unacceptable to most Liberals and to enough Conservatives to split the Conservative Party (1903–06). Under the stress of the Depression Ramsay MacDonald's Labour government (1931) adopted imperial preference. The policy was endorsed by the Ottawa Agreement (1932) and survived with some modifications until Britain joined the European Community (1972).

IMRO A terrorist group formed in 1895 to secure Macedonian autonomy, but after World War I to obtain the transfer to Bulgaria of Greek and Yugoslav Macedonia by means of cross-border raids, assassinations and outrages. The group collaborated with the Croat Ustase to murder King Alexander of Yugoslavia (1934).

India A republic of south Asia. Under the 1950 constitution India renounced dominion status, severed its links with the British crown and established a centralized republic. Nehru's Congress Party won the first election and Nehru remained in power continuously until his death in 1964, establishing a dynasty which has effectively ruled India ever since. His immediate successor, Shastri, died in 1966 and was succeeded in turn by Nehru's daughter, Indira Gandhi. Her rule was interrupted in 1977 by the victory of Desai's Janata Alliance, but was resumed in 1980 and continued up to her assassination in 1984. Her elder son and chosen successor, Sanjay, had died in an air crash in 1980 and his brother, Rajiv, a former airline pilot, became leader of the Congress Party and prime minister. From the time of independence the regime was faced with the apparently insoluble problem of a population increase which outstripped the expansion of industry to provide employment and agriculture to provide food, despite the most strenuous efforts in both directions. Internal stability was briefly affected by an outbreak of terrorism in West Bengal led by the Maoist Naxalite group, but the worst crisis occurred in the Punjab, with Sikh demands for an independent state of Kalistan. In an endeavour to suppress political and communal murders by Sikh extremists, the Indian army stormed the Golden Temple in Amritsar in 1983 and provoked the murder of Mrs Gandhi. Subsequent attempts to resolve the problem did not prove successful. Internationally, Nehru early established himself as leader of the non-aligned nations, a position his successors were unable to maintain. A border dispute with China (1957) culminated in military defeat (1962) and inclined India towards the USSR in the Sino-Soviet dispute, a tendency accentuated by US support for Pakistan. Indian relations with Pakistan were strained after partition and on three occasions led to a state of war. In 1948 fighting broke out in Kashmir when a Hindu ruler chose to incorporate a Muslim state into India. In 1965 fighting over the disputed border in the Rann of Kutch was settled only by Soviet mediation, and in 1971 the Indian defeat of Pakistan brought independence to Bangladesh. In 1974 India became the world's sixth nuclear power. Its army was able to intervene – with dubious success – in Sri Lanka in the 1980s and its navy very effectively to stifle a coup in the Maldive Islands (1988).

Indian Empire This came into existence in 1877 when Queen Victoria was crowned empress of India, imperial power being vested in a viceroy. He ruled British India directly and the somewhat larger area of the princely states through British residents. There was a consistent policy of devolving local powers upon Indian officials and elected representatives under a series of India Acts from 1909 to 1935, the last of these proposing that the self-government foreshadowed in 1918 by the Montagu-Chelmsford Report should take the form of dominion status. Indian political interests came to be represented by the Indian National Congress Party (founded in 1885), which pressed for complete self-government, at a pace too fast for the British administration, in the civil disobedience campaign led by Gandhi. The Congress Party was predominantly Hindu and as early as 1906, the Muslim League had been formed to safeguard Muslim interests. By the 1930s it was calling for an autonomous Muslim state (Pakistan) and laying the foundations of partition. Indians had given the British wholehearted support in World War I. In 1942, following the Japanese conquest of Burma and Malaya and with Japanese armies poised to invade the sub-continent, Gandhi led a 'quit India' movement and an Indian National Army was formed from prisoners-of-war by Subhas Chandra Bose to fight for the Japanese. Clement Attlee's postwar Labour government agreed in principle to independence but hoped to preserve a unitary state. In the event, tensions increased to such an extent that the viceroy, Lord Mountbatten, recommended partition and the creation of two dominions, India and Pakistan (1947). The ensuing population exchanges resulted in large-scale communal massacres. For subsequent history see **India, Pakistan**.

Indochina Geographically, the whole peninsula of southeast Asia, including Burma, Thailand and Malaya, but more loosely applied to what was French Indochina – Laos, Kampuchea and Vietnam.

Indonesia A republic of southeast Asia. The country was colonized by the Netherlands as the Dutch East Indies from the 17th century. The Dutch suppressed native risings in Java (1825), Bali (1906 and 1908) and Borneo (1903–08). The Indonesian Nationalist Party (PNI) was formed by Sukarno in 1927, the year after an abortive communist rising. It collaborated with the Japanese who occupied the country in 1942 and filled the power vacuum which occurred between the Japanese surrender and the return of the Dutch. Having declared Indonesian independence (17 August 1945), the PNI offered armed resistance to the reimposition of Dutch rule until 1949, when the Netherlands formally relinquished all possessions except Western New Guinea (Irian). The dominance of Java, government corruption and economic decline caused disturbances in Sumatra and the other islands (1958), which were suppressed by the army. To divert attention from domestic problems, Indonesia invaded

Western New Guinea (1962), forcing the Dutch to concede a UN presence and the referendum (1969) under which the population opted for incorporation into Indonesia. In 1963 Sukarno opposed the creation of Malaysia by military infiltration into Brunei. In 1965, when the communists attempted a coup, murdering six senior army officers, the army arrested and executed thousands of communists (or alleged communists) and many more were lynched by the mob. Some 750,000 people may have lost their lives in this way. In 1967, the army minister, General Suharto, took over the presidency from Sukarno, ended the 'confrontation' with Malaysia and sought the economic rehabilitation of the Republic. On the Portuguese withdrawal from East Timor (1975), Indonesian troops invaded, suppressed the independence movement and, despite UN disapproval, annexed the territory. By 1988 armed resistance had been brutally repressed, with at least 60,000 deaths from military action or famine.

Industrial Workers of the World (IWW or 'Wobblies') A revolutionary syndicalist trade union movement founded in Chicago (1905), which aimed to unite skilled and unskilled workers to overthrow the capitalist system by means of strikes and other industrial action. Its leaders included Debs, Hayward and Daniel de Leon (1832–1914). The IWW was strongest before 1914, improving working conditions, especially in the lumber camps, and influenced the development of the trade union movement in the United States by unionizing unskilled, migrant and black labour.

Inönü, Ismet (1884–1974), Turkish soldier and statesman. He served in the 1st Balkan War and in the Yemen, distinguished himself at Gallipoli and commanded a corps in Palestine in World War I. Chief of general staff to Mustafa Kemal Atatürk (1920), he commanded the western army which drove the Greeks from Anatolia. In 1922 he represented Turkey as foreign minister at the Treaty of Lausanne. When Atatürk assumed the presidency (1923), Inönü was appointed prime minister, an office he filled until 1937. In 1938, on the death of Atatürk he became president, maintaining Turkey's neutrality during World War II and in 1945–46 fostering the creation of a multi-party system. Defeated in the 1950 elections, he returned as prime minister after the 1960 military coup, holding office during 1961–65. He remained nominal head of the Turkish opposition until the imposition of martial law (1972).

International Bank for Reconstruction and Development The formal title of the World Bank, a specialized UN agency founded (1945) as a result of the Bretton Woods Conference. Member nations – which must belong to the International Monetary Fund – are entitled to receive loans to encourage productive investment and foreign trade and to ease the burdens of international debt.

International Brigades The volunteers who were enlisted to support the Republican government during the Civil War in Spain (1936–39). Although never more than 40,000 effectives, they took part in all the major battles of the war until they were withdrawn in September 1938 at the request of the international non-intervention committee. Such prominent communist leaders as Tito, Ulbricht and the Frenchman, André Marty (1886–1956), served in their ranks.

International Court of Justice The first Hague Conference (see under **disarmament**) established in 1899 the Permanent Court of Arbitration, or Hague Tribunal, to adjudicate in international disputes at the request of the parties concerned. From 1921 it was overshadowed by the Permanent Court of International Justice (World Court), established under the covenant of the League of Nations, and from 1945 by the International Court of Justice, established under the UN charter. These courts are also sited in The Hague, and their judicial function goes beyond the purely arbitrational role of the Tribunal. Valuable as has been the courts' contribution to international law, even those nations accepting their competence have hedged their acceptance with so many provisos as to limit its practical effectiveness.

International Labour Organization A specialized UN agency originally established by the Treaty of Versailles and affiliated to the League of Nations. The ILO remained in being after the demise of the League (1945) and in 1946 continued to work in the United Nations for fair wages, hours and conditions of employment, especially for women and children and, latterly, for migrant labour.

International Monetary Fund A specialized UN agency set up in 1945 in consequence of the Bretton Woods Conference. Working in close conjunction with the International Bank for Reconstruction and Development and with funds subscribed by its members, it helps its members discharge international debts and stabilize their currencies. It facilitates international trade and provides technical assistance to its members in monetary matters.

International Red Cross An international society which cares for the sick and wounded in time of war. The original Geneva Convention (adopted by 12 of the original 16 nations which met to form the society) concerned armies in the field. Subsequently the Hague Conventions extended its principles to cover naval forces and prisoners of war. While national red cross societies are concerned to alleviate domestic sufferings, the work of the International Red Cross has been greatly expanded since World War II to take in the care of refugees from such conflicts as the Arab-Israeli War, the exchange of prisoners-of-war (Korean War and Iran-Iraq Conflict), and relief work in such natural disasters as the Bangladesh cyclones (1970 and 1988) or the Armenian earthquake (1988).

Iqbal, Muhammad (1873–1938), the spiritual founder of Pakistan. A poet, philosopher and religious thinker, Iqbal was elected to the Punjab provincial legislature in 1927 and later (1930) served as president of the Muslim League. He moved from a nationalism advocating Hindu-Muslim unity to a belief in the neccessity of a Muslim homeland.

Iran A republic in southwest Asia. Known as Persia until 1935, from the mid-19th century the country was the scene of intense rivalry between Russian and British interests, only resolved by the Anglo-Russian Agreement (1907), when the country was divided into respective spheres of influence. In 1906 a nationalist revolt forced the shah to grant a liberal constitution but, with Russian help, absolute rule was restored in 1908. Iran remained neutral during World War I but its territorial integrity was violated by both British and Russian troops. The latter were withdrawn after the October Revolution. A British attempt to establish a protectorate was thwarted by France and the United States and by the accession (1921) of Reza Shah Pahlavi. He assumed dictatorial powers and set himself in place of the last Qajar shah whom he deposed. His prewar rapprochement with Germany fuelled British and Soviet fears at a crucial stage of World War II. Iran was occupied by Anglo-Soviet forces and Reza Shah was deposed in favour of his son Mohammad Reza Shah Pahlavi (1941). Despite the Tehran Declaration (1943) recognizing Iranian independence, Soviet troops remained in the north to give support to the People's Republic of Azerbaijan and the Kurdish People's Republic (1945). When they were withdrawn on promise of the grant of oil concessions, the Iranians crushed these puppet regimes (1946). Nationalist feelings became crystallized and in 1951 the prime minister, Mussadegh, nationalized the oil industry (in British hands since 1900). A British blockade brought economic and political chaos, until the oil dispute was settled, with an international consortium to run the industry and share the profits with Iran (1954). For the remainder of the shah's reign an attempt was made, with US backing and with ever-increasing haste, to modernize the country through educational and agricultural reform and through the emancipation of women. The bitter opposition of the clergy and the students erupted in riots in 1963, in the assassination of the prime minister in 1965 and in an attempt on the shah's life. Twelve years later student riots heralded the shah's downfall. In 1978 there were further clashes in the holy city of Qom, violent demonstrations in Tehran demanding the return of the Ayatollah Khomeini and the flight of the Shah and his family (16 January 1979). The Ayatollah triumphed and in April 1979 Iran was declared an Islamic republic. The Shi'ite clergy and the political left combined to eliminate their opponents on a scale and with a severity beyond anything inflicted by the shah, who had fled to the United States. In an endeavour to obtain his return a mob took the US embassy staff in Tehran hostage. An attempted rescue failed humiliatingly and only after the shah had died and Reagan had succeeded Carter as US president were terms for the release of the hostages agreed (1981). Uprisings by the Kurds and the Baluchis and the Soviet invasion of Afghanistan (1979) increased clerical suspicion of left-wing groups. After Iraq, the Soviets' ally, began the Iran-Iraq Conflict (1980) the execution of 'leftist militants' began (1981) and the Tudeh (Communist) Party was banned, its members being imprisoned (1983). The Mujahedin Khalq, the armed opposition to the regime, was responsible in 1981–82 for a number of bomb outrages, including one which killed the prime minister and the president, and, in the ensuing counter-terror, as many as 20,000 of Khomeini's opponents may have been executed. As the war with Iraq dragged on, Iran exported its fundamentalist fighters as a counterweight to the Syrian influence in the Lebanon and in 1987 stirred up religious riots in Mecca. At home there was continuing rivalry among revolutionary factions as rumours of Khomeini's ill–health inspired hopes of succession. Once a cease-fire with Iraq had been arranged in the autumn of 1988, a power struggle developed in which clerical supporters of the Ayatollah were tried and executed together with many hundreds of political prisoners.

Iran-'Contra' scandal In November 1986 it was revealed that Lt-Colonel Oliver North of the US National Security Council had been selling arms to Iran – in defiance of an embargo – in exchange for US hostages and using the profits to replace funds which Congress had cut off from the so-called Contra rebels in Nicaragua. Congressional committees exonerated President Reagan from complicity (February) but censured his ignorance of the operation (November 1987) and his national security adviser, Admiral Poindexter, was forced to resign. The Democrats failed to make this an issue of the 1988 presidential election and its impact had been greatly lessened by the time North was brought to trial (February 1989).

Iran-Iraq Conflict A war (1980-88), with casualties on a World War I scale, initiated by Iraq in an attempt to asert control over the Shatt al-Arab, the waterway leading from the confluence of the Tigris and Euphrates and providing the Iraqi port of Basra with access to the high seas. In 1935, control over the waterway was granted to Iraq, but in 1975, it bargained some of its rights against the cessation of Iranian support for the Kurdish rebellion. In 1980, taking advantage of the revolutionary turmoil in Iran, the Iraqis launched an invasion which, after some initial success, was soon halted by Iran. By 1982 Iran had regained all teritories occupied by Iraq and had in turn invaded Iraqi soil. Iran aimed to overthrow the Iraqi regime by sheer weight of numbers. Iraq relied on superior fire power including chemical weapons. Each side attempted to cut the other's oil exports, bringing repeated attacks upon neutral shipping in the Persian Gulf. In 1987 the Iraqis hit a US warship. In 1988 an American warship accidentally destroyed an Iranian airliner with the loss of over 200 lives. Both sides were by now exhausted. A truce was arranged by the United Nations in August 1988 and peace talks were begun in Geneva.

Iraq A republic of southwest Asia. Until 1918 it comprised three provinces of the Ottoman Empire, which were overrun and occupied by British forces during World War I. When promises of autonomy were delayed, there was a nationalist rising suppressed by the British administration (1920), which later in the year received the League of Nations mandate. In 1921 the Hashemite Feisal I was proclaimed king and by 1926 was governing the country through an elected assembly. In 1930 a 25-year alliance was made with Britain, becoming effective in 1932 when the British mandate ended and Iraq became a member of the League of Nations. During the 1930s the oil industry was firmly established as the source of national wealth, but politics were stormy (the Kurds had been in open revolt during 1922-32) and strong nationalist and Pan-Arab movements began to take shape during the reign of Feisal's successor, King Ghazi (1933-39). Anti-British sentiments grew stronger with the suppression of the Arab Revolt in Palestine and the increase in Zionist colonization and erupted when, during World War II, Rashid Ali's pro-Axis group seized power (1941). Britain reacted promptly to restore the regent and to occupy the country until 1947. In 1948 Iraq shared the defeat of the other Arab states in the war with Israel, and in response to the creation of the United Arab Republic of Egypt and Syria, the young King Feisal II and his prime minister, Nuri es-Said, formed the Central Treaty Organization (1955) and announced the federation of Iraq and Jordan (1958). This prompted a left-wing rebellion in which the king, the former regent and the prime minister were murdered, and General Kassem came to power. He was succeeded by his associate, Colonel Aref (killed in an air crash 1966), who with his brother proclaimed a socialist republic and ruled initially with the backing of the Ba'ath Party until the bloodless coup by General Ahmad Hassan al-Bakr (1914-79) in 1968. Iraq was engaged in the Arab-Israeli War (1973) and the oil embargo which followed it. In 1974, following a confrontation with Iran over the Shatt al-Arab waterway, with Iranian backing the Kurds broke the 1970 truce but were crushed by Saddam Hussein. In 1979 Saddam succeeded to power on the death of al-Bakr and, hoping to take advantage of the revolutionary turmoil within Iran, launched a full-scale invasion on 22 September, thus initiating the Iran-Iraq conflict. Eight years later, having survived the attacks of the numerically stronger Iranians, he compelled them to accept a cease-fire. He then used the Iraqi army to crush Kurdish resistance – allegedly employing chemical weapons. The regime emerged with enhanced prestige, while the political opposition, consisting of dissident Ba'athists, Nasserites, Islamic fundamentalists and communists, remained in opposition in exile in Damascus.

Ireland A republic of western Europe. The early years of the 20th century saw the culminating point of the struggle waged by Irish nationalists to reverse the Act of Union (1800), which had abolished the Irish parliament and had effected a legislative union of Great Britain and Ireland. However, when Asquith's Liberal government introduced the Home Rule bill in 1912 the Protestant minority in the north of Ireland rallied against the threat of submergence by the Catholic majority in the south. By the time the bill reached its third reading in 1914, an armed Ulster Volunteer Force was ready to resist its imposition, and the discipline of the British army appeared to have been affected (see **Curragh Incident**). The outbreak of World War I brought a temporary suspension of home rule. However, following the Easter Rising (1916), Sinn Fein and the IRA conducted a guerrilla war against the British which ended only with the 1921 Treaty which partitioned Ireland into Northern Ireland (see **Northern Ireland**) and the Irish Free State. The Irish Free State came into being on 1 January 1922, but it was immediately riven by civil war betwen those who accepted the terms of the treaty and the intransigent members of the IRA, led by Eamon de Valera, who stood for a united Ireland. Despite the murder of the new Irish prime minister, Michael Collins, the anti-treaty forces were defeated and it was not until 1927 that de Valera and his Fianna Fail Party agreed to enter the Dail. In 1932 de Valera became prime minister and immediately renounced the oath of allegiance to the British crown, provoking a retaliatory British trade war (1932-38). In 1937, in line with his policy for an independent and united Ireland, he promulgated a new constitution for Eire, an independent state within the Commonwealth, but during World War II ensured that Eire remained neutral. In 1948 the Eire prime minister, John Costello, demanded complete independence and the end to partition and, although his claim to jurisdiction over Northern Ireland was rejected, Eire withdrew from the Commonwealth when the Republic of Ireland was proclaimed on 18 April 1949. Domestically, there was tension over such matters as divorce and abortion, resulting from the entrenched position given to the Roman Catholic Church by the constitution, and the economic prosperity of the 1960s was followed by inflation and recession caused in part by the continuing unrest in the north. Indeed, in the late 1980s the Ulster problem continued to dominate Irish politics and seriously to affect relations between the London and Dublin governments.

Irgun Zvai Leumi A Zionist terrorist organization formed before World War II and responsible (1946–48) for over 200 outrages against Britons and Arabs, including the bombing of the King David Hotel in Jerusalem.

Irish Republican Army (IRA) An organization formed by Michael Collins from the survivors of the Easter Rising (1916) and from elements of the Irish Volunteers as the military arm of Sinn Fein. The objective of both was a unified Ireland, for which they fought with the British army and the Black and Tans (1919–21), and with the Free State forces during the civil war (1922–23) which followed partition. Throughout the 1930s they were responsible for terrorist outrages on both sides of the border. The Irish Free State army was employed against them in 1930–31 and Eamon de Valera, their former leader, outlawed the movement and interned its leaders (1936). In 1939 they began a bombing campaign in mainland Britain and during World War II their pro-German policy lost them support, which further decreased after the establishment of the Republic of Ireland in 1949. Except for a brief bombing campaign in the Republic (1957) the organization remained quiescent until the start of the civil rights movement in Northern Ireland (see **Northern Ireland**). Thereafter, it took an active role in destabilizing the province, drawing support from such diverse sources as the United States and Libya. During the period there were splits within the organization. In May 1972 the 'official' IRA declared a cease-fire and the members who did not agree broke away to form the Provisional IRA. Later an even more ruthless group of terrorists split from the 'officials' to form the INLA. The Sinn

Fein Party in Northern Ireland is now the political arm of the IRA and acts as its apologist.

Iron Guard Originally called the Legion of the Archangel Michael, a Romanian nationalist movement organized on military lines, strongly anti-semitic and anti-parliamentarian, which pursued its aims through terror. In 1933 it assassinated the prime minister, Ion Duca, and in 1940 the ex-premier, Nicolae Iorga. In 1938 King Carol II imprisoned the movement's founder, Codreanu, and other leading members who were subsequently shot. In 1940 Antonescu came to power with the help of the Iron Guard but suppressed the movement in 1941.

Isaacs, Rufus Daniel (1860–1935, Marquess of Reading), British states-man. A highly successful barrister, he became a Liberal MP (1904), attorney-general (1910) and lord chief justice (1913), having been cleared of complicity in the Marconi Share Scandal (1912). During World War I he served as special envoy (1917) and special ambassador (1917–19) to the United States. As viceroy of India (1921–26), he was criticized for repressing the passive resistance movement and imprisoning Gandhi. He was briefly foreign secretary in Ramsay MacDonald's national government (1931).

Islam The religion of the Muslims, based on the teachings of the prophet Mohammed. The 20th century witnessed the revival after many centuries of decline and decadence of Islam as a political, philosophical and religious movement. The Pan-Islamic movement was originally ised by the sultans to bolster the tottering Ottoman empire, but later Islamic movements took more specific forms. In Egypt, for example, the introduction of western modes was the catalyst for an Islamic revival, taking the forms of the nationalist Wafd movement, the fundamentalist Muslim Brotherhood and President Nasser's Arab socialism. In the long term, religious fundamentalism may perhaps be the most potent, since its effects are pan-Islamic rather than Pan-Arab and are being felt through-out the Muslim world, where the imposition of strict sharia law, or the threat of this, has caused bitter strife in the Sudan and grave concern to substantial non-Muslim minorities in Nigeria, Pakistan and Malaysia. In the case of Salman Rushdie's novel, *The Satanic Verses*, religious fundamentalism was able to focus Muslim outrage in worldwide demonstrations.

Israel A republic of southwest Asia. The state was created when, in the face of terrorist attacks and failing to receive US support, Britain relinquished its Palestine mandate. The Zionists, who had been granted a Jewish homeland there, proclaimed the state of Israel on 14 May 1948, all parties having rejected the UN plan under which Palestine would have been divided into separate Jewish and Palestinian states and Jerusalem would have become an international city. The Israelis now used force and terror to drive out the Palestinian population, while the neighbouring Arab states – Egypt, Jordan, Lebanon, Syria and Iraq – sent in their armies to crush the infant state. Israeli troops not only repulsed their attackers but, when armistice negotiations were completed in 1949, controlled some 50 per cent more territory, although the old city of [East] Jerusalem remained in Jordanian hands. This uneasy truce was broken in 1956 when, following the nationalization of the Suez Canal, Israel launched a pre-emptive strike against Egypt in collusion with the British and French governments. Israel was compelled by international opinion to withdraw from Sinai and Gaza, but gained an outlet to the Gulf of Aqaba. In 1967, when Nasser blockaded the Gulf of Aqaba and enforced the withdrawal of a UN peacekeeping force from Sinai and Gaza, the Israelis launched a preventive attack. In the Six Day War which followed they drove the Jordanians from East Jerusalem, occupied the West Bank, and ejected the Syrians from the Golan Heights and the Egyptians from Sinai. The Arab nations had from the very start refused to acknowledge Israel's right to exist and hence to negotiate with it. They had supported within their territories the different factions of the PLO which had engaged in acts of terrorism against Israel, and in 1973 Syria and Egypt launched a surprise attack which came within an ace of defeating Israel. Israel's victorious counterattacks in the Yom Kippur War were restrained by the threat of an oil embargo. A truce but no general settlement followed until, in 1977, after the Camp David Talks, Israel agreed to trade territory in Sinai for peace with Egypt. Following its expulsion from Jordan in 1971, the PLO had established itself in Lebanon. To end the raids across the Lebanese border Israel launched a full-scale invasion (1982). The PLO was forced to withdraw its leadership and fighting units, but left behind large refugee camps, in two of which Lebanese Christian militia carried out massacres with the connivance of the Israeli army. By 1983 Israeli forces were withdrawn leaving a border-zone controlled by Israel's Lebanese allies and mercenaries. The occupied territories, including the Gaza strip, remained an outstanding problem and peace efforts involving the United States, Egypt and Jordan foundered on the refusal of Israel to discuss it with the only representatives acceptable to the Palestinians themselves – the PLO. In December 1987 the Palestinians in the occupied territories began an uprising, or *intifada*, which, despite a brutal repression, continued into 1989. In 1988

King Hussein of Jordan renounced any responsibility, as former administrator, for the West Bank. The PLO declared a Palestinian state and its leader, Yasser Arafat, acknowledged Israel, renounced terrorism and sought direct negotiations. These approaches were, however, rebuffed by Israel.

Italy A republic of southern Europe. It did not become a unitary state until 1860, under the royal house of Savoy. In 1900 King Victor Emmanuel III succeeded to the throne on the assassination of his father Umberto I, and reigned until 1946. The first period of his reign, up to World War I, was marked by the political dominance of Giolitti, who presided over a domestic scene of poverty, unemployment and industrial unrest, politicized by anarchists, syndicalists and Mussolini's militant socialists. Despite the successful war with Turkey and the annexation of Libya, Italy had been a loser in the scramble for overseas possessions and this served to sharpen nationalist agitation on behalf of 'Italia irredenta' – Istria and the Trentino still occupied by Austria-Hungary. For this reason Italy broke with the Triple Alliance and entered World War I on the side of the Allies, only to be disappointed in the peace settlement. The origins of Italian fascism lay in this dissatisfaction, in the postwar economic crisis, and in unemployment and industrial and political violence which governments were too weak to control. In 1922 Mussolini came to power. Fascism made the monarchy its servant, violently suppressed all political opposition, embarked on an ambitious programme of public works at home to combat unemployment and, with the Lateran Treaty, healed the breach with the Vatican. Through League of Nations membership, by signing the Kellog-Briand Pact (1928) and by joining France and Britain to protest at the Stresa Conference (1935) against the reintroduction of conscription in Germany, Mussolini sided with the democracies against the rise of Nazi Germany. Indeed, after the assassination of Dolfuss in 1934, his mobilization of Italian forces at the Brenner Pass had had temporarily frustrated Hitler's Austrian ambitions. However, when Italy endeavoured to solve its economic problems by the invasion and conquest of Ethiopia (1935–36), the break with the democracies was irreversible. Italy formed with Hitler the Rome-Berlin Axis and signed – with Germany and Japan – the Anti-Comintern Pact (1937), sending troops and aircraft to assist Franco in the Spanish Civil War (1936–39). In 1939 Italy seized Albania, in June 1940 it declared war on France and Britain, and in October 1940 invaded Greece. However, World War II proved a disaster for Italy and, with its armies defeated and its African colonies captured, in 1943 the country was invaded by the

Allies. After the landings in Sicily (July 1943), the king dismissed Mussolini and appointed Badoglio prime minister. He surrendered to the Allies (September) and declared war on Germany (October). Mussolini was rescued from his mountain prison by German paratroops who set him up in the puppet fascist Republic of Salo, but, with the German defeat imminent, Mussolini was captured and executed by partisans (28 April 1945). Victor Emmanuel's long association with fascism had tainted the monarchy and, although he abdicated in favour of his son, Umberto II, a referendum declared in favour of a republic (2 June 1946). Under the 1947 peace treaty Italy lost its African colonies, Fiume and the Dalmatian territories, but in 1954, despite Yugoslav dissatisfaction, was allotted most of Trieste. Thanks to the immediate assistance of Marshall Aid, the Italian economy made enormous strides after World War II, although the south remained backward despite specific development programmes. The industrial north, however, enjoyed marked prosperity, especially after Italy joined the European Community (1957). In marked contrast was the apparent political instability of a country ruled by 26 governments under 12 different prime ministers during the first 30 years of its republican constitution. Because of splits within the Socialist Party and the rejection of any electoral pact with the communists, from 1946 to 1983 the Christian Democrats, the party founded by De Gasperi, governed through a series of left- and right-of-centre coalitions which, however ephemeral, carried on the government in the face of serious terrorist outrages by the Red Brigades (which in 1978 kidnapped and murdered the former prime minister, Aldo Moro) and by the neo-Fascists, who in 1980 killed 80 in a bomb outrage in Bologna station. In 1983 the Socialist, Bettino Craxi, formed the first non-Christian Democrat government which lasted for nearly four years, until the elections of 1987 replaced it with another Christian Democrat administration.

Ito, Prince Hirobumi (1841–1909), Japanese statesman. As chief minister (1884–88, 1892–96 and 1900–01), he was largely responsible for creating a legislature and civil service, building a fleet and an army, and westernizing Japan. Opposing the nationalism which led to the Russo-Japanese War, he was sent in disgrace as viceroy to Korea, where he was assassinated by a Korean nationalist.

Izvolsky, Alexander Petrovich (1856–1919), Russian statesman. As foreign minister (1906) he helped create the Triple Entente, but in 1908 was outwitted by Austria-Hungary over Austria's annexation of Bosnia-Hercegovina.

J

Jabotinsky, Vladimir Evgenevich (1880–1940), Russian-born Zionist militant. He helped recruit Jewish troops in World War I to drive the Turks from Palestine. In 1925 he left the Zionist executive to form his own revisionist group which demanded unrestricted immigration to a 'Greater Israel' and formed the Irgun Zvai Leumi to fight the British administration and the Arabs.

Jamaica An independent country in the West Indies and a member of the Commonwealth. During the 19th century Jamaica, under British rule since 1655, underwent a severe economic decline, marked by serious disturbances. The tradition of violence was maintained in the 20th century, with sporadic outbreaks of rioting, the worst of which occurred in 1938. Under the 1944 constitution universal adult suffrage was introduced and an elected assembly created. In 1958 Jamaica joined the West Indian Federation, but dissatisfaction with its role, inter-island jealousy and the oratory of Sir Alexander Bustamente took Jamaica out of the federation (1961) to achieve independent status (1962) under Bustamente's Jamaica Labour Party. In 1972 the socialist People's National Party came to power, but Jamaica's economy had been hit by the world recession of the mid-1970s and there was considerable discontent with prime minister Manley's economic policies and his stance in foreign affairs. In 1980, after a particularly violent election, he was defeated by Edward Seaga, the leader of the Labour Party, but returned to power in 1989 on a more moderate platform.

Jammu and Kashmir see **Kashmir**

Japan A constitutional monarchy of east Asia. Following the Meiji Restoration in 1868, the country adopted the policy, promoted by Prince Ito, of grafting western institutions and technology on to traditional stock. The emperor remained supreme and, under him, a legislature and civil service modelled on western exemplars oversaw the creation of a modern industrial state with an efficient army (German-trained) and a British-trained navy. The new-found power had been tried in the Sino-Japanese War (1894–95), from which Japan obtained Formosa (Taiwan) and the Pescadores Islands, and placed Japan on the world stage with its victories in the Russo-Japanese War (1904–05). Japan obtained Port

Arthur and a foothold in Manchuria in consequence and in 1910 annexed Korea. During World War I Japan joined the Allies and as a result obtained German interests in China and the Pacific. During the war the Allies had prevented the execution of the Twenty-one Demands, which would have made China a Japanese protectorate, but in 1931 the League of Nations was powerless to prevent the annexation of Manchuria or, after a fabricated 'incident', the assault on China itself (1937). Japanese armies soon overran most of the country, leaving only the Communist resistance in the northwest and the Kuomintang in the southwest. Military extremists had murdered the prime minister of Japan in 1932 and attempted a coup in 1936. They now pushed Japanese policy in the direction of military alliance with the Axis powers following the Anti-Comintern Pact of 1937. In 1940, after the defeat of France, Japanese forces occupied French Indo-China, preparations for war were accelerated and in December 1941, when a civilian had been replaced as prime minister by General Tojo, Japan launched a surprise attack upon the US naval base at Pearl Harbor. By the end of 1942 Japan had overrun Malaya, Singapore, Burma, the Dutch East Indies (Indonesia), the Philippines and many of the Pacific islands, was threatening India and Alaska, and was able to launch air attacks on Ceylon (Sri Lanka) and Australia. The tide was turned by a series of decisive naval battles and US and Australian ground forces gradually fought their way back across the Pacific, and British and Commonwealth troops recaptured Burma. After the defeat of Germany in 1945 atom bombs were dropped on Hiroshima and Nagasaki to enforce the Japanese willingness to surrender. The USSR declared war and seized Manchuria and the Kurile Islands. Under the terms of the peace treaties signed during the 1950s with its wartime opponents (except the USSR), Japan surrendered all conquests made since the Sino-Japanese War and paid reparations to the Asian nations which it had occupied. The point of dispute with the USSR was the return of the Kuriles, always Japanese territory. A number of leading Japanese were tried and executed as war criminals but the emperor Hirohito remained with limited powers as head of a parliamentary democracy under a constitution which came into effect in 1947. After the signature of the main peace treaty in 1951 the United States undertook to defend Japan – which was permitted only very restricted self-defence forces – and the presence of American bases and the renewal of security treaties between the countries caused violent demonstrations by students and workers during the 1950s. Initially the Social Democrats were in power, but they lost to the conservative Liberals in 1949. The Liberal government remained in power until 1954 when it was replaced by the Democratic wing of the party set up to fight internal party corruption. In 1955 the two wings were reunited as the Liberal Democratic party which has remained in power ever since despite the scandals which forced the resignations of the prime minister, Tanaka, for accepting bribes from the Lockheed Corporation in 1976, and in 1988 of the deputy prime minister, Miyazawa, for insider dealings in the shares of the Recruit Corporation. The country's dominant economic position has been secured by Japanese industry, with an annual 10 per cent increase in the gross national product between 1953 and 1965, and far outstrips the avowedly imperialistic 'Greater East Asia Co-prosperity Sphere' of Japan's military conquests.

Jaruzelski, Wojciech (1923–   ), Polish Communist soldier and political leader. Deported to the USSR (1939), he served in the Soviet-controlled Polish army in World War II. He was promoted chief of general staff (1965–68) and defence minister (1968–83). In February 1981, to meet the economic and social crisis, he assumed office as prime minister and in October was appointed first secretary of the party. His initial approach towards Solidarity was conciliatory, but his proposal that a national alliance council should be formed (November) was followed by the imposition of martial law in December 1981. Although this was eased from time to time and political prisoners were released, it was not lifted until July 1983. In 1985 Jaruzelski became chairman of the council of state and, through a succession of prime ministers, attempted to meet the ever-growing popular dissatisfaction with his regime.

Jellicoe, John Rushworth (1859–1935, Earl Jellicoe), British naval officer. Appointed 2nd sea lord (1912) and from 1914 to 1916 C-in-C of the grand fleet, he won minor victories in the Heligoland Bight (1914) and Dogger Bank (1915), and the decisive action at Jutland (1916). Appointed 1st sea lord in 1916, he was dismissed by Lloyd George for his opposition to the convoy system and served as chief of naval staff for the remainder of the war. He was subsequently governor-general of New Zealand (1920–24).

Jewish Agency An international body formed in 1929 which drew half its members from within Palestine and half from outside members of the World Zionist Federation. It had developed from a group representing Jewish communities in Palestine. It promoted Zionist immigration and investment and provided the nucleus of the first Israeli government in 1948. The creation of a similar Arab agency was vetoed by the British government.

Jinnah, Muhammad Ali (1876–1948), The founder of Pakistan. A barrister, as a member of the Indian National Congress he advocated Muslim-Hindu co-operation. He sat on the viceroy's legislative council (1910–19), joined the Muslim League (1913) and subsequently left the Congress through disagreements with Gandhi's policy and fear of Hindu domination (1934). He transformed the league from a cultural to a political organization, in which he was joined by all other Muslim members of Congress by 1935. At a meeting in Lahore in 1940 Jinnah and the league demanded the partition of the subcontinent and the creation of Pakistan. In 1947, when independence was granted and partition effected, Jinnah was forced to accept a smaller state than he had originally demanded, the goodwill won by his support of the British war effort dissipated by his 'direct action', which caused terrible communal riots in Calcutta in 1946. In August 1947 he became governor general of Pakistan, but died in office in the following year.

Joffre, Joseph Jacques Césaire (1852–1931), French soldier. He saw service in Indo-China, the French Sudan and Madagascar, being appointed chief of general staff and vice-president of the supreme war council (1911). Defeated in the opening battles of World War I, he made a strategic withdrawal which enabled him to counterattack on the Marne (1914). He was made C-in-C of the French army (1915). After the failure of the Battle of the Somme (1916), he was promoted marshal of France and superseded by Nivelle. He subsequently served as chairman of the Allied war council.

John XXIII (Angelo Giuseppe Roncalli, 1881–1963), Italian pontiff, 1958–63. Ordained (1904), he served as a medical orderly and army chaplain during World War I. He subsequently entered the Vatican diplomatic service and, after consecration (1925) as an archbishop, was sent as diplomatic representative to Bulgaria, Turkey and Greece and, in 1944, as papal nuncio to France. Patriarch of Venice and cardinal (1953), he was elected pope in 1958. Concerned to modernize the church and to make the Christian message available to the whole world, he summoned the 2nd Vatican Council (1962), the apex of his pontificate. He was well loved for his ecumenical spirit – as a diplomat he had established friendly relationships with the Orthodox Christians and Muslims – and for his concern for world peace and for social reform and aid to the Third World.

John Paul II (Karol Wojtyla, 1920–), Polish pontiff, elected pope in 1978. During the German occupation of Poland he worked as a forced labourer. Ordained in Rome (1946), he returned to Poland as a parish priest, becoming auxiliary bishop (1958) and finally archbishop of

Cracow (1964). A cardinal (1974), in 1978 he was elected the first non-Italian pope since 1522. He aimed to reinforce the traditional doctrines of the Roman Catholic Church, curbing theological excess whether by the permissive Dutch Church or by the traditionalist Archbishop Lefèbvre (excommunicated 1988), and denouncing the materialisms of both east and west. Despite an assassination attempt (1981), his energy remained undiminished, enabling him to make constant pastoral visits in Italy and abroad.

Johnson, Lyndon Baynes (1908–73), 36th president of the United States (1963–69). A school-teacher, he went to Washington as secretary to a Texan congressman (1932). A strong supporter of Roosevelt's New Deal, he became the Texas director of the National Youth Administration (1935). In 1937 he was elected to the House of Representatives in which he served – with a break for duty in the US navy (1941–42) – until 1948, when he was elected to the Senate. Democratic whip (1951), floor leader (1953) and majority leader after 1954, he failed to obtain the presidential nomination in 1960, but agreed to run as Kennedy's vice-president, succeeding him on his assassination in 1963 and winning a landslide victory in 1964. Always a strong social reformer, supporting the legislation of the Republican president, Eisenhower, he provided social security benefits within a wide range of anti-poverty programmes (1965–66), while his Voting Rights Act (1965) safeguarded the rights of black voters who had already benefited from his radical Civil Rights Bill (1964). This magnificent record was obscured by the Vietnam War, in which he increased US involvement without achieving victory. This failure brought his popularity to a level at which he declined to seek nomination for re-election in 1968, and he retired from political life.

Jordan A kingdom of southwest Asia. Ruled by the Turks until the fall of the Ottoman Empire during World War I, in 1919 the area became part of Feisal I's kingdom. After his expulsion by the French (1920), it was included in the British mandate for Palestine. In 1921 it was specifically exempt from becoming part of the Jewish homeland and was made the emirate of Transjordan, ruled by Feisal's brother, Abdullah Ibn Hussein, who became the first king of Transjordan in 1928. The state changed its name to the Hashemite Kingdom of Jordan, under the treaty of independence with Britain (1946). In 1948, Jordan with the other states of the Arab League, attempted to crush Israel, acquiring in the process the Old City of Jerusalem and territory on the West Bank of the Jordan. Following the assassination of King Abdullah (1951), in 1952 Hussein succeeded his father, Abdullah's mentally defective son, Talal.

In 1958 Jordan formed a short-lived federation with Iraq and, after the overthrow of the Iraqi monarchy, was forced to call for British military assistance to meet threats from Egypt and Syria. In 1963 the United States joined Britain in promising aid when the Syrians supported a revolutionary Jordanian government in exile in Damascus. In 1967 Jordanian forces were driven from East Jerusalem and the West Bank, and Jordan received 450,000 Palestinian refugees. Tension between Hussein and the PLO mounted, fighting broke out in 1968, a ten-day civil war erupted in 1970, and in 1971 the Jordanian army crushed the Palestinians and expelled their guerrillas from Jordan. In the Yom Kippur War, Jordan gave limited support to Syria, but subsequently joined Egypt and the United States in efforts to turn the Camp David agreements into a more durable Middle East settlement. Following the Palestinian uprising in 1987, King Hussein renounced all interests in the occupied West Bank and opened the way for the declaration (1988) of an independent state of Palestine.

Juan Carlos I (1938–), king of Spain from 1975. The grandson of Alfonso XIII, he acceded as a constitutional monarch on Franco's death in 1975. He took Spain from a dictatorship to a parliamentary democracy, which elected a socialist prime minister in 1982, having by his tact and courage rallied the army and the nation against a right-wing coup (1981).

July Conspiracy An abortive attempt by the German anti-Nazi opposition to assassinate Hitler, overthrow the regime and conclude a peace with the Allies. The bomb planted in Hitler's East Prussian headquarters failed to kill him and the conspirators were prevented from seizing power in Berlin. The success of the coup in Paris was short-lived. The Gestapo executed 150 conspirators; 13 others, including Rommel, committed suicide.

K

Kadár, János (1912–   ), Hungarian Communist leader. Minister of the interior (1948–51), he was arrested, imprisoned and tortured (1951). Released on the fall of Rákosi (1954), he was restored to the central committee (July 1956), becoming first secretary of the party (October). During the Hungarian Uprising he first identified himself with Imre Nagy, but defected to the Soviets and presided as prime minister over the trial and execution of its leaders. In 1958 he resigned the premiership (resuming it during 1961–65). He carried out a purge of Stalinists in 1960, but in 1968 supported the Soviet invasion of Czechoslovakia. From 1959 he instituted a more liberal economic policy while retaining strict political control as first secretary. However, economic problems and Gorbachov's political reforms forced his resignation in May 1988.

Kampuchea A republic of southeast Asia. In the 19th century it became a French protectorate. In 1949 it acquired the status of an independent state within the French Union, achieving full independence in 1953. It remained a constitutional monarchy until 1970 when, with US backing, Marshal Lon Nol overthrew the government and proclaimed the Khmer Republic. The prime minister, Prince Sihanouk, fled, set up a government in exile in Peking and put a guerrilla force, the Khmer Rouge under Pol Pot, into the field. After bitter warfare the Khmer Rouge was victorious (1975). Prince Sihanouk returned as head of state, but was driven into exile (1976) when Pol Pot and his associates took power. A combined Kampuchean and (predominantly) Vietnamese invasion (1978–79) established a Vietnamese-controlled administration, the Vietnamese army fighting a war against Khmer Rouge and non-Communist guerrillas supplied by the United States and China. By 1988, the burden of this war had proved too great for the Vietnamese economy and, with the USSR moving towards a rapprochement with China, Vietnam agreed to withdraw its 50,000 troops from Kampuchea. Talks on the future of the country produced no immediate agreement among the parties involved.

Kapp Putsch The putsch led in 1920 by Wolfgang Kapp (1858–1922), a nationalist politician, against the Weimar republic. He seized control in Berlin but was defeated by a general strike by the Berlin workers. Kapp subsequently fled to Sweden, but returned to Germany and died while awaiting trial for treason.

Karamanlis, Constantine (1902–), Greek statesman. He held various ministerial posts 1946–55, being appointed prime minister after the death of Marshal Papagos (1955), and continued in office virtually uninterruptedly until his resignation in 1963. A staunch supporter of NATO, he was given substantial financial support for his schemes for agricultural and industrial development. After the 1967 coup he went into exile in Paris to voice the strongest criticism of the colonels, returning after their overthrow to reintroduce parliamentary government. After electoral victory in 1974 he became prime minister once again, holding office until 1980 when he was elected president. He retired in 1985.

Karolyi, Count Michael (Mihaly Karolyi de Nagykarolyi, 1875–1955), Hungarian statesman. A liberal who became increasingly radical in his views, he was appointed prime minister by the last emperor, Charles, in October 1918 to make a separate peace with the Allies. Provisional president of the Hungarian Republic (November 1918), he surrendered the government to Béla Kun (March 1919) and, on the fall of Kun's dictatorship, he escaped to England. Returning to Hungary (1946), he was appointed ambassador to France (1947), but resigned in 1949 over Communist policy and died in exile.

Kashmir A region in the northern part of the Indian subcontinent. The princely state of Jammu and Kashmir was ruled by a Hindu maharajah, who, despite the fact that three-quarters of his subjects were Muslim, elected to join India after independence and partition in 1947. In the resultant communal violence both India and Pakistan moved in their regular forces and fighting occurred. In 1949 the UN supervisory commission established a cease-fire line but in 1957 India formally annexed the state. Following a boundary agreement between Pakistan and China (1963) which defined the frontiers of Pakistani-controlled, or Azad Kashmir, there were further outbreaks of fighting during 1965. In 1966 the USSR mediated, but no solution was reached and later the Indians marginally improved their position by territorial gains during the 1971 war over the independence of Bangladesh.

Kassem, Abdul Karim (1914–63), Iraqi soldier and politician. He distinguished himself in action against the Kurds and during the 1948 Arab-Israeli War. He led the military coup which overthrew the monarchy (1958) and became prime minister of the new republic. His anti-Egyptian policy lost him support and, having survived a coup attempt in 1959, he was overthrown by a Ba'athist revolt and executed (1963).

Katanga see **Zaïre**

Katyn A village in European Russia near which on 13 April 1943 the German army discovered the mass graves of some 4250 Polish officers. Evidence pointed to their execution by the Soviet secret police and, when the head of the Polish government in exile, General Sikorski, demanded an investigation by the International Red Cross, Stalin used this as a pretext to sever diplomatic relations.

Kaunda, Kenneth David (1924–), Zambian statesman. He entered politics, joined the African National Congress and was imprisoned (1953) for opposing the Federation of Rhodesia and Nyasaland. In 1958 he founded the Zambia African National Congress (and was promptly imprisoned when it was declared illegal) and, on his release in 1960, the United National Independence Party. Its electoral success brought him ministerial office (1962), the end of the federation (1963) and his own appointment as prime minister of Northern Rhodesia (now Zambia) and president of the independent republic of Zambia (1964). An autocratic ruler (Zambia became a one-party state in 1972), he supported the liberation movements which took power in Zimbabwe and Mozambique, and advocated sanctions against South Africa. In the 1980s he faced domestic unrest caused by a worsening economic climate as Zambia moved from reliance upon diminishing copper reserves to an agricultural economy.

Kellog-Briand Pact The agreement, signed 27 August 1927, under which 57 countries, including Germany and two non-members of the League of Nations, the United States and the USSR, formally renounced war as a means of settling international disputes. Since the pact, named after the French foreign minister, Aristide Briand, and the American secretary of state, Frank Billings Kellog (1856–1937), contained no sanctions against violators of its provisions it rapidly became a dead letter.

Kennedy, John Fitzgerald (1917–63), 35th president of the United States. He served in the US Navy during World War II, became a congressman (1947) and a senator (1952), making his mark on the Foreign Relations Committee. In 1960 he won the Democratic nomination and narrowly defeated Richard Nixon in the presidential election. He was the first Roman Catholic and the youngest man to have held the presidency and generated enormous enthusiasm for his New Frontier programme of domestic reform. After the Bay of Pigs fiasco, Kennedy regained his prestige by his firmness in handling the Cuban Missile Crisis (see under **Cuba**) and was subsequently able to conclude a treaty with the USSR (1963) banning the atmospheric testing of nuclear weapons. In Vietnam he left his successor a policy of ever-increasing US involvement. In Latin America and the Third World he instituted American economic assistance in the shape of the Alliance for Progress and the Peace Corps programme. On 22 November 1963 he was assassinated in circumstances which still arouse considerable controversy.

Kennedy, Robert Francis (1925–68), US lawyer and politician, and younger brother of J.F. Kennedy, served as his attorney-general (1961–64). Disagreeing with President Johnson's Vietnam policy he resigned, and in 1968, while running for the presidential nomination, was assassinated by a Jordanian student.

Kenya A republic in East Africa and a member of the Commonwealth. As the East Africa Protectorate (1895), it served as a base for the British campaign in World War I against the neighbouring German colony of Tanganyika and become the crown colony of Kenya in 1920. European exploitation of the best agricultural land in the White Highlands, Asian domination of local commerce and denial of political expression in the white-dominated legislative councils provoked African resentment. In 1928 the Kikuyu formed a central association, of which Jomo Kenyatta was secretary. However, resentment did not erupt into violence until 1952 with the Mau Mau rising. British troops and local police had suppressed the rising by 1957, but during the emergency many of the African nationalist leaders were imprisoned, including Kenyatta. In 1960 a change of British government policy set Kenya on the road to independence, granted in December 1963. In November 1964 Kenyatta's Kenya African National Union was declared the sole party in a one-party state and on 12 December Kenya became a republic with Kenyatta as its president. Kikuyu dominance was resented by the minority tribes and there was considerable unrest in 1969 when the Luo politician and vice president, Tom Mboya, was murdered. It led to the banning of the Communist Kenya Peoples' Union and the arrest of its Luo leader, Oginga Odinga (1911–). Under Kenyatta Kenya enjoyed prosperity and stability, retaining an influential proportion of white setters in agriculture and industry and attracting substantial aid from Britain and the United States. Kenyatta died in 1978 and was succeeded by Daniel Arap Moi. Economic difficulties spawned an abortive coup by air force officers (1982) and a vociferous opposition movement (Mwakenya) levelling charges of incompetence and corruption against the ruling clique. This in turn led to severe repression and, in certain cases, infringement of human rights. In its external politics Kenya maintained a strong, but moderate pan-African line.

Kenyatta, Jomo (*c*1893–1978), first president of Kenya (1964–78). He joined the Kikuyu Central Association and, as its secretary, represented the tribe in talks with the Colonial Office (1929–30). Settling in England (1931) he helped Kwame Nkruma to found the Pan-African Congress in Manchester (1945). He returned to Kenya (1946) to be elected president of the Kenya African Union (1947). Suspected by the British authorities of being behind the Mau Mau rising (1952), he was tried and imprisoned (1953). After serving his sentence he was exiled (1959) until a change of policy brought his release in 1961. Elected president off the newly formed Kenya African National Union (1960), he led negotiations for the constitution under which Kenya achieved self-government (with himself as prime minister) and complete independence as a republic (of which he became president in 1964). He remained president until his death in 1978 and his moderate, if autocratic rule, ensured the initial stability and prosperity of his country.

Kerensky, Alexander Feodorovich (1881–1970), Russian political leader. A lawyer, he entered the Duma (1912). He joined the Socialist Revolutionary Party after the February Revolution (1917), becoming deputy chairman of the Petrograd soviet. He joined the Provisional Government, was minister of justice and then war minister, succeeding Lvov as premier in July 1917. He insisted on continuing the war, failed to tackle urgent economic problems, lost popularity and, although he survived a coup led by General Kornilov, he was driven from power by the October Revolution and escaped abroad.

Khomeini, Ayatollah Ruhollah (1900–), Iranian religious leader. In the 1960s he denounced the shah's reforms in sermons which caused serious rioting. He was arrested and expelled from Iran, living first in Turkey, but during 1965–78 close to Baghdad in the Shi'ite holy city of Najaf. The Iraqis used him in their quarrel with Iran over the Shatt al–Arab waterway, but after the 1975 agreement he was expelled and given sanctuary in France (1978). From Paris he masterminded the fundamentalists who, in conjunction with the Communists and other political groups, overthrew the shah in January 1979. In February he returned in triumph and in April declared Iran an islamic republic. As its *velayat faqih*, or moral supervisor he was the power which sustained or toppled its premiers and presidents and inspired islamic revolutionaries throughout the Muslim world. Despite Iran's defeat in the Iran-Iraq conflict (1980–88) and the containment of his supporters by the Syrian-backed Amal militia in the Lebanon, his influence remains strong among the Shi'ite mujahedin in Afghanistan and he was able to rouse the Muslim world against Salmon Rushdie's allegedly blasphemous novel, *The Satanic Verses*.

Khrushchev, Nikita Sergeyevich (1894–1971), Soviet Communist leader. He was appointed (1938) first secretary of the Ukrainian Communist Party, which he purged on Stalin's orders. Elected to the Politburo (1939), he was responsible for incorporating eastern Poland into the USSR (1939). He subsequently organized resistance behind the German lines in the Ukraine (1941). In 1949 he became first secretary of the Moscow Communist Party. Closely associated with Stalin, after the latter's death he replaced Malenkov as first secretary of the Central Committee, and ousted him from power. In 1956, at the 20th Party Congress, Khrushchev denounced Stalin's crimes and his cult of personality and purged the Central Committee of neo-Stalinists (1957). His aggressive policy towards the United States failed (see **Cuba**) as did his attempt to boost Soviet agriculture in the 'virgin lands' of central Asia. However, it was his quarrel with Mao Tse-tung, bringing with it a threat of war with China, which led to his removal from office (1964) and replacement by Brezhnev and Kosygin. Khrushchev was then allowed to live on in retirement near Moscow.

Kim Il Sung (Kim Sung Chu, 1912–), North Korean Communist leader. After the failure of an armed uprising against the Japanese occupying forces during the 1930s, he escaped to Moscow. In 1945 the Soviets appointed him chairman of the People's Committee of North Korea and in 1948 he became premier of the newly created people's republic. In 1952–53 he engaged in open war with South Korea and thereafter followed a policy of cold war with the south, while skilfully avoiding involvement in the Sino-Soviet dispute and extending his personal autocracy in an extravagant personality cult.

King, Ernest Joseph (1878–1956), US naval officer. Assistant chief of staff to the commander of the US North Atlantic Fleet in World War I, between the wars he acquired expertise in both submarine and air warfare. Appointed commander US naval forces (December 1941), in March 1942 he took up the additional post of chief of naval operations, devising and directing the grand strategy which brought the US navy its victories in the Pacific.

King, Martin Luther (1929–68), US civil rights leader. A Baptist pastor in Montgomery, Alabama, he became famous through his campaign against segregation in the town's buses (1954). As leader of the non-violent civil rights movement, he mounted a massive demonstration in Washington, DC (15 June 1963), and the 60-mile procession from Selma to

Montgomery (March 1964). Awarded the Nobel peace prize in 1964, he was assassinated in Memphis, Tennessee, later the same year.

King, William Lyon Mackenzie (1874–1950), Canadian statesman. A lawyer, civil servant and federal MP for over 40 years from 1908, he served as minister of labour (1909–14) under Laurier whom he succeeded as Liberal leader in 1919. As prime minister (1921–26, 1926–30 and 1935–48), he worked towards the creation of an independent Canada and, although tending to isolationism, staunchly supported Britain in World War II.

Kishi, Nobusuke (1896–1987), Japanese statesman. As the official responsible for Japanese industrial exploitation of Manchuria after 1935 and as the minister of commerce in Tojo's wartime government, he was imprisoned as a war criminal after World War II. Secretary of the Democratic Party he helped weld conservative political factions into the Liberal Democratic Party (1955). In 1957 he became party president and prime minister, resigning both posts in 1960 after public outcry against the US-Japanese Security Treaty.

Kissinger, Henry Alfred (1923–   ), US diplomat and statesman. He taught at Harvard as professor of government (1958–71), acted as consultant and was appointed special adviser on national security (1969–73) by Nixon, whom he had advised during his 1968 presidential campaign. Secretary of state (1973) – serving until 1976 under Nixon's successor, Ford – he influenced foreign policy, helping to arrange the SALT I (1969), the rapprochement with China (1972), the US disengagement from Vietnam (1973 – awarded Nobel peace prize) and the Israeli-Egyptian cease-fire (1973).

Kitchener, Herbert Horatio (1850–1916, Earl Kitchener), British soldier. He served in Cyprus and Palestine and was attached to the Egyptian army (1882), becoming its adjutant-general (1889) and C-in-C (1892). He reconquered the Sudan, defeating the Mahdi at Omdurman, and subsequently ejected the French from Fashoda (1898). Lord Roberts's chief of staff in the Boer War (1899), he succeeded him in command in 1900. C-in-C in India (1902–09) and the effective ruler of Egypt as British agent (1911–14), on the outbreak of World War I he was appointed war minister. Almost alone in realizing that the war would prove a long struggle, he recruited nearly two million volunteers. However, relations with colleagues and subordinates became strained and, since his resignation would have been too severe a blow to public morale, he was sent on a mission to bolster the Russian war effort. His ship struck a mine off the Orkneys and he was drowned.

Kolchak, Alexander Vasilievich (1873–1920), Russian admiral. He served in the Russo-Japanese War and commanded the Black Sea fleet in World War I. Minister of war in the anti-Bolshevik government formed at Omsk in Siberia, he seized power in November 1918 and was recognized as representing the Provisional Government. His campaign to join forces with the interventionists in north Russia failed. He was betrayed to the Bolsheviks and executed by them at Irkutsk.

Kondylis, George (1879–1936), Greek soldier and statesman. He served in the Balkan Wars and during World War I. Minister of war and of the interior (1924–25), he overthrew General Pangalos (1926) and briefly became premier. In 1935 he suppressed a coup attempt by Venizelos and restored the monarchy after a referendum, but was dismissed by the new king.

Koniev, Ivan Stepanovich (1897–1973), Soviet soldier. He commanded the army which held the German attack on Moscow (1941). In concert with Zhukov he directed the offensives which defeated the Germans (1943–44), took Berlin (1945) and eventually effected a junction with Patton's US forces in Bohemia (April 1945). He commanded the Soviet occupation forces in Austria (1945) and Soviet ground forces (1946). He was deputy minister of defence (1950–55), commander of Warsaw Pact forces (1956–60) and subsequently of Soviet forces in East Germany (1961–62). In 1953 he presided at the trial of Beria.

Konoye, Prince Fumimaro (1891–1945), Japanese statesman. President of the house of peers (1933–37) and prime minister (1937–39 and 1940–41), in 1938 he passed the National Mobilization Law and proclaimed Japan's ambitions for a 'new order in east Asia'. In 1940 he made Japan a formal member of the Axis, and in 1945 was sent as peace emissary to Moscow. Although vice-premier of the first postwar cabinet, he was listed as a war criminal but committed suicide before his trial.

Korea A country in east Asia. The Japanese invaded Korea (which had long been under Chinese influence) during the Sino-Japanese War (1894–95) and murdered the last queen of the native dynasty in her palace. During the Russo-Japanese War (1904–05) they moved their troops through the country, which they made their protectorate in 1905 and formally annexed in 1910. Their brutal colonial regime exploited the natural resources, established an industrial base, and aroused armed opposition from the Koreans. From 1919 a provisional Korean government was established in Shanghai under Syngman Rhee. In 1938 Kim Il Sung led a Communist guerrilla uprising. After World War II, Soviet forces occupied the north of the country and US forces the south. Efforts to reunite the country after free elections in both occupation zones were consistently blocked by the USSR and, in 1948 separate republics came into being, divided by the 38th parallel which demarcated US and Soviet zones. For subsequent history see **Korean People's Democratic Republic, Korea, Republic of.**

Korean People's Democratic Republic (North Korea) This was proclaimed on 9 September 1948, as a Communist, one-party (Korea Workers' Party) state under the leadership of Kim Il Sung. Following the withdrawal of Soviet and American forces (1949), he attempted in 1950 to unify the country by an armed invasion of the south (see **Korean War**). After the 1953 armistice North Korea remained implacably hostile to the United States. Despite an agreement with the Republic of Korea (South Korea) in 1972 to seek reunification by peaceful means, there were allegations of North Korean incursions, subversion attempts and terror attacks, including the assassination of the South Korean foreign minister in Rangoon (1983). Relations became very strained over the decision to hold the 1988 Olympic Games in Seoul, but eased when, at the end of the year, there were direct talks on reunification. Moreover, in 1989 meetings were held in Peking with American representatives.

Korea, Republic of (South Korea) Came into existence on 15 August 1948 with the nationalist, Syngman Rhee, as president. After the Korean War the problems of resettling refugees and rebuilding a shattered economy proved increasingly beyond the powers of his government, despite lavish international aid. Discontent with its corruption, with unemployment and inflation led to increasingly angry demonstrations which forced Rhee into exile (1960). He was succeeded by two weak civilian governments until, in 1962, the military seized power under General Park Chung Hee. His rule entailed the loss of many liberties, but encompassed the transformation of South Korea into one of the most powerful industrial states in east Asia. Opposition to his rule grew, particularly among students, and after he was accidentally shot dead by his intelligence chief (1979), martial law was declared and the opposition leader, Kim Dae Jung, was arrested. Students led an uprising at Kwangju (1980), which was brutally suppressed by Chun Doo Hwan, the new president. Constitutionally Chun's presidential term of office expired in 1988 and his party nominated Roh Tai Woo to succeed him. The elections, held in 1987 against a background of extreme violence, were won by Roh, largely because the opposition vote was split. This violence continued – with a break for the Olympic Games in the summer – to the end of 1988. President Roh promised an inquiry into the Kwangju massacres and carried out a government reshuffle, but in the face of demands that he call ex-President Chun to account, was unable to ease the growing tension.

Korean War On 25 June 1950 North Korean forces invaded South Korea and speedily took Seoul, the capital, occupying virtually all the republic except for a small area around the port of Pusan. Since the USSR was boycotting the Security Council, the United Nations was able to assemble 15 member states to assist South Korea. Their troops, directed by General MacArthur under a unified command in which US forces predominated, launched a counter-offensive from Pusan in September while landings were made at Inchon, behind the North Korean lines. UN forces swept north but, in his determination to overthrow the Communist regime, MacArthur neglected the Chinese warning to halt his advance. A massive Chinese attack (November 1950–January 1951) captured Seoul and drove the UN forces below the 38th parallel. Counterattacks in January and, in response to further Chinese onslaughts, in April and May, established the UN troops slightly to the north of the old frontier. President Truman had replaced MacArthur with General Ridgway (April) who conducted negotiations for an armistice in July 1951. Two years later a truce was signed between Chinese and US representatives, ending a war which cost the lives of over three million servicemen and civilians on both sides.

Kreisky, Bruno (1911–), Austrian statesman. Serving as a diplomat, he helped to negotiate the 1955 Austrian State Treaty, and was minister of foreign affairs (1959–66). Chairman of the Socialist Party (1967), he became chancellor in 1970, holding office until 1983.

Kronstadt Revolt A mutiny by sailors of the Soviet navy at the headquarters of the Baltic fleet which broke out in March 1921. The sailors supported the demands of peasants and workers for freedom under the Bolshevik government. The revolt was suppressed by Trotsky, but Lenin's New Economic Policy relaxed some of the harshness of the regime.

Kun, Béla (1886–c1937), Hungarian communist leader. He served in the Hungarian army, was taken prisoner by the Russians (1915), joined the Bolsheviks and returned to Hungary as a communist agitator. In 1919 he overthrew the Karyoli government, establishing a communist dictatorship, raising a Red Army and invading Slovakia. The Allies forced him to evacuate his conquests and the Romanian army drove him from Budapest to take refuge in Vienna. In 1920 he was allowed to leave Austria for the USSR where he worked for the Comintern. A victim of Stalin's purges, he was rehabilitated in 1958.

Kuomintang A moderate socialist party organized by Sun Yat-sen (1912) which established revolutionary governments in Canton (1918 and 1921). From 1922 it received aid from the Comintern and in 1924 formed a coalition with the Communists. In 1928 Chiang Kai-shek became chairman and C-in-C of the Kuomintang, having purged the Communists (1927), and began the civil war. From 1928 to 1947 the Kuomintang was recognized as the government of China (with its capital at Nanking), but after World War II the corrupt regime was swept from the mainland and from 1949 remained in power only in Taiwan.

L

Labour Party   British political party. During the 19th century successful candidates sponsored by the Labour Representation League (1869) had been absorbed into the Liberal Party. In 1900 a socialist grouping comprising the Trades Union Congress, the Fabian Society, the Independent Labour Party and the Social Democratic Federation formed the Labour Representation Committee which became the Labour Party after the 1906 election in which 29 of its candidates were successful. The party increased its representation in parliament in 1910. During World War I Ramsay MacDonald's pacifism became a handicap, but the party gained experience through Arthur Henderson (1863–1945), and George Barnes (1859–1940), who held office in Lloyd George's coalition. Following a split in the Liberal Party, Labour became the official opposition (1922) and in 1924 MacDonald formed a minority Labour government, but lost the election later that year (see **Zinoviev Letter**). In 1929 he led a second Labour government, but split the party in 1931 when he formed a coalition with the Conservatives. Under the leadership of George Lansbury (1932–35) and Clement Attlee the party's ideology became more firmly socialist and committed to a nationalization programme and, until almost too late, resolutely pacificist. Only the outbreak of the Spanish Civil War brought home the threat from Nazi Germany. During World War II Labour leaders held high office in Churchill's coalition government and in 1945 won a sweeping electoral victory which made important changes to British society by the nationalization of major industries, the introduction of the welfare state and an enhancement of the power of the state to direct and control. Labour was out of office between 1951 and 1964 and 1970 and 1974 but had established a political climate of a mixed economy, welfare and full employment, considerable state control and strong political influence by the trade union movement. The governments of Wilson and Callaghan (1974 to 1979) highlighted the reasons for the almost total eclipse of the party in the 1980s – lack of competence in handling the grave economic crises of those years, deep divisions within the party on defence and the common market, the infiltration of a party dedicated to parliamentary democracy by organizations dedicated to its overthrow, and the undue and stultifying influence of the trade unions. After electoral defeat in 1979, the party chose Michael Foot as its leader (1980) and, following further defeats, replaced him with Neil Kinnock (1983).

Lange, David Russell (1942–), New Zealand political leader. A lawyer by profession, he became an MP in 1977. Leader of the Labour Party (1983), he took office as prime minister and foreign minister after his 1984 electoral victory. His application of the 1985 regional treaty declaring the South Pacific a nuclear-free zone caused tension with France (see **Rainbow Warrior**) and, by banning nuclear-powered or nuclear-armed warships from New Zealand waters, he made the ANZUS Treaty a dead letter. His advocacy of free market principles caused some stress within his own party.

Lansdowne see **Petty-Fitzmaurice, Henry, 5th Marquess of**

Laos A republic of southeast Asia. In 1893 the French established a protectorate over the region (comprising two kingdoms and a principality divided since the beginning of the century between the Siamese and the Annamese), which was occupied by the Japanese (1942). The Japanese authorities proclaimed its independence (1945), leaving a nationalist movement in control when they withdrew. The French re-established their protectorate (1946), granting autonomy within the French Union (1949) and complete independence (1953). In the interim the northern half of the country had been taken by the Pathet Lao, a communist and nationalist movement led by ex-Prince Souphanouvong, from the neutralist government of the ex-prince's half-brother, Prince Souvanna Phouma (1901–84). In 1957 the Pathet Lao joined the government, but this coalition collapsed in 1959. Throughout the 1960s coup followed counter-coup, involving neutralist, Pathet Lao and rightist forces with increasing North Vietnamese support for the Pathet Lao. As the United States grew more deeply involved in the Vietnam War, Laos itself became a battleground when South Vietnamese troops invaded (1971) to counter North Vietnamese penetration. A ceasefire in 1973 ceated a neutralist-Pathet Lao coalition, but once North Vietnam had captured Saigon and won the Vietnam War, the communists took over completely (1975). On 2 December the People's Democratic Republic was proclaimed, with ex-Prince Souphanouvong as its president, but effective control was exercised by the Vietnamese. During 1988 this control began to be relaxed as their forces started a slow withdrawal.

Lateran Treaty The agreement between the Italian government and Pope Pius XI recognizing the sovereignty of the Holy See in the Vatican City and regulating the position of the Roman Catholic Church in Italy by means of a concordat (1929). It brought to an end the hostility between church and state dating from the seizure of Rome (1870) during the reunification of Italy.

Lattre de Tassigny, Jean-Marie Gabriel de (1889–1952), French soldier. He commanded the 14th Infantry Division (May-June 1940). Interned by the Germans (1942), he escaped to North Africa. He led the French 1st Army from the time of the landings in the south of France (1944) right up to the German surrender, at which he was the French representative. He was subsequently high commissioner and C-in-C in Indochina (1950–52).

Latvia A Baltic republic of the USSR. Incorporated into the Russian Empire by the end of the 18th century, Latvia was particularly active in the 1905 Revolution. The country suffered severely in World War I, but the fall of the German and tsarist empires enabled it to expel their forces and to declare independence (1918). Following a peace treaty with the USSR, a democratic republic was created under the 1920 constitution but never became firmly established. In 1934 Karlis Ulmanis, the prime minister, established a dictatorship. In 1940 Latvia was annexed by the USSR under the Nazi-Soviet Pact, which established a communist regime – reimposed after liberation from the German occupation (1941–44). The response of the Latvians to Gorbachov's reforms (1988) was muted by 'Russification', which had made them a minority in their own land.

Laurier, Sir Wilfred (1841–1919), Canadian statesman. A barrister, he became a federal MP (1884) and Liberal Party leader (1887). As prime minister (1896) – the first French Canadian and Roman Catholic to hold the office – he worked to establish a Canadian identity, encouraging links between the French- and English-speaking communities and urging Canadian independence in defence and foreign affairs. In 1911 he was defeated on a proposed commercial treaty with the United States but remained leader of the Liberal opposition until his death.

Lausanne, Treaty of The agreement (24 July 1923) which officially ended the state of war between the Allies and Turkey. Following the Chanak Crisis (1922), the Treaty of Sèvres had become a dead letter. Under the new treaty Turkey regained some of the territories ceded to Greece under the earlier agreement and renounced all claims to the former possessions of the Ottoman empire. Compulsory exchanges of population beween Greece and Turkey were also arranged.

Laval, Pierre (1883–1945), French politician. A socialist (1914–19) and then an independent socialist deputy and senator (1924–40), he held various ministerial posts (1925–30). Prime minister and foreign minister (1931–32 and 1935–36), he was forced to resign over the Hoare-Laval Pact of December 1935 and his unpopular economic policy. In 1940 he helped bring the Third Republic to an end and became vice president of the new French State. He was replaced by Darlan (1941) but, on German insistence, was recalled to the Vichy government (1942), and as minister of the interior, foreign minister and minister of information adopted a policy of whole-hearted collaboration. After the war he was arrested by the Americans, handed over to the French, tried and executed.

Law, Andrew Bonar (1858–1923), British prime minister. A Conservative MP (1900–23), he supported tariff reform. As party leader (1911), he strongly opposed Home Rule. During World War I he was colonial secretary in Asquith's coalition cabinet (1915–16) and chancellor of the exchequer and leader of the House of Commons (1916–19) under Lloyd George. Lord privy seal (1919–22), he resigned Conservative party leadership (1921) only to resume it the following year and head the rebellion against the continuation of Lloyd George's coalition. He became prime minister in October 1922, but was forced to resign in the following May because of deteriorating health.

Lawrence, Thomas Edward (1888–1935), British soldier and archaeologist. Having gained a knowledge of the middle east before World War I, in 1916 he was sent to Jeddah to act as liaison officer with the Emir Feisal in his revolt against the Turks. He directed raids against Turkish communications and key centres, acting on the right flank of Allenby's advance through Palestine and Syria, and entering Damascus on 1 October 1918. Until 1922 he worked for the Arab cause as delegate to the Peace Conference (1919) and adviser to the Colonial Office (1921–22). In 1922 he enlisted in the RAF under the name of Ross, transferring to the Tank Corps and rejoining the RAF in 1923. He served in the ranks until 1935 and was killed in a motorcycle accident shortly after his discharge.

League of Nations An organization for international co-operation established after World War I. The last of President Wilson's 'Fourteen Points' had been the creation of 'a general association of nations ... under specific covenants' and this was effected in the League of Nations instituted at the Paris Peace Conference (1919), with its headquarters in Geneva. The objectives of the league were to settle international disputes by arbitration and to further international co-operation, and it was able to make useful progress in world health, the care of refugees, efforts to suppress white slavery and drug trafficking and fair employment (through the International Labour Organization). It also was able to settle some international disputes. However, the league was powerless to enforce its arbitration, since economic sanctions were generally ineffective and it lacked the support of its begetter, the United States. The USSR was a member only from 1934 to 1940 and Germany from 1926 to 1933, while such states as Brazil (1926), Japan (1933) and Italy (1936) walked out when their actions were criticized. Thus the league was unable to prevent the Chaco War (1932–35), Japan's seizure of Manchuria (1931) and invasion of China (1937), Germany's remilitarization of the Rhineland (1936) and the Anschluss (1938), or to mediate in the Spanish Civil War (1936–39) or the Russo-Finnish War (1939). Efforts, too, to achieve international disarmament were equally useless. The organization remained in being during World War II, its functions being absorbed (1946) by the United Nations.

Lebanon A republic at the eastern end of the Mediterranean. As part of the Ottoman Empire it was disturbed by strife between its Druze, Maronite Christian and Muslim Arab inhabitants. After World War I it came under a French mandate. In 1926 it was granted a republican constitution and in 1936, under a treaty with France (ratified only in 1941 after the expulsion of the Vichy regime), complete independence was guaranteed after a three-year period. Independence became effective in 1943. Lebanon joined the rest of the Arab League in declaring war on Israel (1948) but took no part in the fighting and remained neutralist. The United States intervened in 1958 to support the pro-western President Camille Chamoun (1900–87) against a Pan-Arab revolt and in 1962 there was an unsuccessful coup by pro-Syrian elements. However, Lebanese prosperity and stability were not seriously affected until the Six Day War, the Israeli occupation of the West Bank and the massive influx of Palestinian refugees into southern Lebanon (1967), where their camps provided the base for guerrilla raids on northern Israel. During 1968–69 these provoked Israeli counter-measures which increased in severity after the expulsion of the PLO from Jordan (1970). Israeli attacks paid no regard to Lebanese safety and the Christian Phalangist militia turned against the PLO (1975–76) until checked by Syrian intervention in 1976. From then on Lebanese factions became pawns in the power struggles of Arab states and of Israeli politics. The key events were: Israeli withdrawal from southern Lebanon (leaving a surrogate defence force – the Christian militia) and the arrival of a UN peacekeeping force (1978); the Iranian revolution (1979) and the birth of the fundamentalist Shi'ite terrorist organization, Hizbollah; a full-scale Israeli invasion (June 1982) and the siege of PLO strongholds in Beirut; the arrival of western peacekeeping forces following the evacuation of the PLO (August); the massacre by Christian militia of Palestinian refugees in camps in Israeli-occupied Beirut (September 1982); suicide lorry bomb attacks on US and French troops (1983); the withdrawal of Israeli troops from Beirut (1983); the withdrawal of the peacekeeping force (1984); the Syrian attempt to take control of the PLO, the attack by their Amal militia on the refugee camps (1985) and the attempt to starve the survivors into submission (1987). In the interim Beirut was the scene of constant factional violence and the taking of Western hostages. By the end of 1988 even the facade of a Lebanese government had been destroyed and there were separate Muslim and Christian governments in Beirut, with the Syrians intervening against the Christians.

Leclerc (Philippe Marie de Hauteclocque, 1902–47), French soldier. He escaped to join de Gaulle in London (1940), becoming governor of the French Cameroons which he rallied to the Free French cause. He captured Kufra from the Italians (1941) and led a Free French force from Chad to join Montgomery in Tunisia (1943). He took part in the Normandy landings and, with the 2nd Armoured Division, liberated Paris. As C-in-C in Indo-China he received the Japanese surrender (1945). Appointed inspector-general of French forces in North Africa (1946), he was killed in an air crash in the following year. He was posthumously promoted marshal of France.

Lee Kuan Yew (1923–), Singaporean political leader. A lawyer, he founded his People's Action Party (1954) and, on independence (1959), became Singapore's first prime minister, taking Singapore into the Federation of Malaysia (1963), but withdrawing two years later in consequence of political disputes. His strongly autocratic regime brought great prosperity to Singapore but with increasing danger of infringement of human rights.

Lend-Lease Act The act passed by the US Congress on 11 March 1941 to permit the president to sell, transfer, lend or lease armaments to the United Kingdom (and subsequently to China and the USSR), repayment to be 'in kind or property, or any other direct or indirect benefit which the President deems satisfactory'. The United States was thus able to set on foot its war production eight months before it entered World War II and obtain substantial indirect economic and political benefits. In 1942 a reverse lend-lease system was introduced for the supply of US forces overseas. President Truman brought the act to an end in August 1945 with the introduction of Marshall Aid.

Lenin (Vladimir Ilyich Ulyanov, 1870–1924), founder of the USSR.

Banished while a law student for his revolutionary activities, he completed his studies and practised in St Petersburg (Leningrad). Exiled to Siberia (1887) for political agitation, on his release he left Russia (1900), and visited Belgium, England and France, before settling in Geneva. In 1903 he headed the majority (Bolsheviks) when the Social Democratic Party split over his proposal that only a disciplined party of professional revolutionaries could bring socialism to Russia. He returned to Russia to organize the St Petersburg Soviet during the 1905 Revolution, escaping to Finland in 1907 and returning to Geneva to wage a pamphlet war against his opponents within the movement. He saw the outbreak of World War I as an opportunity to overthrow capitalism and accepted the invitation of the German general staff to return to Russia in 1917. After the failure of the February Revolution Lenin escaped to Finland, but in the October Revolution overthrew the Provisional Government and as chairman of the council of people's commissars became head of state. In 1918 he concluded the humiliating Treaty of Brest-Litovsk with the Germans and moved the seat of government to Moscow. He now undertook the tasks of suppressing all opposition to the Bolsheviks, of exporting the revolution to Germany, Poland and Hungary, and of spreading communist influence worldwide through the creation of the Comintern (1919). Although Lenin failed in his foreign ventures, he was completely successful at home, defeating the White Russians and suppressing all internal opposition. His repressive regime and the failure of socialist economic policies caused unrest. After the Kronstadt Revolt (1921), Lenin felt it wise to introduce a measure of liberalization in his New Economic Policy. His illness and early death leave unresolved the question of whether he would have allowed the NEP to continue or whether he would have reimposed a strict communist regime like his successor, Stalin.

Leopold III (1901–83), king of the Belgians (1934–51). Having made unavailing efforts to mediate at the outbreak of World War II (1939), he took command of the Belgian army when German forces invaded but was forced to surrender (28 May 1940). He was placed in custody by the Germans, with whom he refused to collaborate. Although he had kept his allies informed, his surrender in 1940 was branded as 'treason' for wartime propaganda purposes by the British and was used to stir republican sentiments by the postwar Belgian socialist government. The king was not allowed to return and abdicated in favour of his son Baudouin (1950).

Liaquat Ali Khan (1895–1951), first prime minister of Pakistan. Called to the English bar (1922), he joined the Muslim League (1923), becoming its general secretary (1936) and a close associate of Jinnah. He served on the United Provinces legislative council (1926–40) and the central legislative assembly of India (1940–46), and played an important part in the negotiations which led to Indian independence and the creation of Pakistan (1947). In 1948 he succeeded Jinnah as prime minister, and Jinnah's early death and his own assassination (1951) seriously affected Pakistan's development.

Liberal Party A British political party created during the 19th century. Representing the industrial and commercial interests of unfettered capitalism, it had been gradually brought by Gladstone to accept responsibility for the urban working class, enfranchised by the Conservatives. In the early 20th century, under prime ministers Campbell-Bannerman and Asquith and with Lloyd George as chancellor of the exchequer, the Liberals introduced a whole series of important social reforms (1906–14). The seeds of Liberal decline were sown by the disputes between Asquith and Lloyd George in World War I and the intrigues with the Conservative Party, through which Lloyd George displaced his rival and became prime minister in a coalition government (1916). The Labour Party reaped the benefit of these internal squabbles and became the official opposition in 1922. During the 1930s there was a further decline when many Liberals allied with the Conservatives in the National Government (1931), support continuing to fall away during and after World War II as the radical elements became absorbed into the Labour Party. In 1976 David Steel was elected to the leadership by a ballot of party members (unique at this time among British political parties) and his pact with the Labour Party enabled the Callaghan government to survive until 1979. In 1981 the Liberal Party voted in favour of an electoral alliance with the newly formed Social Democrats. However, although this alliance gained some success in local government elections, in the general elections of 1983 and 1987 it failed to capture the anti-Tory vote, despite the poor showing of the Labour Party. The 1987 election had proved a particular disappointment and Steel now proposed a merger of the two parties. He was strongly opposed by the Social Democrat leader, David Owen, but in the event both parties agreed to the merger which was effected in 1988, the Liberal Party becoming known as the Social and Liberal Democrats.

Libya A republic of north Africa. Italy seized the country from the Ottoman Empire in the Libyan War (1911–12) and, after pacification, began a major series of public works (1930), encouraged Italian immigration and settlement. In 1939 Libya was made an integral part of Italy and limited citizenship granted to the Muslim population. During World War II the country became a battlefield and remained under British military administration (following its capture in 1943) until 1951. It then became the first independent state to be created by a resolution of the UN General Assembly. The emir of the Senussi was made the constitutional monarch of a federation as King Idris I. Although Libya joined the Arab League in 1953, defence treaties permitted Britain and the United States to retain bases in the country. In the 1960s Libyan society underwent a profound change, with the development of the oil industry and the influence of Nasser's revolution in neighbouring Egypt. In 1969 a group of junior officers seized power and deposed the king. Colonel Muammar al-Qaddafi was their leader and from that date Libyan history became a reflection of his political ideas and ambitions.

Libyan War The war between Italy and Turkey (1911–12). In 1900 Italy and France came to a secret understanding that, in return for allowing the French a free hand in Morocco, Italy should be allowed to acquire the Turkish provinces of Tripoli and Cyrenaica (modern Libya). In 1911, with the Moroccan crisis unresolved, Italian forces landed at Tripoli, defeating the Turkish garrisons commanded by Enver Bey, and by 1912 had annexed the country. At the same time the Italians seized Rhodes and the other islands of the Dodecanese.

Lie, Trygve Halvdan (1896–1968), Norwegian statesman. A lawyer by profession, he was minister of justice (1935–39), minster of trade (1939–40) and foreign minister (1940–45). Appointed first UN secretary-general in 1946 (re-elected 1950), he unavailingly urged the admission of Communist China to the United Nations and had an important share in organizing the UN force in Korea (1950). Lie resigned in 1953 to return to Norwegian politics, where he once again held office (1963–68).

Liebknecht, Karl, see under **Spartakist Rising**

Lin Piao (1908–71), Chinese Communist soldier and political leader. He served in the Northern Expedition as a Kuomintang officer but joined the Communists when the two parties split (1927). In 1947–48 he defeated Kuomintang forces in Manchuria and in 1950–52 commanded the Chinese 'volunteers' in Korea. He was promoted marshal (1955), defence minister (1959) and succeeded Liu Shao-chi as heir apparent to Chairman Mao. In 1972 it was announced that he had instigated in an abortive plot against Mao (1971) and been killed in an air crash while trying to escape to the USSR.

Lithuania A Baltic republic of the USSR. By the end of the 18th century this once powerful state had been completely absorbed by Russia. A national revival – inspired by the Roman Catholic clergy – brought frequent collisions with the Russian authorities during the 19th century and, after the tsarist collapse, there was a short-lived German-protected Lithuanian kingdom (February 1918). With the German defeat, a republic was proclaimed in November 1918, which survived the attacks of the Red Army and the German Freikorps, although the Poles seized Vilnius (1920) and Lithuania remained technically at war with Poland until 1927. Lithuania became a dictatorship under Augustine Voldemaras (1926–29) and Antanas Smetona (1929–39), who by 1938 had made it a corporate state. Under the Nazi-Soviet pact Lithuania was incorporated into the USSR (1940). During World War II Lithuania was occupied by the Germans (1941–44) and the Jewish population was largely exterminated. With the return to Soviet control, the postwar period saw the Roman Catholic church subjected to heavy persecution, but the spirit of nationalism remained alive and there was strong pressure for independence when Gorbachov's reforms began to take effect in the 1989 elections.

Little Entente   The name derisively given by a Hungarian journalist to the series of alliances between Czechoslovakia and Yugoslavia (1920), Czechoslovakia and Romania (1921), and Yugoslavia and Romania (1921), consolidated by treaty (1929). These agreements aimed to restrain Hungarian attempts to revise the Treaty of Trianon and to prevent the restoration of the Hapsburg monarchy. The countries concerned co-operated both economically and militarily, but their alliance fell apart when Hitler occupied Czechoslovakia (1938).

Litvinov   (Maxim Maximovich Meir Walach, 1876–1951), Soviet statesman. He joined the Social Democrats (1898), was imprisoned for revolutionary activities (1901) and escaped (1902). He settled in England (1908) after joining the Bolsheviks and taking part in the 1905 Revolution. After the October Revolution he was appointed Soviet spokesman in London, returning to Moscow (1918). As chief assistant to the commissar for foreign affairs (from 1926) and as Soviet delegate at the League of Nations (from 1934) he was largely responsible for the direction of Soviet foreign policy towards collective security, signing a Franco-Soviet Treaty and a non-aggression pact with Czechoslovakia (1935). In the Soviet policy switch after Munich (1938) he was replaced by Molotov, serving as Soviet ambassador in Washington (1941–43) and deputy foreign minister (1943–46).

Liu Shao-chi   (c1898–c1973), Chinese Communist leader. Sent to Moscow where he joined the Communist Party (1921), he returned to China to organize industrial agitation. He was elected to the central committee (1927) and the Politburo (1934). As leading party theoretician he became principal vice-chairman of the party (1949) and in 1959 succeeded Mao Tse-tung as chairman, although ranking second to him in the party hierarchy. During the Cultural Revolution he was superseded as Mao's heir by Lin Piao and in October 1968, deprived of all his offices, disappeared completely from public life. In 1974 his death was announced by the Chinese press.

Lloyd George, David   (1863–1945, 1st Earl), British statesman. A Liberal MP (1890–1945), as president of the board of trade in Campbell-Bannerman's government (1905), he began the series of social reforms which he continued as chancellor of the exchequer in Asquith's administration (1908). In 1909 the rejection by the House of Lords of his budget, with its provisons for social insurance, raised the constitutional crisis settled by the Parliament Act (1911). During World War I he became minister of munitions (1915) and of war (1916), before ousting Asquith and taking the premiership in a coalition government with Conservative support (1916). As prime minister he vigorously prosecuted the war, rejecting any attempts (1916 and 1917) at a negotiated peace. Having gained an overwhelming electoral victory for the coalition in 1918, he attended the peace conference, moderating Wilson's idealism and Clemenceau's harshness. He negotiated the treaty which led to the establishment of the Irish Free State (1922), but, too heavily dependent upon Conservative support, was unable to survive the Chanak Crisis. The fall of the coalition government marked the end of Lloyd George's active political career, but he remained leader of the Liberals (1926–31) and then of the Independent Liberals. Although he had sympathized with German grievances and had visited Hitler in 1936, after Munich he became a strong opponent of appeasement.

Locarno Treaties   A series of treaties, signed in 1925, which guaranteed the boundaries of France, Belgium and Germany as defined by the Treaty of Versailles, provided that the borders between Germany and Czechoslovakia and Poland might be changed only by international arbitration, while France signed separate mutual defence pacts with Poland and Czechoslovakia, and Germany was promised admission to the League of Nations. Hitler denounced the treaty when he remilitarized the Rhineland (1936).

Lockheed Aircraft scandal   The revelation in February 1976 by a US Senate subcommittee that the Lockheed Aircraft Corporation had paid out 22 million dollars in bribes to officials in Japan, Turkey, Italy and the Netherlands in order to further the sales of its aircraft. Prince Bernhard (consort of the queen of the Netherlands) was forced to resign his public and private posts because of his involvement, while in Japan the former prime minister, Tanaka, was indicted for receiving a bribe of $1.6 million.

Lomé Convention   The trade agreement signed on 28 February 1975 (and subsequently renewed) between the European Community and an original 46 (the number was later increased) Third World countries, by which their products were given free entry to the EC, while European Community members agreed to provide sums of money in development aid.

London, Treaties of   (1) The treaty (May 1913) which ended the first Balkan War and under which Turkey in Europe was limited to an area around Constantinople, the state of Albania was formed and Macedonia divided between Greece, Serbia and Bulgaria. Bulgarian disagreement with the last provision led to the second Balkan War in which Bulgaria lost its share of Macedonia under the Treaty of Bucharest (August 1913). (2) The secret treaty of 25 April 1915 between Britain, France, Russia and Italy under which Italy was to enter the war on the Allied side within one month in return for a promised postwar settlement which was to give Italy the Austrian provinces south of the Alps (Italia irredenta), Trieste, parts of the Dalmatian coast and its offshore islands, the Albanian port of Valona and full sovereignty over the Dodecanese, with part of Turkish Asia Minor, colonial gains in Africa and a share of war indemnities. The treaty was denounced by President Wilson when the Bolsheviks published its terms after the October Revolution. Britain and France reneged on their commitments at the Paris Peace Conference, thus arousing Italian resentment and easing the way for Mussolini's climb to power.

Long March   The epic journey undertaken by Chinese Communists in 1934–5. By the summer of 1934 the Kuomintang had encircled the Communists in central China (Kiangsi Province). Some 90,000 men with their dependants broke out and headed west into Kweichow province. Here Mao Tse-tung was elected leader and determined to march to the Shensi Soviet base in the far northwest. Despite the most formidable natural obstacles and attacks by the Kuomintang and local warlords during much of the 6000 miles covered, a third of the original marchers reached Shensi, which was to prove a secure base to which other Communist forces rallied.

Longo, Luigi (1900–80), founder of the Italian Communist Party (1921). Inspector-general of the International Brigades during the Spanish Civil War, he returned to Italy during World War II to organize the Communist partisan units. An MP (1948), he was deputy secretary of the Italian Communist Party (1945–64) and secretary-general from 1964 until his retirement as party president (1972).

Lon Nol (1913–85), Kampuchean head of state. Army chief of staff and minister of defence (1955–66), he was premier (1966 and 1969), and first vice president (1967). In 1970 he deposed Prince Sihanouk and seized power with US backing. Having failed to suppress the Communist Khmer Rouge guerrillas, he fled the country shortly before their final victory.

Ludendorff, Erich (1865–1937), German soldier. As Hindenburg's chief of staff on the eastern front in World War I, he planned his victories (1914–15) and when the latter was appointed to supreme command of the German armies (1916), he went with him as quartermaster general, in virtual control thereafter of the entire German war-machine. When the Allies held his March 1918 offensive and their counter-offensive broke his armies, Ludendorff was dismissed and fled to Sweden. In 1919 he returned to take part in the Kapp Putsch (1920) and in Hitler's Munich Putsch (1923). A Nazi member of the Reichstag (1924–28) and unsuccessful candidate for the presidency (1925), he broke with Hitler and spent his latter years in retirement.

Lugard, Frederick John Dealtry (1858–1945, 1st Baron), British soldier and colonial administrator. He saw service in the Afghan War (1878–80), the Sudan (1884–85) and Burma (1886–87) and explored Uganda (1890–92). As commissioner for Northern Nigeria (1894), he raised the West African Frontier Force (1897) and by 1903 had imposed law and order. Governor of Hong Kong (1906), he returned to Nigeria as governor (1912–19), welding both north and south into a single administrative unit. Lugard was the apostle of indirect rule, by which control was exercised through existing native institutions.

Lumumba, Patrice Hemery (1925–61), was the first prime minister of the Republic of the Congo (now Zaïre). A permanent member of the committee of the All-African People's Conference and president of the Congolese People's Movement, he left the country temporarily (1959) and on his return was briefly imprisoned by the Belgian authorities. The chief negotiator for Congolese independence (1960), he came to power as prime minister, with his arch rival, Kasavubu, as president. After the army mutiny and the secession of Katanga, Lumumba appealed for aid to the United Nations and to the USSR. He was dismissed by Kasavubu, placed under house arrest by Colonel Mobutu and, after escape and recapture (1960), sent to Katanga where he was shot, allegedly while trying to escape.

Luthuli, Chief Albert John (1889–1967), African nationalist leader. Chief of the Zulu Abasemakholweni tribe (1936) and a convinced Christian, he advocated non-violent opposition to racial discrimination and continued to do so within the African National Congress, which he joined (1946), and of which he was elected president (1952). When he refused to resign the post, the authorities deposed him from his chieftainship. Having led the campaign of passive resistance to apartheid, he was with some 150 other critics of the government tried for treason (1956). In 1959 he was banished to his village and in 1960 the ANC was made illegal. In 1962 his statements to the media were banned and in 1967 he was killed, accidentally it is alleged, by a train. He had been awarded the Nobel peace prize in 1960.

Luxemburg, Rosa see under **Spartakist Rising**

Lvov, Prince Georgi Yevgenyvich (1861–1925), Russian administrator. Before World War I he had played a prominent part in the development of local government in tsarist Russia. He was, however, quite unfitted to head the Provisional Government formed after the February Revolution (1917), being an idealist with a strong aversion to violence and, after the Petrograd rising in July 1917 was suppressed, he made way for Kerensky's moderate socialist government. Lvov died in exile in Paris.

Lyautey, Louis Hubert Gonsalve (1854–1934), French soldier. He served in Algeria (1879–82), Indo-China (1893–95), Madagascar (1896) and Algeria (1903–12). In 1912 he was appointed resident general in the newly created French protectorate over Morocco. Briand's war minister (1916–17), he returned to Morocco, staying there until his retirement in 1925 after the defeat of Abd el-Krim. A devout Catholic with a profound respect for Islam, he aimed to an assimilation of the two cultures, which his successors mistakenly took to be western dominance.

Lyons, Joseph Aloysius (1879–1939), Australian statesman. Labour prime minister of Tasmania (1923–1928), he became a federal MP (1929). In 1931 he broke with the Labour Party to form the United Australia Party, a coalition group which came to power in 1932. As prime minister from 1932 until his sudden death in 1939, he introduced a three-year defence programme (1934), which was to prove vital to Australia in World War II.

M

MacArthur, Douglas (1880–1964), US soldier. He served in the Philippines and Japan and as an aide to President Theodore Roosevelt (1906–07). He was attached to the US army general staff (1913–17) and in World War I was chief of staff of the 42nd Division and commanded the 84th Infantry Brigade (1918). Between the wars he held various appointments in the United States and the Philippines, retiring in 1937. He returned to active duty in July 1941 as commander US forces in the Far East and, after a heroic defence of the Philippines against the Japanese (December 1941-March 1942), was ordered by Roosevelt to withdraw to Australia to command Allied Forces South West Pacific. On 12 September 1945 he received the Japanese surrender and as commander of the Allied Powers in Japan, directed the occupation. A rare example of the American proconsul, he helped to build a new and peaceful Japan, but his high-handed ways lost him friends in Washington. As C-in-C UN forces in Korea (1950), he cleared the South of invaders and pressed towards the Yalu River, risking Chinese intervention. When it came he sought permission to bomb Chinese bases in Manchuria. Truman was not prepared to risk war with China and when MacArthur publicly disputed his refusal, Truman dismissed him on 11 April 1951. He unsuccessfully sought Republican presidential nomination (1948 and 1952).

McCarthy, Joseph Raymond (1908–57), US Republican senator. Elected in 1946, he sprang from obscurity in 1950 with the claim that he had evidence of communist infiltration of the State Department. Although a Senate investigation cleared the department, he continued his campaign and helped to swing the 1952 elections to the Republicans. In January 1953 he was appointed chairman of the Senate permanent investigations subcommittee and now conducted a witch-hunt against communists and their alleged sympathizers. When attacked (October 1953), the US army countered. His credibility was destroyed by televised hearings and he was censured by the Senate. McCarthy's rash attacks on President Eisenhower brought an end to his discreditable campaign.

MacDonald, James Ramsay (1866–1937), British statesman. He joined the Social Democratic Federation (1885), the Fabian Society (1886) and the Independent Labour Party (1894). He helped to organize the Labour

Representative Committee and was its first secretary (1900–12). He became a Labour MP (1906) and led the Parliamentary Labour Party (1911–14), but his pacificism lost him both influence and his seat in the 1918 election. He returned to parliament in 1922, when he became leader of the opposition, and in January 1924 formed a minority Labour government in which he was both prime minister and foreign secretary. He lost the October election (see **Zinoviev Letter**). In 1929 Labour again returned to power. MacDonald refused to adopt the socialist measures proposed by his cabinet colleagues against the Depression and formed a National government (1931) in coalition with the Conservatives. He came increasingly to rely on their support and yielded the premiership to their leader, Baldwin, in 1935, although he was to remain in the cabinet until his death.

Machel, Samora (1933–86), 1st president of Mozambique. He joined the independence movement, Frelimo, and was sent (1963) to Algeria for training as a guerrilla. On his return to Mozambique he was so successful that he became Frelimo's C-in-C (1968) and president, when the Portuguese granted independence (1975). Until his death in an air crash he held power in a one-party state racked by economic decline and an increasingly bitter war with the Renamo guerrillas.

Macmillan, Maurice Harold (1894–1986, 1st Earl of Stockton), British statesman. He served and was three times wounded in World War I. He was a Conservative MP (1924–29 and 1931–64). A progressive social reformer and critic of his party's foreign and defence policy in the inter-war years, he was a junior minister in Churchill's wartime coalition. He entered the cabinet as minister resident in North Africa (1942), easing tensions between de Gaulle and the Americans and handling the problems of the Italian surrender and the liberation of Greece. Minister of housing (1951–54), minister of defence (1954–55), foreign secretary (1955) and chancellor of the exchequer (1955–57) under Churchill and Eden, he succeeded Eden as prime minister (1957), winning the 1959 election and remaining in office until his resignation from ill-health in 1964. During the early years of his administration he presided over full employment and an expanding economy, but by its close it faced economic uncertainty and the taint of the Profumo affair. Macmillan accepted the independence movement in Africa and his 'wind of change' speech (1960) accelerated its progress. After his retirement he became the Conservative's elder statesman, and as Earl of Stockton expressed a progressive attitude to social issues at variance with that of the Conservative government.

Maginot Line A system of fortifications along France's eastern frontier originally conceived in 1925 and begun under the direction of André Maginot (1877–1932) as minister of war (1929–32). Because of Belgian opposition the fortifications did not cover the Belgian frontier, while the rough terrain of the Ardennes was considered protection in its own right. It was precisely in these areas that the line was outflanked by the German blitzkrieg in 1940, having already contributed to the defensive mentality which lost the battle of France.

Magsaysay, Ramon (1907–57), Philippines political leader. A guerrilla leader against the Japanese occupation forces in World War II, he was appointed provincial governor (1945) and elected to the Philippine Congress (1946–50). As secretary of national defence under President Quirino he quelled the Communist Hukbalahap rebels by a combination of armed force and a land resettlement programme. Elected president (1953), he combined a policy of co-operation with the United States with land and governmental reform. He was killed in an air crash while running for a second term.

Makarios III (Mikhail Khristodoulo Mouskos, 1913–77), archbishop, ethnarch and political leader. Elected bishop of Khition (1948) and archbishop of Cyprus (1950), he supported Enosis and was exiled by the British on suspicion of aiding the terrorist campaign. In 1957 he was released and from 1958 began to campaign for Cypriot independence rather than unification with Greece. Having helped to create the republic of Cyprus, he became its first president (1959; re-elected 1969 and 1973) but, by opting for independence, antagonized many of his supporters. There were attempts on his life culminating in a coup, backed by the Greek government, which forced Makarios into exile in July 1975 and led to the Turkish invasion and the partition of the island. Makarios returned in December but was unable to resolve the situation before his death in 1977.

Malan, Daniel François (1874–1959), South African statesman. A Calvinist minister turned newspaper editor (1914), he entered parliament as a Nationalist (1918) and held office in the Herzog coalition (1924–33). He introduced legislation to make Afrikaans an official language and attempted to have the Indian minority repatriated. As leader of the opposition (1934–39 and 1940–48) he expressed Afrikaans nationalist hostility to South Africa's entry into World War II. When his Nationalist Party won the 1948 election and he became prime minister, he was able to implement its racial theories. He was responsible for introducing the oppressive system of apartheid and when the South African Supreme

Court held such policies unconstitutional (1952) he legislated to make parliament superior to the courts. He remained prime minister until his retirement in 1954.

Malawi An independent African Commonwealth country, formerly known as Nyasaland. It became a British protectorate in 1891. In 1915 a small-scale African revolt was easily suppressed and the region moved forward to greater African participation in government until Dr Hastings Banda led the bitter opposition to the Federation of Nyasaland and Rhodesia. This created a state of emergency (1959–60). The federation was ended in 1963 and Nyasaland achieved independence as Malawi on 6 July 1964, with Dr Banda as prime minister. In 1966 Malawi became a republic with Dr Banda as president, an office made life-long in 1971. Having suppressed attempts to overthrow him in 1965 and 1971, Banda remained firmly in power operating a moderate and essentially pragmatic policy towards his neighbours, including South Africa, with which his country had strong trade links.

Malaysia An independent Commonwealth federation comprising (1) West Malaysia and (2) East Malaysia, established on 16 September 1963 and originally including Singapore (which left the federation in August 1965).

(1) **West Malaysia** comprises the 19th century crown colony, the Straits Settlements (then including Singapore) and the Federated Malay States. Following Japanese occupation in World War II, the British established first the Union of Malaya (1946) and then the Federation of Malaya (1948) which was immediately faced by a Communist insurrection. During the Malayan emergency (1948–60) British and Commonwealth forces under General Sir Gerald Templer defeated the guerrillas and on 31 August 1957 Malaya gained its independence. Its new prime minister, Tunku Abdul Rahman, directed the closing stages of the guerrilla war and became the founding father of the wider federation of Malaysia (1963).

(2) **East Malaysia** comprises all former British protectorates and colonies (with the exception of the Sultanate of Brunei) in the northern section of the island of Borneo. (The former Dutch possessions in the south are now known as Kalimantan and form part of Indonesia.) British North Borneo (Sabah) was made a protectorate in 1882 and joined Malaysia in 1963, while Sarawak was the area granted by the Sultan of Brunei to the 'White Rajah', James Brooke in 1841. It became a British protectorate in 1888 but remained under the control of the Brooke family until 1946 when it was ceded to Britain and became a crown colony. In

1962 an armed left-wing insurrection against the proposed federation with Malaya spread from Brunei, but was put down by British troops and in the following year federation was effected. The whole region was occupied by the Japanese in World War II. The Federation of Malaysia was faced by an immediate challenge from Indonesia, the 'confrontation' or invasion of East Malaysia, contained and defeated with the aid of Commonwealth forces, followed by sporadic border warfare which ended with the fall of Sukarno (1966). In 1968 there was tension when the Phiippines laid claim to Sabah. However the main problem facing the federation has not been economic (it enjoys considerable prosperity), but ethnic. A substantial Chinese and a small Indian minority tend to dominate commerce and the professions, creating resentment among Malays. Similarly the Malays' privileged position entrenched under the constitution and their dominant political role causes grave Chinese and Indian concern. These ethnic tensions erupted into race riots in Kuala Lumpur (1969) and fears of Chinese economic exploitation have been used by politicians, including the present prime minister, Dr Mahathir Mohamad, to bolster his increasingly autocratic rule.

Malenkov, Georgi Maksimilianovich (1902–79), Soviet statesman. He was Stalin's trusted assistant in the destruction of the kulaks (1929) and in the Great Purge (1935–38). He was a member of the central committee (1939) and candidate member of the Politburo (February 1941), a member of Stalin's war cabinet, a full member of the Politburo, deputy prime minister and second secretary of the Party (1946). Regarded as Stalin's heir, on the death of the dictator (1953) he was outmanoeuvred by Khrushchev, who became first secretary. In 1955 the failure of his agricultural policy caused his replacement as prime minister and in 1957 he was stripped of his functions as an 'anti-party' opponent of Khrushchev, exiled and later (1961) expelled from the party. He spent his later years in retirement in Moscow.

Malinovsky, Rodion Yakovlevich (1898–1967), Soviet soldier. During World War II he commanded the counter-offensive at Stalingrad (1942) and the armies which liberated southern Russia, took Bucharest and forced the Romanian armistice (August 1944), besieged Budapest and finally captured Vienna (April 1945). After the German surrender Malinovsky commanded the armies which occupied Manchuria, became C-in-C of the Soviet army and deputy defence minister (1956), succeeding Zhukov as defence minister (1957) and holding the post until his death.

Malta An island in the Mediterranean and an independent Commonwealth country. The British formally annexed the island in 1814. Malta was always of prime strategic importance and became a major base for the British Mediterranean fleet. During World War II it was blockaded and heavily bombed by Axis forces and after the relief of the island (March 1942), the entire population was awarded the George Cross for its heroism (April 1942). Until full independence was granted (1964) the island had known periods of self-government (1921–36 and 1953–58), punctuated by political violence leading to colonial status or rule through emergency powers. After independence Malta faced grave economic problems due to the closing of its naval dockyards and the strained relations between the Maltese and British governments. Despite arrangements by which Britain and its NATO allies agreed (1972) to lease these facilities over a seven-year period, after the end of the agreement the Maltese government flirted with the Communist bloc and with Libya. Although dockyard employment remained an issue, the economy was becoming increasingly geared to take advantage of the tourist trade. Domestic politics were full-blooded and often violent between the Nationalists – under whose leader, Dr Borg Olivier, independence was won – and Dom Mintoff's Labour Party. These became increasingly bitter immediately prior to Mintoff's resignation because of ill-health (1984) after Labour gained a majority of seats on a minority of votes in the 1981 elections. In 1986 the prime minister, Dr Bonnici, brought in a constitutional measure which guaranteed a majority of seats to the party polling the most votes. Through this system in the 1987 elections the Nationalists came to power, under their leader Eddi Fennech Adami.

Manchukuo The name given to the Chinese provinces making up Manchuria (together with the province of Jehol) which the Japanese army invaded in 1931. Their puppet regime expanded the heavy industry of the region to provide their armies with the weapons and munitions required for war with China (1937) and the United States and the western allies (1941). In 1945 the Red Army expelled the Japanese and the region was restored to Chinese rule.

mandates A trusteeship system established by the League of Nations for former German colonies and provinces of the Ottoman Empire under which specific member states became responsible for guiding the territories towards self-government at rates consistent with their development. The league function was inherited by the UN Trusteeship Council.

Mandela, Nelson (1918–), black South African nationalist leader. Son of a chief, in 1952 he left the law for full-time membership of the executive of the ANC, continuing to work underground after the organization was banned (1961) and until his arrest and imprisonment in 1962. During his sentence he was tried (October 1963-June 1964) for treason under the Suppression of Communism Act and sentenced to life imprisonment, becoming the symbol of the anti-apartheid movement. In 1988 he was treated for tuberculosis contracted in prison, and was subsequently accorded a lighter regime.

Manhattan Project see under **nuclear energy**

Manila Pact see **South East Asia Treaty Organization**

Manley, Michael Norman (1924–), Jamaican statesman. The son of Norman Washington Manley, he inherited his leadership of the People's National Party in 1969, having been active as a trades union leader, senator (1962–67) and member of the Jamaican House of Representatives. He was prime minister during 1972–80 and from 1989.

Manley, Norman Washington (1893–1969, Jamaican statesman. A distinguished lawyer, he founded the left-wing People's National Party (1938) and as chief minister (1955–59) put through a programme of land reform and industrial and tourist development. As president of the West Indies Federal Labour Party (1957 61) he helped to found the West Indies Federation, only to see it destroyed by his cousin and life-long political rival, Alexander Bustamente. After Jamaican independence he became leader of the opposition. His son, Michael Norman Manley, succeeded him as head of the PNP in 1969.

Mannerheim, Baron Carl Gustav Emil (1867–1951), Finnish soldier and statesman. He was commissioned in the Russian imperial army, serving in the Russo-Japanese War and World War I. He commanded the Finnish forces in the war of independence against the Bolsheviks (1918), headed the provisional government and retired after failing to win the presidential elections (1919). He remained president of the Finnish defence council and was responsible for the Mannerheim Line which held the Soviet invasion for 13 weeks during the winter 1939–40. He commanded Finnish forces in alliance with Germany against the USSR (1941–44) and was elected president to negotiate an armistice with the Soviets (1944) and to switch to the Allied side (March 1945). He resigned (1946) because of ill-health.

Manstein, Erich von Lewinski von (1887–1973), German soldier. He was von Rundstedt's chief of staff in Poland (1939). He planned the breakthrough in the Ardennes which won the battle of France (1940). He captured the Crimea and attempted to break the siege of Stalingrad (1942). His plan for a strategic withdrawal was overruled by Hitler. He was dismissed from his command (March 1944). Although imprisoned (1949–53) by a British war crimes tribunal, in 1958 he helped advise on the reconstruction of the German army.

Mao Tse-tung (1893–1976), Chinese Communist leader. A founder member of the Communist Party (1921), during the Communist-Kuomintang alliance he was director of the Kuomintang Peasant Movement Training Institute (1926). After the two parties split (1927) Mao led a peasant uprising in Hunan. Between 1928–30 he broke new ground by organizing the peasants rather than the industrial workers and in 1931 was elected chairman of the Soviet Republic of China. When the Kuomintang attacked his base in Kiangsi province, Mao led his followers to safety in the remote northeast on the famous Long March (1934–35). Here Mao organized the armed struggle against the Japanese invaders (1937–45) and Chiang Kai-chek's forces, first in guerrilla warfare (1945–46) and then in set-piece battles which ended in total victory and the expulsion of the Kuomintang from the mainland (1949). Mao became chairman of the People's Republic on its proclamation in October 1949 and suppressed all opposition to his rule by summary executions, imprisonment and forced labour. Initially relying on Soviet aid, Mao was forced to find his own solutions to China's problems when that aid was withdrawn after Mao's denunciation of Khrushchev's 'revisionism' (1956). A measure of liberalization – the '100 Flowers Campaign' (1957) – was followed by the 'Great Leap Forward'. Its failure brought Liu Shao-chi to the chairmanship of the People's Republic, but Mao retained party chairmanship and was thus able to launch the Cultural Revolution which brought down Liu. By his actions Mao had created the People's Republic; by his writings he became enormously influential throughout the Third World and among Marxists who had become disillusioned with Soviet-style Communism.

Marconi scandal In 1912 the Marconi Company was commissioned by the British government to set up wireless links throughout the then British Empire. The managing director was a brother of the attorney general, Sir Rufus Isaacs, which led to rumours of 'insider' dealings by Sir Rufus and others. A select committee reported (1913) that members of the cabinet, including Isaacs and Lloyd George, had bought shares in the American Marconi company. Although exonerated from charges of corruption, they tendered their resignations, which the prime minister, Asquith, refused.

Marcos, Ferdinand Edralin (1917–   ), Philippines statesman. A lawyer, he was elected to Congress as a Liberal (1949), and was a delegate to the

UN (1954; 1960–62). Elected president as a Nationalist (1965), he was re-elected (1969) and after declaring martial law and assuming dictatorial powers (1972) made himself president for life. Initially a reformer of land tenure and government abuses, his constant battle with Communist insurgency and urban terrorism led him to condone the creation of private armies and ever-increasing corruption in which he and his wife Imelda were themselves involved. In 1983, his opponent, Benigno Aquino, was assassinated at Manila airport. Public outrage was such that Marcos was forced to stand for re-election in 1986. The results were disputed. The United States withdrew its backing and his opponent, Aquino's widow, Corizon, ousted him with the support of the people and of the army. Marcos went into exile in Hawaii.

Marshall, George Catlett (1880–1959), US soldier and statesman. He was a staff officer in World War I and became Chief of Staff US Army (1939). He was responsible for the expansion of the US army and for its strategic employment in all theatres of World War II. He attempted unsuccessfully to end the civil war in China (1945). As Truman's secretary of state (1947–49) he initiated the Marshall Plan. He was secretary of defence during the Korean War (1950–51), and helped form NATO (1949). He is the only general to have been awarded the Nobel peace prize (1953).

Marshall Plan (European Recovery Program) This was promoted by secretary of state George Marshall, instituted at the Paris Economic Conference (1947) and put into effect by President Truman (1948). Through it the United States granted over $12 billion in aid to different European countries, including neutrals, such as Sweden, Switzerland and Turkey, as well as World War II allies and enemies. Aid was offered to but denounced by the USSR and its satellites. The plan succeeded in speeding European economic recovery from the devastation of the war and in so doing deprived the strong communist parties in Italy and France of the social discontents on which to build revolution.

Masaryk, Ján Garrigue (1886–1948), Czechoslovak diplomat. Son of the philosopher Thomas Garrigue Masaryk, he was ambassador in London (1935–38). He was foreign minister in the Czech government in exile (1940), retaining the post both in the immediate postwar Czechoslovak government and in that of Klement Gottwald after the communist coup in 1948. He had tried to keep a balance between the USSR and the Western Allies. He died from a fall from a window in the foreign ministry in Prague, but whether this was suicide, accidental or deliberate murder has never been determined.

Masaryk, Thomas Garrigue (1850–1937), Czechoslovak philosopher and patriot. He was professor of Philosophy at the Czech University in Prague. In 1882 he joined the Young Czech Party and became an Austrian MP (1891–93). He founded the Czech People's (later Progressive) Party which sought Czech equality and autonomy within an Austro-Hungarian federation of nationalities. He was elected to parliament (1907). He opposed the annexation of Bosnia-Hercegovina (1908) and with Eduard Beneš escaped abroad on the outbreak of World War I and formed the Czechoslovak National Council. On the collapse of the Austria-Hungary in 1918, Masaryk became the first president of the republic and remained in office until he retired (1935) and was succeeded by Beneš.

Massey, William Ferguson (1856–1925), New Zealand statesman. He emigrated to New Zealand in 1870 and established himself as a farmer. He entered parliament (1893), became chief whip (1895) and leader (1903) of the conservative Reform Party. He was prime minister (1912–25, in coalition 1915–19). A strong supporter of the empire, he favoured a continuation of the wartime links forged with Britain and was reluctant to join the League of Nations, although New Zealand subsequently became a member.

Matteotti, Giacomo (1885–1924), Italian socialist leader. He was an MP (1919), secretary-general of the Socialist party (1924) and a prominent opponent of fascism. His murder by fascist extremists (probably beyond Mussolini's control and against his wishes) led to demonstrations which were used by him as a pretext for tightening his rule, the murderers receiving token sentences in 1926.

Mau Mau A secret society formed (1948) in Kenya among members of the Kikuyu tribe to drive interlopers (both black and white) from traditional tribal lands. Their campaign started in 1952 and, although combined military and police action had crushed it by 1954, the state of emergency (during which Jomo Kenyatta was imprisoned on charges of managing the movement) lasted until 1960. During this time Africans suffered the bulk of the casualties and killed most of the 11,000 Mau Mau who died.

Maximilian, Prince of Baden (1867–1929), German political leader. He became chancellor (1918), formed a coalition government and opened peace negotiations with the Allies. In the disorder after the Kiel mutinies he advised Kaiser Wilhelm II to abdicate and when he refused to do so, Prince Maximilian announced his abdication (9 November) and handed over government to Ebert.

May Fourth Movement A march by 5000 Peking University students on 4 May 1919 against the clause in the Treaty of Versailles awarding to Japan the lease of the former German treaty port of Kiaochow. Demonstrations and strikes spread to Shanghai and there was a national boycott of Japanese goods. The Chinese refused to sign the treaty; intellectuals began to reject traditional philosophies in favour of foreign ones, including Marxism, while the political consciousness of the nation was aroused.

Mboya, Thomas Joseph [Tom] (1930–69), Kenyan nationalist leader. A Luo trade unionist, he joined Kenyatta's Kenya African Union (of which he became treasurer). He was elected general secretary of the Kenya Federation of Labour (1953), was an elected member of the Kenya Legislative Council (1957) and became president of the All African People's Conference in Ghana (1958). In 1960 he merged his Kenya Independence Movement with Kenyatta's Kenya African National Union and and after independence served as minister of labour (1962–63), of justice and constitutional affairs (1963–64) and of economic planning (1964–69). His experience, moderation and ability marked him as the successor to Kenyatta and serious rioting followed his murder in 1969.

Meany, George (1894–1980), US trade union leader. He was secretary-treasurer (1939) and president (1952) of the American Federation of Labor (AFL). When it merged (1955) with the Congress of Industrial Organizations (CIO) he was elected president of the AFL-CIO and subsequently re-elected unopposed. His quarrel with the Democratic party and neutrality in the 1972 presidential election has been held responsible for Nixon's landslide victory.

Meir, Golda (Golda Meyerson, née Mabovitz, 1898–1978), Israeli political leader. She emigrated from the United States to Palestine (1921), was active in the kibbutz movement, trade unionism and socialist politics. She was head of the General Federation of Jewish Labour (1936). When the state of Israel was declared she served as ambassador in Moscow (1948), was minister of labour (1949–56), foreign minister (1956–66) and, on the death of Levi Eshkol in 1969, became prime minister. Her immense personal popularity enabled her to rally the nation in the Yom Kippur War (1973), but later she was criticized for Israeli unpreparedness and resigned in 1974.

Menderes, Adnan (1899–1961), Turkish statesman. A lawyer and farmer, he entered politics in 1932 and helped to found the Democratic Party, Turkey's first opposition party (1945). As prime minister (1950) he strengthened ties with the West, brought Turkey into NATO (1952) and eased Graeco-Turkish tensions over Cyprus (1959). Seeking dictatorial powers to meet an economic crisis, he was overthrown by an army coup

(1960), tried for breach of the constitution and, with two of his ministers, hanged in prison in 1961.

Mendès-France, Pierre (1907–82), French statesman. He was a Radical-Socialist deputy (1932–40), held junior office under Blum (1938) and played a leading role in the French resistance and held office in de Gaulle's provisional government. A deputy (1946–58) under the Fourth Republic, as prime minister and foreign secretary (1954–55), he helped control inflation, brought the war in Indo-China to an end and negotiated the independence of Tunisia. He was minister of state (1956) but failed to win a seat in the assembly (1958) and was expelled from his party (1959). Having opposed the return of de Gaulle, in 1959 he joined the Unified Socialist Party, backing Mitterand's campaign for the presidency and became the elder statesman of the non-communist left.

Menelik II (1844–1913), emperor of Ethiopia (1989–1913). He crushed the Italian invasion at Adowa (1896), conquered the Muslim southern provinces, moved the capital to Addis Ababa and began the modernization of Ethiopia.

Mensheviks see under **Bolsheviks**

Menzies, Sir Robert Gordon (1894–1978), Australian statesman. A barrister, attorney-general, minister of railways and deputy prime minister (1932–34) of Victoria. He was a Federal United Australian (later Liberal) Party MP (1934) and attorney-general (1935–39). After a bitter internal wrangle he succeeded Lyons as leader of the party and prime minister (1939). In 1941 he was deposed by his own cabinet. He reorganized the UAP as the Liberal Party, returned to power in 1949 and remained prime minister until his retirement in 1966. His firm support for the Commonwealth (of which he came to be regarded as the elder statesman) was matched by his co-operation with the United States in regional defence pacts for the Pacific and South East Asia.

Mesopotamia The area roughly corresponding with modern Iraq, scene of a British campaign against the Turks in World War I.

Metaxas, Iohannis (1871–1941), Greek soldier and statesman. He served in the Graeco-Turkish (1897) and Balkan (1912–13) Wars. As chief of staff he was dismissed for his pro-German sympathies when Greece entered the war (1917). He led a coup (1920), was exiled (1923–24) and joined the royalists and, after the restoration of the monarchy (1935), became prime minister (1936), dissolving parliament, instituting a dictatorship and making himself premier for life (1938). He increased military and administrative efficiency, developed agriculture and undertook a large programme of public works and his death early in 1941 left Greece leaderless on the eve of the German invasion.

Mexico A Central American republic. During the 19th century Mexico suffered from US intervention (losing 40% of its northern territories to the United States after the war of 1846–48) and from the French who briefly imposed the Emperor Maximilian (1862–67) and from the attendant evils of economic backwardness and political instability. The successful armed revolt of Porfirio Díaz who ruled from 1876 to 1880 and from 1884 to 1911, initiated a period of economic expansion which profited Díaz, his supporters and the foreign companies exploiting Mexican resources but left the mass of the people in poverty. In 1911 Díaz was overthrown, but his successor, Huerta, was unable to control the revolution, and political instability and US interventions ensued until the coming to power of Plutarcho Calles in 1924. In 1934 he was supplanted by Lazaro Cardenas, but the National Revolutionary Party, which he founded in 1929 and which became the Institutional Revolutionary Party (PRI) in 1946, remained (and still remains) the party of government. Despite the PRI's revolutionary past – the anti-clericalism of Calles, the nationalization of the oil industry by Cardenas (1938) and his land reforms – it has ossified and begun to atrophy in power. As the strength of the opposition has grown, so the PRI has found it necessary to resort to electoral violence and fraud. A high birth-rate, crippling foreign debts and falls in the price of oil (Mexico's major source of wealth) combined to produce a crisis which brought the PRI to its lowest level of popular support in the 1988 presidential elections.

Mihajlovic, Draza (1893–1946), Yugoslav soldier. He served in the Serbian army in the Balkan Wars (1912–13) and in World War I. He organized the Chetniks (Serbian guerrillas) to resist the Axis occupation (1941) and was appointed minister of defence by the government in exile. Ethnic and political differences divided his movement from Tito's partisans, who attacked them. Some Chetnik units sought Axis aid and Allied recognition was withdrawn. In 1946 Mihajlovic was tried and shot for treason although there was no positive proof that he personally had collaborated with the Axis.

Milner, Alfred (1854–1925, 1st Viscount Milner), British colonial administrator. He was high commissioner in South Africa and governor general of Cape Colony (1897–1906). By his support for British settlers in the Boer Republics he helped precipitate the Boer War; when it was over he worked to repair the moral and material damage it had caused. While he was colonial secretary (1919–21), his theories of education for self-government strongly influenced colonial administration.

Minto, Lord see **Elliot-Murray-Kynynmund, Gilbert John**

Mitterand, François Maurice Marie (1916–), French statesman. He distinguished himself in the Resistance during World War II. He became a deputy (1946) and held office virtually continuously in different governments 1947–58. He voted against the return of de Gaulle, led the left-wing Socialist opposition and was an unsuccessful presidential candidate (1965). He lost the leadership of the left (1968–71), but formed an alliance with the Communists to contest the 1974 presidential election in which he failed to defeat Giscard d'Estaing. In 1981 he succeeded and, with the left victorious in the assembly elections was able to form a Socialist government. The position was reversed in 1986 and, until 1988, Mitterand was forced to co-habit with a right-wing prime minister who reversed many of his policies. However, he triumphed over a divided right in 1988 and was once more able to govern (the fourth president of the French fifth Republic) through a Socialist prime minister.

Mobutu, Sese Soko (Joseph Désiré Mobutu, 1930–), political leader of Zaïre. He joined Lumumba's nationalist movement in 1956, was chief of staff to the Force Publique, the army of the newly independent Belgian Congo (1960) and deposed Lumumba (1960). He staged a further coup in 1965, assumed the premiership (1966) and established a presidential regime of which he became first president. In 1971 he began a programme of 'national authenticity' under which geographical and personal names were Africanized. His original energy and sense of discipline lapsed to the extent of tolerating widespread corruption within his administration as his politics have moved steadily to the left.

Mohammed Reza Shah Pahlavi (1919–80), shah of Iran (1941–79). He succeeded his father Reza Shah Pahlavi, who was deposed by the British for his German sympathies (1941), an act which made him favour United States interests. In 1949 he escaped assassination by a member of the (Communist) Tudeh party and in 1953 he was briefly forced into exile by supporters of Mossadegh. From 1963 onwards he attempted an ambitious programme of modernization, but his educational reforms produced a class of left-wing intellectuals which resented his authoritarian regime. His agrarian reforms alienated the landowners, while his emancipation of women outraged religious prejudice. In 1979, the unrest drove the shah into exile and an Islamic Republic was established under the Ayatolla Khomeini. The shah, refused refuge by his former friends, died of cancer in Egypt on 27 July 1980.

Moi, Daniel Arap (1924–), Kenyan political leader. A schoolteacher from the minority Kalenjin tribe, he became Kenyatta's vice-president (1967–78), and succeeded him on his death in 1978. His party, the Kenya

National African Union, has been attacked for its corruption and inability to manage the economy and for its subservience to the west. In 1982 Moi survived a coup by air force officers, but subsequently outlawed opposition parties and since 1986 has shown a tendency to infringe the rights of those suspected of belonging to so-called subversive organizations.

Mollet, Guy (1905–75), French political leader. He was a schoolteacher and resistance fighter. He became mayor of Arras (1945), a deputy (1946) and secretary-general of the French Socialist Party (1946–69), holding office in various governments. As prime minister (1956–57) he granted virtual independence to French possessions in Black Africa, but adopted a hard line on Algeria. He weathered the Suez Crisis and signed the Treaty of Rome. At first he supported the return of de Gaulle and served as his minister of state, but entered the opposition in 1959, backing Mitterand's candidacy for the presidency (1965).

Molotov (Vyacheslav Mikhailovich Skriabin, 1890–1986), Soviet statesman. He joined the Bolsheviks (1906), was exiled (1909–11) and was one of the founders of *Pravda* (1912). He was again exiled (1915) but escaped to join the October Revolution. He rose rapidly in the party as an associate of Stalin. He was a candidate member (1921) and full member (1926–53) of the Politburo, chairman of the Council of People's Commissars (1930–41) and he replaced Litvinov as foreign minister (1939–49). He negotiated the Nazi-Soviet Pact and attended the Yalta and Potsdam Conferences. He became vice chairman of the council of ministers (1949–56). After Stalin's death Khrushchev made him foreign minister again (1953–56), but when he joined the opposition he was deprived of party office (1957) and given minor posts (1957–61) until his expulsion from the party (1962). He was re-admitted as a pensioner member in 1984.

Monnet, Jean (1888–1979), French economist and administrator. He served on the Inter-Allied maritime commission in World War I. He was deputy secretary-general of the League of Nations (1919–23). He was a consultant (1923–38), arranging stabilizing loans and helping to reorganize the economies of Poland and Romania, and a member of the British Supply Council in Washington (1940–43). In 1947 he produced the Monnet Plan for the reorganization of French industry and later prepared the Schumann Plan which laid the foundations of the European Coal and Steel Community. He was the father of the European Community, and its first president (1950–55), resigning to become chairman of the Action Committee for a United States of Europe (1956).

Montagu-Chelmsford Reforms Suggested by the report (1919) in which Edwin Montagu (1879–1924), secretary of state for India, and Lord Chelmsford (1868–1933) recommended the establishment in British India of an elected legislature with some governmental responsibilities, ideas which were accepted and incorporated in the India Act (1919).

Montenegro A constituent republic of Yugoslavia, within which is the enclave which remained unconquered by the Ottomans, who acknowledged Montenegrin independence (1799). The last of its dynasty of reforming rulers was Nicholas I (1841–1921) who ruled as prince (1860–1910), enlarging his domain after the Russo-Turkish War, and as king (1910–18), further extending his territory after the Balkan Wars. He joined Serbia in World War I, saw his country occupied by Austria and was driven into exile. In 1918 he was deposed by a national congress which voted for incorporation within Yugoslavia.

Montgomery, Bernard Law (1887–1976, 1st Viscount Montgomery of Alamein), British soldier. He served as an infantry officer on the Western Front in World War I. In the World War II he commanded the 3rd Division during the Battle of France (1940) and the 8th Army in Egypt (1942), gaining the victory of El Alamein and driving the Axis forces from North Africa (1943). After the conquest of Sicily and the invasion of southern Italy, in December 1943 he returned to Britain to plan the invasion of Europe in which he was commander ground forces (June–August 1944). Thereafter he commanded 21 Army Group in northwest Europe and, temporarily, two US armies during the Battle of the Bulge. On 24 March 1945 his troops crossed the Rhine and on 4 May he accepted the surrender of all German forces in northwest Europe. He was CIGS (1946–48) and Deputy Supreme Commander NATO Forces in Europe (1951–58). He established a reputation as the greatest British military commander of World War II, publishing controversial memoirs (1958).

Montreux Convention An agreement signed in July 1936 under which Turkey was permitted to refortify the Dardanelles and Bosphorus, revising the Treaty of Lausanne in this respect and in that of the aggregate tonnage of warships passing through the straits in time of peace.

Morley-Minto Reforms The recommendations of the secretary of state for India, Viscount Morley (1838–1923), and of the viceroy, Lord Minto (see **Elliot-Murray-Kynynmund**), that Indians should be admitted to legislative councils and be eligible to serve on the viceroy's executive council and on the advisory council of the secretary of state for India.

This step towards Indian participation in responsible government was incorporated into the India, or India Councils Act (1909).

Moro, Aldo (1916–78), Italian political leader. A Christian Democrat MP (1948), he became leader of his party (1959). As foreign minister (1965–66, 1969–72, 1973–74) he played a prominent part in the European Community, and as prime minister (1963–68 and 1974–76) he governed through a coalition with the socialists. After his resignation he became an influential elder statesman in his party but was kidnapped and murdered by Red Brigades.

Morocco A kingdom of North Africa. After the French conquest of Algeria (1830–44) the country was open to commercial penetration by the European powers, but Mulay Hasan (sultan, 1873–94), while modernizing his kingdom, successfully played on the jealousies of those powers to prevent any one of them imposing a colonial regime. However, the intemperate actions of imperial Germany (see **Algeciras Conference**, **Agadir Incident**) enabled the French, by making concessions to Britain and Italy, to impose a protectorate (1912). (Spain was allotted spheres of influence.) During 1912–25, under the French resident-general, Lyautey, a system of indirect rule brought the whole country under the control of the sultan. Limited European immigration provoked the revolt of Abd el-Krim (1921–26), after which the French took a more visibly dominant role in the administration. This was challenged by the emergence of the Istiqlal Party in the 1930s and nationalism was strengthened by the French reverses in World War II. In 1952 there were serious riots, repressed by the French, but pressure for independence continued to grow. Following the Indo-China debacle and the Algerian nationalist uprising, it was granted by France (March) and Spain (April) 1976, the sultan becoming King Muhammad V. His prestige was sufficient to check the influence of the left-wing Istiqlal Party. On the accession of his son, Hassan II, in 1961 the movement, in alliance with the trade unions, was ruthlessly suppressed after the Casablanca riots (1965) and its exiled leader, Ben Barka, kidnapped and murdered in Paris. In 1971 and 1972 there were abortive military coups against the monarchy which re-established its prestige in 1975 by the seizure of the Spanish Sahara. This united the country in the face of short-lived hostilities with Algeria (1976) and a protracted war with the Polisario Front attempting, with Algerian and Libyan support, to create an independent state in the former Spanish colony. After 13 years of stalemate, in 1988 both sides agreed that a referendum on the future of the territory should be held under UN supervision. In 1989 Morocco reached agreement with Mauretania,

Tunisia, Algeria and Libya on the formation of a Maghreb Community.

Morrison, Herbert Stanley (1888–1965, Baron Morrison), British statesman. He was secretary of the London Labour Party (1915–47), mayor of Hackney (1920–21), a member of the London County Council (1922). As its leader (1934–40) he created the publicly owned London Transport system. He was engaged in large-scale slum clearance and created the 'green belt'. He became a Labour MP (1923, 1929–31 and 1935–49), was briefly minister of transport in MacDonald's Labour government (1931), and was minister of supply (1940) and home secretary (1940–45) in Churchill's wartime coalition. Morrison drafted much of the programme which brought a Labour government to power in 1945. He was lord president of the council and deputy prime minister (1945–51), and foreign secretary (1951). An able parliamentarian and an outstanding administrator, he saw his ambitions twice thwarted when Attlee (1935) and Gaitskell (1955) defeated him in elections for leadership of the Labour Party.

Mosley, Sir Oswald Ernald (1896–1980), British politician. He served in World War I and was elected to parliament as a Conservative (1918) and as an Independent (1922–24). He joined the Labour Party (1924) and was an MP (1926–31). As chancellor of the Duchy of Lancaster (1929) he resigned from MacDonald's government (1930) when his proposals to overcome the Depression by state control and public investment in industry were rejected. The failure of his New Party in the 1931 elections drew him to the idea of the corporate state and in 1932 he formed the British Union of Fascists. This developed on Nazi lines, provoked riots and was thoroughly anti-Semitic, and during World War II Mosley was interned (1940–43). In 1947 he founded the Union Movement, twice stood unsuccessfully for Parliament (1959 and 1966), and retired to France to become an advocate of European unity.

Mossadegh, Muhammad (1880–1967), Iranian political leader. He served as a provincial governor, finance minister (1921) and foreign minister (1923–25) under Reza Shah Pahlavi, but retired from politics when the latter assumed the throne. He returned (1943) to lead the National Front. On coming to power, he nationalized the oil industry (1951). British reprisals provoked a crisis in which Mossadegh was overthrown by a military coup, arrested, tried and imprisoned (1953). After his release (1956) he retired from political life.

Mountbatten, Louis Francis Albert Victor Nicholas (1900–79, 1st Earl Mountbatten of Burma), British naval officer. He served in World War I, commanded the 5th Destroyer Flotilla (1939), and was chief of combined operations (1942), directing raids on occupied Europe and initiating plans for the invasion. He became Supreme Allied Commander South East Asia (1943). As last viceroy of India (1947) he accelerated the pace of independence and became the first governor-general of India (1947–48). He resumed his naval career as 1st Sea Lord (1955–59) and chief of defence staff (1959–65). As a great-grandson of Queen Victoria and uncle of Queen Elizabeth II's consort, the Duke of Edinburgh, he was a trusted adviser to the royal family. He was murdered by the IRA.

Mozambique A republic of southwest Africa. A Portuguese colony from 1498, it was laxly controlled until the 19th-century scramble for Africa when, in an attempt to link the colony with the west African colony of Angola, the Portuguese laid claim to what is now Zimbabwe and Malawi. They were forced to renounce these by the British ultimatum of 1890, but from then until about 1920 consolidated their rule of the country in a series of bitter colonial wars. Nationalism gained momentum after World War II, the different groups uniting in 1962 to form Frelimo and begin a guerrilla war against the Portuguese in 1964. By 1974 the war-weary Portuguese began to look for a political solution. After the revolution in Portugal a transitional government was formed to prepare for the creation of the independent People's Republic of Mozambique, proclaimed on 25 June 1975. The Marxist military commander of Frelimo, Samora Machel, became the first president, nationalizing all private property (1976), declaring Mozambique a one-party state (1977) and attempting to set up a socialist regime. His support for Robert Mugabe's ZANU guerrillas in their war with the white-dominated government in Rhodesia brought repeated retaliation and Rhodesian support for the opposition Renamo guerrilla movement. After the collapse of the Smith regime in Rhodesia (1980) Renamo was supported by the South African government, while Machel's regime received vital assistance from Zimbabwe. The guerrilla war devasted large areas of the country, bringing famine and halting all economic development. In 1984 South Africa agreed to withdraw support for Renamo in return for Mozambique's ceasing to aid the ANC. In 1986 Machel was killed in an air crash. His successor, Joaquim Alberto Chissano, appeared to have turned the tide against Renamo in the context of peace initiatives (1988–   ) for southern Africa as a whole.

Mubarak, Mohammed Hosni (1928–   ), Egyptian political leader. As air force C-in-C (1972–75) he gained prestige in the Yom Kippur War. He became vice-president (1975–81) and succeeded to the presidency after the assassination of Anwar Sadat (1984), continuing his pro-Western policy, despite Arab hostility and attempts at subversion by Islamic fundamenalists.

Mugabe, Robert Gabriel (1924–), Zimbabwean political leader. A schoolteacher, he became deputy secretary-general of Joshua Nkomo's Zimbabwe African People's Union (ZAPU) on its foundation (1961). He was imprisoned (1962) but escaped to Tanzania. He returned to Rhodesia and, after detention (1964–74), made his way to Mozambique to lead the guerrillas of his Zimbabwe African National Union (ZANU) in the Patriotic Front in alliance with ZAPU. Following the ceasefire in December 1979, Mugabe led ZANU to electoral victory and became Zimbabwe's first prime minister (4 March 1980). With skill and determination he divided the white Conservative Alliance of Zimbabwe and crushed by force Nkomo's ZAPU, until in 1987 he was able to make the necessary constitutional changes and on 31 December 1987 was voted the first executive president of a one-party state. He was a firm advocate of sanctions against South Africa and gave military aid to Mozambique. At the same time he maintained his ties with the west, attempted to retain the remaining white settlers and dealt severely with corruption within ZANU.

Muhammad V, Ibn Yusuf (1909–61), sultan (1927) and king of Morocco (1957–61). During World War II he refused to implement the Vichy regime's anti-semitic regulations. He showed his sympathy for the Istiqlal Party and his support of the independence movement led the French to exile him (1953). In the face of an armed uprising they restored the sultan in 1955 and granted Morocco its independence (1956).

Mukden incident On 18 September 1931 the Japanese army guarding the South Manchurian railway seized the province on the pretext that a section of line had been blown up by saboteurs. The action was taken independently by the Japanese military as the first step in their East Asian campaign of aggression.

Munich Conference (1938) Talks held at Munich between Britain, France, Italy and Germany, where, without the participation of the Czechoslovak government, it was agreed to accede to Hitler's demand that the Sudetenland should be incorporated into Germany.

Munich Putsch An attempt by Hitler to overthrow the government of Bavaria (8–9 November 1923). General Ludendorff was a co-conspirator. Police suppressed the rising by force, 16 of the Nazis were killed and Hitler was tried and imprisoned. The 'Beer-hall Putsch' became part of the Nazi legend.

Muslim Brotherhood A politico-religious organization founded in Cairo

(1920) by Hasan al-Banna. Islamic fundamentalist in outlook, the brotherhood accepted western science and technology, but called for a specifically Islamic society which was neither socialist nor capitalist. During World War II Hasàn al-Banna aided the Axis and after the war acted against the Egyptian monarchy, assassinating two prime ministers (1945 and 1948) before he was himself assassinated (1949). Having helped to bring down King Farouk, the brotherhood was disbanded by Nasser (1954) for its refusal to accept a secular state. After an attempt on Nasser's life in October of that year, it was brutally suppressed but never destroyed. It gathered support to organize the assassination of President Sadat (1981). In 1982 members of the brotherhood were ruthlessly crushed when they attempted a revolution against the Ba'ath socialists in Syria.

Mussolini, Benito Amilcare Andrea (1883–1945), Italian fascist leader. As a socialist he was imprisoned for organizing strikes against the Libyan War (1911), becoming editor of the socialist party paper (1912). Having first followed the party line of neutralism in World War I, in 1915 he made a complete turn-about, was expelled from the party and founded his own paper to urge Italian intervention. When Italy declared war on the Central Powers he saw active service until his discharge with wounds in 1917. In 1921 Mussolini formed the Fascist Party from groups of ex-servicemen he had organized as a nationalist counterbalance to communism and socialism. With the connivance of the authorities, he seized power in Milan (1922) and organized the 'March on Rome'. Appointed prime minister by King Victor Emmanuel, Mussolini allowed a limited opposition to his coalition of fascists and nationalists until the opposition parties withdrew in protest at the murder of Matteotti (1924), leaving the way clear for the introduction of the corporate state (1925–26), confirmed in 1928 when the Fascist Party became the sole legal political party and Mussolini himself became solely responsible to the king. The measures with which Mussolini supplemented his programme of public works to alleviate Italy's economic ills – colonial expansion and his invasion of Ethiopia (1936) – alienated British and French public opinion and made Mussolini seek an alliance with Hitler. Mussolini brought Italy into the war on the Axis side (June 1940), but the damage to Italian arms in Africa and in Greece soon reduced him to total dependence upon Hitler. After the Allied invasion of Italy (1943), Mussolini was overthrown and imprisoned by Badoglio. Rescued by the Germans, he became the puppet head of the Republic of Salo in North Italy and on the German collapse was shot by partisans while attempting to escape to Switzerland (28 April 1945).

Mustafa Kemal (Kemal Atatürk – 'Father of the Turks', 1881–1938), Turkish soldier and statesman. He served in the Libyan and Balkan Wars, but held aloof from the Young Turk Movement, perhaps through hostility to Enver Pasha. In World War I he distinguished himself by his victories at Gallipoli (1915) and against the Russians in the Caucasus (1916). In 1919 at Samsun he initiated a nationalist revolution against the dismemberment of Turkey by the Allies. Having signed an armistice with France (1920), Mustafa Kemal expelled the Greeks from Asia Minor (1920–22, see **Chanak Crisis, Smyrna**). In 1923 he deposed the Sultan, signed the Treaty of Lausanne and was declared president of the Republic, founding the People's Republican Party, the sole legal political party. In 1924 the caliphate was abolished and Turkey became a secular state. Polygamy was banned, Roman script substituted for Arabic, the Koran was to be recited in Turkish and religious courts were abolished. Western dress was made compulsory. On the economic plane, foreign businesses were nationalized and a state bank founded, but the estates of wealthy landowners remained intact. In foreign affairs Mustafa Kemal re-established Turkey's international standing and by his harsh authoritarianism tried to root out the religious and administrative customs which had brought down the Ottoman empire.

N

Nagy, Imre (1896–1958), Hungarian political leader. He was taken prisoner in World War I by the Russians, became a communist, returned to Hungary, went underground after the fall of the Bela Kun regime and escaped to Moscow (1930). Returning with the Red Army in 1944, he became minister of agriculture and, briefly, minister of the interior, succeeding Rákosi as prime minister in 1953. Turned out of office and expelled from the party as a Titoist (1955), he was brought back by popular support during the Hungarian rising to head a government and to propose political pluralism, withdrawal from the Warsaw Pact and a neutral status. When the Red Army crushed the uprising, Nagy took refuge in the Yugoslav embassy and, on leaving it under promise of safe conduct, was arrested and shot after a secret trial.

Nahas Pasha, Mustafa (1876–1965), Egyptian political leader. As head (1927–52) of the Wafd Party he was five times prime minister between 1928 and 1952. As prime minister in 1951 he denounced the 1936 Anglo-Egyptian treaty but, following the anti-British riots in 1952, he was dismissed by Farouk. Although he expressed support for the military regime which overthrew the king he was forced to disband the Wafd and was himself imprisoned (1953–56). On his release he retired from politics.

Nakasone, Yashiro, see under **Recruit Cosmos Scandal**

Namibia A country of southwest Africa. It was proclaimed a German protectorate in 1884 and then known as German South West Africa. From the 1890s there were outbreaks of violence beween European settlers and the native Africans, culminating in a rising against the Germans by the Herero tribe (1904–08), in which some 54,000 of the Herero population of about 74,000, and another 20,000 black Africans, lost their lives. In World War I the area was occupied by South Africa and after the war was assigned to it to be administered under mandate. In 1945 South Africa refused to transfer its mandate to UN trusteeship and from 1948 attempted to integrate South West Africa into South Africa. In 1966 the United Nations passed a resolution ending the South African mandate and in 1968 decreed that South West Africa should be known as Namibia. South Africa ignored these resolutions and rulings and proceeded to implement its own plans for the administration of the country. However, from 1966 onwards it had to contend with the SWAPO guerrilla movement (mainly drawn from members of the Ovambo tribe), operating from bases in southern Angola. From 1980 onwards South African forces began to launch deeper and deeper strikes into Angola against SWAPO camps and to back the UNITA rebels. Late in 1988 South African, Angolan and Cuban representatives met in Geneva under UN auspices and agreed on independence for Namibia and the withdrawal of South African forces conditional upon a phased evacuation of Angola by the 50,000-strong Cuban expeditionary force. In March 1989 UN troops arrived to supervise elections for a Namibian parliament.

Nash, Walter (1882–1969), New Zealand political leader. English-born, he was elected to the national executive of the Labour Party (1919), became an MP (1929–60), minister of finance (1935–49) and deputy prime minister (1940–49). He succeeded Peter Fraser as leader of the opposition (1950), formulating the social security policy which returned a Labour government in 1957, of which he was prime minister until 1960.

Nasser, Gamal Abdel (1918–70), Egyptian soldier and statesman. He formed (1942) what became the Free Officers Movement, its aims including the overthrow of the monarchy and the corrupt power of the major landowners (held responsible for defeat in the Arab-Israeli War of 1948), independence from Britain, the development of Arab socialism, and pan-Arabism. Many of these Nasser realized when, following the military coup which overthrew Farouk (1952), he ousted the nominal leader of the movement, General Neguib, and assumed full control (1954). His agrarian reforms broke up the large estates and he suppressed the old political parties. He compelled the British to evacuate their Suez Canal bases and initiated the Aswan high dam scheme to expand agriculture and introduce industrialization. His socialism incurred the enmity of the Muslim Brotherhood (ruthlessly suppressed after its attempt on his life in 1954). When the west withdrew its support from the Aswan dam, Nasser nationalized the Suez Canal. The Anglo-French and Israeli military response was defeated diplomatically by US and Soviet intervention. Although Soviet aid now replaced that of the west, Nasser maintained the neutralism which had made him a leader at the Bandung Conference. His pan-Arabism was expressed in the United Arab Republic, a short-lived union with Syria (1958–61), and in his support for the revolutions which overthrew the Iraqi monarchy and established the Yemeni Arab Republic. From 1961 he launched a programme limiting private property and extending state control of industry. His popularity survived humiliating defeat in the Six Day War (1967), which drew Egypt closer to the Soviet camp, when Soviet weapons and advisers were brought in to rebuild the shattered Egyptian forces. Nasser maintained his prestige throughout the Arab world until his sudden death (1970) and his influence continued.

National Aeronautics and Space Administration (NASA) see under space flight

National Health Service A comprehensive health service providing free diagnosis and treatment of illness at home or in hospital, denistry and ophthalmic service by act of parliament introduced by Attlee's Labour government (1946) and becoming effective from 5 July 1948. Despite charges for prescriptions, glasses and dental treatment (constantly raised since their introduction in 1951), the ever-increasing sums which successive governments had to find for the service, failed to keep pace with cost-inflation and the increasing price of high-tech treatments. The ill-advised reforms of the Heath government (1970–74) produced an unwieldy and inefficient administrative structure and the innumerable and powerful sectional interests made radical reform both difficult and politically inexpedient.

Nationalist Party A South African political grouping. Founded by General Herzog (1914–15) as the political expression of Afrikaanerdom, it joined the coalition government (1924–33) which imposed an industrial colour bar. The governing party since 1948, it disenfranchized the Cape Coloured voters (1951), made South Africa a republic, forced its withdrawal from the Commonwealth (1961) and built up the structure of apartheid. When both internal and external pressures forced the Nationalists to liberalize their policies to some degree, hardliners broke away in 1982 to form the Conservative Party which, after the 1987 election, had become the official opposition and made considerable inroads into nationalist support on the far right of the party.

National Socialism see **Nazi Party**

Nazi Party Formed as the National Socialist German Workers' Party (1920) from the German Workers' Party, under Hitler's leadership it survived the fiasco of the Munich Putsch (1923), gave him electoral backing to become chancellor (1933) and grew from 176,000 members in 1929 to two million (1933) and six million (1944). Its ideology was set out by Hitler in his *Mein Kampf* and may be encapsulated in its slogan, *Ein Volk, ein Reich, ein Führer*. 'One people' (*ein Volk*) embraces both pan-Germanist emotion and the theory of the Aryan master race; 'one empire' (*ein Reich*) looks back to the Holy Roman Empire and forward to the

'New Order' in Europe when Germany was to rise from defeat, regain its rightful place in the world and acquire living space (*Lebensraum*) in the east; 'one leader' (*ein Führer*) focused loyalty and devotion upon Hitler himself. In the structures which it imposed, Nazism borrowed much from fascism (the organs of the corporate state, party militias) and from communism (secret police methods, and concentration and labour camps). Officially banned by the constitution of the German Federal Republic, nazism bequeathed a legacy of misplaced national pride, racial hatred and anti-semitism to extremist political organizations all over the world.

Nazi-Soviet Pact   The agreement signed on 23 August 1939 between Nazi Germany and the USSR. It marked a complete reversal of Soviet policy, which had hitherto looked to collective security with the western democracies against German expansion eastwards. Partly through disgust with the Munich Agreements and partly out of a wish to weaken capitalism by involving the west in war with Germany, Stalin agreed to a non-aggression pact with Hitler, with clauses allowing the USSR to annex the Baltic republics, Bessarabia and eastern Poland. In return Stalin assisted the German war effort, but his misplaced trust in Hitler's intentions was shattered in June 1941 when Germany invaded the USSR.

Negrín López, Juan   (1887–1956), Spanish political leader. An academic, he became a socialist MP (1931) and finance minister (1936). At the height of the Civil War (1937), he became prime minister of the republican government which fled from Madrid, first to Valencia and then to Barcelona. Overthrown by a communist coup, Negrín went to France (1939) and remained head of the republican government in exile until 1945.

Nehru, Jawaharlal   (1889–1964), Indian statesman. He received an upper-class English education and was called to the bar. When he returned to India he became politically active after the Amritsar massacre (1919). He was Congress Party president 1929 (the first of three terms), spent 9 years in prison and had long periods of preventative detention between 1921 and 1945 for instigating civil disobedience. This included imprisonment (with Gandhi) for refusing to aid the British war effort without the promise of immediate Indian independence. He helped negotiate the terms of independence and after partition became prime minster of India (1947–64). He fought communalism, established an industrial base and – his greatest achievement – founded a parliamentary democracy based on the rule of law. In foreign affairs he became one of the leaders of the non-aligned Afro-Asian group. The Indian defeat in the border war with

China (1962) diminished his standing at home, but he established a ruling dynasty through his daughter, Indira Gandhi.

Nenni, Pietro (1891–1980), Italian socialist leader. Imprisoned (1911) for his protest against the Libyan War, he joined the Socialist Party (1921), becoming editor of its newspaper and secretary-general. With the advent of Mussolini he went into exile in France (1926), fought in the Spanish Civil War (1936–39) and was imprisoned by the Germans (1943). On his release he re-formed the Socialist Party, became secretary-general (1944–66) and president (1966–69) of a Unified Socialist Party. Allied with the communists (1947–56), he broke with them after the Hungarian uprising (1956). He supported Moro's Christian Democrats (1964), splitting his party and causing it heavy electoral losses (1968). Nenni held office in a number of postwar governments and stood (1971) unsuccessfully for president.

Netherlands A constitutional monarchy of northwestern Europe. It was ruled by a succession of female sovereigns – Queen Wilhelmina (1880–1962), who came to the throne in 1890 and abdicated (1948) in favour of her daughter, Juliana (1909–   ), who abdicated (1980) in favour of her daughter, Beatrix. Neutral during World War I, the country was invaded by the Germans in May 1940, suffering considerably during liberation by British and Canadian troops (1944–45). A series of postwar coalition governments saw the restoration of Dutch prosperity and the dismantling of the third largest European colonial empire. The Dutch East Indies gained their independence as Indonesia (1949), to which Dutch New Guinea was added (1962), the Netherlands Antilles were granted autonomy (1954) and Surinam (Dutch Guiana) its independence (1975). The Netherlands was in the forefront of European unity as a founder member of NATO (1949), of Benelux (1947) and of the European Community.

Neuilly, Treaty of The agreement concluded on 27 November 1919 between the Allies and Bulgaria, formally ending World War I hostilities. Under its terms Bulgaria made minor territorial concessions to Greece, Yugoslavia and Romania, paid limited reparations and had its army limited to 20,000 men.

New Deal The principles pledged in 1932 by Franklin D. Roosevelt as a 'new deal' for the American people and, to which as president, he gave effect in a three-stage reform programme. This first (1933–34) halted the effects of the depression and provided recovery and relief through agricultural, business, financial and banking regulation, price stabilization and an extensive programme of public works. The second stage (1935–

37) emphasized social legislation, many measures being blocked by the Supreme Court as unconstitutional, while the third (1938) became a defence of gains already made against opponents' charges of 'creeping socialism' and opposition to exorbitant public spending, high taxes and the growing power of the federal authorities.

New Economic Policy (NEP) The economic programme instituted by Lenin at the 10th Party Congress in the USSR (1921). It relaxed the regime's rigid and inept economic management in the face of discontents, riots and the Kronstadt Revolt. Until 1929 private enterprise was allowed to flourish and agricultural output increased accordingly – never to recover from Stalin's brutal collectivization.

Ne Win, U (Shu Maung, 1911–), Burmese soldier and political leader. He joined a Japanese–supported nationalist group (1941), but later fought the Japanese as commander of the Burmese Independence Army. After independence (1948), he became minister of defence; he deposed U Nu (1958) to become prime minister (1958–60, 1962–74). Under the 1974 constitution, Ne Win became president – his 'Burmese Way to Socialism' reducing the country to a police state, with insurrection on its borders and economic stagnation – until toppled (1988) by student uprisings.

New Zealand An independent Commonwealth country in the South Pacific. It was first colonized by Britain in 1840. Notwithstanding the Treaty of Waitangi (1841) which guaranteed the Maori possession of their land in return for recognition of British sovereignty, there were land disputes and wars with the settlers. Although relations between the races remained reasonably good, in the postwar years the movement for Maori rights gathered strength. New Zealand was a pioneer of social legislation, granting women over 21 the right to vote (the first country to do so) in 1893 and beginning a comprehensive programme of social welfare in 1898. During both World Wars it staunchly supported Britain and supplied contingents to the wars in Korea and Vietnam. Britain's entry into the European Community seriously upset the balance of New Zealand trade in agricultural produce and prime minister Holyoake strengthened links with Australia. New Zealand was always a strong supporter of Pacific defence, but its membership of the ANZUS Pact was nullified by the non-nuclear policies of prime minister Lange.

Nicaragua A republic of Central America. It gained its independence of Spain (1821), but was thereafter frequently subject to interference from and occupation by the United States which stationed a force of marines there (1916–33). In 1936 Anastasio Somoza became dictator. Until his assassination (1956) he ruled the country as if it were his personal property and his style was continued by his sons, who supported American business interests and professed anti-communism. This ensured US backing until their violations of human rights alienated the Carter administration and united the Roman Catholic Church, professional classes and the trade unions in support of the Sandinista Liberation Front. In 1979 this guerrilla movement drove out General Anastasio Somoza Debayle and established a provisional government with a majority in the ruling junta. As in Cuba, a popular uprising was hijacked by the Marxists who in 1982 declared a state of emergency and imposed press censorship. The creation of a Marxist state on the American mainland was seen as a direct challenge to the United States by President Reagan, whose extreme measure of mining Nicaraguan waters (1984) was repudiated by the US Senate. Congress became lukewarm to the idea of providing funds for the anti-government 'Contra' guerrillas, based in neighbouring Honduras, leading to the Iran-Contra scandal (1986). Public opinion became alienated by Contra atrocities and by 1988 the Sandinista forces had achieved the upper hand. However, a combination of guerrilla attacks, a US economic embargo and government inefficiency caused a breakdown of the economy. Discontent erupted in massive demonstrations in July 1988.

Nicholas II (1868–1918), tsar of Russia (1894–1917). A cousin of King George V, he married Alexandra of Hesse, whose autocratic character encouraged him to resist reform. The tsarina's German antecedents made the autocracy unpopular in World War I. The tsar's assumption of supreme command (1915) associated him with defeat and he was forced to abdicate (15 March 1917). The imperial family was placed under arrest and finally murdered by the Bolsheviks (16 July 1918).

Nigeria A West African Commonwealth country. The separate British protectorates established over Northern and Southern Nigeria (1906) were amalgamated in 1914 to form the Protectorate and Colony of Nigeria. Lord Lugard's system of indirect rule preserved the differences between the Muslim north and the Christian and animist south, but did not prevent the achievement of independence (1960) and the proclamation of a republic (1963), with Dr Azikiwe as first president. However, tribal and regional loyalties placed the federation under growing stress. In January 1966 Ibo army officers staged a coup in which the federal prime minister and the prime ministers of the northern and western regions died. In July Hausa officers staged a successful countercoup, followed in September by massacres of Ibo traders in the Hausa north. In May 1967 the Ibo Eastern Region seceded from the federation as the independent state of Biafra, which was reintegrated (1970) after bitter fighting, much bloodshed and starvation. A military government remained in power until 1975; then, after a series of military coups, a civilian government was restored in October 1979. Economic problems arising from the fall of oil prices and government corruption combined to create unrest and in 1984 the army once more seized power and instigated a rigorous purge of corrupt officials. In August 1985 General Ibrahim Babangida became president of the ruling Army Council and worked to establish economic recovery through state and private enterprise with a view to returning to civilian rule in 1992. Nigeria was affected by the Islamic revival which provoked riots and loss of life in Kaduna in the north (1987), and the moves in 1988 to introduce Sharia law were a potential source of division and violence.

Night of the Long Knives   Hitler's own description of the night of 29–30 June 1934 in which he used his SS to eliminate the Brown Shirts (SA) of Captain Ernst Roehm as well as a number of his other Nazi rivals. The purge of the radical element made the Nazi Party more acceptable to the German army and to the industrialists. There were over 100 victims including the former chancellor, General von Schleicher, and his wife.

Nimeiry, Gaafur Muhammad al-   (1930–   ), Sudanese soldier and political leader. A leader of a left-wing military coup (1969), he became president and after suppressing a Communist revolt (1971) ended his policy of alignment with Libya. He was elected to a second term (1977), but the civil war in the south, the influx of refugees from Ethiopia and government corruption forced him to relinquish power to a civilian administration (1985).

Nimitz, Chester William   (1885–1966), US admiral of the fleet. After Pearl Harbor (1941) he commanded the US Pacific Fleet until final victory over Japan. He succeeded Admiral King as chief of naval operations (1945) and, after his retirement (1947), headed the UN commission which enquired into the Kashmir dispute (1949).

Nixon, Richard Millhouse   (1913–   ), United States political leader. A lawyer, he served in the US navy in World War II (1942–46). He became Republican representative (1946) and senator (1950). As Eisenhower's vice-president (1952) he gained invaluable experience of international diplomacy, including a public debate with Khrushchev in Moscow (1959). In 1960 he was narrowly defeated by Kennedy for the presidency and also lost the election for governor of California (1962). Nixon returned to the law, but won both the Republican nomination and the 1968 presidential election, becoming 37th president. In office he achieved a ceasefire in Vietnam (1973) – but only after invading Kampuchea (1970) and Laos (1971), and by bombing North Vietnam and mining its harbours – and visited Peking (February) and Moscow (May 1972). The Peking visit ended a diplomatic isolation of over 20 years; the second initiated SALT 1 and resulted in major trade agreements. In 1972 he was re-elected to the presidency by a landslide vote which carried 49 of the 50 states of the union. His second term began inauspiciously when his vice-president, Agnew, resigned because of a financial scandal (December 1973), while he himself was driven out of office over the Watergate affair.

Nkomo, Joshua (1917–), Zimbabwean politician. He was president (1961) qf the Zimbabwe African People's Union (ZAPU), imprisoned (1963–64) and placed under restriction until 1974. On the failure of talks with the Smith regime (1976), he committed ZAPU to fighting in the guerrilla war alongside Mugabe's ZANU in the Patriotic Front. ZAPU was defeated by ZANU in the 1980 elections, but Nkomo served in Mugabe's first government briefly as minister of home affairs and then as minister without portfolio. In 1982 Mugabe began to destroy Nkomo's political base among the Matabele and Nkomo went abroad (1982–83). On his return both he and his party were gradually absorbed by ZANU into the one-party state (1987).

Nkrumah, Kwame (1909–72), first president of Ghana. He was educated in the United States and in England, where he became involved in Pan-African and nationalist politics. He returned home to become general secretary of J.B. Danquah's United Gold Coast Convention Party (1947). He founded his own Convention People's Party (1949). His militant campaign of strikes and demonstrations for immediate independence caused him to be imprisoned (1950) by the authorities but, when the CPP won a sweeping election victory (1951), he was released to become prime minister (1952). In 1957 he secured independence and in 1960 made Ghana a republic, of which he was the first president. An acknowledged leader of the Pan-African movement, he briefly united Ghana with Guinea (1959) and Mali (1960) and, as a leading proponent of non-alignment, obtained aid from both the United States and the USSR. In 1961, following a succession of strikes, he assumed command of the armed forces and, after he had survived assassination attempts, his rule became more remote and more paranoid. His extravagant schemes of self-glorification in elaborate public works at a time of economic hardship brought financial chaos and rampant inflation. Nkrumah was overthrown while visiting Peking (1966). He spent a period of exile in Guinea and died while under medical treatment in Romania (1972).

North Atlantic Treaty Organization   (NATO) The alliance created at the height of the Cold War, on 4 April 1949, by Belgium, Canada, Denmark, France, Iceland, Italy, the Netherlands, Norway, Portugal, the United Kingdom and the United States; it was joined by Greece and Turkey (1952), the German Federal Republic (1955) and Spain (1982). Because of tension with Turkey on the Cyprus issue, Greece withdrew its forces during 1964–80, while France withdrew (1966) as a gesture of independence by de Gaulle. The treaty was a defensive alliance to meet the threat of Soviet conventional military strength and relied on its retaliatory nuclear strategy. It was a major force in preserving peace in Europe but its future was in question in the light of the effect of Soviet conventional and nuclear force reductions (1988–89) on western unity.

North Borneo   see **East Malaysia** under **Malaysia**

Northern Ireland   An integral part of the United Kingdom, which came into being (1922) as a result of the northern Protestants' refusal to accept a Catholic majority. In consequence, its borders were so drawn as to include only those six counties in which Protestants could return a majority to the Northern Ireland parliament at Stormont and ensure their control of local councils. The Catholic minority was kept down politically by gerrymandering and socially by discrimination in employment and housing. Sporadically the IRA launched terrorist attacks in protest against partition. Such hard-line policies relaxed when Captain Terence O'Neill became prime minister (1963), but he failed fully to satisfy Catholic expectations and he deeply alarmed the hard-line Unionists who reacted by trying to suppress the Catholic Civil Rights movement. Sectarian violence was actively promoted by some notorious Protestant demagogues, and in 1969 the British army was brought in to protect the Catholic minority from the violence of the Protestant majority. Since the army kept order regardless of sectarian affiliation, suppression of Catholic counter-violence – and notably the IRA bombing campaign which erupted in September 1970 – inevitably 'provoked' the IRA and the first British soldiers were murdered in February 1971. Thereafter the IRA – Officials, Provisionals or the splinter INLA – has waged a campaign of violence and provoked counter-violence by Protestant paramilitaries. They have carried their campaign into mainland Britain and against service personnel and installations in West Germany, but despite the human and economic cost, it has failed in its basic aim of forcing the withdrawal of British troops from the north. Nor have the security forces been able to do more than to contain the violence. Internment (introduced in 1971) had proved a failure by 1975;

intimidation of jurors was met by the introduction (1972) of courts in which a single judge sat without a jury, but convictions on the evidence of informers were not sustained. Nor have the different political solutions proved any more effective. In March 1972 the Stormont government was dissolved and direct ru2e by London imposed. In December 1973, the British prime minister, Edward Heath, inaugurated the Sunningdale Agreement under which a power-sharing executive was created including Ulster Unionists and members of the Catholic SDLP. The reactions of the Protestant majority proved decisive and power-sharing was blocked by strikes and demonstrations. A further attempt in 1982 to evolve a similar power-sharing assembly proved equally abortive. In 1985 talks between the British and the Dublin governments resulted in an Anglo-Irish agreement, which gave the government of the Republic certain rights of consultation in respect of the North in return for closer co-operation on security. Given the security stalemate and the political deadlock, the most recent initiative has been towards a more genuine unionism, with Northern Ireland repsented in Westminister by members of the same political parties as the rest of the United Kingdom – an initiative cold-shouldered by the mainland parties.

Northern Rhodesia see **Zambia**

Novotny, Antonin (1904–75), Czechoslovak political leader. He joined the Communist Party (1921), was arrested and survived a term in Mauthausen concentration camp (1941–45). He took part in the Communist coup (1948) and after the fall of Slansky became first secretary of the Party (1953–68) and president (1957–68). A rigid Stalinist, his devotion to heavy industry caused an economic crisis (1961–63). Although Novotny attempted to placate the growing opposition by abandoning the third five-year plan, he could not contain the discontent. He resigned the party secretaryship to Dubček and the presidency to General Svoboda when the Czech army refused to act against the dissidents in the Prague Spring of 1968.

Nu, U (Thakin Nu, 1907–), Burmese political leader. He led the Burmese nationalist movement against the British authorities and was imprisoned by them (1942). Released by the Japanese, he became foreign minister of their puppet government, but at the same time organized anti-Japanese guerrillas. He became the first prime minister of an independent Burma (1948–56, 1957–58 and 1960–62) but he was ousted (1958 and 1962) by military coups led by Ne Win who imprisoned him (1962–66). On his release he was exiled.

nuclear energy The process of nuclear fission was discovered (1938) by

Hahn and Strassmann, elucidated (1939) by Meitner and Frisch and the first sustained nuclear chain reaction achieved by Fermi (1942). The potential of nuclear energy as a weapon of war was immediately perceived and the British and American governments pooled their scientific resources in the Manhattan Project under Robert Oppenheimer to produce an atomic bomb. This was successfully tested in July 1945 and employed against Hiroshima (6 August) and Nagasaki (9 August 1945) to end the war against Japan. Soviet intelligence, through such spies as Klaus Fuchs and the Rosenbergs, were able to obtain the necessary information to produce their own weapon (1949) and subsequently Britain (1952), France (1960), China (1964) and India (1974) have all produced atomic weapons of their own. Despite the provisions of the Nuclear Non-proliferation Treaty, South Africa, Israel and (possibly) Pakistan are all believed to have developed nuclear weapons. Both tactical and strategic nuclear weapons are deployed by the superpowers which increasingly see the need for their control and reduction to the point of elimination (see under **disarmament**). Nuclear reactors as propulsion units for ships have been virtually confined to submarines, and the peaceful use of nuclear energy has been to generate electric power. Nuclear power stations have been installed in many countries throughout the world in an endeavour to provide power more cheaply than by the burning of fossil fuel and with less damage to the atmosphere. However, cost savings have proved illusory, the disposal of radioactive waste has caused grave environmental problems and the safety of the power stations themselves has been called in question following the disastrous fire at the Soviet nuclear power station at Chernobyl (1986).

Nuremberg Laws Regulations promulgated at the 1935 Nazi Party congress depriving Jews of their civic rights and forbidding marriage and sexual relations between Jews and non-Jews. Persons of partly Jewish descent were restricted in a more limited degree.

Nuremberg Tribunal see **war crimes**

Nuri es–Said (1888–1958), Iraqi general and political leader. He served as chief of staff to the Emir Feisal in the Arab Revolt and when the emir was made king of Iraq (1921) he trained the Iraqi Army and served as prime minister (from 1930). After defeat in the Arab-Israel War (1948), he quelled the unrest by dissolving all political parties and executing four leading Iraqi Communists. In response to the Egyptian revolution and to Soviet support of Kurdish nationalism, he joined the Bagdhad Pact (1955), but when he created the Arab Union of Iraq and Jordan, in reply to the UAR of Egypt and Syria, it provoked a military revolt. The king and his uncle were murdered and Nuri himself was done to death in revolting circumstances.

Nyasaland see **Malawi**

Nyerere, Julius Kambarage (1921–   ), political leader of Tanzania. He founded the Tanganyika African National Union (1954) which won the 1958 and 1960 elections and became prime minister when Tanganyika achieved independence (1961). He was elected president of the Republic of Tanganyika (1962) and of the new Republic of Tanzania formed by the union of Tanganyika with Zanzibar (1964), converting the country to a distinctive brand of Christian socialism until his resignation in 1985. By then the state of the economy called for the intervention of the International Monetary Fund. He was succeeded by Ali Hassan Mwinyi, but retained leadership of the sole legal political party, the Revolutionary Party. An idealist, he has been a consistent opponent of apartheid and proponent of African unity, forming a customs Union with Uganda and Kenya (1967), and supporting his fellow socialist Obote in exile and in power in Uganda.

O

Obote, Apollo Milton (1925–), Ugandan political leader. Active as a trade unionist in Kenya, he returned to enter the Legislative Council (1957) and to found the Uganda People's Congress (1960). After independence he became prime minister (1962) and, having deposed the Kabaka, president (1966). He was overthrown by Idi Amin (1971) and went into exile in Tanzania. After the overthrow of Amin, Obote returned, took power after fraudulent elections (1980), continued Amin's policy of violence and fled after the 1985 coup. His first term as president had seen the failure of his socialist schemes, the second civil war as his rival Museveni tried to redress fraud by force.

Obregón, Alvaro (1880–1928), Mexican political leader. A supporter of Madero against Díaz, in 1913 he sided with Carranza, but when the latter tried to take power permanently (1920), Obregón led the revolt which overthrew him, becoming president in his turn. He introduced important agrarian and educational reforms and, having engaged in a bitter struggle against and persecution of the Church was assassinated by a militant Catholic.

October Revolution The revolution in Petrograd which brought Lenin and the Bolsheviks to power in 1917. Since the Gregorian calendar was not adopted until 1918 it takes its name from its Julian dates (25–26 October), not its Gregorian (6–7 November).

Oder-Neisse Line The present frontier between Poland and the German Democratic Republic agreed at the Yalta and Potsdam conferences and running along the rivers of these names. The new frontier was to compensate Poland for the annexation of its eastern territories by the USSR. The six million German inhabitants of the area were expelled by the Poles. The German Federal Republic did not recognize the frontier until 1970.

oil embargo see **Organization of Petroleum Exporting Countries**

Organisation de l'Armée Secrète see under **Salan, Raoul Albin Louis**

Organization for Economic Co-operation and Develoment (OECD) An enlargement of the OEEC (see below) by the inclusion of the United States and Canada, formed 14 December 1960 to extend development aid from the industrialized nations to the Third World. Later members are Japan (1964) and Finland (1968); Australia, New Zealand and Yugoslavia are associate members.

Organization for European Economic Co-operation (OEEC)   Formed on 16 April 1948 by Belgium, Denmark, France, Greece, Iceland, Ireland, Italy, Luxembourg, the Netherlands, Norway, Portugal, Sweden, Switzerland, Turkey and the UK, with the FRG (1955) and Spain (1959), to implement the objectives of its title. It formed the basis of the EEC and EFTA and lapsed after the creation of the OECD.

Organization of African Unity   Established at the Pan-African Conference in Addis Ababa (Ethiopia) in 1963, and with permanent headquarters there. Its original 32 members were pledged to mutual support and co-operation and to the eradication of colonialism from Africa.

Organization of American States   A regional grouping of American states to promote the joint welfare of its members which was formed at the 9th Pan-American Conference at Bogotá (April 1948) as a successor to the Pan-American Union, as the International Bureau of American Republics (founded 1899) became known in 1910. While it has been critical of US attempts to dominate the affairs of the hemisphere, it was equally critical of Soviet attempts to penetrate it via Cuba. In 1961 it established the Alliance for Progress.

Organization of Petroleum Exporting Countries   Formed in 1960 by the major oil exporters (excluding Canada and the USSR) to control development, output and oil prices and to regulate the terms on which western oil companies operate. In 1967–68 the Middle East and North African oil-producers formed the Organization of Arab Petroleum Exporting Countries (OAPEC), which imposed an oil embargo on the United States, the United Kingdom and the German Federal Republic for supporting Israel in the 1967 war, with grave consequences for the world economy. The search for fresh sources of supply and new sources of power has tended to undermine OPEC's efforts to control the price of oil by restricting production, efforts further undermined by the need of oil revenues to finance the Iran-Iraq conflict or to service the foreign debts of Third World countries.

Orlando, Vittorio Emanuele   (1860–1952), Italian political leader. An MP (1897–1925), he had held various ministerial posts before being appointed prime minister in 1917 after the Italian defeat at Caporetto. He resigned in 1919 when France and Britain failed to honour the secret Treaty of London (1915). Orlando retired from politics when Mussolini came to power (1925), but returned to the Senate (1948–52).

Ottawa Economic Conference   Convened on the initiative of Canadian prime minister Bennett in July-August 1932 to meet the problems of the Depression by a system of Imperial Preferences which would modify the tariffs introduced by the United Kingdom in February 1932 in favour of the dominions.

Ottoman Empire   see **Turkey**

Oxfam   Formed in Oxford in 1942 by a group of private citizens concerned to alleviate the famine in Greece, it has since the war expanded its activities to fight hunger world wide. It is the first of the many private organizations in the industrial nations dedicated to channelling help from their citizens to the Third World.

Oxford and Asquith, Earl of,   see **Asquith, Herbert Henry**

P

P 2 see **Propaganda Due**
Pahlavi see **Mohammed Reza Shah Pahlavi** and **Reza Shah Pahlavi**
Pakistan A republic in the Indian sub-continent created by the partition
of British India in 1947. Originally it comprised West Pakistan (the
present republic) and East Pakistan (see **Bangladesh**) which were
separated geographically by the republic of India. After the premature
deaths of its founding fathers, Jinnah (1948) and Liaquat Ali Khan
(assassinated 1951), Pakistan was ruled by an increasingly inept civilian
government which was terminated in 1958 when the army, under
General Ayub Khan, took charge. Strained relations with India erupted
in fighting in Kashmir (1965) and alignment with Peking. Military rule
ended in strikes and riots when General Yahya Khan succeeded (1969).
To allay the civil disorders he held elections, but annulled them when the
Awami League won an overwhelming victory in East Pakistan. East
Pakistan seceded; India intervened and defeated the Pakistani army.
Bangladesh was proclaimed and Pakistan left the Commonwealth when it
recognized the new republic. The deputy premier, Zulfiqar Ali Bhutto,
assumed absolute control of [West] Pakistan. He reached agreement with
Bangladesh and with India (1973) and instituted a period of civilian rule
which ended when the army took over to end four months of disorder
(1977). A military council elected General Zia al-Haq president, arrested
the government and opposition leaders, and tried and executed Butto for
complicity in a political murder. The Soviet invasion of Afghanistan
(1979–80) afforded Pakistan an opportunity of retaliation for Afghan
encouragement of a breakaway Pathan state (Pushtunistan) by support
for the mujahedin. In 1985 martial law was relaxed and non-party
elections held. In August 1988 General Zia was killed in an air crash and
following elections in November, Z. A. Bhutto's daughter, Benazir,
became prime minister with the victory of her Pakistan People's Party.
Palestine A former Turkish province captured by British and Dominion
forces with the aid of Arab irregulars during World War I and placed
under British mandate by the League of Nations (1920). The expansion
of 19th and early 20th century Zionist settlements was encouraged by the
Balfour Declaration (1917) and the promise of a 'Jewish homeland',

itself hardly compatible with the promise of independence which had incited the Arabs to rise against the Turks. The period of the British mandate was one of increasing tension culminating in an armed Arab uprising in 1937, and in 1939 the mandate was recognized as unworkable by the British government (Peel Report) because of the incompatibility of Arab and Zionist interests. World War II postponed the inevitable crisis and in 1947 the British placed the problem in United Nations hands in the face of Zionist terrorism and illegal immigration, and Arab refusal to contemplate partition of the country and the creation of separate Arab and Jewish states.

For the self-declared state (1989) west of the Jordan river see **West Bank**.

Palestine Liberation Organization (PLO) A movement formed in Jordan in May 1964 to co-ordinate Arab resistance within Israel, the aspirations of refugees and the aims of the different guerrilla groups. Since 1969 the PLO has been controlled by its chairman, Yasir Arafat, despite attempts to unseat him by leaders of different factions within the movement, and efforts by other Arab governments to direct the movement in their own interests. In 1970 the failure of an attempted coup in Jordan cost the PLO many casualties and forced them to move (under Syrian patronage) to Lebanon. Arafat's own faction, Al Fatah, as well as the more extreme Black September Movement (Abu Nidal) and the Popular Front for the Liberation of Palestine (George Habash) launched guerrilla attacks upon Israel and perpetrated international acts of terrorism. To counter these, Israel invaded Lebanon and drove out and dispersed Arafat and his fighters (1982). However, Palestinians in Israel continued to regard the PLO as their representative and Arafat was elected provisional president (April 1989) of the Palestinian state (Gaza Strip and West Bank) and proclaimed a meeting of the Palestine National Council in Algiers (November 1988). Although the PLO renounced terrorism and accepted UN Resolution 242 guaranteeing Israel secure borders, Israel continued to refuse to negotiate with its leaders.

Panama A Central American republic set up in 1903 by secession from Colombia and with the backing of the United States. In return, American interests then leased in perpetuity the zone through which they constructed the Canal linking the Caribbean with the Pacific Ocean. The United States was also authorized to intervene in Panamanian affairs and did so three times between 1908 and 1918. From the 1960s the Panamanians agitated for the return of the Canal Zone and, after the breaking of diplomatic relations (1963–64) and protracted negotiations,

President Carter reached agreement whereby the zone would be returned to Panama on 1 January 2000.

Pankhurst, Mrs Emmeline (née Goulden, 1858–1928), British suffragette. She founded the Women's Social and Political Union (1903); many of its members were gaoled for their militancy, and she was sentenced to three years' penal servitude (1913). During World War I she encouraged women to enter industry and the armed forces. She worked for child welfare in Canada (1919–26), left the Independent Labour Party when women were enfranchised (1918), joined the Conservatives and was adopted as a candidate shortly before her death. Her eldest daughter, Dame Christabel (1880–1958), was her mother's lieutenant in the suffrage movement; her second daughter, Sylvia (1882–1960), became the champion of the Ethiopian cause (1936) , while her third daughter, Adela (1885–1960), became an noted Australian feminist.

Papadopoulos, George (1919–), Greek political leader. A colonel in the junta which seized power in 1967, he took over as premier after King Constantine's unsuccessful counter coup, and suppressed all political opposition, ruling by decree, imprisoning and torturing his opponents. In 1973, following an abortive attempt by naval officers to overthrow his regime, he declared Greece a republic and himself the president. Student riots, put down by the army, and the worsening economic situation made him resign the presidency (1973) and, when the junta's plot to overthrow Archbishop Makarios and proclaim enosis in Cyprus went awry, the army was forced to relinquish power (1974). Papadopoulos, who was subsequently put on trial with some 20 other members of his government, was sentenced to death, but later reprieved and given a life sentence.

Papagos, Alexander (1883–1955), Greek soldier and statesman. He served in the Balkan Wars, became war minister (1935), then Chief of Staff (1936), and defeated the Italian invasion (1940) but was captured by the Germans (1941). After his release (1945) he become C-in-C of the Greek army. Having successfully concluded the Civil War, he resigned (1950) to enter politics, founding the right-wing Greek Rally. As prime minister (1952–55) he strengthened Greek alliances with the West (in particular with the United States), reached agreements with Yugoslavia and Turkey (1954), and improved relations with Bulgaria and Albania.

Papandreou, Andreas (1919–), Greek statesman. Son of George Papandreou, he became a naturalized American citizen (1944) and a university lecturer in economics, but returned to Greece (1960) and entered politics and served in his father's government. Accused by the

Papadopoulos regime of leading a left-wing opposition movement, he was imprisoned without trial (1965); after release under an amnesty (1967), he went into exile and formed an anti-government movement. He returned to Greece (1973) to head the Panhellenic Socialist Movement (PASOK) in opposition to the Karamanlis government. PASOK won the 1981 elections on a stridently anti-American platform and this anti-Americanism and his overtures to the Soviet bloc caused concern among his NATO allies. Re-elected in 1985, he eased relations with Turkey and reached agreement with the United States on defence matters. However, economic mismanagement and financial scandals beset him in the run-up to the 1989 elections.

Papandreou, George (1888–1968), Greek politician. Minister of the interior (1923) and of education (1929–33), he founded the Democratic Socialist Party (1935), but was exiled (1926; 1936–40), and imprisoned in World War II (1940–44), before escaping to join the resistance and head the government in exile (1944–45). Although he was opposed to Communism, at the liberation he was forced to resign because of his left-wing sympathies. He held office, but did not become premier again until 1963 and 1964–65. His attempt to purge right-wing extremists from the army was blocked by King Constantine II and he was forced to resign. When the colonels seized power (1967), he was briefly imprisoned.

Paraguay A South American republic. After it gained independence from Spain (1811), in an attempt to gain access to the sea, it engaged in a war with Brazil, Uruguay and Argentina (1865–70) which ended in defeat and the loss of approximately half the population. By 1912 the country had regained a measure of stability, but the victory over Bolivia in the Chaco War (1932–35) was only won at considerable economic cost. A succession of civilian governments and the military dictatorship of General Morinigo (1940–47) was ended in 1954 when General Stroessner (1912–   ) came to power. He provided Paraguay with a degree of stability at the cost of considerable curtailment of personal and civic liberties, until a deteriorating economy from 1982 onwards put increasing pressure on the regime with opposition from the Church, his political opponents, the United States government and street demonstrations. In February 1989 he was overthrown by the army C-in-C, General Rodriguez, whose subsequent election as president was denounced as fraudulent by the opposition.

Paris Peace Conference (18 January 1919–10 August 1920). The conference held at the end of World War I at which the structure of the League of Nations was determined and Allied peace terms were dictated by the 'Big Four' (Britain's Lloyd George; France's Clemenceau; Italy's Orlando, and the United States' Wilson). These terms which were embodied in the Treaties of Versailles (Germany), St Germain (Austria), Neuilly (Bulgaria), Trianon (Hungary) and Sèvres (Turkey) were to cause considerable bitterness, since they were seen by the vanquished to be imposed upon them by the victors rather than negotiated.

Paris Conference (25 April–12 July 1946). The meeting between the foreign ministers of Britain, France, the USSR and the United States at which the terms for the Treaty of Paris (*see below*) were settled but at which no agreement could be reached on the German question. These terms were later agreed at a meeting (29 July–15 October) of the 21 nations which had defeated the Axis powers in World War II.

Paris, Treaty of The treaty signed on 10 February 1947 by the 21 victorious Allies in World War II with the Axis Powers (excluding Germany, Japan and Austria) under which all were charged with denazification and the payment of reparations. Italy conceded territory in the Alps to France, in Istria to Yugoslavia and the Dodecanese islands to Greece and renounced its colonies; Bulgaria withdrew to her pre-1941 frontiers; Romania ceded Bessarabia and Bukovina to the USSR; Hungary ceded Transylvania to Romania, and Finland ceded territories to the USSR.

Park Chung Hee (1917–79), South Korean president. As a major-general he became chairman of the military junta which overthrew the civilian government (1961). Elected president (1963, 1967 and, after constitutional amendments, 1971), in 1972 he declared martial law allegedly to put through economic reforms, but in fact to increase still further dictatorial powers ruthlessly exercised in arbitrary arrests and torture. Park's wife died in an unsuccessful attempt upon his life in 1974, and in 1979 Park himself was assassinated.

Parliament Act The measure passed under threat by Asquith (and with the agreement of George V) that the king would create 250 new Liberal peers to enable the act to be voted through the House of Lords where the Conservative majority had been used to block Lloyd George's 'People's Budget' of 1909 and other reforming legislation. Under the Parliament Act (1911) the House of Lords was deprived of any power over money bills and could only impose its veto over other measures for three (later reduced to two) sessions of Parliament, while the maximum duration of an elected House of Commons was reduced from seven to five years. The unforeseen effect of the act was to allow any political party with a majority of seats (but not neccessarily of votes) to impose its will upon the country without any constitutional check upon its power.

partisans see **resistance movement**

Pasic, Nikola (c1845–1926), Serbian statesman. He founded the Radical Party (1881) and was exiled for his opposition to King Milan (1883–89) but became prime minister (1891–92) under King Alexander. Exiled (1899), he returned to power on the accession of Peter I and from 1903 directed a Pan-Slav policy which became violently anti-Austrian after the annexation of Bosnia-Hercegovina (1908). His dream of a 'Greater Serbia' was realized in the creation of Yugoslavia, but his insistence on Serbian hegemony as prime minister (1921) aroused the bitter resentment of Croats and Slovenes.

Patton, George Smith (1885–1945), US soldier. He commanded a tank brigade in World War I. A specialist in armoured warfare, in World War II he commanded (1942–43) a tank corps in Tunisia and the US 7th Army in Sicily. In 1944–45 'Old Blood and Guts' headed the US 3rd Army which he led through France, over the Rhine, across Bavaria and into Czechoslovakia, but was held back to allow the Red Army to capture Prague. After the German surrender he was transferred from the governorship of Bavaria for alleged leniency to former Nazis. He was killed in a car accident on 21 December 1945. Aggressive and self-opinionated, he was one of the greatest commanders of armoured forces of World War II.

Paul VI, Pope (Giovanni Battista Montini, 1897–1978), 260th pontiff (1963–78). Ordained in 1920, he served in the Vatican secretariat of state and became Archbishop of Milan (1954). In 1958 he was created cardinal by Pope John XXIII whom he succeeded in 1963. The first pope to travel extensively outside Italy, he reconvened the 2nd Vatican Council, reorganizing the Roman Curia (1967) and introducing the vernacular into the liturgy (1969). Despite his emphasis upon papal infallibility, the celibacy of the clergy and his ban on artificial methods of birth control, he has been blamed for failing to defend the traditional dogma and discipline of the Church.

Pavelic, Ante (1889–1959), Croat politician. He led the extreme wing (Ustase) of the Croat nationalist movement against Serbian hegemony. Exiled, he organized the murder of King Alexander in Marseille (1934). During World War II he headed the brutal puppet regime set up by the Axis powers in Croatia, escaping in 1945 to Argentina and dying in exile in Spain.

Peace Corps The United States government agency established by President Kennedy (1961) to assist the Third World in meeting its needs for trained manpower by means of volunteers working within the countries concerned.

Pearson, Lester Bowles (1897–1972), Canadian statesman. An academic, he entered the diplomatic service (1928) and played an important part in setting up the UN (1944–45), leading the Canadian delegation, presiding over the General Assembly (1952–53) and acting as mediator in the Palestine Crisis (1947) and in the Arab-Israeli War (1956) for which he was awarded the 1957 Nobel Peace Prize. A Canadian MP (1948), he was secreatary of state for external affairs (1948–57), playing a key role in the formation of NATO. He led the Liberal opposition (1958–63), succeeding Diefenbaker as prime minister (1963–68), and resigning in favour of Pierre Trudeau.

Peel Commission, Report of the   see **Palestine**

Perez de Cuéllar, Javier (1920–   ), 5th secretary-general of the UN. A Peruvian diplomat, he was ambassador to the USSR (1969–71) and to the UN (1971–75). He served as Waldheim's special representative in Cyprus (1975–76) and as UN undersecretary (1979–81), succeeding Waldheim as secretary-general (1982; re-elected 1986). Despite the failure of his Falklands peace plan (1982), his patient negotiations brought a truce to the Iran-Iraq conflict and Soviet withdrawal from Afghanistan (1988) and independence for Namibia (1989).

Perón, Juan Domingo (1895–1974), Argentinian president. A colonel in the junta which came to power in 1943, he became secretary of labour, and later minister of war and vice president. As president (1946–55) his programme of 'Peronism' was calculated to appeal to the urban industrial worker through generous welfare legislation, to the Church by its emphasis upon Catholicism, to the Army by its call to leadership in South America and to the patriotism of all by its anti-Americanism and its aim to make Argentina self-sufficient and master in its own house by the nationalization of foreign business interests. His wife, the actress Eva Duarte (1919–52), ran his social welfare programme, gaining fervent support among the urban workers through her personal qualities, but incurring the enmity of the army. Her death was a serious blow to Perón's popularity, and having become embroiled with the Church and outraged moderate opinion by repressive measures against his opponents, he was forced from power and into exile in 1955. The Perónist Party recovered to elect him to the presidency (1973–74), and survives both as a philosophy and as a powerful political force.

Pershing, John Joseph (1860–1948), US soldier. He served against the Apache and Sioux, in the Spanish American War (1898), in the Philippines (1899–1903; 1906–13) and against Pancho Villa in Mexico (1916–17). In 1917 he commanded the American Expeditionary Force in France, and later was chief of staff (1921–24).

Peru   A South American republic. It gained its independence from Spain in 1824, then suffered the government of wealthy oligarchs or military dictators who repressed such popular movements as APRA (Alianza Popular Revolucionaria Americana, founded 1924). When legalized, APRA held a parliamentary majority from 1945–48, used to back the moderate president, Bustamente. In 1948 and 1962 the army intervened to check APRA-supported moves to the left, but in 1963 Fernando Belaunde Terry (1912–) and his Popular Action party came to power and intitiated a series of social, educational and land reforms. His subservience to American interests lost him popularity and he was overthrown by a military coup in 1968. The army ruled until 1980 when the restoration of civilian rule saw the return to power of Belaunde and his Popular Action party, to be replaced by APRA in 1985. Faced by galloping inflation and a crushing burden of international debt, Peru's problems have been compounded by the Maoist Sendero Luminoso guerrilla movement.

Pétain, Henri Philippe   (1856–1951), French statesman. In World War I he took part in the battle of the Marne (1914) and commanded in Artois and Champagne, but made his name as the defender of Verdun (1916). Superseded by Nivelle (1916), he resumed command of the central army group (1917) having suppressed a mutiny in the French army. He was made marshal of France (1918) and defeated Abd el-Krim in Morocco (1925). In 1939 he was appointed ambassador to Spain (Franco had served under him in joint operations in Morocco), but was recalled by Reynaud and appointed deputy premier in an effort to rally the French people (May 1940). On 17 June 1940 he accepted the premiership, concluded an armistice with the Germans, abolished the Third Republic and became head of the French state established at Vichy. In 1942 the Germans made him appoint Laval premier and he was drawn into ever closer collaboration with them. After the invasions by the Allies, he was abducted by the Germans (August 1944), but managed to make his way from Sigmaringen to Switzerland and then surrendered to the French authorities (April 1945). He was convicted of treason and sentenced to death (August 1945), but his sentence was commuted to life detention in a fortress and he died on the Ile d'Yeu in 1951. His role was highly controversial and he has had many posthumous apologists.

Petty-Fitzmaurice, Henry Charles Keith   (1845–1927, 5th Marquess of Lansdowne), British statesman. He held office under Gladstone, was governor-general of Canada (1883–88); then viceroy of India (1889–94) and secretary for war (1895–1900). As foreign secretary (1900–05), he broke Britain's diplomatic isolation by alliances with Japan (1902) and the Anglo-French Agreement (1904). In 1917 he advocated a negotiated settlement to World War I which was repudiated by the British government.

Philippines, Republic of the A southeast Asian archipelago. It was ruled by Spain until the United States took it in the Spanish-American War, and it was ceded to them under the Treaty of Paris (1898). Filipino nationalists led by Emilio Aguinaldo, who had almost secured independence before American intervention, now had to resume the struggle. Although the Americans conceded self-rule and recognized the Filipino right to independence (1916) and established (1934) a constitution which provided Filipino autonomy under an elected president, the US high commissioner still retained some powers of veto. It was only after the archipelago had been liberated from Japanese occupation (1941–45), that a genuinely independent Philippine Republic came into being (4 July 1946), which was forced to make large concessions to US naval, military and business interests. Rural poverty incited the Communist-led Hukbalahap guerrilla movement which was finally defeated in 1950 by Ramon Magsaysay, who became an $ble, reforming president. While the Philippines maintained a strong anti-communist stance (they had joined SEATO in 1954), American influence and sovereignty over US bases were issues which divided the country and provoked anti-American demonstrations during the 1960s. In 1965 Ferdinand E Marcos became president and began an increasingly repressive and corrupt rule which lasted until 1986, when Mrs Corazon Aquino won a disputed presidential election. An influential section of the army, realizing that the Marcos regime had now lost American support, backed the popular rising which drove Marcos from power into exile in Hawaii. President Aquino inherited a state of civil war with the Muslim Moros and Communist guerrillas, lurking sympathies for Marcos within the army – resulting in a major mutiny in 1987 – and an ailing economy.

Pibul Songgram (1897–1964), Thai soldier and statesman. He led the military coup (1932) which changed Thailand from an absolute to a constitutional monarchy under a ruling elite. Premier (1938–44 and 1948–57), he supported the Japanese in World War II (temporarily annexing the eastern provinces of Kampuchea) and on his return to power adopted a pro-western, anti-communist policy. Ousted in a coup (1957), he went into exile in Japan, where he became a Buddhist monk (1960).

Pieck, Wilhelm (1876–1960), German statesman. Social Democrat (1895), founder member of the German Communist party and MP (1928), he escaped to France on Hitler's rise to power (1933). He moved to the USSR, having succeeded Thälmann as party secretary (1935), and became general secretary of the Comintern (1938–45). He returned with the Red Army, set up the German Democratic Republic, and was elected its first president (1949). He remained in office until his death.

Pilsudski, Josef (1867–1935), Polish soldier and statesman. Exiled to Siberia (1887–92) on suspicion of a plot to assassinate Tsar Alexander III, on his release he resumed his socialist and nationalist activities, seeking Japanese support (1904) for a Polish revolt. During World War I he recruited the Polish Legion to fight for the Central Powers. Briefly imprisoned by the Germans (1917), he returned to Warsaw to proclaim an independent Polish republic (1918). Given dictatorial powers, he expelled the Red Armies and expanded Poland's eastern frontier, remaining army C-in-C until 1923, having resigned his political powers (1922) following peace with the USSR and the election of a president (1921). In 1926 he led a military coup, serving as prime minister (1926–28 and 1930), but exercising real power as war minister from 1926 until his death in 1935.

Pinochet Ugarte, Augusto (1915–   ), Chilean general and head of state. He led the CIA-backed coup which ousted the Marxist regime of President Allende (1973), purged communist and socialist elements from the administration, and established an authoritarian regime. He repaired the economic damage of his predecessor's socialist policies at the cost of serious violations of human rights. In 1986 he survived an assassination attempt but lost a referendum (1988) on the question of his standing as sole presidential candidate in the 1989 elections.

Pius XII, Pope (Eugenio Pacelli, 1876–1958), 258th pontiff (1939–58). Ordained in 1899, he entered the Vatican diplomatic service, becoming papal secretary of state (1930). He denounced totalitarianism, but was forced to work with totalitarian regimes in order to forward the humanitarian role of the Vatican in World War II. In the post-war world he protested vainly against the persecution of Catholics by the Communist powers and in Italy fostered support for the Christian Democrats against the resurgence of the Communist Party.

Poincaré, Raymond (1860–1934), French statesman. Deputy (1887–1903) and senator (1903–13, 1920–29), he became prime minister and foreign secretary (1912–13). Elected president in succession to Fallières (1913), he was concerned to play more than a ceremonial role. To meet the German menace, he helped to raise the conscription period to 3 years (1913) and strengthened French military alliances with Russia and the United Kingdom. In World War I to counter defeatism (1917) he appointed Clemenceau premier, despite their incompatibility. After his term of office, Poincaré returned to the Senate. As prime minister (1922–24) and foreign secretary he sent French troops into the Ruhr. When this failed to obtain payment of reparations he was forced to accept the Dawes Plan. The worsening economic situation brought him back in 1926, when his drastic deflationary measures brought stability but lost him support and he was forced to resign (1929) shortly before his death.

Poland East European republic reconstituted in 1918 from the monarchy which disappeared in the 18th century and on land which was four times divided by Prussia, Austria and Russia (1772, 1793, 1795, 1815). Polish independence was successfully defended by Marshal Pilsudski against the invasion of the Red Army, and confirmed by the Treaty of Riga (1921) which defined the Polish-Soviet frontiers. Pilsudski dominated Polish political life between the wars and, recognizing the Nazi menace, signed a 10-year non-aggression pact with Germany (1934). In breach of this agreement, the Germans invaded (1939) and World War II began. Poland was swiftly overrun and, under the terms of the Nazi-Soviet Pact, once more partitioned. The Nazi regime was particularly brutal, but a government in exile continued the struggle with units formed from Poles who had escaped in 1939 and from a corps formed in the USSR from the survivors of such KGB murders as the Katyn Massacre and the gulags. In 1944 as the Soviet advance reached the Polish borders, the Soviets established a puppet government at Lublin and disowned the London government in exile. The Polish resistance, the Home Army, took the field with the approach of the Red Army. Once their purpose had been served, the units were disarmed and their members imprisoned by the Soviets, who allowed the Germans to crush the Warsaw Rising (August-October 1944), while their own troops remained inactive on the outskirts of the city. In consequence the Soviets were able to impose a puppet Communist government, headed by Boleslaw Bierut (1892–1956), which agreed to their eastern borders following the Curzon Line. In compensation for this loss of territory the western frontier was fixed on the Oder-Neisse Line and the German inhabitants of the region were expelled. Since World War II Polish antipathy to the Russians has been reinforced by the failure of the Communist governments to resolve the country's economic problems and to allow its people to exercise their basic civic rights. These dissatisfactions have expressed themselves in the consistent and constructive opposition of the Roman Catholic Church, the growing disillusion of students and intellectuals, and strikes and demonstrations by the workers. The first of these (1956) caused the downfall of Bierut; his successor, Gomuĺka, was toppled by the serious riots of 1970, while his successor, Edward Gierek, did not survive the failure of his own economic policy, and was replaced in 1980 after the strikes and disorders which saw the birth of Solidarity. Government concessions bred increased unrest and the fear of Soviet intervention. General Jaruzelski (appointed prime minister, February 1981), imposed martial law in September and arrested and imprisoned the leaders of Solidarity, provoking an American trade embargo. Despite demonstrations when martial law was relaxed during the summer of 1982, by the following summer it had been lifted, only to be replaced by equally stringent internal security laws. By 1986 General Jarulzelski was claiming that Solidarity had been broken, but the movement remained a powerful force. In 1988 the prime minister, Zbigniew Messmer was replaced by Mieczyslaw Rakowski, as the Polish economy took a deeper plunge. Early in 1989 talks began, and on 3 April agreement was reached legalizing Solidarity and allowing free elections to a parliament with a built-in (65%) Communist majority in the lower house.

Polisario Front see under **Morocco**

Polish Corridor A strip of German territory along the lower reaches of the Vistula awarded to Poland under the Treaty of Versailles to allow the new republic access to the Baltic Sea. Polish refusal to grant Germany an extraterritorial German corridor across the Polish Corridor was used as a pretext for the German invasion (1939) which started World War II.

Pol Pot (Saloth Sar, 1928–   ), Kampuchean head of state. After studying in Paris (1950–53), he returned to become secretary-general of the Kampuchean Communist Party (1963), raised the Khmer Rouge guerrillas and took power when the capital, Phnom Penh, fell (January 1975). The perverted ideology of his regime did some three million of his countrymen to death before he was driven out by the Vietnamese (1975). The Khmer Rouge continued to receive Chinese support and conducted guerrilla warfare from their bases in Thailand. Although discredited, Pol Pot continued to plan for a return when the Vietnamese completed their withdrawal in 1989.

Pompidou, Georges Jean Raymond (1911–74), French statesman. A former schoolmaster, he was active in the Resistance in World War II. He became a banker – director general of Rothschild's (1956–62) – and was made educational adviser to de Gaulle (1944–46). He was appointed head of de Gaulle's cabinet office (1958) – helping to conclude the Evian

Agreements – and member of the Constitutional Council (1959–62). In 1962 he succeeded Michel Debré as prime minister and leader of the Gaullist party, skilfully handling the student riots in May 1968, only to be dismissed by de Gaulle in July. Elected to succeed de Gaulle as president (1969), his austerity measures met French economic problems, and he reversed Gaullist foreign policy by voting for British admission to the European Community. He died suddenly of cancer in 1974.

Popular Fronts   (1) The belated move in 1935 by the Comintern (see **Doriot, Jacques**) to create an alliance of 'bourgeois' left-wing and communist parties to combat the threat of nazism and fascism.

(2) In Spain, the Republican governments of Azana, Caballero and Negrín, overthrown by Franco in the Spanish Civil War (1936–39), were popular front governments.

(3) In France, Léon Blum headed a coalition of left-wing parties (1936–37), rallied opposition against fascists and right-wing extremists and introduced important social legislation governing working hours and wages, nationalization of the railways and reorganization of the Banque de France. Blum and his successor, Chautemps, lost the support of the far left when economic problems halted their social legislation and they adopted a policy of non-intervention in Spain. The movement ended with Blum's second brief premiership (March–April 1938).

(4) Between 1938 and 1947 Chilean popular front governments instituted important social reforms.

Portal, Charles Frederick Algernon   (1893–1971, 1st Lord Portal), British Marshal of the Royal Air Force. He served with distinction in World War I and, as chief of air staff (1940–46), helped to shape the strategy of the air war in World War II.

Portsmouth, Treaty of   The agreement signed in Portsmouth, New Hampshire, in 1905 to end the Russo-Japanese War. Britain and the United States, who acted as mediators, granted Japan a free hand in Korea and the cession of Russian territories and bases in return for acceptance of the Open Door Policy in China and freedom of action for the Americans in the Philippines.

Portugal   A West European republic proclaimed on 5 October 1910 with the overthrow of the monarchy (founded 1128) and the flight of King Manuel II (1889–1932). Despite a liberal constitution, the administration remained inefficient and corrupt and governments unstable until in 1926 Marshal Carmona came to power. He remained head of state until his death (1951), the real power being exercised from 1928–68 by Dr Salazar, whose 'New State' brought stability and social and economic improvement at the price of some infringements of personal and civic freedom. His successor, Dr Caetano, was faced by the spontaneous move towards greater freedom at home and by the strains of colonial wars in both Angola and Mozambique. Both coincided in the Armed Forces Movement which staged a successful coup in April 1974, the junta under General Spinola managing to steer a middle course between right and left wing extremism. In 1976 the first free elections since the 1920s returned a minority socialist government under Mario Soares. Despite economic problems and a succession of short-lived governments after 1978, genuine democracy survived. Soares returned to power in 1983 and took Portugal into the European Community (1985) and was elected president (1986). However his socialist party was defeated in the 1987 elections and replaced as governing party by the Social Democrats under Anibal Cavaco Silva.

Potsdam Conference   The first post-war summit conference between the United States, the USSR, and the United Kingdom. It discussed German reparations, the structure of the occupation administration and the Soviet entry into the war against Japan. At Potsdam, Truman informed Stalin of the existence of the atom bomb. During the course of the conference (16 July-2 August 1945), Churchill was defeated in the British elections; he and Eden departed and Attlee and Bevin took their places (from 24 July).

Primo de Rivera, José Antonio   (1903–36), Spanish politician. The lawyer son of Miguel Primo de Rivera, he became an MP and founder of the Falange (1933). In 1936 he was arrested on the orders of the popular front government, summarily tried and executed. He became the martyr to Franco's cause.

Primo de Rivera y Orbaneja, Miguel   (1870–1930, Marques de Estella), Spanish soldier and statesman. Before his appointment (1922) as captain-general of Catalonia he served in Morocco, Cuba and the Philippines. In 1923 he led a successful coup against the government, suspended the constitution and formed a military junta which King Alfonso XIII accepted. He reversed Spanish defeats in Morocco, installed military governors to counter provincial separatism and revived the economy with a massive series of public works. His economic policies foundered with the Wall Street Crash (1929). There were unsuccessful attempts to overthrow him and eventually the king dismissed him and he died in exile (1930).

Prohibition   The ban on the manufacture and sale of alcoholic drinks in the United States. During World War I, and in the absence of many male voters on service overseas, the temperance movement succeeded in passing through the US Congress (1917) the 18th Amendment to the Constitution, prohibiting the manufacture and sale of intoxicating liquors. The amendment came into force on 16 January 1920 and, being unenforceable in the cities and large towns, was largely ignored. The supply of illicitly distilled or imported liquor provided the financial base for organized crime. Prohibition was repealed by the 19th Amendment (5 December 1933).

Propaganda Due [P2] A secret and illegal Italian masonic lodge whose Grand Master, Licio Gelli, was supected of financing the neo-fascists and other right-wing groups. He fled the country in 1980 when sought for fraud (for which he was subsequently extradited and convicted) following the failure of the Banco Ambrosiano, when the activities of the P2 Lodge came to light and brought down the government of the day.

Pu-yi, Henry (1906–67), last Manchu emperor of China (as Hsuan T'ung, 1908–12) and first and last emperor of Manchukuo (as K'ang Te, 1934–45). After his abdication (1912), he took refuge in the Japanese concession of Tientsin (1925) to escape rioting in Peking; later he was taken to Manchuria by the Japanese and made emperor (1934). Although a figurehead, he was arrested and imprisoned by the USSR (1945–50), then by the Chinese (1950–59). On his release he worked in Peking as an archivist.

Q

Qaddafi, Muammar al- (1938–), Libyan head of state. As a captain, he led the group of junior officers which overthrew King Idris in the 1969 coup and made himself C-in-C and chairman of the Revolutionary Command Council. The four-fold inspiration of his highly personal rule has been Islamic fundamentalism which has led him reintroduce Sharia law and turn Benghazi cathedral into a mosque, Pan-Arabism which has led him to interfere in the affairs of Egypt, the Sudan and Tunisia and to support the Palestinian cause against Israel, and a consistently anti-western and specifically anti-American policy. This led him to support the more extreme terrorist movements, including the IRA, and to provoke armed conflict with the United States, leading to air battles over the Gulf of Sirte (1981) and the retaliatory bombing of Tripoli (1986). His aid to the rebels in Chad covered his annexation of a mineral-rich strip in the north of that country, from which his troops were driven (1987). Qaddafi has suppressed all internal opposition and, despite his devotion to Islam, ordered the murder of the Grand Mufti of Tripoli, and has sent assassins to kill Libyan opponents in exile in western Europe.

Quebec Canadian city and scene of two conferences in World War II between Churchill, Roosevelt and their chiefs of staff to plan the Normandy Landings (1943) and the shift of forces from Europe to the Pacific and southeast Asia after the defeat of Germany (1944). Quebec is also the centre of the French-speaking Canadian population and of the separatist movement.

Quezon, Manuel Luis (1878–1944), first president of the Commonwealth of the Philippines. He joined Aguinaldo's nationalist insurrection against Spain (1899), continuing the fight for independence (1901) after the United States annexed the Philippines, and was briefly imprisoned. After qualifying as a lawyer (1903), he was appointed a provincial governor, and led the majority Nationalist party in the assembly (1907–09). As Philippine commissioner in the United States (1909–16), he lobbied continuously for independence; the measure of self-government and the promise of ultimate independence granted (1916) were largely due to his efforts, as was the passage of the Act of Congress creating the Commonwealth of the Philippines (1934). On his return (1916), he was elected to the Philippine Senate, of which he became president. In 1935 he was elected president of the new commonwealth. Re-elected in 1941, he escaped from the invading Japanese and headed the Philippine government in exile in the United States, where he died in 1944. The province of Tabayas was renamed Quezon and the capital of the Philippines Quezon City in his honour.

Quisling, Vidkun (1887–1945), Norwegian soldier and politician. After retiring from the army (1923), he became an Agrarian Party MP, and was defence minister (1931–33). He founded the Nazi-inspired National Unity Party (1933), which was the only legal party in Norway under the German occupation (1940–45). He discussed a possible coup d'état with Hitler (1939), and betrayed Norwegian defences to German agents (1940). Prime minister of the puppet Norwegian government established by the Germans (1942), after the German surrender (1945), he was arrested, tried and executed for treason.

R

Radical, Parti [also **Parti Radical-Socialiste**] The major French political party (founded 1875) of the Third Republic. It began as the republican opposition to the Second Empire, continued under the Third Republic as a defence against a royalist or Bonapartist restoration, and came to represent the mass of the French people. It was republican, anti-clerical, individualistic, defensive of the rights of private property, yet open to social reform. The party weathered the divisions caused by the Dreyfus Affair and broke with the socialists in 1905. Its members formed the bulk of most governments until 1940, in alliance with both right (Poincaré) and left (Blum). It was the party of Clemenceau, Herriot and Daladier, but suffered the fate of the Third Republic with which it was so closely associated. It enjoyed a revival with the restoration of the republican regime (1945), but never regained its old influence and broke up during the 1970s.

Raeder, Erich (1876–1960), German naval officer. Admiral Hipper's chief of staff in World War I, he was responsible between the wars for rebuilding the German navy, but its inability to mount Operation Sealion (1940) and his identification with a surface fleet caused Hitler to make Doenitz C-in-C in his place (1943). His sentence of life imprisonment by the Nuremberg Tribunal (1946) was commuted in 1955 because of his ill health.

Rahman, Sheikh Mujibur (1920–75), first prime minister of Bangladesh. Secretary-general (1953) and president (1966) of the opposition Awami League, he was imprisoned for a total of 10 years during his battle for East Pakistan autonomy. In 1971 Bhutto charged him with treason and imprisoned him, but he was released in 1972 after Indian intervention, the defeat of the Pakistani army and the declaration of an independent Bangladesh. He refused the presidency to become prime minister, and attempted to introduce a democratic form of socialism but it degenerated into a dictatorship (January 1975) in the face of the overwhelming economic and social problems. In August 1975 he was overthrown in a military coup and murdered with other members of his family.

Rainbow Warrior The ex-trawler belonging to Greenpeace, the environmentalist group, which was due to lead a protest flotilla into the French

Pacific nuclear test zone, but was sunk by two explosions in Auckland harbour on 10 July 1955, in the second of which a photographer was killed. Two French agents were arrested, tried and sentenced to 10 years' imprisonment, severely straining Franco-New Zealand relations. Later the French government negotiated their release into French custody on a Pacific island for a fixed period of years. Relations were again impaired when they were released on the pretext of ill health.

Rajk, Laszlo (1909–49), Hungarian Communist leader. He fought with the International Brigade in the Spanish Civil War and escaped to France where he was interned (1939); on his return to Hungary he became first secretary of the Communist Party (1941), and was imprisoned by the Gestapo (1942–45). As minister of the interior (1946) he helped destroy the Peasants' Party. In 1948 he became foreign minister but was seen as a rival by Rákosi, who had him executed for Titoism after a show trial (1949). In 1956 he was officially rehabilitated.

Rákosi, Mátyás (1892–1971), Hungarian Communist leader. He became a Communist while a prisoner of war in Russia. A commissar in Béla Kun's government (1919), he escaped to Austria then returned secretly to Hungary (1925) to work underground. He was imprisoned for his activities (1927), and released to the USSR (1940). He returned with the Red Army (1945), and became secretary-general of the party and deputy premier in the non-Communist government. A hard-line Stalinist, he rapidly eliminated the non-Communist politicians as well as party rivals such as Rajk, and dominated political life from 1949-53. On the death of Stalin he was succeeded as prime minister by Imre Nagy, but he still retained great influence and became premier again in 1955. In the Hungarian Uprising (1956) he fled the country, his ruthless use of the secret police having made him particularly odious. He was expelled from the party (1962) and died in the USSR.

Rapallo, Treaties of (1) An agreement reached on 12 November 1920 between Italy and Yugoslavia on territorial differences. They pledged their opposition to any restoration of Hapsburg rule.

(2) The agreement concluded between German and Soviet delegations, on 16 April 1922, following an economic conference in nearby Genoa, under which they re-established diplomatic relations, renounced all financial claims on each other and pledged joint co-operation (defined in secret clauses as including the training in the USSR of aircraft and tank crews, Germany being forbidden tanks and warplanes by the Treaty of Versailles).

Rasputin (Grigori Yefimovich Novykh, c1872–1916), Russian faith-healer. His reputation took him to St Petersburg (1903) and brought him to the notice of the tsarina, who was desperate to find a cure for her son's haemophilia. His treatment appeared to work and, despite a well-deserved reputation for sexual and alcoholic excesses, the monk became one of the inner court circle (1905). Rasputin shamelessly used his influence and association with him discredited the tsar and the Orthodox church. Eventually he was murdered by a group of noblemen, but by that time he had fatally compromised the tsar and his family in the eyes of the Russian people.

Reading, Marquess of see Isaacs, Rufus Daniel

Reagan, Ronald Wilson (1911–), 40th president of the United States. A sports journalist and film actor, he was six times president of the Screen Actors' Guild (1947–51; 1959). A Democrat supporter of Eisenhower, he joined the Republican Party (1962) and served two terms as governor of California (1966–74). He won 44 states in the 1980 presidential election, and was re-elected (1984) with a decisive majority of all classes except the blacks. His domestic policy followed the pattern set in California – cuts in the federal budget for welfare, education and housing – reflecting the nationwide conservative swing. He revived the economy and cut unemployment, but at the cost of a large adverse balance of trade. His foreign policy was strongly anti-communist with increased defence spending and initiation of the so-called 'Star Wars' project. In Central America it was less than successful, but in US-Soviet relations the initial hard line paid off in the establishment of easy personal relations with Gorbachov and in important disarmament agreements in the final year of his presidency (1988). His uncompromising attitude towards terrorism was dented by the Iran-Contra scandal, but he remained immensely popular and his real achievement may have been to restore to Americans a belief in themselves.

Recruit Cosmos Scandal A large-scale Japanese financial scandal. In order to turn his business data service into an electronic data base, the chairman of the Recruit Cosmos Corporation bribed leading members of the Japanese ruling Liberal party to allow him to lease at favourable rates the government-owned Nippon Telephone and Telegraph's digital lines between major cities. Bribery took the form of allocating Recruit Cosmos stock to favoured politicians, who were able to sell out at high profit after the company went public in 1986. The scandal came to light in 1988 and involved the chairman of NTT (who resigned), the former premier Nakasone, and some 16 other politicians, including current members of the cabinet such as the deputy premier and the finance minister, the justice minister and the Economic Planning Agency's director-general (who resigned), the speaker of the Japanese parliament and the prime minister.

Reichstag Fire The destruction, by arson, on 27 February 1933, of the Reichstag, the lower chamber of the federal parliament of Germany. Hitler used the fire as the pretext to outlaw the German Communist Party and to assume dictatorial powers (23 March 1933). A simple-minded Dutchman, Marinus Van der Lubbe, who had apparently started the fire, was executed, but the communists tried with him were acquitted when the Bulgarian, Dimitrov, suggested that the fire had been started at Nazi instigation.

Renner, Karl (1870–1950), Austrian statesman. A Social Democrat MP (1907), he headed the provisional government after the abdication of the Emperor Charles I (1918). Chancellor (1919–20), then speaker of the Austrian parliament (1931–33), he went underground after the Anschluss. Premier and foreign minister of the provisional Austrian government (1945), he was elected president (1945), remaining in office until his death.

reparations The financial compensation demanded from Germany and its allies under the treaties imposed by the Paris Peace Conference (1919–20) after World War I. In practical terms they proved a dead letter (see **Dawes Plan, Young Plan**), while economically they caused inflation, recession and deep bitterness, particularly among the Germans, thus facilitating the rise of the Nazi Party. After World War II reparations took the form of seizures of assets and industrial plant by the victors from the vanquished, although West Germany has paid substantial reparations to Israel for the loss of Jewish lives and property during the Nazi regime.

Republican Party US political party formed in 1854 by the opponents of slavery, and which successfully preserved the Union after the secession of the Confederates and the Civil War (1861–65). Republican presidents were in office between 1861 and 1913, with Democratic interludes (1885–89, 1893–97). Until the beginning of the 20th century the differences between Democrats and Republicans – except over slavery – had been less of policies than of personalities. But the rise of the Populists and the capture of the Democratic Party by this radical wing in the 1890s set it in opposition to a Republican Party which was the mouthpiece for conservative economic policies, big business interests and isolationism. These effectively negated the internationalist policies of Woodrow Wilson (1913–20), but the Republican administrations of Harding, Coolidge and Hoover (1920–32) were tainted by corruption (Teapot

Dome scandal) and discredited by their inability to meet the crises of the Wall Street Crash and the Depression. Not until 1952, when Eisenhower was elected, was there a Republican president, but then followed the Democratic presidencies of Kennedy and Johnson. Nixon's victory in 1968 marked the swing in American politics to the right, interrupted by the Watergate affair, but continued from 1980 by Reagan and Bush.

resistance movement The name given during World War II to the spontaneous opposition to the Nazi regime which occurred throughout occupied Europe. Organized by the British SOE and the American OSS and assisted by agents infiltrated into their respective countries, these movements supplied military intelligence, assisted the escape of prisoners of war, engaged in acts of sabotage and assisted the Allies by co-ordinating armed uprisings with the liberation forces. German counter-intelligence virtually nullified the Dutch resistance, but the Norwegians were successful in sabotaging German nuclear research and the Poles provided advance information on the V-weapons and won imperishable glory in the Warsaw Uprising. After the surrender of Italy, it was chiefly Communist partisans who fought the Germans and fascist militia, and captured and executed Mussolini. In France the FFI played a vital role in the success of the landings in Normandy and Provence and in the liberation of their country. Communists had collaborated with the Germans until the invasion of the USSR, but after 1941 the efforts of their units (generally adopting the name of partisans) had two goals, the defeat of the Axis and the establishment of a Communist government in their country. To this end their first task was often physically to eliminate any other resistance movement, successfully accomplished in Yugoslavia by Tito and in Albania by Hoxha. In Greece the attempt failed – although it left a legacy of civil war – while in France efforts were stifled by the establishment of a committee directed from London, and by the incorporation of units of the FFI into the regular FFL for the liberation of Alsace and the final defeat of Germany.

Reuther, Walter Philip (1907–70), US trade union leader. He organized the United Automobile Workers (of which he became vice-president in 1942 and president, 1946), was elected vice-president of CIO (1946) and, as president (1952), engineered the merger with AFL (1955). Vice-president of AFL-CIO, Reuther's belief that the trade union movement should support such causes as civil rights (1963) set him against the AFL-CIO president, George Meany, who held that unions should be strictly non-political. Reuther was killed in an air crash (1970).

Revolution of 1905 The uprising in Russia in which opposition groups formed a temporary alliance. The underlying causes of unrest were the refusal of the tsar to introduce constitutional reform, the hardships inflicted on the peasants and workers by tax increases during the Russo-Japanese War and the humiliating defeat of Russia by the Japanese. The catalyst was Bloody Sunday, 22 January, when troops opened fire on a peaceful demonstration. The tsar's promises of constitutional reform failed to quell the wave of strikes, demonstrations and terrorist incidents or the calls for independence within the Russian Empire from Poland, the Baltic provinces, Finland and Transcaucasia. In June the crew of the battleship *Potemkin* seized the vessel and murdered their officers, and indiscipline affected other naval and military units. By October European Russia was gripped by a general strike and at the month's end the tsar was forced to grant a constitution. Lenin and others had hoped to change this 'bourgeois revolution' into a 'socialist revolution', but these concessions satisfied the majority. Isolated groups continued the struggle but they were ruthlessly suppressed.

Reynaud, Paul (1878–1966), French statesman. Republican deputy (1919, 1928–40), he held office (1930–32) and was Daladier's minister of justice and later finance minister (1938) when he put in hand economic reforms and tried to prepare France for war. In March 1940 he became prime minister, took over the ministry of defence, replaced Gamelin by Weygand and agreed joint operations in Norway with Britain, but the French defeat forced his resignation (16 June). Interned by the Vichy authorities, he was arraigned at the Riom trials and deported to Germany (1942–45). Re-elected to the assembly (1946–62), he became finance minister (1948) and deputy premier (1953–54).

Reza Shah Pahlavi (Reza Khan, 1877–1944), shah of Iran. As a general, he led a successful coup (1921), became prime minister (1923), and negotiated an agreement for the withdrawal of Soviet troops (1921) and (1924) of the British. In 1925 he overthrew the last shah of the Qajar dynasty, taking his place as first of the Pahlavis. An absolutist, he aimed to reform and modernize national institutions and to encourage industry and education. His allegedly pro-German tendencies caused Soviet and British troops to occupy the country in 1941. He was deposed in favour of his son Mohammed Reza and exiled to South Africa, where he died.

Rhee, Syngman (Yi Seung Man, 1875–1965), first president of the republic of Korea [South Korea]. Imprisoned (1897–1904) by the Japanese for nationalist activity, on his release, he studied in the United States. Then he returned to Korea (1910) to resume the struggle for independence. He fled to the United States (1912), worked for independence and came to head a government in exile, returning in 1945. He was president from 1945 to 1960. After the Korean War his dictatorial, corrupt and inefficient rule roused widespread opposition. He rigged the 1960 presidential elections in his own favour, but was forced out of office by violent riots and went into exile in Hawaii.

Rhineland According to the Treaty of Versailles (1919) the region was to be placed under military occupation until 1935 and, thereafter, the area 50 km to the east of the River Rhine was to be a demilitarized zone. The German foreign minister, Stresemann, persuaded the French to evacuate the area in 1930. Although Germany had accepted demilitarization in the Treaty of Locarno (1928), in 1936 Hitler sent troops into the Rhineland. Britain and France protested, but took no positive action.

Rhodesia see **Zimbabwe**

Rhodesia and Nyasaland, Federation of An attempt to integrate the peoples, agriculture, industries and economies of Nyasaland (Malawi), Northern Rhodesia (Zambia) and Southern Rhodesia (Zimbabwe) into a single political unit. It came into being in 1953, but foundered on the attitudes of Southern Rhodesia to and discriminatory legislation against black Africans. It was formally dissolved in December 1963 when it became apparent that there could be no mutual agreement on a policy which would satisfy the aspirations of all citizens.

Rhodesia, Northern see **Zambia**

Rhodesia, Southern see **Zimbabwe**

Ribbentrop, Joachim von (1893–1946), German politician. After serving in World War I, he became a wine-merchant and married into the Henkell champagne family. He joined the Nazi party (1932), impressing Hitler with his knowledge of foreign affairs and became ambassador to Britain (1936–38). As foreign minister (1938–45), he helped form the Rome-Berlin Axis and extend it to Japan, and signed the Nazi-Soviet Pact (1939). Vastly unpopular in Britain, he failed to gauge British opinion and this miscalculation helped to precipitate World War II. He was tried at Nuremberg and hanged as a war criminal.

Riga, Treaties of (1) Between Latvia and the USSR (1920), which recognized Latvian independence. (2) Between Poland and the USSR (1921) ending the war between the two states and fixing Poland's eastern frontier. Both treaties were eventually nullified by the consequences of the Nazi-Soviet Pact (1939).

Riom Trial The trial in February 1942 of prominent politicians and soldiers (including Blum, Daladier, Reynaud and Gamelin) by the Vichy regime, which charged them with the responsibility for France's declaration of war in 1939 and its defeat in 1940. The accused, however, so turned the tables that proceedings were halted in April. They were returned to prison and subsequently deported by the Germans.

Röhm, Ernst (1887–1934), German politician. Wounded in World War I, he helped Hitler form the National Socialist Party (1919), recruiting the party's strong-arm men, the SA or Brownshirts. He took part in the Munich Putsch (1923) and was sent to prison briefly after its failure. He went to Bolivia (1925–30), after quarrelling with Hitler over the role of the SA which Röhm wished to retain as his private army. After Hitler came to power (1933), Röhm wanted to absorb the regular army into the SA. Hitler had him shot (with many of his followers) in the Night of the Long Knives (1934).

Rokossovsky, Konstantin Konstantinovich (1896–1968), Soviet marshal. He was born in Warsaw and commissioned in the Imperial Russian Army, but joined the Bolsheviks (1917) and served with the Red Army in the Far East during the civil war. Purged (1937), but rehabilitated (1940), he distinguished himself during World War II at Moscow, Stalingrad and Kursk and 'liberated' Poland, standing by while the Polish Home Army was destroyed in the Warsaw Uprising. Appointed Poland's defence minister (1949) and, from 1952, its deputy premier and a symbol of Soviet domination, he was forced to resign when Gomulka came to power. He returned to the USSR (1956) and was appointed inspector-general in the ministry of defence (1961).

Roman Catholic Church In 1870 the Church ceased to be a temporal power when the Papal States were annexed to the new kingdom of Italy; simultaneously the 1st Vatican Council promulgated the dogma of papal infallibility. Between 1870 and the 2nd Vatican Council (1962) the Church had to adapt itself not only to its own changed circumstances but to those which followed from a general secularization of society. Anticlericalism, which produced the separation of Church and state in various Catholic countries, and the expulsion of religious orders (especially in the field of education) or restrictions upon their activities, degenerated into outright persecution in such countries as Mexico, the USSR and its satellites, China and Vietnam. By no longer being identified with the ruling powers, the Church has been able to stand aloof from both capitalism and socialism, and in the encyclicals of Leo XIII (1891), Pius XI (1931), John XXIII (1961) and Paul VI (1967) to preach social responsibility and social justice and to encourage its application in the formation of Christian Democrat parties (especially since World War II). The concern, too, of Pius XI and Pius XII to establish local hierarchies in what were then colonial territories enabled the Church to distance itself from the colonial powers. While it has been in constant and consistent opposition to atheistic Marxism, its dilemma has been its attitude to equally tyrannous but nominally Christian governments, particularly in Latin America. Priests and religious, in their defence of the poor, have become the victims of right-wing death squads in such countries as Brazil and El Salvador. The danger for the Church has been that in opposing one oppressor they risk – as in Cuba and Nicaragua – introducing another, a danger which liberation theology courts. If the change from temporal to spiritual authority has been made slowly but surely, the exercise of that spiritual authority still has to be determined. The rigid disciplines which had governed the Church until his day, motivated John XXIII to call a council which would bring the Church up to date. If the reforms of Vatican II overstepped the bounds of prudence, and if John Paul II now adopts a more traditional view of church discipline and doctrine, it is to strike a balance and to provide a framework essential for an organization with a worldwide mission.

Romania   A republic of eastern Europe. The nucleus of the country, the principalities of Moldavia and Wallachia, obtained autonomy under Turkish suzerainty at the Congress of Paris (1856). They were united (1861–62) under the rule of John Cuza (deposed in a coup 1866), gained full independence under his successor Carol I (1878) and were proclaimed a kingdom (1881). The monarchy survived internal disorder, foreign interference and a corrupt bureaucracy. Neutral in the first Balkan War, Romania took part in the second to profit territorially from the Bulgarian defeat. In World War I it remained neutral until 1916, when it joined the Allies and was immediately defeated. It declared war again on 9 November 1918 in time to profit from the peace settlement with territorial gains from Austria, Hungary and Russia. In 1919 Romanian troops helped to put down Béla Kun's regime in Hungary. Between the wars Romania formed part of the Little Entente but, geographically and commercially, German influence was bound to predominate over the wartime rapprochement with France. The rise of the Iron Guard made parliamentary government unworkable and King Carol II imposed a dictatorship (1938). In World War II German pressure forced Carol to abdicate (1940) and Antonescu brought Romania firmly into the Axis camp, joining the invasion of the USSR in 1941. German defeats and the appalling loss suffered by Romania allowed Carol's son King Michael to overthrow Antonescu, to make a separate peace with the Soviets (1944) and to declare war on Germany. He was allowed to retain his throne and a pluralist regime until 1947, when he was forced to abdicate. Romania became a people's republic under Gheorghiu-Dej and the full apparatus of the socialist state was imposed. In 1965 his successor Ceauşescu renamed the country a socialist republic in which he maintained an increasingly repressive regime characterized by an exaggerated personality cult, economic failure and stagnation, international debt and the persecution of national minorities (especially Hungarian). His foreign policy has shown considerable independence of the USSR.

Rome, March on   Faced by the threat of civil war, on 29 October 1922 King Victor Emmanuel II invited Mussolini to form a government. Catching the overnight express from Milan, Mussolini arrived in Rome to take office and brought 25,000 of his Blackshirt followers (mainly by rail) to stage a victory rally on 31 October.

Rome, Treaty of   The treaty establishing the Common Market and signed by the original members of the European Community on 25 March 1957, governing the terms on which later applicants were admitted.

Rome-Berlin Axis   see **Axis powers**

Rommel, Erwin   (1891–1944), German soldier. He served in World War I and was an infantry instructor between the wars. His handling of the 7th Panzer Division in the Battle of France (1940) led Hitler to appoint him to command the Axis forces in North Africa after Graziani's defeat by Wavell (1941). His Afrika Korps initially achieved a string of victories until they were held by Auchinleck and defeated by Montgomery at El Alamein (1942). Rommel was recalled before the final German defeat in Tunisia (1943) to command Army Group B in northern France at the time of the Allied landings. On 17 July 1944 he was severely wounded when the RAF machine-gunned his staff car. Believing that he had knowledge of the July Conspiracy, if not actively involved, the Gestapo compelled him to commit suicide in October 1944.

Roosevelt, Franklin Delano   (1882–1945), 32nd president of the United States. A Democrat state senator for New York (1910–13), he became assistant secretary to the Navy under Woodrow Wilson (1913–20). In 1921 he was stricken by poliomyelitis, which left him crippled for the rest of his life. Despite this handicap he re-entered politics, won the Democratic nomination in 1932 and defeated Hoover for the presidency which he held for the rest of his life, being elected for second (1936) and – unique in the 20th century – for third (1940) and fourth (1944) terms. He took office in the depths of the Depression, but his New Deal policy and latterly the rearmament programme restored American self-confidence and the economy. Between the outbreak (1939) of World War II and America's entry (1941) he supported Churchill as closely as he was able through Lend-Lease and the Atlantic Charter. Only with the benefit of hindsight can blame be attached to his trust in Stalin and Chiang Kai-chek, his treatment of de Gaulle and his support for the rapid decolonization of the overseas possessions of his erstwhile allies. He died suddenly and was succeeded by Truman. In March 1905 he had married his distant cousin, **Anna Eleanor Roosevelt** (1884–1962). She assisted him in his political career and was herself a tireless worker for many causes – women's and youth organizations, slum housing and unemployment, and human welfare worldwide. She was US delegate to the UN (1945–53; 1961) and largely instrumental in drawing up the Declaration of Human Rights (1948).

Roosevelt, Theodore (1858–1919), 26th president of the United States. As President McKinley's assistant secretary to the navy (1897), he oversaw preparations for the war with Spain in which he was to win fame with his rough-riders in Cuba (1898). Governor of New York state (1898–1900), he became McKinley's vice-president, succeeding him on his assassination (1901). Although a Republican, he was aware of the need for reform and during his first and second terms (he was elected in 1904) he tackled the scandals of big business, activating anti-trust legislation, refusing the use of federal troops as strike-breakers and defending the natural resources of the United States against greedy over-exploitation. In foreign politics he mediated successfully in the Russo-Japanese War (1906) and was instrumental in calling the Algeciras Conference (1906), but in Latin-American affairs he adopted the 'big stick' policy, specifically over the Panama Canal. In 1908 he temporarily retired from politics to make a world tour. His return caused a split in the Republican Party when the more conservative Taft was preferred as presidential candidate (1912) although Roosevelt gained more votes. The Democrat Wilson was elected.

Rosenberg, Alfred (1893–1946), German politician. He was principal theoretician of the Nazi Party, which he joined in 1919, and editor of the party newspaper (1921). His neo-pagan, racist theories supplied Hitler with a 'basic philosophy and culture'. Rosenberg worked in the foreign office (1933–41) and, having always been a strident anti-Bolshevik, was then appointed minister for the eastern occupied territories. He was condemned for war crimes at Nuremberg and hanged.

Round Table Conferences see **Simon Report**

Rundstedt, Karl Rudolf Gerd von (1875–1953), German soldier. A staff officer in World War I, he helped to rebuild the German army, retiring in 1938. Recalled in 1939, he directed the Polish campaign, the battle of France (1940) and the invasion of the Soviet Union (1941). He resigned in November 1941 when Hitler decided to continue the offensive against Moscow, but was recalled to command German forces in the west (1942). After the Normandy landings he was superseded, but regained Hitler's favour by presiding over the court martial of the July conspirators. He directed the surprise offensive in the Ardennes (1944). He was held prisoner by the British (1945–49) on suspicion of war crimes, but released on grounds of health.

Rusk, David Dean (1909–   ), US secretary of state. He served in southeast Asia in World War II, then entered the diplomatic service (1946), and succeeded Alger Hiss at the UN (1947). As assistant secretary of state for far eastern affairs (1950), he played a major part in Truman's decision to commit US forces in Korea. From 1952–61 Rusk was president of the Rockefeller Foundation. Secretary of state (1950–69) under Kennedy and Johnson, he supported the 1963 Test-Ban Treaty with the USSR, but, believing that force should be met by force, and with freedom of action in far eastern affairs, Rusk bears considerable responsibility for US involvement in Vietnam.

Russia see **Union of Socialist Soviet Republics**

Russo-Finnish War The conflict between Finland and the USSR in 1939–40. Taking advantage of the Nazi-Soviet Pact, the USSR made extensive territorial demands on Finland in September 1939. When these demands were rejected, the USSR alleged that Finland had shelled its troops, denounced the non-aggression pact of 1932 and opened hostilities on 30 November. The Finns put up a stiff resistance, but despite foreign aid and sympathy were forced to capitulate and to cede territories under the peace treaty of March 1940.

Russo-Japanese War The conflict between Russia and Japan in 1904–05. Confident in their ability to defeat the Japanese, the Russians refused to negotiate spheres of influence in Korea and Manchuria where the two nations were rivals. In response the Japanese launched a surprise attack upon Port Arthur (February 1904), capturing the Russian base in January 1905. This was followed by the decisive land battle at Mukden (February-March 1905) and the sea battle at Tsushima (May 1905). These defeats precipitated the Revolution of 1905 in Russia and, after American mediation, peace was concluded by the Treaty of Portsmouth (1905).

S

Sabah see **East Malaysia** under **Malaysia**

Sadat, Anwar al- (1918–81), Egyptian soldier and statesman. He joined the Free Officers Movement and helped Nasser to power in 1952, and as vice president succeeded him (1970). He liberalized the regime, and won prestige from his successes against Israel in the Yom Kippur War (1973). His peace initiative (1977) and the conclusion of a treaty with Israel relieved the Egyptian economy but led to the country's expulsion from the Arab League. He was assassinated by a Muslim fanatic (1981).

St Germain, Treaty of The peace settlement concluded 10 September 1919 between the Allies and Austria under which Austria lost one third of its German-speakers in territories ceded to Italy, Yugoslavia, Czechoslovakia, Poland and Romania, and was forbidden any form of union with Germany.

St Laurent, Louis Stephen (1882–1973), Canadian statesman. Liberal MP (1941), attorney-general (1941–46) and minister for external affairs (1946–48), he succeeded Mackenzie King as prime minister (1948–57). He made Canada a founder member of NATO and engaged the United States in exploiting the economic potential of the St Lawrence Seaway.

Sakharov, Andrei Dimitrievich (1921–), Soviet physicist. He helped to create the Soviet hydrogen bomb. During the 1960s he adopted an anti-nuclear stance and his protests on behalf of peace and against repression in the USSR earned him (1980) a spell of internal exile. On his release he continued to campaign for human rights and is the most prominent Soviet dissident. He was nominated by the Academy of Sciences to the Congress of People's Deputies (1989).

Salan, Raoul Albin Louis (1899–1984), French soldier. He served with the Free French in World War II, in Indo-China (1945–53) and in Algeria where he was C-in-C (1958). Convinced that the Algerian nationalists could have been suppressed, he formed the terrorist OAS and when its revolt against Algerian independence failed in Algiers (1961), he tried to have de Gaulle assassinated (1962). He was imprisoned for treason but pardoned in 1968.

Salazar, Antonio de Oliviera (1889–1970), Portuguese head of state. A professor of economics, he became Marshal Carmona's finance minister

(1928), restoring financial stability and, from 1932, assumed, as prime minister, dictatorial powers to establish (1933) a corporatist state. Although he supported Franco in the Spanish Civil War, Salazar leased the Azores as a base for the Allies in World War II. Colonial wars in Angola and Mozambique drained the prosperity he had given Portugal and the repressive nature of his regime became all the more apparent before his retirement from political life following a stroke (1968).

Sandino, Augusto Cesar (1895–1934), Nicaraguan revolutionary. He joined the Liberal revolution in 1916 and carried his protest against American intervention to undefeated guerrilla warfare (1927–33) against the US Marines. After their withdrawal he was treacherously murdered by Somoza, but became 'patron' of the anti-Somoza forces (Sandinistas) who seized power in Nicaragua (1979).

San Francisco Conference see **United Nations**

Saragat, Giuseppe (1898–), Italian statesman. A socialist opponent of Mussolini, he went into exile until the Italian surrender (1943). As president of the constituent assembly he helped to draw up the republic's constitution (1946). He split the Socialist Party (1947) and as leader of the anti–Communist Democratic Socialists held various government offices before his election as president (1964–71).

Sarawak, see **East Malaysia** under **Malaysia**

Sato, Eisaku (1901–75), Japanese statesman. A Liberal MP (1948), he held various ministerial posts (1952–64) and succeeded Ikeda as premier in 1964. Although he negotiated the return of Okinawa to Japan, the retention by the United States of bases on the island caused such violent anti-American riots that he was forced to resign (1972).

Saudi Arabia Middle Eastern kingdom created (1932) by Ibn Saud of the strict Wahabite sect of Islam. Oil was discovered in 1936 and commercial production by the American company, Aramco, began in 1938, bringing immense wealth and power to the ruling family. Although a member of the Arab League, the country took little part in the Arab-Israeli wars. It provided financial assistance to the Palestinian cause, but its attempts since 1981 to act as a mediator foundered on the hostility of Syria and on the suspicions of other Arab states of Saudi links with the United States. Initially a supporter of the Nasserite revolution, the Saudis' Islamic fundamentalism opposed Arab socialism in the Yemen (1962–70). During the Shah's regime, the Saudis backed Iran against socialist Iraq, but with the advent of the Islamic revolution they changed sides, offering support in the Iran-Iraq conflict. The fear of destabilization by Iran of the Shia minority in Saudi Arabia was highlighted by the serious riots by Iranian pilgrims in Mecca (1979 and 1987).

Savage, Michael Joseph (1872–1940), New Zealand statesman. A trade unionist, he became an MP in 1919 and leader of the Labour Party in 1933, to which he rallied the neglected farming interests. In consequence he won the elections of 1935 and 1938 and became the first Labour prime minister, holding office from 1935 until his sudden death in 1940.

Schacht, Horace Greeley Hjalmar (1877–1970), German financier. At the crisis of German inflation (1923) he substituted the rentenmark, based on the theoretical mortgage value of all land and industry, for the worthless currency. Having stabilized the mark, balanced the budget and negotiated foreign loans under the Dawes Plan, he introduced the reichsmark based on the gold standard. He was president of the Reichsbank (1929–30, when he resigned as an opponent of reparations and during 1933–39, when he resigned as an opponent on financial grounds of Hitler's rearmament programme). He supported the Nazis and served as minister of the economy (1934–37). He was sent to a concentration camp (1944–45) for suspected complicity in the July Conspiracy. He was cleared of war crimes by the Nuremberg tribunal.

Schlieffen Plan The war plan prepared by the chief of the German general staff, General von Schlieffen (1833–1913), to defeat the French by an outflanking move through Holland and Belgium. General von Moltke (1848–1916) modified it, so that in 1914 the German invasion violated only Belgian neutrality. This was a factor in the plan's failure and the subsequent German defeat on the Marne. In 1940 the original plan was implemented and the error of a premature drive on Paris and neglect of the Channel ports was avoided in the victorious battle of France.

Schmidt, Helmut (1918–), German chancellor. He entered the Bundestag as a Social Democrat (1953), becoming party leader (1967). He served as defence (1969) and finance minister (1972) in Willy Brandt's cabinet and succeeded him as chancellor (1974–82).

Schuman, Robert (1886–1963), French statesman. A prewar deputy who escaped from deportation to Germany (1942), he was a member of the assembly (1945–62) and served as premier (1947–48). As foreign minister (1948–53) he laid the foundations of the European Community with the Schuman Plan for the pooling of French and German coal and steel industries, and continued to work for unity as president of the European Movement and in the European Parliament at Strasbourg.

Schusnigg, Kurt von (1897–1977), Austrian chancellor (1934) in succession to Dolfuss who had appointed him minister of justice (1932). He strove to keep the balance between left- and right-wing extremists, but his attempt to prevent the Anschluss by a plebiscite was foiled by Hitler's invasion of Austria (1938). Schusnigg was imprisoned by the Germans until 1945.

Sealion, Operation The code name for the German invasion of England (1940), foiled by the victory of the RAF in the Battle of Britain. Moreover, the German naval C-in-C, Raeder, was unwilling to risk the operation against the strength of the Royal Navy.

Security Council see **United Nations**

Seeckt, Hans von (1866–1936), German soldier. He distinguished himself as a commander on the eastern front in World War I, becoming head of the German army (1920). With Soviet help and under the Treaty of Rapallo he circumvented the Treaty of Versailles in respect of the army's numbers, training and equipment. In 1926 Hindenburg forced his resignation and he later acted as military adviser to Chiang Kai-chek (1934–35).

Sendero Luminoso ('Shining Path'). A Peruvian guerrilla movement. It followed the teachings of Mao Tse-tung and during the 1980s built up a large following among the Andean Indian peasants, financed its operations by alliance with drug traffickers and begun to establish urban cells. It posed an ever-growing threat to the Peruvian government.

Senghor, Leopold Sedar (1906–), first president of Senegal. A major poet, he has been as dominant in the field of francophone African literature as in the political life of French West Africa. He sat as deputy in the French national assembly (1945–58), formed the majority Senegalese political party and, on independence, became the republic's first president (1960–80).

Serbia see **Yugoslavia**

Sèvres, Treaty of Peace treaty imposed on Turkey by the Allies on 10 August 1920 under which, *inter alia*, Greece was granted administrative rights in Asia Minor and the Kurds and Armenians autonomy and independence. It was rejected by Mustafa Kemal Atatürk, whose victory over the Greeks made these provisions a dead letter. See **Lausanne, Treaty of**.

Shamir, Yitzhak (Yitzhak Yzernitshy, 1914–), Israeli statesman. He emigrated from Poland to Palestine (1935), joined the terrorist Irgun Zvai Leumi, and followed Abraham Stern when he formed the Stern Gang (responsible for the murders of Lord Moyne and Count Bernadotte), of which Shamir became operational director. He entered politics in 1973 and after the resignation of Begin succeeded to the leadership of the right-wing Likud Party and to the premiership (1983) which he shared

(1984–88) with the Labour leader Peres (prime minister 1984–86) until the 1988 elections placed him at the head of government.

Sharpeville An African township outside Johannesburg where, on 21 March 1960, security forces opened fire on a demonstration killing 67 and wounding some 200 demonstrators, to provoke the first significant international condemnation of apartheid. The 'Sharpeville six' Africans, found guilty of murder as having 'common purpose' with the mob which killed the deputy mayor of Sharpeville (1985), were reprieved (1988) after prolonged agitation for clemency both at home and abroad.

Shepard, Alan Bartlett, Jr (1923–), US admiral and astronaut. He served at sea in World War II and flew as test pilot. The first American (and second man) to be launched into space (5 May 1961), he commanded the lunar landing mission in 1971.

Shultz, George Pratt (1920–), US secretary of state. A professor of economics, he acted as adviser to three presidents and was Nixon's secretary of labor (1969) and secretary of the treasury (1972–74). In June 1982 he succeeeded Alexander Haig as secretary of state, an office he filled with conspicuous success through the rest of Reagan's terms as president.

Sian Incident The kidnapping in 1936 of Chiang Kai-shek by army officers. He was kept prisoner until, through the negotiations of Chou En-lai, he had agreed to make common cause with the Communists against the Japanese.

Siegfried Line The name borrowed from a World War I defence system and applied to the fortifications along the Franco-German frontier erected (1936–38) by the Germans in response to the Maginot Line.

Sihanouk, Norodom (1922–), Kampuchean prince and political leader. King of Cambodia (1941), he negotiated independence from the French (1953). He abdicated in his father's favour (1955) to become prime minister and to attempt to preserve his country's independence from the North Vietnamese and the United States during the Vietnam war. Overthrown by a CIA-backed coup (1970), he headed a government in exile in Peking until Pol Pot seized power (1975), when he returned to suffer house arrest. Following the Vietnamese invasion (1979), he headed a government in exile and attempted to negotiate a Kampuchean political structure after the Vietnamese withdrawal (1989).

Sikorski, Wladyslaw (1881–1943), Polish soldier and statesman. Chief of general staff (1922), head of state (1922–23) and minister of war (1924–25), he ceased political activity and went into exile in France when Pilsudski seized power (1926). During World War II he became C-in-C of Poles in France and later in the United Kingdom. He was killed in an air crash shortly after the USSR had broken off diplomatic relations over the Katyn massacre.

Simon Report Published in 1930, it contained the findings of the commission chaired by Sir John Simon (1873–1954) recommending increases in responsible government in India, which were developed at the round table conferences (1931–32).

Singapore Asian republic. Purchased by the East India Company in 1819, the island became a crown colony as part of the Straits Settlements (1867–1946). From self–governing colony (1946–59) Singapore became an independent state (1959–63) and then joined Malaysia (1963–65), but left the federation on the grounds of discrimination against the Chinese who form the majority of its population. Under the British, Singapore was developed as an international port and a major base – its easy capture (1942) by the Japanese was the most humiliating defeat suffered in World War II – and it expanded as a financial and trading centre under Lee Kuan Yew, who has led it in his autocratic style from self-government to its present independent prosperity.

Sinn Fein Irish republican political party. Founded by Arthur Griffith (1902), it did not come into its own until the Easter Rising of 1916 and the events leading to the treaty (1921) which created the Irish Free State. Its leader, De Valera, would not accept the terms of the treaty and civil war resulted. From 1927 (when De Valera entered the Dail) until 1938 (when it became the political arm of the IRA) the party was in eclipse, but has come into prominence in its new role since the troubles in Northern Ireland (1969).

Sino-Japanese War Without formal declaration of war, the Japanese used the pretext of a clash between their troops and the Chinese at the Marco Polo Bridge near Peking (7 July 1937) to invade the country. Although they occupied large areas, they encountered stubborn resistance from Mao Tse-tung's Red Armies and the Kuomintang (Nationalist) troops of Chiang Kai-shek who, between them, tied down over a million Japanese troops. The Japanese formally surrendered to Chiang Kai-shek on 9 September 1945.

Six Day War A pre-emptive strike by Israel (5–10 June 1967). It destroyed the Arab air forces on the ground, took East Jerusalem and the West Bank from Jordan and the Golan Heights from Syria, and by the reoccupation of Sinai closed the Suez Canal.

Slansky, Rudolf Salzmann (1901–52), Czech Communist leader. He joined the party (1921) and as its general secretary (1945–51) played a leading part in the coup in which Gottwald seized power (1948). In 1951, in line with Stalin's anti-Semitic purge, he was falsely accused of plotting to overthrow the government and, after a show trial, was hanged with seven other Jewish defendants, including the ex-foreign minister Vladimir Clementis.

Slim, William Joseph (1891–1970, 1st Viscount Slim), British soldier. He served in World War I and commanded British and Indian forces in the Middle East (1940–41). In 1942 he commanded the withdrawal from Burma and, from 1943, with the 14th Army, defeated the Japanese and liberated Mandalay and Rangoon. CIGS (1948–52) and governor-general of Australia (1953–60), he was one of the greatest British commanders in World War II.

Smith, Ian Douglas (1919–), Rhodesian politician. He served in the RAF in World War II and entered Rhodesian (1948) and federation politics (1953), founding the Rhodesian Front party in 1961 and becoming prime minister in 1964. When negotiations with Britain for independence foundered on the issue of white supremacy, he made a unilateral declaration of independence (1965). He suppressed black nationalism within Rhodesia and fought a successful war against Nkomo's and Mugabe's guerrillas. When further talks with Britain finally broke down he declared Rhodesia a republic (1970), but after nine years was forced to accept an interim black government under Bishop Muzorewa. In Robert Mugabe's Zimbabwe Ian Smith led the white Conservative Alliance of Zimbabwe, but his influence was gradually eroded and in 1987 he was suspended for 'racist utterances' while visiting South Africa.

Smuts, Jan Christian (1870–1950), South African statesman. A leader of Boer commandos (1901–02), he later worked with Botha for reconciliation. As minister of defence (1910–19) he repressed a Boer rebellion and directed the campaigns against the Germans in South West and East Africa during World War I. As a member of Lloyd George's war cabinet he took part in the Paris Conference (protesting against the harshness of the peace terms inflicted on Germany). On Botha's death he succeeded him as prime minister (1919–24). Defeated in 1924 by Herzog, he joined him in a coalition as minister of justice (1933) and when Herzog opposed entering World War II, Smuts succeeded him (1939), remaining premier until his defeat by the Nationalists in 1948. By his neglect of domestic policy for international statesmanship – he served in Churchill's war cabinet and was concerned with the formation of both the League of Nations and the UN – he left the way open for apartheid.

Smyrna   Turkish port [Izmir] in Asia Minor. It had a substantial Greek population when allocated to Greece under the Treaty of Sèvres. When the Greeks, encouraged by Lloyd George, invaded Asia Minor (1920) and were routed by the Turks (1922), Smyrna was recaptured and those of its inhabitants who survived the ensuing massacres were forced to emigrate to Greece under the Treaty of Lausanne.

Soares, Mario Alberto Nobre Lopes   (1924–   ), Portuguese statesman. A lawyer exiled (1970–74) by Caetano for his defence of opponents of the regime, he became leader of the Socialist Party (1973) and as foreign minister (1974–75) after the military coup of 1974 negotiated the independence of Portugal's African colonies. He was premier of coalition governments (1976–78, 1983–85) and was elected president in 1986.

Social Democratic Party   A British political movement which was formed in 1981 as a centre party by four former Labour cabinet ministers (Roy Jenkins, Shirley Williams, David Owen and William Rodgers), disavowing the extreme left-wing penetration of their old party. Roy Jenkins was elected leader (1982) and was succeeded by Owen (1983). Success in local elections was not matched on the national scale when fought in alliance with the Liberal Party. In 1988 the Liberal leader suggested a merger of the two parties. Owen rejected it and remained head of a diminished party after many of his followers, led by Jenkins and Williams, joined what became known as the Social and Liberal Democrats.

Socialist parties   Of the 19th century political theorists who looked to a system of common ownership to alleviate the injustices of laissez-faire capitalism, Karl Marx (1818–83) proved the most influential and from his writings a complete system of philosophy was developed. Marx espoused revolutionary socialism, embodied in Communist parties, and in consequence of Lenin's foundation of the 2nd International, evolutionary socialists broke away to form the parties – Socialist, Social Democrat, etc – which from time to time formed pre-World War II popular front governments (France; Spain) or postwar administrations in all western European countries. These postwar Socialist governments (Helmut Schmidt in West Germany, François Mitterand in France, Bettino Craxi in Italy, Felipe Gonzales in Spain) have come to power by abandoning the vestiges of Marxism and by accepting the open market economy.

Solidarity   The free Polish trade union movement born in the Gdansk Lenin Shipyard in 1980 and led by Lech Walesa. It obtained many concessions from the government, but was banned when General Jaruzelski imposed martial law and its leaders were imprisoned (1981). Government action appeared to have suppressed the union and to a degree discredited its leaders, but in the economic and political crisis of 1988 it emerged as the channel for popular discontent and helped negotiate the 1989 political settlement.

Somalia   Republic in the Horn of Africa created by the amalgamation of the former colonies of British and Italian Somaliland into a UN Trust Territory granted independence in 1960. The new state endeavoured to expand to include Somalis in adjacent territories. The French thwarted the incorporation of French Somaliland by referendum; the Kenyans retained their frontier after border clashes; and only in the Ethiopian province of the Ogaden was the struggle continued. After the military coup which brought Mohammed Siyad Barrah to power in 1969, the USSR gave support in return for military facilities, but changed sides with the advent of a Marxist regime in Ethiopia (1977). Ethiopia turned the tables by supporting the anti-government Somali National Movement in northwest Somalia where guerrilla warfare erupted into large-scale fighting in 1987 and 1989.

Somoza   The family which effectively ruled Nicaragua from 1936 until 1979 through command of the National Guard. Anastasio Somoza Garcia (1896–1956) seized power in a coup (1936) and established his dictatorial rule (holding the presidency 1937–47; 1950–56) and enjoying the support of the United States until his assassination (1956). He was succeeded by his son, Luis Somoza Debayle (1922–67; president 1957–63), who relaxed the more repressive aspects of his father's rule but ensured that the family remained in power through his younger brother, Anastasio Somoza Debayle (1925–80; president 1967–72; 1974–79). Like his father he exercised power through command of the National Guard, but his corrupt regime was overthrown by the Sandinistas and he himself assassinated in Paraguay where he had taken refuge.

Soong Mei-ling   (c1897–), Chinese political leader. A member of an influential American-educated Christian merchant family, in 1927 she married Chiang Kai-shek, whom she converted to Christianity and thereafter played an important role in the Kuomintang, by rallying financial and political support in the United States through the notorious China Lobby. Although her influence declined after the Nationalist defeat, the Lobby was able to frustrate for many years any rapprochement between the United States and Communist China.

Souvanouvong, Prince   (c1909–), Laotian president. He joined the nationalist movement after World War II, founding the Communist Pathet Lao (1950) which fought first the French and then the neutralist government of his half-brother, Prince Souvanna Phouma (1901–84).

Allied to the North Vietnamese, when the latter took over in Vietnam and Cambodia (1975), the Pathet Lao assumed power, abolished the monarchy and made the prince president of the Lao People's Democratic Republic.

South Africa, Republic of (1) **Union of South Africa,** formed in 1910 after the Boer War, comprised the old Boer republics and the British colonies. Its first prime minister, Botha, was an advocate of co-operation between British and Afrikaaners who supported Britain in World War I. He was succeeded by Smuts, who lost power in 1924 to Herzog, a Nationalist who curtailed the rights of non-whites. Smuts joined him in coalition (1934) but succeeded him in 1939 when he opposed South Africa's entry into World War II, in which its forces were to distinguish themselves. In 1948 he was defeated and the Nationalists came to power and imposed their system of apartheid.

(2) **Republic of South Africa.** In 1960 a referendum of white voters narrowly decided to leave the Commonwealth and the independent republic was proclaimed on 31 May 1961. Its domestic policies have met with international disapproval and protest expressed in bans on sporting and cultural links with the republic and demands for economic sanctions. Over a period this has led to the withdrawal of multinational companies from South Africa and in consequence some relaxation of the harsher provisions of apartheid. Its discriminations against non-whites have provoked protest and repression in the riots at Sharpeville and Soweto and in a campaign of sabotage by the African National Congress. Banned within the republic, the ANC has operated from neighbouring states, against which South Africa has responded by its support for Ian Smith's regime in Rhodesia, and the UNITA and Renamo guerrillas operating against the Communist governments of Angola and Mozambique. South African policy has, however, always been directed towards establishing a modus vivendi with its black neighbours and moves in conjunction with the UN, the United States and the USSR to settle the Namibian and Angolan problems (1988) were followed by approaches towards Mozambique and the possibility of talks with the ANC.

South East Asia Treaty Organization (SEATO) A mutual security pact signed at Manila in 1954 by Australia, France, New Zealand, Pakistan, the Philippines, Thailand, Britain and the United States. Members including France and Britain ignored its provisions in relation to Vietnam and, Pakistan having withdrawn in 1973 and France in 1974, it was decided to phase out the organization in 1975.

South Tirol see **Trentino-Alto-Adige**

South West Africa see **Namibia**

Soweto A black township on the outskirts of Johannesburg in which riots broke out on 16 June 1976 against the compulsory teaching of Afrikaans in schools. In three days of violence nearly 250 non-whites were killed and some 1100 injured. The anniversaries have regularly produced violent protest.

Spaak, Paul Henri Charles (1899–1972), Belgian prime minister. A socialist, elected deputy in 1932, he became minister of transport in 1935 and premier of a coalition government (1938–39). Although he was later twice premier (1946; 1947–49), he was an outstanding foreign minister (1938–49, 1954–57 and 1961–66), helping to form the Benelux Union and presiding over the UN Assembly (1946). He made a great contribution to Europe's unity as president of the consultative assembly of the Council of Europe (1949–51) and to its defence as secretary-general of NATO (1957–61).

space flight The 'space race' began after World War II, the USSR placing the first satellite in orbit (Sputnik 1: 4 October 1957), and conducting the first manned space flight (Vostok 1 with Yuri Gagarin: 8 April 1961). Although the USSR was the first to transmit TV pictures and to land instruments on the moon (Luna series 1959–66), the United States was the first to land men, in the Apollo 11 (Neil Armstrong: 21 July 1969). Subsequently the Soviets seemed to have concentrated upon establishing space stations (Salyut programme), while NASA, for the United States, developed space shuttles, starting with Columbia (April 1981) and continuing despite the disaster to Challenger (1986). Both the USSR and the United States have sent probes to Mars, Venus and Saturn and both have investigated space-launched missiles, while Reagan's Strategic Defence Initiative envisaged an invulnerable satellite defence system for the United States.

Spain A kingdom of southwestern Europe. **(1) Bourbon restoration**. After a short-lived republic (1873–74), the Bourbons were restored in the person of Alfonso XII. He was succeeded in 1886 by his son Alfonso XIII who resigned (but did not abdicate) in 1931. During his reign there was considerable industrial unrest, anarchist outrage and a rise in anti-clericalism. Spain remained neutral in World War I, but suffered humiliating defeats in Morocco from Abd el–Krim and, in response to Catalan separatism (1923), Primo de Rivera instituted his dictatorship.

(2) Second Republic. In 1930 Prima de Rivera was overthrown, the king resigned and Zamora became president. Domestic problems increased in scale and violence and the election of a Popular Front government in 1936 provoked an army mutiny. The Nationalist forces were led by Franco (with German and Italian support), the Loyalists receiving help from the USSR and from left-wing sympathizers throughout the world in the International Brigades.

(3) **Nationalist government**. The republic fell with the loss of Barcelona (January) and the fall of Madrid (March 1939) and the flight of the government and its supporters. Franco became Caudillo. Although he sent the Blue Division to fight for the Axis on the Russian front, he kept Spain neutral in World War II and broke Spain's postwar diplomatic ostracism through leasing Spanish bases to the United States.

(4) **Constitutional monarchy**. In 1969 Franco named Prince Juan Carlos as his successor and he became king on the Caudillo's death (1975). The king personally suppressed a right-wing coup attempt in 1981 and Spain has moved to a parliamentary democracy under a socialist premier (1982). Major problems inherited from Franco have been the continuing dispute with Britain over Gibraltar and the failure to end the long campaign of murder and terror by the Basque separatist movement, ETA.

Spartakist Rising The insurrection by the Spartakist Group in Germany, which comprised socialists who broke with the Social Democrats over the party's attitude to World War I and, led by Karl Liebknecht and Rosa Luxemburg (both b.1871), transformed themselves into the German Communist Party. They instigated a general strike and revolt in Berlin (January 1919) which was suppressed and both Liebknecht and Luxemburg were murdered.

Spiegel affair In 1962 the west German magazine *Der Spiegel* published an article critical of the German army, the Bundeswehr. The defence minister, Franz Josef Strauss, had the deputy editor and the author of the article tried for treason. They were acquitted. Strauss's abuse of his powers permanently damaged his political career and the affair forced the resignation of Chancellor Adenauer in the following year.

Sri Lanka Asian republic known until 1972 as Ceylon. In 1795 Britain occupied the original Dutch settlements, declaring the island a Crown Colony (1798) and bringing it completely under British control in 1815. Concessions to the independence movement which had come into being during World War I were made in the constitutions of 1931 and 1946, before the island obtained full independence within the Commonwealth in 1948. As an independent republic the island has been riven by the demands of the Tamil minority for parity with the Singhalese, which expressed themselves in rioting in 1958 and have developed in the 1980s

– following Mrs Badaranaike's pro-Singhalese policy (1970–77) – into separatist demands for a Tamil state. These were backed by terrorist outrages and guerrilla warfare by the Tamil Tigers, whose power was suppressed but not destroyed by the despatch of an Indian peacekeeping force (1987). The other divisive force has been the Marxist JVP whose rebellion was crushed in 1971 but who emerged in 1988 to attempt in Singhalese areas (as the separatists did in Tamil areas) to disrupt the presidential elections. Despite considerable violence these resulted in the election of the prime minister, Ranasinghe Premadasa. There was renewed violence early in 1989 in a bloody but unsuccessful effort to halt parliamentary elections.

Stalin (Josef Vissarionovich Djugashvili, 1879–1953), Soviet dictator. Intended by his mother for the Orthodox priesthood, he was appointed by Lenin to the Bolshevik central committee (1912), after distinguishing himself as a revolutionary in Georgia and twice escaping from exile. Freed from deportation (1913–17) by the revolution of March 1917, he played a subordinate role in the October revolution but as a commissar played a notable part in the defence of Tsaritsin (Stalingrad) against the Whites (1918). In 1921 he was elected to the key post of secretary-general to the central committee and after Lenin's death manipulated his colleagues to obtain the banishment of Trotsky (1929) and achieve supreme power. This he exercised with complete brutality. Forced industrialization and the collectivization of agriculture – 'socialism in one country' – employed deportation and deliberately induced famine. In the 'great terror' Stalin eliminated his rivals after show trials in Moscow (1936–38) and 'purged' the army and the party. Misplaced confidence in Hitler's undertakings in the Nazi-Soviet Pact (1939) almost lost him the war when the Germans invaded the USSR, but with victory and the imposition of Communist rule on eastern Europe, Stalin's personality cult reached megalomania. He continued his terror policy in the Leningrad affair and in the anti-Semitic 'doctors' plot and before his death in 1953 was responsible for the deaths of between 20 (western estimates) and 12 million (Soviet admissions) of his fellow citizens or of deportees from eastern Europe and the Baltic republics by execution or by the inhuman regime of his concentration camps (gulags), in which many millions more suffered and survived.

Stauffenberg, Claus Schenk von (1907–44), German soldier. Severely wounded in Tunisia (1943), as a staff colonel he joined the July conspiracy and deposited the bomb intended to kill Hitler in his East Prussian HQ. The attempt failed and he was arrested and shot the same evening.

Stern Gang   see under **Shamir, Yitzhak**

Stolypin, Piotr Arkadevich   (1862–1911), Russian statesman. As Tsar Nicholas's prime minister and minister of the interior (1906–11) he attempted to create a loyal peasantry by his land reforms and policy of colonizing Siberia. In consequence he alienated the right while failing to win over the liberals whom he had shocked by his ruthless suppression of terrorism and agrarian revolt. He was assassinated by a double agent in the secret police.

Strategic Arms Limitations Talks (SALT)   see under **disarmament**

Strategic Defence Initiative (Star Wars Programme)   see under **space flight**

Strauss, Franz Josef   (1915–88), West German statesman. A Christian Social Union member of the Bundestag (1947–78), the sister party of Adenauer's Christian Democrats, he served as minister for nuclear issues (1955–56) and as minister of defence (1956–62) where he had the unpopular task of re-forming a German army. Despite his many gifts his impulsive behaviour in the *Spiegel* affair seriously affected his political career and, although he served as finance minister (1966–69), he failed in a bid to be elected chancellor (1980) and had to be content with the office of prime minister in his native Bavaria (1978–88). This flawed giant was one of the creators of the German Federal Republic.

Stresa conference   A meeting between the prime ministers and foreign ministers of France, Italy and Britain during 11–14 April 1935 where agreement was reached to oppose any further violation of the Treaty of Versailles after Germany had reintroduced conscription. The alliance foundered on the Italian invasion of Ethiopia six months later and Mussolini then formed the Rome-Berlin Axis (1936). Earlier, in 1932 a 16-nation economic conference had also been held at Stresa.

Stresemann, Gustav   (1878–1929), German statesman. He became an MP in 1907 and founded the German People's Party in 1918; as chancellor (1923) and as foreign minister (1923–29) he worked to reconcile Germany with its victors. His acceptance of the Dawes (1924) and Young (1929) Plans, his part in the Locarno Pact (1925) and his signature of the Kellog-Briand Pact (1928) succeeded in restoring Germany to the world community with its entry into the League of Nations (1926).

Strijdom, Johannes Gerhardus   (1893–1958), South African prime minister. Nationalist MP (1929–58), from 1934 he led the extreme Afrikaaner wing and as prime minister (1954–58) was an enthusiastic exponent of apartheid. His disenfranchisement of the Cape Coloured voters, the Group Areas Act, extension of apartheid to the universities, attempts to crush all liberal and black opposition and contempt for world opinion marked him from his predecessor, Malan, and his successor, Verwoerd.

Sudan African republic. The spread of Anglo-Egyptian influence southwards into the Sudan, checked by the revolt of the Mahdi (1881) and the death of General Gordon at Khartoum (1885), was completed by Kitchener's victory at Omdurman (1898) and an Anglo–Egyptian condominion was established. Under pressure for independence after World War II a legislative assembly was established and elections were held (1948) which brought to power the Independence Party. Independence was granted in 1956, but the predominantly Christian and animist south, fearing Muslim domination by the north, had risen in a revolt (1955) which lasted until 1972 when President Nimeiry granted the province semi-autonomy. When in 1983 the president imposed sharia law on the whole country, the south once again rose in revolt and an increasingly bitter war was waged by Colonel John Garang's Sudan People's Liberation Army. Within five years trade and agriculture had ceased and much of the population, reduced by starvation, had fled north or to Ethiopia. The Democratic Union Party, the moderate group in the civilian government which had replaced Nimeiry's regime in 1986, held talks with the the SPLA in 1988, but the prime minister, under the influence of the fundamentalist National Islamic Front, at first refused to accept the agreement. Under army pressure a new government withdrew this refusal and formal talks were opened (1989).

Sudetenland The German-speaking region of northern Bohemia which was transferred from Austro-Hungarian rule to Czechoslovakia by the Treaty of St Germain. After Hitler came to power in Germany he financed Henlein's Sudeten-German Party to agitate against Czech rule and to press for union with Germany, an aim achieved by the Munich Agreement (1938). After World War II the Czechs recovered the area and the German population was expelled.

Suez Canal crisis Under an Anglo-Egyptian agreement of 1954 Britain agreed to withdraw its troops from the Canal Zone, which they had guarded since 1882, by 13 June 1956. On 26 July Nasser nationalized the canal in response to the withdrawal of western financial backing for the building of the Aswan dam. There were half-hearted negotiations while the British and French governments colluded with Israel. Israeli forces launched an attack in Sinai (29 October). An Anglo-French ultimatum called on both sides to cease military action and, when Egypt rejected this, Anglo-French aircraft attacked Egyptian bases (31 October) and their paratroops were dropped round Port Said (5 November). The collapse of sterling and the hostility of the United States put paid to the operation. The career of the British premier, Eden, was ended by this humiliation, and Nasser's prestige in the Arab world correspondingly enhanced.

suffragettes see under **women's rights**

Suharto (1921–), Indonesian soldier and president who fought with the Japanese during World War II and with the anti-Dutch guerrillas (1945–49). As chief of staff (1965) he crushed an alleged pro-Chinese Communist plot in which hundreds of thousands of suspected left-wingers were slaughtered. From 1966 he assumed more and more of President Sukarno's powers until he finally supplanted him and was elected president in 1968 (re-elected 1971, 1977, 1983). Suharto reversed Sukarno's policies, strengthening political and economic ties with the west and retained power despite the corruption of his administration and its violation of human rights, especially since the Indonesian occupation of Portuguese Timor (1975).

Sukarno (1901–70), Indonesian statesman. He founded the Indonesian independence movement (1927) and was imprisoned and exiled by the Dutch for his activities. During World War II he co-operated with the Japanese and on their surrender to the Allies declared Indonesian independence (1945), which was not achieved until protracted guerrilla warfare forced the Netherlands into recognition (1950). As president, Sukarno's policy of 'guided democracy' masked an incompetent dictatorship which destroyed the country's prosperity, drew it increasingly within the the Sino-Soviet and (after 1956) Chinese orbit and involved it in a pointless armed confrontation with Malaysia (1963–65). In 1965 the army crushed an alleged Communist plot and its commander, General Suharto, eased Sukarno from power.

Sun Yat-sen (1866–1925), Chinese revolutionary. After the failure of a revolt against the Manchus (1895) Sun escaped abroad, founding the Chinese United League on the principles of nationalism, democracy and socialism which was later developed into the Kuomintang. Summoned to China by the successful 1911 revolution, he resigned the office of president of the new republic to which he had been elected (1912) to the warlord Yuan Shih-kai (1859–1916). Having failed in an attempt to overthrow Yuan, he escaped to Japan, returning to Canton in 1917 where he was proclaimed president of a nationalist government. He organized the Kuomintang on Soviet lines, allied with the Chinese Communist party, set up the Whampao Military Academy and received Soviet help to organize the Northern Expedition designed to overthrow the Peking warlords. However, he died of cancer before Chiang Kai-shek was able to achieve this final objective on his behalf.

Sykes-Picot Agreement A secret agreement on behalf of the British and French governments through their respective representatives, Sir Mark Sykes and Georges Picot, signed on 16 May 1916. It ran clean counter to the promises made to Arab leaders by T. E. Lawrence in that it defined the countries respective spheres of interest in the non-Turkish provinces of the Ottoman Empire and, in the event of its defeat, granted Syria and the Lebanon to France. It has given rise to continued Arab suspicion of Britain's Middle East policy.

Syria Middle East republic. A province of the Ottoman Empire, it was allocated under the Sykes-Picot Agreement to the French who, after expelling Feisal (1920), received a League of Nations mandate. During 1925–27 there were serious revolts against the French presence and Syrian aspirations were not satisfied by the 1930 constitution. Accordingly, under agreement reached in 1936, Syria was to be granted autonomy. When the French failed to implement the terms of the treaty and ceded Alexandretta to Turkey so serious a situation arose that the constitution was suspended. During World War II British, Dominion and Free French forces occupied Syria when the Vichy regime appeared on the point of granting the Axis powers bases in the country and in 1944 the Free French conceded independence. When there was delay in implementing the agreement, fighting broke out (1945) and Franco-British forces were evacuated under UN supervision (1946). Syrian defeat in the Arab-Israeli war (1948) discredited the government and a series of coups produced a military dictatorship (1951–54). To forestall the tendency of its left-wing members towards a Soviet alliance, a new civilian government joined Egypt to form the United Arab Republic (1958). Three years later the UAR foundered and a series of coups eventually brought a Ba'ath Socialist military government to power (1963). But the Ba'ath party was itself divided and, after Syria's defeat in the Six Day War (1967), General Hafiz al-Assad of the nationalist faction seized power (1970) and has ruled Syria ever since. His policy has been dictated by the Syrian aim of dominating the Lebanon by its control of the Shia Amal militia and of influencing the Palestinian question by support of the extremist groups opposed to the more moderate policy of the PLO, while at the same time continuing its inveterate feud with the Iraq Ba'athists.

T

Taft, William Howard (1857–1930), 27th president of the United States. A lawyer, he was the first American civil governor of the Philippines (1901–04) and was Theodore Roosevelt's secretary of war (1904–08). In 1908 he won the presidential election for the Republicans, but lost to Woodrow Wilson in 1912 after Roosevelt had split the Republicans. In 1921 Harding appointed him chief justice of the US Supreme Court, an office which he filled with distinction until his death.

Taiwan [Portuguese name **Formosa**] An island annexed by Japan (1895) and returned to China (1945) which became the refuge of the defeated Chinese Nationalists (1950). Here Chiang Kai-shek established the Republic of China which until 1971 occupied a seat on the UN security council, claiming to be the legitimate Chinese government. During 1954–78, the United States was committed to the defence of the island, but following the US rapprochement with the People's Republic and the death of Chiang Kai-shek (1975), such support was gradually withdrawn. The island was governed by the Kuomintang under martial law imposed in 1949 and lifted only in 1987, shortly before the death of Chiang's son and successor, Chiang Ching-kuo (c1909–88), in a programme of political reform aimed to match the economic prosperity enjoyed by the island. Tension between the two Chinas was eased and a delegation visited Peking in May 1989.

Tanaka, Kakuei (1918–), Japanese prime minister. A wealthy building contractor, he became a Liberal Democratic deputy in 1947, minister of finance (1962–64) and of international trade and industry (1964–72), and prime minister (1972–74). Forced to resign because of a scandal over party political contributions, he was indicted for accepting bribes in the Lockheed scandal (1976) and, although convicted (1983), still retained influence in his party.

Tanganyika see under **Tanzania**

Tanzania East African republic formed in 1964 by the union of the island of Zanzibar with the mainland republic of Tanganyika, following a left-wing coup which overthrew the elected government. Tanganyika, formerly German East Africa, became a League of Nations mandate under that name after World War I. The British administration developed the economy and led the country towards independence (1961), the prime minister, Julius Nyerere, becoming the first president of the republic (1962) and retaining the office after the creation of Tanzania. His vice president was Sheikh Abeid Karume (1905–72), chairman of the Zanzibar Revolutionary Council, whose increasingly authoritarian rule on the island led to his assassination. In 1985 Nyerere resigned the presidency, but retained chairmanship of the ruling Revolutionary Party.

Tariff Reform League   see **Imperial Preference**

Teapot Dome scandal   In 1921 President Harding transferred from the US navy to the interior department the Teapot Dome and Elk Hill oilfields (reserved for the US navy). The secretary of the interior, Albert Fall (1861–1944), was convicted of accepting bribes (1929) when, after the death of Harding, it was revealed that he had accepted loans from two oil developers (acquitted of of bribing the secretary) in return for leases on the fields.

Tedder, Arthur William   (1890–1967, 1st Baron Tedder), British air chief marshal. He transferred from the infantry to the RFC during World War I and as commander of the Middle East air forces (1940–43) during World War II contributed to the victories in North Africa and to the successful invasions of Sicily and Italy. Appointed Eisenhower's deputy in 1943, he ensured the contribution of the Tactical Air Force to victory in Europe (1943–45).

Tehran Conference   The meeting (28 November–1 December 1943) between Stalin, Roosevelt and Churchill at which agreement was reached on operations against Germany and the USSR pledged support against Japan following the German defeat.

Templer, Sir Gerald Walter Robert   (1898–1979), British military commander. He served in both world wars and in Iraq (1919–21) and Palestine (1936). As high commissioner and director of operations, Federation of Malaya (1952–54), he turned the tide of Communist insurrection and initiated the policies which were to end the emergency. He was chief of the imperial general staff (1955–58).

Tereshkova, Valentina Vladimirovna   (1937–   ), Soviet cosmonaut. The first woman in space (Vostok VI, 16 June 1963), she proved women's abilities as cosmonauts. She was head of the Soviet Women's Committee (1968) and a member of the Praesidium of the Supreme Soviet (1974).

Test Ban Treaty   see under **disarmament**

Thailand   [known as **Siam**, 1781–1939] Southeast Asian kingdom. Thailand maintained its independence throughout the 19th century as a buffer between the British (Burma and Malaya) and the French (Indo-China). The first parliamentary constitution was granted in 1934. In 1938 Pibul Songgram became prime minister and remained in power until 1957. His successors maintained his pro-American stance and under the SEATO Treaty (1954) supported the United States in the Vietnam war with troops and base facilities. Communist guerrilla activities in the north and south of the country, which had posed serious problems in the 1970s, were virtually extinguished by 1987 and the withdrawal of Vietnamese forces from Kampuchea (1988) eased tensions on the border and offered a solution to the problem of the Kampuchean refugees.

Thälmann, Ernst (1886–1944), German Communist. A trade unionist, he became a Communist deputy in 1924 and as party secretary twice stood against Hindenburg in presidential elections. Having refused to form a popular front with the Social Democrats, when the Nazis came to power (1933) he was arrested and imprisoned. Ten years later he was transferred to Buchenwald where he died.

Thant, U (1909–74), Burmese diplomat. He was Burma's permanent representative at the UN (1953–61), when he was elected acting secretary-general of the UN on the death of Dag Hammarskjold and confirmed in office (1962). His highly successful first term included solutions to the Cuban missile crisis (1962), settlement of the civil war in Zaïre (1963), the despatch of a UN peace-keeping force to Cyprus (1964) and the cease-fire in the Indo-Pakistan War (1965), but his second term was marred by war in Vietnam and the Middle East and further conflict between India and Pakistan. In 1972 he declined a third term.

Thatcher, Margaret (née Roberts, 1925–), British prime minister. Conservative MP (from 1959) and minister of education (1970–74) under Edward Heath, she succeeded him as leader of the Conservative Party in 1975. She won the 1979 election to become Britain's first woman premier and was re-elected in 1983 and 1987 with substantial majorities. She resolved the problems of Zimbabwe (1979), handled the Falklands Crisis (1982) with resolution and courage, reasserted British interests in the European Community and established herself as a European spokeswoman in her dealings with Reagan and Gorbachov. At home she reduced inflation and revived the economy after the stagnation of the last Labour administration. However, lack of any effective parliamentary opposition allowed the government to adopt an increasingly authoritarian tone and to apply its monetarist policies with a not always appropriate rigidity in its privatization of public utilities and reform of the NHS.

Thieu, Nguyen Van (1923–), Vietnamese soldier and politician. He joined the Viet Minh (1945) but left them to serve in the French army (1946–54) and then in that of South Vietnam, in which he rose to divisional commander (1963). A reluctant member of the junta which overthrew President Diem (1963), he was elected president (1967) and when his increasingly authoritarian and corrupt regime collapsed on the withdrawal of US support (1975), he escaped to exile abroad.

Thorez, Maurice (1900–64), French Communist leader. A miner, he was a founder-member of the French Communist Party in 1920 and became secretary-general in 1930. As deputy (1932) he later worked to to form the Popular Front government (1936). Called up in 1939, he made his way to Moscow (where he spent the war) and was sentenced to death as a deserter (amnestied in 1944). When the Communists gained the largest proportion of votes in the 1945 and 1946 French elections he served as vice-premier (1946–47) and then went into opposition. A hard-line Stalinist, his subservience to the Soviet line lost the party much support. He was succeeded as secretary-general shortly before his death.

Tibet Mountainous country between India and China. Its spiritual ruler, the Dalai Lama, had been the nominal vassal of the Chinese since 1715, but from c1900 had enjoyed virtual independence until 1950 when the Chinese invaded and imposed a Communist regime. Fears that they would kidnap the Dalai Lama prompted the Tibetans to revolt and the Dalai Lama to flee to India (1959). From that date Chinese rule imposed collectivization (with a three-year famine, 1959–62), entailing mass immigration of Chinese, reducing the Tibetans to second-class citizens and, especially during the Cultural Revolution, the systematic destruction of Buddhist monasteries and shrines and the murder of monks and nuns in concentration camps. Although since 1985 more overt oppression has been alleviated, basic grievances remain and produced violent disturbances and more violent repression in the capital, Lhasa, in 1988–89.

Tirpitz, Alfred von (1849–1930), German grand admiral. As navy minister (1897–1916) he was responsible for the creation of the German high seas fleet and for the arms race with Britain. When the kaiser refused to commit the fleet to action, Tirpitz advocated unrestricted submarine warfare, resigning when this was opposed by Bethmann-Hollweg. From 1924–28 he sat in the Reichstag as a Nationalist deputy.

Tito (Josip Broz, 1892–1980), Yugoslav Communist leader. A Croat, he was taken prisoner by the Russians in World War I but escaped to join the Red Army and returned to Yugoslavia in 1920 to work for the Communist Party. After imprisonment (1928–34), he went to the USSR, reorganized the Yugoslav Communist Party (1937) and, after the German invasion in 1941, returned to lead the Communist partisans in eliminating Mihajlovic's Chetnik resistance movement and in defeating the occupying forces and their Croat auxillaries. In 1945 he took control of the government, abolished the monarchy and made Yugoslavia a federal republic. He liquidated the opposition, but was denounced by Stalin as a deviationist (1948) and expelled from Cominform. He was now able to exert influence (along with Nehru and Nasser) among the nonaligned nations and, without in any way modifying the repressive nature of his rule, to open a dialogue with the west and to introduce a slightly more liberal economic regime.

Togliatti, Palmiro (1893–1964), Italian Communist leader. A lawyer and founder member of the Italian Communist Party (1921), he took refuge in the USSR (1926) after Mussolini came to power. He worked for Comintern and acted as political commissar in Spain during the Civil War (1937–39). In 1944 he returned as head of the Italian Communist Party, holding ministerial office between 1944–46. When Communists were excluded from government he led the left-wing opposition as head of the largest Communist Party in the west. He was also its most influential leader, advocating greater independence for national parties and sowing the seed of Euro-Communism.

Togo, Heihachiro (1846–1934), Japanese admiral. One of the founders of Japanese naval power, he studied in England (1871–78), served in the Sino-Japanese War (1895) and defeated the Russian Pacific fleet at Port Arthur (1904) and Baltic fleet at Tsushima (1905) during the Russo-Japanese War. He was subsequently chief of naval staff and a member of the supreme war council.

Tojo, Hideki (1884–1948), Japanese general and statesman. He led the militarist party from 1931, becoming war minister (1940) and prime minister (1941). He authorized the attack on Pearl Harbor (1941) and was Japan's wartime dictator until American successes moved the Emperor Hirohito to force his resignation (1944). After the Japanese surrender he attempted suicide but was tried and executed as a war criminal.

Tonkin Gulf resolution Following attacks by North Vietnamese torpedo boats on US destroyers in the Gulf of Tonkin, the Congress resolution of 7 August 1964 authorized the administration to take all necessary action to defend the United States and its SEATO allies. Presidents Johnson and Nixon used the resolution to involve the United States in full-scale war in Vietnam.

Trades Union Congress (TUC) With the growth of trade unionism in

Britain from the 1850s the TUC was formed in 1868. Individual unions affiliated to it and it provided a forum for policy discussion among unions and a channel of communication between organized labour and elected government. The TUC embodied the growth of the movement up to and during World War I and thanks to such unionists as Ernest Bevin, and more particularly to its secretary-general from 1926–47, Walter Citrine (1887–1983, 1st Baron Citrine), was able to restore the prestige of the movement after the disastrous defeat it had suffered in the General Strike (1926). Since the movement's political levy provided the bulk of the Labour Party's finances, the TUC was able to play an increasingly important role in formulating the social policy of postwar Labour governments and in modifying that of the Conservatives. The growth of trade union power and the privileged position which it enjoyed in law led to calls for reform. In 1969 the Labour government issued the White Paper, *In Place of Strife*, but the proposals were stifled by TUC opposition. The introduction by the Conservatives of the Industrial Relations Bill (1971) provoked widespread industrial unrest, the TUC expelling 20 unions who registered under the provisions of the bill (1973). The return of the Labour government in 1974 marked the high point of TUC power. Under the so-called Social Contract the TUC agreed to a policy of wage control in return for the repeal of the Industrial Relations Bill and no further restriction of union rights. This misuse of power in pursuit of sectional interests allowed the Conservatives continuously to restrict the rights of trades unionists since the 1980 Employment Act. The TUC has so far failed to respond to the very different industrial world created by the Thatcherite economic revival except by the negative refusal of co-operation. This provides the government with a justification for continuing to ignore the voice of organized labour.

Transjordan see **Jordan**

Transkei A Black African homeland ('Bantustan') within South Africa. In 1963 it was separated from Cape Province and granted semi-autonomy, the decisions of its assembly being subject to the veto of the president of South Africa. In 1976 it was granted formal independence. Transkei was the first of nine projected homelands, but their independence has been ignored by the international community.

Trenchard, Hugh Montague (1873–1956, 1st Viscount Trenchard), British marshal of the RAF. As an infantry officer he saw service in India and during the Boer War. Joining the RFC in 1912, during World War I he commanded it in France (1915–18). As an advocate of an independent air force he became the 'Father of the RAF' when it was created in 1918. He was chief of air staff (1921–29) and after his retirement became a reforming commissioner of the Metropolitan Police (1931–35).

Trentino-Alto-Adige A region in northeast Italy comprising the provinces of Trento and Bolzano and ruled by Austria until 1866. Trento then passed to Italy and Austria began a policy of Germanization in Bolzano which roused the Italian minority. When, by the Treaty of St Germain, Bolzano came under Italian rule a similar policy of Italianization aroused the German-speaking population. The long history of racial disharmony brought an agreement in 1971 granting the province considerable autonomy, but minor conflicts continued.

Trianon, Treaty of Peace treaty with Hungary signed 4 June 1920 under which the new republic was forced to pay reparations, was restricted as to the size of its army and lost over two-thirds of the territory of the prewar kingdom of Hungary. While many of the lost lands were non-Magyar, the Hungarian population of Transylvania (ceded to Romania) suffered as a minority and as late as 1988 their treatment caused resentment and formal protests by the Hungarian government.

Tripartite Pact Treaty signed between Germany, Italy and Japan (27 September 1940) pledging mutual assistance between the Axis powers and Japan. Subsequently Hitler compelled his European allies to adhere to the pact.

Triple Alliance An alliance formed by Germany, Austria-Hungary and Italy in 1882 and to which Romania adhered (1883). Diplomatic efforts by the Triple Entente (*see below*) succeeded in detaching Italy and Romania from this alliance in World War I.

Triple Entente The diplomatic counterpoise to the Triple Alliance, formed by Britain, France and Imperial Russia. In 1904 France (already in alliance with Russia) signed the Treaty of London (the Entente Cordiale) and in 1907, Britain and Russia settled their differences in Asia and the Triple Entente came into being.

Trotsky, Leon (Lev Davidovich Bronstein, 1879–1940), Russian revolutionary. He served terms of imprisonment in Russia (1898, 1905) from which he escaped to engage in revolutionary activity in Europe, but returned in the revolutions of 1905 and 1917 to head the St Petersburg/ Petrograd soviets. As commissar for foreign affairs he resigned over the Brest-Litovsk Treaty to become a brilliantly successful commissar for war (1918). He became Stalin's chief rival for the succession to Lenin, but Stalin used his position as secretary-general to expel Trotsky from the party (1927) and then to banish him (1929). Exiled first to Turkey and then to Norway, Trotsky was murdered by one of Stalin's agents in his final home in Mexico City. As an advocate of permanent revolution he has been the inspiration of many violent Marxist revolutionary splinter groups.

Trudeau, Pierre Elliott (1919–), Canadian prime minister. A lawyer specializing in labour and civil rights cases, he became a Liberal MP in 1965. He served as minister of justice (1967–68) under Lester Pearson and succeeded him as prime minister (1968). In that year he won a landslide electoral victory. A strong federalist, he suppressed Quebec separatism (1970) but lost votes in 1972 and headed a minority government until regaining a majority in 1974. Defeated in 1979, he returned to power in 1980 and during this term of office negotiated the complete independence of Canada from Britain. He was politically able, but his high government spending damaged the Canadian economy. He retired in 1984.

Trujillo Molinas, Rafael Leonidas (1891–1961), Dominican dictator. Chief of staff of the National Guard (1927), in 1930 he led a coup which placed him in absolute power for the next 30 years. He ruled by terror and corruption. To deter illegal immigration from neighbouring Haiti he sent the Dominican army across the border (1937) and massacred some 15,000 peasants. He was assassinated in 1961.

Truman, Harry S. (1884–1972), 33rd president of the United States. As a Democratic senator (1934) he supported the New Deal and in 1944 was selected as Roosevelt's running mate, succeeding him on his sudden death in 1945. The new president concluded the war in Europe, attended the Potsdam Conference, and brought the war with Japan to a speedy end by authorizing the use of nuclear weapons. In foreign affairs he resolutely opposed Soviet expansionism through Marshall Aid (1947), a four-point programme of aid to underdeveloped countries (1949) and by the foundation of NATO (1949); but his domestic reforms (his 'Fair Deal' continuation of the New Deal) were blocked by the Republicans. In 1950 he was re-elected against all expert prevision. Once again his domestic policy was blocked and undermined by McCarthy's witchhunt, but abroad he halted Communist aggression in Korea (1950) and asserted presidential authority by dismissing General MacArthur (1951). He retired to private life in 1953.

Truman Doctrine In March 1947 – in the context of the Greek civil war caused by an attempted Communist coup – President Truman pledged American aid to 'free peoples . . . resisting attempted subjugation by armed minorities or by outside pressures'.

Tshombe, Moise Kapenda (1919–69), Congolese politician. When the Congolese Republic was proclaimed, with the backing of Union Minière he formed the secessionist Republic of Katanga of which he became president (1960). The central government (with UN aid) regained control in 1963 and Tshombe fled the country, but was recalled in 1964 and was premier until overthrown in 1965 by General Mobutu. He went into exile in Spain, was condemned to death *in absentia* for treason in 1966 and, after the aircraft in which he was flying was hijacked to Algeria (1967), died there in prison.

Tukhachevsky, Mikhail Nikolayevich (1893–1937), Soviet marshal. An officer of the Imperial Guard, he joined the Bolsheviks (1918) and became their most brilliant soldier, serving in the civil war in command of the 5th Army and in the Soviet Polish War (1920). In 1921 he suppressed the Kronstadt Revolt. By 1937 he had been promoted to marshal and was people's commissar for defence when he was arrested, court-martialled and shot on forged evidence supplied by a Nazi double agent – the first of some 20 generals and 35,000 officers to be executed in Stalin's purge of the Red Army.

Tunisia North African republic. A semi-autonomous province of the Ottoman Empire under its hereditary ruler, the bey, it became a French protectorate in 1881 and remained such until 1956, when it became independent. Its first prime minister, Bourguiba, who had led the independence movement since the 1930s, abolished the rule of the bey (1957), to become president (an office to which he was regularly re-elected until declared president for life in 1975). The French maintained bases in Tunisia until 1962 and during the Algerian war (1958–61) some 1,000 Tunisians were killed in clashes with the French. Under Bourguiba Tunisia pursued a moderate line in Arab affairs which led to tension with the more extreme policies of Algeria and Egypt in the 1960s and to conflict with Libya (1980). In 1982 it housed the headquarters of the PLO (expelled from the Lebanon) and in 1985 was the victim of an Israeli attack directed against Yasir Arafat. Bourguiba's moderate policies were continued by his successors who in 1989 signed the agreement setting up the Maghreb Union.

Tupamaros see under **Uruguay**

Turkey A republic of western Asia. (1) **Ottoman Empire**. From a high point at the end of the 17th century – when it controlled the Balkans, southern Russia, Armenia, Georgia, the Middle East and most of North Africa – the sultanate of Abdul Hamid II was everywhere in decline. In 1908 the Young Turk revolution attempted to arrest the process, but the new Sultan Mehmet V saw Libya taken by the Italians (1911) and Turkey's possessions in Europe reduced to the area around Constantinople (Istanbul). The German alliance which drew Turkey into World War I on the side of the central powers compounded the disaster and culminated in the humiliating Treaty of Sèvres.

(2) **Republic of Turkey**. Those who found the treaty unacceptable formed a provisional government in Ankara (1920) with Mustafa Kemal Atatürk as president. Having defeated the Greeks (September 1922), he deposed the sultan (November), negotiated the Treaty of Lausanne with the Allies and declared Turkey a republic (1923), abolishing the spiritual power of the caliph (1924). Atatürk imposed a reforming, secular and authoritarian regime and his work was continued by his successor Inönü who preserved Turkish neutrality during World War II until February 1945, when it declared war on the Axis. In 1950 Menderes came to power in free elections, but the army was forced to intervene in 1960 and 1971 when public order was threatened, and continues to hold the ultimate authority in the president, General Evren. Soviet pressures in 1947 ensured Turkey's alignment with the west. Turkish troops distinguished themselves in Korea and Turkey became a member of NATO (1952) and of the Baghdad Pact (1955). Despite the Balkan Pact (1954) with Yugoslavia and Greece, relations with the Greeks were embittered over the Cyprus dispute and specifically the Turkish invasion (1974) and the establishment of a breakaway Turkish state in the north of the island. A further cause of friction was the 1987 dispute over oil exploration in the Aegean and Greek opposition was an obstacle to the Turkish application (1987) to join the European Community.

U

Uganda East African republic. Commercial penetration in the 19th century led to the establishment in 1894 of a British protectorate dividing the area into five provinces. One of these, Buganda, had been the most powerful enclave under its hereditary rulers, the Kabakas, and in consequence enjoyed a more independent position which the British administration attempted to diminish during the 1920s and 1930s. In the post-World War II atmosphere of decolonization, the Kabaka was exiled (1953–55) without suppressing the movement for Bugandan independence. After Uganda itself became independent (1962), Buganda enjoyed considerable autonomy, and when it became a republic, the Kabaka was the first president (1963). The prime minister, Milton Obote, in his drive towards a single-party state, deposed and drove the Kabaka into exile (1966) and his repression of the Baganda began the break-up of the state which was accelerated when Idi Amin deposed Obote (1971) and expelled the Asian community. The fall of Amin (1970) and the return of Obote as president (1980) marked the continuing disintegration of Uganda. In 1985 Obote was overthrown in a bloodless coup by the army, the military government in its turn being superseded by the National Resistance Army led by Yoweri Museveni, whom Obote had cheated of power in the rigged 1980 election. Museveni and the NRA worked to restore order and had so far succeeded as to allow free elections to be held in February 1989.

Ulbricht, Walther (1893–1973), German Communist leader. A trade unionist, he joined the Communist Party in 1919 and became a Communist deputy (1928–33). When Hitler came to power in 1933 he fled to the USSR, returning in 1945 with the Red Army to establish a Communist state. As deputy premier (1949) and as chairman of the council of state (1960) of the GDR, but more particularly as secretary-general of the Socialist Unity Party, he enforced a rigidly repressive and Stalinist regime, provoking the workers' rising (1953), building the Berlin Wall (1961) and sending East German troops to crush the Czech revolt (1968). In 1971 he was succeeded as secretary-general by Erich Honecker.

Union of Soviet Socialist Republics   The successor state of:

(1) **The Russian Empire**. During the second half of the 19th century, Russian territorial expansion reached its limits in central Asia and the Far East. Industrialization grew rapidly and, with the building of the Trans-Siberian Railway (1891–1905), fresh areas were opened for settlement and exploitation. All these processes were continued under Count Witte, while Stolypin attempted to create a class of landowning peasantry. This steady progress was interrupted by the Russo-Japanese war (1904–05), by the 1905 revolution and by the reactionary policy of Tsar Nicholas II, who repeatedly undermined and repressed the attempts to liberalize the regime through the Duma. The loyalty to the tsar kindled by the outbreak of World War I was soon spent in defeat, inflation and food shortages, and Nicholas was forced to abdicate after the revolution of February 1917.

(2) **The Provisional Government**. Formed under Prince Lvov and continued under his successor Kerensky, it lacked the strength to enforce its policy of continuing the struggle in the face of increasing war weariness and the active opposition of the Bolsheviks and other revolutionary forces, and was overthrown in the October Revolution (7 November 1917).

(3) **The Soviet regime**. To consolidate the power of the Bolshevik revolution Lenin was forced to seek peace at any price at Brest-Litovsk (1918) and then to crush the counter-revolution in the civil war (1918–20) and to regain those parts of the tsarist empire which had seized the opportunity to declare their independence. Poland, the Baltic republics and Finland succeeded, but by 1921 the Soviets had re-established Russian rule in the Ukraine, Belorussia and Transcaucasia. 'War Communism' which had provoked the Kronstadt Revolt was relaxed in favour of the New Economic Policy until Stalin came to power after the death of Lenin (1925) and forced collectivization and industrialization at enormous human cost.

Foreign policy under Litvinov had sought accommodation with the western democracies against Nazism and Fascism and supported Popular Front governments, but following the Munich Agreement (1938), Molotov concluded the Nazi-Soviet Pact (1939) under which the USSR was able to recover former tsarist possessions in Poland and the Baltic republics. The German invasion (1941) was held only at great cost and final victory in the Great Patriotic War, in which the USSR was sustained by supplies from the west, was achieved only by immense heroism and self-sacrifice by the Russian people.

World War II left the USSR in control of central Europe and most of the Balkans and in confrontation with the United States. In the ensuing Cold War, the protagonists were restrained by the nuclear deterrent but used their proxies to fight their wars. A striking feature of postwar Soviet policy was the expansion of the Soviet navy from a coastal defence force to an ocean-going fleet; policy in, for example, Somalia or Vietnam, was directed to obtaining base facilities for operations in the Indian Ocean and the China Sea.

After the death of Stalin (1953), Khrushchev attempted a measure of liberalization, but was removed from power (1964) by the old guard. The Brezhnev era saw an accumulation of economic problems for the USSR. This enormous and successful expansion of Soviet power placed an intolerable burden on the economy. In addition to the massive forces of the Warsaw Pact in Europe, the breach with China over Khrushchev's revisionism had led to a military build-up in the Far East. Economic and military aid, too, had to be provided to the states in which, to a greater or lesser degree, the USSR had established a foothold – Ethiopia, Mozambique, Angola and (initially) Somalia in Africa; Cuba and Nicaragua in Central America; Nasser's Egypt, and Syria and Iraq in the Middle East; and Vietnam in Southeast Asia. The enormously successful space programme further distorted the balance of the industrial economy. Finally, the complete failure of agriculture to feed the Soviet people meant the expenditure of hard currency upon grain from the United States and other capitalist countries.

The accession to power of Mikhail Gorbachov (1985) and the failure of the Red Army to pacify Afghanistan (1979–89) paved the way for political and economic reconstruction (*perestroika*) and for a fuller and more frank exposure of the defects of the system in the form of 'openness' (*glasnost*). To cut back military expenditure a rapprochement with the United States aimed to reduce and ultimately to eliminate nuclear weapons and to reduce conventional force levels in Europe. Quarrels with China were settled and the USSR also looked to play a part in the Middle East peace process. Domestic reforms included human rights and an elected Congress of People's Deputies, from which the Supreme Soviet would be chosen. These reforms seem designed to give the appearance of greater democracy within a system still controlled by the Communist Party, but the 1989 elections revealed the depth of popular discontent with its performance. Perestroika also stimulated nationalist movements in the Baltic republics, the Ukraine, Moldavia, Georgia and Armenia (the last two erupting into serious nationalist and ethnic riots in 1988–89).

United Arab Republic   The name borne by the short-lived union between Syria and Egypt (1958–61), which was retained by Egypt until 1971.

United Kingdom   European constitutional monarchy. The diamond jubilee of Queen Victoria (1897) marks the high point of British power and prestige. Industrial and commercial enterprise and the most powerful fleet in the world had enabled Britain to dominate world trade and to plant an empire worldwide during the 19th century. By the end of the century Germany was beginning to overtake Britain industrially and to challenge its supremacy at sea. The Boer War (1899–1902) severely affected British prestige and the years leading up to World War I, although marked by important social reforms, were marred by bitter industrial strife and by the problem of Irish Home Rule. Victory in World War I was achieved at enormous cost and recovery was deeply affected by the Wall Street crash (1929) and the ensuing worldwide Depression. When recovery came towards the mid-1930s it was significant for the future that it came to the south of the country and in light engineering and service industries, while the traditional coal, steel and heavy engineering continued to decline.

The interwar years were notable for the recovery of the trade union movement from the nadir of the General Strike (1926) and for the eclipse of the Liberals as the Labour Party became the alternative party of government, while the break-up of empire began with the independence of southern Ireland as the Irish Free State (1922).

Britain survived World War II thanks to American intervention and to the diversion of German efforts to the unsuccessful task of conquering the USSR. The defeats suffered by the British at Japanese hands were fatally damaging to imperial prestige and the British Empire was dismantled with indecent speed and the enthusiastic co-operation of the United States, former dominions and colonies for the most part remaining within the Commonwealth. Although this process began with Indian independence (1947), Britain was unprepared to exchange an imperial role for the leadership of Europe and, believing that its so-called special relationship with the United States was of particular importance, held aloof from the creation of the European Community – only seeking to join the Treaty of Rome when France had a leader in de Gaulle and West Germany's economic miracle had given it industrial pre-eminence. Since joining the Community in 1973 Britain has been seen to be less than wholehearted in some of the processes of European integration. Concommitant with these developments was the introduction of semisocialism by Attlee's Labour government (1945), developing into Butskellism, a cosy cohabitation of left and right in succeeding Conservative and Labour administrations.

Economically the growth of trade union influence, through the TUC, was to prove disastrous. The 'social contract' between the TUC and the Wilson government left British industry in no position to face the world economic crisis caused by the Arab oil embargo (1974) and the Wilson and Callaghan administrations were under the humiliating obligation of subjecting their foreign and domestic policy to US approval and their financial plans to the IMF in order to maintain government.

The Conservative governments of Margaret Thatcher were initially sustained by the prestige of the Falklands victory (1982) and restored a degree of prosperity and sense of purpose and direction, aided by the exploitation of North Sea oil and gas. This was at the cost of high unemployment and the sharpening of the divide between a prosperous south and a decaying north. However, they failed in their turn to find any solution to the continuing violence in Northern Ireland, and the problems of inner city decay sharpened racial tension. This sense of alienation has led to renewed calls for Welsh and Scottish devolution.

United Nations In 1941 Roosevelt described the alliance fighting the Axis powers as the United Nations. These countries formed the nucleus of the organization planned at Dumbarton Oaks, at Yalta and at San Francisco to replace the League of Nations and which came into being on 26 October 1945. With permanent headquarters in New York, the UN comprises a general assembly, a deliberative body of member states, and the security council, with five permanent members (China, France, Britain, the United States and USSR) and ten members chosen by the general assembly for two-year terms. Although the UN has been able to assemble and deploy peacekeeping forces (see **Cyprus, Lebanon, Zaïre**) – a power which the League of Nations lacked – it has suffered to a lesser degree the same paralysis of the earlier organization in the veto on its actions exercised by the security council. Effectively it can act only if both the USSR and the United States approve. Nonetheless its secretaries-general (see **Hammarskjöld, Lie, Perez de Cuéllar, Thant**) have played an important part, if not in securing general agreements, at least in furthering bilateral treaties between contending powers. Their conciliatory role reflects the work of the UN agencies (*see below*) in the work of international relief and economic development and co-operation. See also **International Bank for Reconstruction and Development, International Court of Justice, International Labour Organization, International Monetary Fund**.

United Nations Educational Scientific and Cultural Organization (UNESCO)
By the 1980s many western governments believed that bad management, financial extravagance and politicization were preventing the organization from achieving the purposes for which it had been established in 1946. In 1984 the United States withdrew, followed in 1985 by Britain and Singapore, but it was to be hoped that their return would follow the appointment of a new director-general (1987) and a reform of the organization.

United Nations Relief and Rehabilitiation Administration This operated between 1943–49 to bring relief to war-devasted areas of Europe and the Far East and to aid the repatriation of displaced persons. Its functions have been transferred to such organizations as UNICEF, the International Refugee Organization and the FAO. Palestinian refugees are the responsibility of the United Nations Relief and Works Agency for Palestinian Refugees, established in 1950.

United States North American Federal republic. Following the war between the states (1861–65), which preserved the union, mass immigration from Europe provided the labour to exploit the natural resources of the continent. By the end of the century the republic shared the imperialist sentiments of Europe and annexed Hawaii (1898) and acquired the Philippines and other Spanish Pacific colonies as a result of its victory in the Spanish-American War (1898). Theodore Roosevelt typifies the policy of aggressive intervention in Central American affairs (see **Colombia, Cuba, Mexico, Nicaragua, Panama**). Under Woodrow Wilson the United States entered World War I on the Allied side, but his idealistic efforts through the League of Nations to establish justice in international relations were unsupported at home. During the 1920s the United States reverted, under Harding and Coolidge, to isolationism in foreign affairs and to unrestricted speculation which provoked the Wall Street crash and the Depression.

Roosevelt's New Deal helped to restore the national economy which was fully developed as the United States became the arsenal of World War II before itself entering the conflict after the Japanese attack on Pearl Harbor (1941). After World War II the former great powers of Europe were eclipsed and the United States became the representative of liberal democracy in opposition to the totalitarian forces of the USSR. Possession by each side of nuclear weapons deterred direct confrontation, each power building a series of defensive alliances (NATO, SEATO, Warsaw Pact) and supporting their clients in armed struggles in the Americas (Cuba, El Salvador, Nicaragua), the Middle East (Afghanistan,

Egypt, Israel, Iraq, Syria) or southeast Asia (Korea, Thailand, Taiwan, Vietnam).

While great power rivalry proved ruinous to the Soviet economy, US government funding of expenditure on the arms and space races has seriously handicapped the United States in its commercial rivalry with Japan and to a lesser degree the European Community. The rapprochement between the superpowers effected during Reagan's second presidential term (1985–89) was perhaps a measure of their exhaustion.

Uruguay South American republic. It joined the Argentinian revolt against Spain (1810), breaking away to proclaim its own independence (1814) which it ultimately achieved in 1828 after Brazilian occupation from 1820. The relative stability enjoyed during most of the 20th century as a result of the reforms of Batlle y Ordóñez ended in the economic decline of the 1960s and 1970s and the emergence of the Marxist Tupamaros. In 1973 the military took power and in order to crush urban terrorism operated a dirty war similar to that of their counterparts in Argentina. It succeeded, but only at the cost of grave infringements of human rights and although a civilian government was restored in 1985 the threat of military takeover remained, in the face of constant agitation to repeal the amnesty law protecting members of the Uruguayan armed forces from prosecution for human rights violations.

Ustase Croat terrorist movement formed by Ante Pavelic in 1929, responsible for the murder of King Alexander of Yugoslavia (1934) and for atrocities against Jews, Serbs and Communists in the puppet state of Croatia during World War II. It survived to commit sporadic outrages against Yugoslav officials and buildings in Europe and Australia.

V

Vargas, Getulio Dornelles (1883–1954), Brazilian president. Elected in 1930, he instituted a right-wing dictatorship and a form of corporate state. He sent Brazilian troops to assist the Allies in World War II and was overthrown by their officers (1945). He was returned to power on a left-wing programme (1950) but was deposed and committed suicide (1954) when it failed.

Vatican Council, The Second The council summoned by Pope John XXIII in 1962 to 'modernize' the Roman Catholic Church. Before it was closed by his successor, Pope Paul VI, it had achieved such major reforms as the introduction of a vernacular liturgy; the collegiality of Pope and bishops; creation of national synods in which there was lay participation; greater involvement of the laity; encouragement of the ecumenical movement; and denunciation of anti-Semitism.

Venezuela South American republic. Venezuela first gained independence from Spain in 1821 as part of the Federal Republic of Greater Colombia, from which it broke away (1830). From 1908 until 1935 it was ruled by the dictator Juan Vicente Gomez. Democratic reforms initiated by Raoul Betancourt (1947) were overthrown in the 1948 coup which established the dictatorship of Colonel Jiménez. Betancourt was returned to power in 1959 and despite left-wing terrorism in the 1960s laid the foundations of a democratic electoral system which survived. Venezuelan prosperity being based on oil (first exploited 1922), the fall of world prices in the 1980s imposed considerable economic strain and a burden of external debt.

Venizelos, Eleutherios (1864–1935), Greek statesman. He led the revolution in Crete (1905) which resulted in its union with Greece (1908). Summoned to Athens, he became a reforming premier (1909–15) who led Greece through the Balkan Wars. Forced to resign by the pro-German King Constantine in 1915, he formed a provisional government in 1916 and forced the king's abdication (1917). He resigned (1920) on the return of the king but his followers forced the king's abdication after the defeats in Asia Minor and proclaimed a republic (1924). Venizelos became premier again (1928–32) but royalist pressures and the effects of the Depression led to his resignation. He fled to Paris after the failure of a rising against the restoration of the monarchy and died there. His son, Sophocles Venizelos (1894–1964), was briefly premier three times after World War II.

Vereeniging, Treaty of The agreement which ended the Boer War (31 May 1902) by bringing the Boer republics under British sovereignty on promise of self-government and grants to repair war damage.

Versailles, Treaty of Signed on 28 June 1919, the treaty embodied the peace terms with Germany. Under it all German colonies were placed under League of Nations mandate; Alsace-Lorraine was returned to France and there were minor territorial concessions to Belgium, Czechoslovakia and Poland; the Saar and Rhineland were occupied and demilitarized; Germany was to pay war reparations and its army and navy were to be restricted, with a ban on aircraft, tanks, submarines, capital ships and chemical weapons. Germany was to admit war-guilt. The treaty was signed under protest, its provisions circumvented and ultimately rejected by Hitler.

Verwoerd, Hendrik Frensch (1901–66), South African prime minister. A professor of psychology (1927–37), he became editor of the Nationalist *Die Transvaler* (1937–48), a senator (1948), minister of native affairs (1950), responsible for enforcing apartheid, and prime minister (1960–66), taking South Africa out of the Commonwealth and declaring a republic (1961). He was assassinated by a crazed Portuguese East African.

Victor Emmanuel III (1869–1947), king of Italy (1900–45). He invited Mussolini to form a government (1922) and remained a figurehead under the fascists who declared him emperor of Ethiopia (1936) and king of Albania (1939). Although his order for the arrest of Mussolini brought down the regime (1943), he was too tainted by his association with the dictator and abdicated (1945).

Vietnam Southeast Asian republic. Vietnam became a French protectorate in 1885 and, together with Laos and Kampuchea, was administered as part of French Indo-China (1887–1940). In World War II the Japanese occupation (1940–45) ended with their proclamation of Vietnamese independence under Bao Dai who abdicated power to Ho Chi Minh. Under the Potsdam Agreement the country was to be divided along the 16th parallel, the north to be occupied by the Chinese, the south by the British. French recognition of the Hanoi government was followed by the replacement of the British by French forces, the declaration of a provisional government in the south at Saigon and the start of the Vietnam War (1946).

Following the French defeat at Dien Bien Phu (1954), the Geneva agreements created the Democratic Republic of Vietnam (North) and the Republic of Vietnam (South). In the face of Communist subversion from the north, the United States gave increasing military and economic aid to a succession of governments but was eventually forced to negotiate an armistice (1973). When these talks were broken off (1974) the north launched a final offensive which resulted in the capture of Saigon (1975).

In 1976 the country was formally reunited as the Socialist Republic of Vietnam. In the south members of the former regime were 're-educated' in concentration camps, while the refugee 'boat people' were prepared to face the hazards of storm and piracy to escape the regime. Initially supported by China, Vietnam chose the Soviet side in the quarrel between the two powers and, with this support, established a protectorate over Laos, invaded Kampuchea (1978), and engaged in a brisk border war with China (1979). The rapprochement between China and the USSR and the Soviet unwillingness to shoulder the cost of the occupation of Kampuchea led to a Vietnamese withdrawal and to an easing of the regime in the hope of attracting western aid.

Vietnam War   The conflict falls into two phases. (1) *The Indo-China War* from 1946–54 when Ho Chi Minh's Viet Minh (led by General Giap) responded to the return of the French and the bombardment of Haiphong (1946) by a sustained guerrilla war. Finally, when the French challenged the Viet Minh by the establishment of the fortress outpost of Dien Bien Phu, Giap answered with a regular siege in which the French were forced to surrender. (2) *The Vietnam War*, properly speaking, stems from this French defeat when the Communist north attempted to subvert the regime in the south by infiltrating North Vietnamese troops and supplies to sustain their southern Vietcong guerrillas. US support for the south was substantially increased by Kennedy, and Johnson used the Gulf of Tonkin Incident (1964), when US warships were attacked by the North Vietnamese, to introduce US naval, military and air forces into the conflict. The Communists were contained and their Tet offensive (1968) defeated, but they gained a moral victory by arousing the mass of the American public against the war. The American withdrawal, begun in 1969, was covered by the invasions of Kampuchea and Laos (1970), by the bombing of the north and the mining of its harbours. The south was unable to sustain Communist pressures in the absence of US forces (1973) and was finally defeated by the Communist offensive which took Saigon (1975).

Villa, Francisco [Pancho]   (Doroteo Arango, *c*1877–1923), Mexican revolutionary and folk hero. A bandit, his fighting skills (1910–11) brought down Díaz, and helped bring Carranza to power (1914). He quarrelled with Carranza, was defeated (1915) and returned to banditry. When his men killed US citizens and made an incursion into the United States, Villa was pursued unsuccessfully by General Pershing for 11 months (1916–17). He continued armed opposition against Carranza but made peace with his successor (1920). He was assassinated in 1923.

Voroshilov, Kliment Yefremovich (1881–1969), Soviet marshal. He joined the Bolsheviks (1903), took part in the 1905 Revolution, and was distinguished as a Red Army commander in the Civil War (1918–20). He served as people's commissar for the navy (1925–34) and for defence (1934–40), and was promoted to marshal in 1935. During World War II he commanded the northern front. A close associate of Stalin, he was president of the USSR (1953–60) until forced out by Khrushchev, who also expelled him from the central committee. He was reinstated in 1966 after the fall of Khrushchev.

Vorster, Balthazar Johannes (1915–83), South African prime minister. Gaoled (1942–44) during World War II for pro-Nazi activities, he became a Nationalist MP (1953) and as minister of justice (1961–66) he tightened and extended the laws against subversion. Succeeding Verwoerd as prime minister in 1966, he continued his apartheid policy at home but was more conciliatory in his foreign policy. Appointed president (1978) he was forced to resign (1979) when implicated in a financial scandal.

W

Wafd Egyptian Nationalist political party founded by Zaghlul Pasha (c1850–1927) in 1919 to secure independence from Britain. Zaghlul became prime minister (1924), but British and court influence forced his resignation. On his death (1927) Nahas Pasha became party leader. Despite the party's nationalism, it was reinstated by the British as a counterpoise to the Axis sympathies of the Egyptian court in World War II. Although a focus of nationalist and antimonarchical sentiment, it was suppressed by Nasser (1952)

Waldheim, Kurt (1918–), Austrian president. Serving in the German Army in World War II, he was wounded on the eastern front (1941) and thereafter served as intelligence officer in the Balkans (1942–45). He entered the diplomatic service in 1945 to become Austrian ambassador at the UN (1964–68, 1970–71) and foreign minister (1968–70). For ten years he was fourth secretary-general of the UN (1972–82). He was elected president of Austria in 1986 despite allegations that he had been involved in war crimes while serving in the Balkans.

Walesa, Lech (1943–), Polish trade union leader. Dismissed (1976) for his part in the Gdansk shipyard strikes, he formed the free trade union Solidarity. Imprisoned (1981–82) when the union was suppressed, Walesa seemed to have gone into eclipse after his release, but remained a leader of the banned union and in 1988–89 emerged to lead the delegation negotiating with the government for reform of the regime.

Wall Street crash see **Depression**

war crimes Military law sanctions the punishment of those guilty of atrocities against prisoners or civilians as, for example, Lt Calley convicted (1971) for the massacre of the villagers of My Lai in the Vietnam War. After World War II the dubious precedent was set for the victors to try the vanquished for planning aggressive war and for genocide, slave labour, organized looting and the maltreatment and murder of prisoners of war. The tribunal set up at Nuremberg in August 1945 by France, the USSR, Britain and the United States tried the major war criminals (lesser offenders were brought before military courts in the countries in which the offences had been committed). After hearing evidence, sentence was passed and a number of the guilty hanged or sentenced to imprisonment (1946). Similar trials of Japanese war criminals were held before an 11-nation tribunal in Tokyo (1946–47). Although such trials have been held to infringe national sovereignty and to try individuals for acts which were legal in the national context at the time they were committed seems a doubtful procedure, the nature of the crimes tried at Nuremberg and Tokyo demanded extraordinary punishment.

Warsaw Pact An agreement signed 14 May 1955 (in response to West Germany's joining NATO) betweeen the USSR, Albania (declined co-operation 1961, left Pact 1968), Bulgaria, Czechoslovakia, GDR, Hungary (sought to leave the pact 1956), Poland and Romania. It formalized the command structure of the Soviet and east European armed forces which engaged in regular joint manoeuvres and were used to suppress the Czech revolt (1968).

Warsaw Uprising The Polish insurrection in 1944. Despite the fact that members of the Polish Home Army, the non-Communist resistance led by General Komorowski (1895–1966) in World War II, had been arrested and disarmed when the Red Army liberated Poland in the summer of 1944, as Marshal Rokossovsky's forces approached Warsaw, on August 1 1944, the general ordered an uprising to facilitate the capture of the city. Two-thirds of Warsaw was initially captured, but Soviet forces remained inactive on the far side of the Vistula and over a two-month period allowed the Germans to destroy the city and crush the Home Army. The heroic Polish defence could only be supplied by air and the Soviets denied the Allies the use of captured bases in Poland for this purpose. General Komorowski was forced to surrender on 3 October and Stalin's purpose of destroying the non-Communist resistance had been achieved.

Washington Naval Treaties The Washington Conference (1921–22) between France, Italy, Japan, Britain and the United States, produced a series of agreements limiting the size of capital ships and aircraft carriers, establishing a ratio of capital ships between the five navies and applying the rules of surface warfare to submarines. Such arms reductions came to be negated by the territorial ambitions of Japan and Nazi Germany.

Watergate The name of the apartment block in Washington, DC, housing the Democratic Party headquarters. On 17 June 1972 five men were arrested for breaking and entering to install bugging devices. Further investigation revealed that they had been authorized to do so by the US attorney general, John Mitchell, and uncovered a mass of illegal activities on behalf of the Republican Party. President Nixon had instituted the practice of taping all White House conversations and when this became known these tapes were demanded under subpoena by the investigating committeee. They revealed that the president had full knowledge of attempts to cover up the affair – which had forced the resignation of his advisers and associates – and his opponents made full use of this to force his resignation (1974). His successor, Gerald Ford, granted a pardon for any and all crimes he might have committed while in office, thus sparing Nixon the ordeal of impeachment. Mitchell and presidential advisers Haldeman and Erlichman were convicted and imprisoned (1975).

Wavell, Archibald Percival (1883–1950, 1st Earl Wavell of Cyrenaica and Winchester), British military commander. He served in the Boer War, and on Allenby's staff in World War I, and commanded British forces in Palestine during the Arab revolt (1937–39). As C-in-C Middle East in World War II he drove the Italians from Eritrea, Ethiopia and Cyrenaica (1940–41), but the German invasion of the Balkans, the Iraq uprising and the need to send expeditionary forces to Greece and against the Vichy regime in Syria so stretched his limited resources that he was driven back to Egypt in 1941. Exchanged with Auchinleck as C-in-C India (1941), he became governor-general and viceroy of India (1943–47) and prepared the country for independence. Despite his qualities as soldier and proconsul he never enjoyed the full confidence of the government.

Weimar Republic see under **Germany**

Weizmann, Chaim (1874–1952), first president of Israel. Born in Russia and educated in Switzerland, he became a British subject in 1910. A scientist, he was director of the Admiralty laboratories (1916–19) in World War I. An active Zionist, he helped procure the Balfour Declaration (1917) and became leader of the movement as president of the World Zionist Organization (1920–31; 1935–46). President of Israel (1948–52), he founded the Weizmann Institute near his home in Rehoboth.

Welfare State see **Beveridge, William Henry**

West Bank An area to the west of the river Jordan, originally forming part of Palestine, which remained in the hands of its inhabitants after the Arab-Israeli War (1948). It was administered by Jordan until it was annexed by Israel after the Six Day War (1967). The establishment of Jewish settlements (in defiance of the Geneva Convention) in 1977 aroused protests from both Britain and the United States. The Palestinians chafed under Israel occupation and in December 1987 began a series of violent protests in their demands for free elections and an end to Israeli occupation. In 1988 Jordan renounced any claims to administer the area – it had provided salaries for the local officials – and the PLO declared the region a Palestinian state of which Yasir Arafat was named provisional president (1989).

West Germany see **German Federal Republic**

West Indies Federation A scheme proposed (1947) under which British colonies in the Caribbean should proceed to independence in association rather than individually. It was implemented in 1958 but rapidly foundered on inter-island jealousy – the capital was in Trinidad to Jamaican disgust – and fears that the more prosperous islands would have to bear the burden of their poorer neighbours. Jamaica withdrew after a referendum (1961) and the federation collapsed (1962), individual members gaining their independence and some of the smaller islands forming the West Indies Associated States.

Westminster, Statute of British parliamentary act (1931) which established the basis of the Commonwealth of independent nations owing allegiance to the British crown and with legislatures on an equal footing with that of Britain.

Weygand, Maxime (1867–1956), French military commander. Weygand served as Foch's chief of staff throughout World War I. He became military adviser to the Poles (1920), high commissioner in Syria (1923), chief of the French general staff (1930), and retired in 1935. Returning to active duty in World War II, he was called from command of the Mediterranean theatre (May 1940) to replace Gamelin as French C-in-C. He refused to surrender in the field but recommended the government seek an armistice. As Pétain's delegate in North Africa (1940–41) he signed an agreement with the United States which was to facilitate the Allied landings (1942). Arrested and deported to Germany (1942), after the war he was arraigned by de Gaulle but obtained a complete discharge and quashing of all charges (1948).

Whitlam, Edward Gough (1916–), Australian prime minister. A lawyer, he served in the RAAF in World War II and became an MP in 1952. He was elected leader of the Labor Party in 1967 and later served as prime minister (1972–75). In asserting Australian individuality he withdrew troops from Vietnam (1973) and attempted to buy back British and American economic interests. His seeming trend to republicanism alienated many of the states and his economic policy caused splits in his own party and was tainted by financial scandal. In consequence of parliamentary deadlock, the governor-general dismissed Whitlam (1975) and appointed the leader of the opposition, Malcolm Fraser, as caretaker premier. When Labor lost the 1975 and 1977 elections Whitlam resigned the party leadership.

Wilhelm II (1859–1941), emperor [kaiser] of Germany and king of Prussia (1888–1918). Having forced the resignation of Bismark (1890), the kaiser dominated his successors. His aims to extend Germany's military, naval, colonial and economic power were confused by tactless inconsistency. The traditional hostility of the French was sharpened by his interference in Morocco (see **Agadir Incident**), while his encouragement of the Boers, of the Ulster Protestants (see **Home Rule**) and especially his programme of naval expansion turned Britain towards its hereditary enemy in the Anglo-French Agreement (1904). Personal friendship with Tsar Nicholas II was negated by German support of Austria-Hungary in the Balkans. All contributed to the crisis of 1914. During World War I the kaiser was overshadowed by his commanders, Hindenburg and Ludendorff, and after the German defeat was forced to abdicate and take refuge in the Netherlands. The Dutch rejected demands for his surrender and he remained in exile until his death.

Wilson, James Harold (1916– , Baron Wilson of Rievaulx), British prime minister. Initially an academic, Wilson was a civil servant during World War II and served as a Labour MP for over 30 years (1945–76). He resigned as president of the Board of Trade (1947–51) when charges were imposed on the NHS. Defeated by Gaitskell (1960) in elections for party leadership, he succeeded after his death (1963) and served twice as prime minister (1964–70, 1974–76). His first administration withdrew British forces east of Suez, applied unsuccessfully to enter the EEC and failed to halt UDI in Rhodesia (Zimbabwe). At home there was economic crisis, devaluation and increasing TUC influence. His second administration made worse the economic crisis which it had inherited and was subjected to the humiliating controls of the US administration and of the TUC. In 1976 Wilson resigned and retired from political life in circumstances never fully explained.

Wilson, Thomas Woodrow (1856–1924), 28th president of the United States. An academic, he was president of Princeton university (1902–10) and governor of New Jersey (1911–12). His progressive reforms in both posts won him the Democratic nomination and rifts in the Republican Party the 1912 presidential election (he was re-elected in 1916 on the pledge of US neutrality in World War I). In office he introduced legislation to curb the unrestricted powers of big business in antitrust and trade union laws and introduced the 18th and 19th amendments (prohibition and votes for women). He was involved in border clashes with Mexico and imposed US protectorates on Haiti (1915) and the Dominican Republic (1916). In 1917 unrestricted submarine warfare and the intrigues revealed by the Zimmerman Telegram brought the United States into the war on the Allied side. Wilson's Fourteen Points were very influential in forming the peace treaties, but Congress refused to ratify the Treaty of Versailles, keeping the United States out of the League of Nations. In campaigning against this isolationism, Wilson suffered a breakdown (1921) and was an invalid for the rest of his life.

Witte, Count Sergei Yulievich (1845–1915), Russian statesman. As the minister responsible for Russian economic and financial affairs (1892–1903) he fostered industrialization and the exploitation of the Far East through the building of the Trans-Siberian railway (1891–1905) and the negotiation of foreign loans. Dismissed by the tsar (1903), he was recalled after the 1905 Revolution to negotiate the Treaty of Portsmouth and to become prime minister with an elected Duma. Although he suppressed the revolutionary movement he was regarded as too liberal by the tsar and dismissed (1906).

women's rights During the 20th century there has been a spectacular change in the status and role of many women throughout the world, diffused from the upper and middle classes in the west and spread to other cultures. In Britain higher education became available to women in the 19th century and, until the vote was granted to women over 30 in 1918, there was a major campaign for women's suffrage, which leaders such as Emmeline Pankhurst conducted with increasing violence up to World War I. During the war women's claims to equal treatment were enhanced by their contributions to the war effort in industry, in the services and in agriculture. In 1919 the Sex Qualification Removal Bill opened to them the professions such as the law – in which women only began to make their mark after World War II. In 1928 an equal franchise was granted and in 1931 the civil service was opened to them, although they were not to be granted equal pay until 1955, 11 years after the teaching profession. Women's rights were extended during World War II and particularly by the changed moral climate of the postwar world in which birth control whether by contraception or by abortion (legalized 1967) became a social norm. The Equal Opportunities Commission, created 1973, advanced women's rights in the Sex Discrimination and Equal Pay Acts (1975) but these chiefly affected single or working women and some anomalies respecting married women still await reform.

Wood, Edward Frederick Lindley (1881–1959, 1st Earl of Halifax), British statesman. A Conservative MP (1910), he held ministerial office (1922–25) and was created Lord Irwin (1925) and appointed viceroy of India (1926–31). He negotiated with Gandhi, promising dominion status for India (1929) and persuading him to join the Round Table Conferences (1931). Leader of the House of Lords (1935), he held office (1935–38) and as Chamberlain's foreign secretary (1938–40) supported the disastrous policy of appeasing Hitler. During World War II he served as ambassador to the United States (1941–46).

World Bank see **International Bank for Reconstruction and Development**

World Council of Churches This organization of Protestant and Orthodox churches formed in 1948 and joined by Roman Catholic members after the Vatican II (1969) provided a forum for the discussion of matters of mutual concern in the religious, social, economic and political spheres. The council has been particularly concerned with the problems of the Third World – causing some scandal by its support of armed liberation movements – and has been a vocal opponent of apartheid.

World Court see **International Court of Justice**

World Health Organization A specialized UN agency. It was founded on 7 April 1948 with the aim of aiding 'the attainment by all peoples of the highest possible levels of health'. Full membership is not confined to members of the UN but open to all sovereign states, and associate membership is open to non-self-governing territories. The WHO is the successor of the Health Office of the League of Nations (1923).

World War I Precipitated by the assassination of the Archduke Franz Ferdinand at Sarajevo, World War I had its origins in the mutual suspicions and rivalries of the European powers. The French sought revenge on Germany for the humiliations of 1870; the Austrians feared the influence of Pan-Slavism on their domains; Britain feared the commercial, colonial and naval challenge of imperial Germany, while a confident and expansionist Germany saw in war a means of world domination. These factors were intensified by the reversal of alliances by which Britain was allied with its traditional enemies and rivals, France and Russia, and Germany was the ally of Austria-Hungary. In consequence, when the Serbs refused an Austrian ultimatum and Austria declared war (28 July), Russia mobilized in support of Serbia and Germany declared war on Russia in support of Austria (1 August) and on Russia's ally, France, on 3 August. German violation of Belgian neutrality brought Britain's declaration (4 August) and the three Allies declared war on Austia-Hungary on the 5, 11 and 13 of August respectively. Having allowed German warships to take refuge in the Bosphorus, Turkey was brought into the war on the side of the Central Powers on 29 October 1914.

The main theatres of war were the eastern and western fronts in Europe and the Balkans, but in addition the Japanese (who declared war on 23 August) captured Germany's concessions and colonies in China and the Pacific. Britain campaigned against the Turks in Mesopotamia and Palestine and against the German colonies in East and Southwest Africa, failing to defeat the Germans in the former but capturing the latter (1915); and Anglo-French and Franco-Belgian forces took the German West African colonies Togo (1914) and the Cameroons (1916).

The war at sea took the form of an Allied blockade of the Central Powers, raids on merchant shipping by German surface vessels and (until the introduction of the convoy system in 1918) an increasingly successful counterblockade by unrestricted German submarine warfare. In 1914 the German Pacific squadron annihilated its British counterpart at the battle of Coronel, only to share the same fate in the battle of the Falklands. The British grand fleet won minor victories at the Heligoland Bight (1914) and the Dogger Bank (1915), but the German high seas fleet, whose growth had caused such alarm, returned to port after the Battle of Jutland (1916), mutinied (1918) and scuttled itself in Scapa Flow after the armistice.

The European War. Operating on interior lines, the strategy of the Central Powers was to hold one front while concentrating strength to deliver the decisive blow on the other. Accordingly, while Hindenburg's victory at Tannenberg and that of von Mackensen at the Masurian Lakes halted the Russians in the east, the main German thrust was through Belgium in an endeavour to outflank the French, capture Paris and achieve a lightning victory. By compromising the original Schlieffen plan and turning too soon on Paris, the Germans exposed their own flank and were defeated in the battles of the Marne and the Aisne. Both sides now engaged in 'the race to the sea' and when the British defeated the final German attempt to turn their northern flank at the first Battle of Ypres open warfare ended and both sides settled down to siege warfare in trench lines running from the North Sea to the Swiss frontier.

On the eastern front the Russian offensive, held by the Germans, had gained ground against the Austro-Hungarians in Galicia and captured Lemberg, while in the Balkans the initial successes of the Austrians over the Serbs had been balanced by the victories at Cers and Rudnik and the recapture of Belgrade. Such successes were short-lived. In 1915, while their armies held the British attacks at Neuve Chapelle (March), Ypres (April) and Loos (September) and the French offensives in the Champagne (February, September) and in the Artois (May), the Central Powers drove the Russians out of Poland and Lithuania, regained ground in Galicia and, having put half the Russian army out of action, occupied the line they would hold at the time of the Treaty of Brest-Litovsk. The entry of Bulgaria on their side enabled their forces to eliminate Serbia (October); a Franco-British force sent to Salonika to support the Serbs was ineffectual. Equally vain were efforts to force the Straits and bring aid to Russia, first by the passage of a fleet through the Dardanelles and, when this failed, by landings (April) on the Gallipoli peninsula to take Constantinople. After bitter fighting and heavy casualties the force was withdrawn by early 1916.

1916 was a year of senseless carnage on the western front. Continuous attacks and counterattacks on Verdun from February to December cost the French 360,000 men and the Germans 335,000, and in the Anglo-French offensive on the Somme (July-November) the losses were 600,000 and 267,000 respectively. On the Eastern Front Brusilov's offensive against the Austro-Hungarians (June-August) failed from lack of munitions after brilliant initial success. Romania, which had entered the war on the Allied side, was as rapidly knocked out but the Italians, who had declared war on the Central Powers in 1915, were able to defeat Austrian attacks on the Isonzo.

In March 1917 the German armies on the western front withdrew to the prepared defences of the Hindenburg line and, although the Canadians took Vimy Ridge, the Allied attack at Arras (April) failed, while at Cambrai the initial success of the tanks could not be exploited. Meanwhile the failure of Nivelle's offensive at the Chemin des Dames lowered French morale to the point of mutiny. In order to relieve pressure on the French, British and Canadian troops continued their attacks on Passchendaele in the third Battle of Ypres in the face of impossible weather conditions and incurred 300,000 casualties (July-November). In Italy the Austrians won the battle of Caporetto and a Franco-British force had to be sent to support the shattered Italians. On the eastern front, despite some success in Galicia (July), the appalling losses suffered by the Russians had broken their morale. After the October Revolution a truce was agreed (November).

Russia had been knocked out of the war, but in 1917 the United States had joined the Allies. By the end of the year the first American troops had landed in France and 1918 was a race between their arrival and the transfer of troops from the eastern front for the final German offensive. In the event the Germans were able to launch their grand attack in March, overwhelming the British 5th Army and driving for the Channel ports. But the Allied lines held and in a series of counterattacks, of which Haig's troops bore the brunt, the Allies defeated and drove back the German armies until the Armistice (11 November). On the Italian front, the Allies crossed the Piave (June) and, by the victory of Vittorio Veneto (October), forced the Austrians to an armistice (3 November). In the Balkans, Franchet-d'Esperey's Franco-British forces forced Bulgaria to capitulate (19 September), threatened Constantinople and brought the Turks to accept an armistice (30 October).

The War With Turkey. In addition to the Gallipoli campaign (*above*), the Russians fought the Turks with mixed fortunes in the Caucasus, and British and Dominion troops were engaged on two fronts. In 1914 an expeditionary force, landed to protect British interests in the Persian Gulf, advanced within 24 miles of Baghdad (November 1915), but was driven back and besieged at Kut (December), finally surrendering in April 1916. Fresh forces engaged the Turks, took Baghdad (1917) and by the armistice had reached the borders of Turkey and Syria. In Egypt a Turkish attack on the Suez Canal was repulsed (February 1915) and by August 1916 the Turks had been driven from Sinai to the Palestine frontier. In April 1917 Allenby launched the campaign which, with the aid of T. E. Lawrence's Arab irregulars, was to clear the Turks from Palestine (Jerusalem captured 9 December 1917) and Syria and win the final victory at Megiddo (September 1918).

During World War I the major developments in land warfare were the use of chemical weapons (poison gases and flame-throwers) and of the tank. At sea there were mines and torpedoes and submarine warfare; but the most significant development was that of aircraft – from frail unarmed reconnaissance machines in 1914 to an arm which could be used in close support of land or naval operations (on aircraft carriers) and for long-range strategic bombing.

Peace treaties with the defeated Central Powers were: Versailles (Germany, 28 June 1919); St Germain (Austria, 10 September 1919); Neuilly (Bulgaria, 27 November 1919); Trianon (Hungary, 6 June 1920); and Sèvres (Turkey, 10 August 1920 – superseded by the Treaty of Lausanne, 24 July 1923).

The belligerents raised between them some 65 million men and lost about 8.5 million dead and 2.1 million wounded, while some 10 million civilians are believed to have perished either in the war itself or in the Spanish influenza epidemic which followed. The war destroyed the German and Russian empires and broke up the Dual Monarchy.

World War II The immediate cause of the war was the German invasion of Poland (1 September 1939). France and Britain were treaty-bound to come to Poland's defence and declared war on Germany (3 September). The attack on Poland was the culmination of Hitler's expansionist programme which had remilitarized the Rhineland (1936), acquired Austria through the Anschluss (1938) and annexed Czechoslovakia after the Munich Agreements (1938). The risk of war on two fronts having been eliminated by the Nazi-Soviet Pact (August 1939), Poland was rapidly overrun and partitioned between Germany and the USSR.

In the west came the 'phoney war', with no more than patrol action until April 1940 when the Germans occupied Denmark and Norway. An Anglo-French force landed in Norway on 14 April but was forced to withdraw on 2 May. In consequence of their defeat Chamberlain was replaced as prime minister by Churchill. On 10 May the German panzers turned the Maginot line by striking through the Ardennes and rapidly reached the Channel coast, cutting off the BEF and the French troops who had advanced to meet the simultaneous invasion of Belgium and the Netherlands. The Dutch capitulated on 15 May, the Belgians on 28 May, and during 27 May–4 June the BEF was evacuated from the beaches of Dunkirk. Between the 4–8 June the Germans broke down the last French defences; the government fled to Bordeaux and signed an armistice (22 June), under which the north and west were occupied, central, southern and southeastern France, the so-called free zone, being governed by Pétain's Vichy regime.

As a preliminary to his invasion of Britain Hitler sought to establish air control but was defeated in the Battle of Britain (July-October). Instead he turned to night bombing and to a submarine blockade in the Battle of the Atlantic which grew in intensity, long-range aircraft and wolf-pack tactics taking an increasing toll of shipping. Only after May 1943 (when 108 ships were sunk for the loss of one U-boat) did countermeasures begin to take effect and by 1944 the battle was won.

Mediterranean War. In June 1940 Italy entered the war and, although by August it had occupied British Somaliland and crossed the borders of Egypt, the Sudan and Kenya, between December 1940 and January 1941 Marshal Graziani had been routed in the Western Desert. During January–May Wavell's troops liberated Ethiopia and forced an Italian surrender in East Africa.

The Royal Navy meanwhile had neutralized the French fleet by the bombardment of Mers-el-Kebir and the internment of the squadron at Alexandria and immobilized much of the Italian fleet when torpedo aircraft attacked its base at Taranto (1940) and inflicted further loss at the battle of Cape Matapan (1941). Despite constant air attack, Malta remained unconquered and from it crippling attacks were launched on the convoys supplying the Axis forces in North Africa. Although preoccupied by his plans to invade Russia, Hitler as a preliminary sent forces to support the Italians whose invasion of Greece (October 1940) had been driven back into Albania. Yugoslavia was invaded and occupied (9 April) and by the end of April the Germans had defeated the Greek army, occupied the country and forced the evacuation of the small British expeditionary force. Between 20 May and 1 June, an airborne invasion seized Crete. On 14 February Rommel's Afrika Korps had landed in North Africa and, weakened by the Greek expedition, Wavell's forces had by 12 April been driven back to the Egyptian frontier. He left a garrison at Tobruk which withstood siege until relieved by Auchinleck's November offensive, which regained Cyrenaica, only to be driven back in 1942. Only his defensive victory at El Alamein (June 1942) saved Egypt.

1941 marked a turning point. In June Hitler invaded the USSR and in December the Japanese attack on Pearl Harbor (*see below*) brought the United States into the war.

The Eastern Front. Despite British warnings the Red Army was taken by surprise when the Germans launched Operation Barbarossa on 21 June 1941, postponed from 15 May by their Balkan operations. The Germans and their allies swept forward on a wide front which, by the end of the year, had carried them to Leningrad in the north and to the Crimea in the south. Zhukov halted them before Moscow and regained some ground, but in 1942 the German advance continued, occupying the Crimea, pressing into the Caucasus and reaching the Volga at Stalingrad (September).

War in the Pacific and the Far East. On 7 December 1941 the Japanese attacked Pearl Harbor, crippling the US Pacific fleet with the fortunate exception of its aircraft carriers, and invaded Malaya and the Philippines where the fortress of Corregidor held out until May 1942. In December Guam, Wake Island and the Gilberts had been seized. By January 1942 the Japanese had conquered Malaya; in February Singapore fell; the Dutch East Indies had been overrun by March and Burma by May 1942. In January New Guinea was invaded and by July, with the capture of Guadalcanal and the Aleutians, the furthest point of Japanese conquest had been reached. But the tide had already been turned by American naval victories in the battles of the Coral Sea (May) and Midway (June), the latter decisive by its destruction of Japanese naval air power.

In August 1942 MacArthur began his 'island-hopping' counterattack from Guadalcanal, until in 1945 he had taken the Japanese islands of Iwojima (February) and Okinawa (April) and was poised to invade

Japan, having in the meantime cleared New Guinea, won the naval victory of Leyte Gulf and returned to the Philippines. In Burma the final Japanese thrust had been halted at Kohima and Imphal (1944). Slim's 14th Army then fought its way back into Burma, recapturing Rangoon (May 1945). In August 1945 atom bombs were dropped on Hiroshima and Nagasaki and on 14 August Japan surrendered.

Victory in Europe. 1942 marked the turning-point of the war in the USSR and North Africa as it had done in the Pacific. In North Africa Montgomery defeated Rommel at El Alamein (October) and in November the Allies landed in Morocco and Algeria. The respective armies converged in Tunisia, following up the defeated Axis forces (May 1943) by the conquest of Sicily (July-August) and the invasion of Italy (surrendered 8 September). However, the decisive action took place at Stalingrad where the Red Army's counter-offensive forced the surrender of the German 6th Army (2 February 1943) and began the series of victories which would take the Russians to the Elbe. Following the decisive tank battle of Kursk (July) the Red Army entered the Ukraine, recapturing Kiev (November), and by January 1944 had also raised the siege of Leningrad and reached the Polish frontier. Allied support for the Soviets had taken the form of saturation bombing of Germany and of the supply of war materials, heavy losses being suffered on the Arctic convoys.

The second front was opened by the Normandy landings (6 June 1944). After bitter fighting the Allied forces broke out of the beachhead, liberating Paris (25 August) and effecting a junction (12 September) with the forces which had landed in Provence (15 August). Belgium was liberated (September), but the plan to cross the Rhine and sweep across the North German plain was abandoned after the failure of the airborne attack on Arnhem (September).

In the east, the Red Army forced the capitulation of Finland (19 September) and Romania (12 September), entered Sofia on 18 September and effected a junction with Tito's partisans in Yugoslavia (15 September). Belgrade was liberated (20 October), but in Hungary the Germans held out in Budapest until 13 February 1945.

In December 1944 von Rundstedt launched the final German offensive in the Ardennes and was pushed back after fierce fighting in the Battle of the Bulge. In Italy German forces put up a stubborn resistance to the Allied advance up the peninsula at Anzio and Monte Cassino before the fall of Rome (June 1944). In January 1945 the Red Army entered East Prussia and Czechoslovakia; in March the Allies crossed the Rhine and forced the surrender of the German armies in the Ruhr (17 April); on 20 April the Red Army smashed the Oder-Neisse defences and entered Berlin (22 April); on 25 April Patton's men met Koniev's troops on the Elbe; on 29 April the German armies in Italy surrendered and on the following day Hitler committed suicide in Berlin. On 8 May the unconditional surrender of Germany was ratified in Berlin.

Some 92 millions were probably mobilized by the belligerents and estimates for the war dead – including civilians – vary from 35 to 60 millions. The proportion of civilians to service personnel was higher than in World War I because of indiscriminate air attacks and the murderous policies of the Nazi regime which killed some 5.7 million Jews in the holocaust. One consequence of the war was the disappearance of the British, Dutch and French colonial empires.

Y

Yahya Khan, Agha Muhammad (1917–80), Pakistani soldier and president. He served in the Middle East and Italy in World War II, and after independence fought in Kashmir. As chief of general staff (1957–62) he helped to bring Ayub Khan to power (1962). As C-in-C of the Pakistan army (1966) he was appointed martial law administrator and assumed the presidency (1969) but his efforts to preserve the unity of the country were thwarted by Awami League success in the 1970 election. After the secession of Bangladesh he resigned, retiring from public life after release from house arrest (1972–74).

Yalta Conference The meeting at the Crimean resort (4–11 February 1945) at which Stalin agreed to the proposals of Churchill and Roosevelt that the USSR should drop its objections to the creation of the UN, join the war against Japan after the defeat of Germany, and accept the creation of occupation zones in Germany which included the French. In return, Polish frontiers were defined on the Oder-Neisse and Curzon Lines and central Europe and the Balkans (except Greece) were conceded to be a Soviet sphere of influence.

Yamomoto, Isoroku (1984–1943), Japanese naval officer. As C-in-C of the combined fleet he planned and executed the attack on Pearl Harbor (1941) and was defeated at the Battle of Midway (1942). Regarded as a dangerous adversary, he was killed when his aircraft was ambushed and destroyed over the Solomon Islands, his movements having been plotted by American code-breakers.

Yemen comprises two Middle East republics. (1) **Yemen Arab Republic** (North Yemen), where Seidi Imam Yahya ibn Mohammad came to power in 1918 and ruled until he and two of his sons were killed in a revolt (1948). His eldest son the Imam Ahmed regained control, joined the UAR (1958–61) and obtained aid from the Soviet bloc for his anti-British activities. On his death (1962) the Arab republic was proclaimed, but the country relapsed into a state of civil war (1962–70) in which the opposing factions were backed by Saudi Arabia and Egypt. There followed a period of political instability until July 1978 when the current president, Colonel Ali Abdullah Saleh, came to power. In 1984 oil deposits were discovered and agreement was later reached with the United States to assist in their exploitation. Long-standing discussion for possible union with South Yemen (*see below*) continued fruitless, given its disturbed political state.

(2) **The People's Democratic Republic of Yemen** comprises the former Crown Colony (1937) of Aden and the desert hinterland. The importance of Aden as a British naval base declined with the withdrawal of Britain from the Far East after World War II and in 1967, following two years of guerrilla warfare, Britain withdrew and the People's Republic was formed. It was given its present name in 1970 when a new and more strictly Marxist regime came to power. Personal and political rivalries which had simmered in the ruling elite erupted in 1986 when the president tried to eliminate one of his predecessors, but was himself forced to flee to North Yemen in the short but savage civil war which followed.

Yom Kippur War   In October 1973 Egypt and Syria launched a surprise attack on Israel on the Day of Atonement (Yom Kippur) which came within an ace of victory. Thanks to an airlift of weapons and ammunition from the United States, Israel was enabled to launch a counteroffensive which swept into southern Syria, crossed the Suez Canal and trapped an Egyptian army on its eastern bank. An oil embargo imposed by OPEC on the west forced a cease-fire and Israeli withdrawal.

Yoshida, Shigeru   (1878–1967), Japanese prime minister. A diplomat and former ambassador to Britain, imprisoned (1944) for urging Japan to seek peace, he became foreign minister in the first post-war government and then prime minister for virtually the entire period 1946–54. He introduced the constitutional, political and economic structures which have been the basis of subsequent Japanese stability and prosperity.

Young Plan   After the failure of the Dawes Plan for German reparations the plan of the US industrialist, Owen D. Young (1874–1962), was adopted (1930) to scale down the amount of reparations and phase repayment over a set period. The plan became a dead letter almost immediately in consequence of the Depression. Hitler repudiated reparations after he came to power (1933).

Young Turk Revolution   The rising led by a group of reformist army officers belonging to the movement revived in 1903, which overthrew the sultan, Abdul Hamid (1908–09). The leaders, Enver Pasha, Mehmed Talaat (1874–1921) and Ahmed Djemal (1872–1922), dominated the liberal politicians when the 1876 constitution was restored and a parliament summoned. They grew more powerful after the Balkan Wars and strengthened the ties with Germany which brought Turkey into World War I on the side of the Central Powers.

Yugoslavia Balkan federal republic. It was formed in 1918 as the Kingdom of the Serbs, Croats and Slovenes, following agreement by their national representatives at the Corfu Conference (1917). The initiative had come from Serbia, a Turkish province (1521) granted autonomy (1829) and independence (1878). Its ruling Prince Milan proclaimed himself king (1882), but his Obrenovic dynasty perished with the assassinations of Alexander and his Queen (1903). His successor, Peter I Karadjordjevic, and his premier, Pasic, formed the Balkan League and emerged victorious from the Balkan Wars, but their pan-Slav policy alarmed Austria-Hungary and was a major cause of World War I. Serbia initially repelled the Austrian invasion, but was overwhelmed when Bulgaria joined the Central Powers (1915). Serbia was the dominant force in the new country, whose name was changed to Yugoslavia (1931) under the dictatorial rule of Alexander I of the Serbian royal family. His assassination (1934) was instigated by Ante Pavelic's Ustase movement, epitomizing the strains in the new state between the dominant Orthodox Serbs and the Catholic Croats and Slovenes (former members of the Dual Monarchy). Under the regency of Prince Paul Yugoslavia moved more closely into the Axis orbit and it was the overthrow of the regent which prompted the German invasion (1941). After a bitter guerrilla war in which Tito eliminated the royalist Mihajlovic and liberated the country from Axis forces, Yugoslavia became a Communist state.

The future of Trieste was a potential flashpoint between Yugoslavia and the west until agreement was reached in 1954 and Tito supported the Communist guerrillas operating in northern Greece until his breach (1948) with Stalin, who resented the independence of the Yugoslav party. Tito liberalized the regime without completely relinquishing party political and economic control. After his death (1980) the defects of the system became apparent. Political cohesion was lost in a leadership which rotated between the federal chiefs and an economy which was neither state-controlled nor a genuine free market enjoyed the worst of both systems. In 1988 the problems of a stagnant economy and a sharply rising rate of inflation were compounded by ethnic unrest. Claims that Serbs were being harassed by the Albanian majority in the autonomous Kosovo region of the Serbian republic roused strong Serbian emotions. The (Albanian) party leaders in Kosovo were dismissed (1988) and, after severe rioting (1989), arrested on charges of separatism, and the autonomous powers of the province were strictly curtailed. Unrest continued, while Croats, Slovenes and Montenegrins all grew concerned at this resurgence of Serb hegemony.

Z

Zaghlul Pasha   see **Wafd**

Zaïre   Central African republic. During the 1870s the International Association of the Congo (an organization formed to hide the interests of Leopold II of Belgium) began operations in the area and by 1885 Leopold was able to proclaim the Independent State of the Congo, of which he was head. In return for loans granted by the Belgian parliament (1889, 1895) to finance its exploitation, Belgium was given the right to annex the Congo in 1901, but did not exercise it until 1908, by which time reports were widely circulated of gross abuses by the companies to whom Leopold had granted concessions. Within the colony, known as the Belgian Congo, the worst of these abuses were removed, but the colonial administration failed to provide more than primary education for the Africans, and white settlers were the dominant force. The post-World War II tide of African autonomy and independence created (1955) a nationalist movement led by Joseph Kasavubu (1910–69) and Patrice Lumumba. The authorities panicked in the face of violent nationalist unrest (1959) and hastily granted independence to the Republic of the Congo (1960).

With the departure of the Belgian administrators there was a complete breakdown of government. Belgian troops were flown in to protect their nationals from attack and a UN peacekeeping force was sent. Colonel Mobutu now seized power, Kasavubu was forced from office and Lumumba was handed over to the secessionists in Katanga and murdered (1961). Kasavubu returned to power in 1961 and with UN aid overcame Moise Tshombe's regime in Katanga. When UN forces were withdrawn (1964) an alliance between Kasavubu and Tshombe provoked widespread revolt. Mobutu once more returned (1965) to a power which he has maintained despite revolts (1966, 1967, 1978). In 1971, under his policy of Africanization, the republic was renamed Zaïre. Relations with Belgium (to which Zaïre was heavily in debt) remained strained after independence and reached their nadir early in 1989.

Zambia   Independent Central African Commonwealth country. The territory was administered by Cecil Rhodes's British South Africa Company (1890–1924) when it became the crown colony of Northern Rhodesia.

African labour brought in to exploit the copper deposits (discovered in the 1920s) was subjected to much discrimination and reacted by strike action (1935, 1940, 1956) and by the formation of the Northern Rhodesia African Congress (1948). Its moderate leadership was unable to prevent the formation of the Federation of Rhodesia and Nyasaland (1953–63) and made way for Kenneth Kaunda's militant United National Independence Party, which gained independence for the region as the Republic of Zambia (24 October 1964).

Kaunda has remained continuously in power ever since, a firm opponent of apartheid and supporter of African liberation movements. His application of sanctions against the Smith regime in Rhodesia caused economic problems, aggravated by the fall in world copper prices, and Zambia is faced by the difficulties inherent in diversifying from mining to agriculture. Zambia has been a single-party state since 1971 when the opposition United Progressive Party was banned and when all political parties except UNIP were outlawed.

Zanzibar East African island forming, with Tanganyika, the republic of Tanzania. It was formerly ruled by sultans whose mainland territories were incorporated into Tanganyika (then German), Kenya and Italian Somaliland, when Britain obtained a protectorate by treaty (1890). Rule was exercised through the sultan by a British consul-general (1890–1913) and resident (1913–63). In 1963 Zanzibar gained first self-government and then independence, with the sultan as head of state. In 1964 John Okello led a revolt of the African population which forced the sultan into exile and ended Arab dominance. A militant left-wing government nationalized the land, imposed one-party rule and merged with Tanganyika to form Tanzania.

Zapata, Emiliano (c1879–1919), Mexican revolutionary. He supported Madero against Porfirio Díaz (1910) on a programme of land reform, for which he later fought Madero, Huerta and also Carranza by whose emissaries he was treacherously murdered. His call for the return of Indian land to his fellow Indians won him wide support and for long he controlled wide areas of the country. He was the inspiration of the agrarian and Indian cultural movements at the heart of Mexican revolutionary nationalism, a legend in his lifetime and a folk hero after his death.

Zhivkov, Todor (1911–   ), Bulgarian president. He joined the Communist Party (1932) and served as partisan leader during World War II, leading the coup which overthrew the monarchy (1948). First secretary of the party (1954), he was prime minister (1962–71) and president (1971–   ) of Bulgaria, which he maintained as the faithful ally of the USSR.

Zhukov, Georgi Konstantinovich (1896–1974), Soviet marshal. He joined the Red Army (1918) after service in World War I and distinguished himself in the civil war (1918–20). After graduating from the Frunze Military Academy in 1931 he served as an adviser to the Republicans in the Spanish civil war (1937–38) and commanded the armoured forces in Manchuria which defeated the Japanese (1938–39). After the Russo–Finnish war (1939–40) he became chief of staff of the Red Army, deputy commissar for defence and candidate member of the Politburo. The outstanding Soviet commander in World War II, he held the German attack on Moscow (1941), mounted the Stalingrad counteroffensive (1942), led the relief of Leningrad (1943), commanded the offensives which crossed the Czech frontier (March 1944) and reached the suburbs of Warsaw (August). However, on Stalin's orders he did not capture the city until January 1945 when the uprising had been crushed. Having captured Berlin (May 1945) he signed the German surrender and became C-in-C of Soviet occupation forces (1945–46). He was demoted by Stalin but promoted to defence minister by Khrushchev (1955), who stripped him of office two years later. He was rehabilitated after the fall of Khrushchev (1965).

Zia ul-Haq, Mohammed (1924–88), Pakistani soldier and president. Promoted general and chief of staff (1976) by Zulfikar Ali Bhutto, he overthrew his patron in the violence after the disputed 1977 election, tried him and had him hanged for conspiracy to murder. General Zia now assumed the presidency, (1978), banned political parties and trade unions and controlled the media under martial law which remained in force until 1985, when public discontent forced him to allow non-party elections (1986). A devout Muslim, Zia strongly supported the mujahedin guerrilla movement against Soviet occupation of Afghanistan. He was killed in an air crash in August 1988, when facing considerable political pressure from Bhutto's daughter, Benazir.

Zimbabwe Independent Central African Commonwealth country. Until 1923 the area was administerd by Cecil Rhodes' British South Africa Company which obtained a charter (1889), sent settlers (1890) who founded Fort Salisbury (now Harare) and defeated the Ndebele (1893, 1896–97) and the Shona (1896–97). The white settlers having rejected union with South Africa in a referendum (1922), the area became the self-governing colony of Southern Rhodesia, which in 1953 joined the Federation of Rhodesia and Nyasaland. African rights had always been ignored and when the United Federal Party made modest proposals for African political advancement it was defeated by the white-supremacist

Rhodesian Front in the 1962 elections. In consequence of their victory and those of African nationalist movements among its other members, the Federation collapsed in 1963. In 1964 Ian Smith became leader of the Rhodesian Front, won the 1965 elections and, when negotiations with Britain broke down, made a unilateral declaration of independence (UDI). Britain made ineffectual efforts to end UDI and when it requested the UN to impose sanctions (1969), Smith retaliated by making Rhodesia a republic (1970). After the collapse of further talks (1971), with South African support Rhodesia held its own against sanctions and the guerrilla attacks of the Patriotic Alliance of Joshua Nkomo and Robert Mugabe until 1979. Withdrawal of South African support and pressure from the United States led to talks at which terms were agreed for a cease-fire and free elections. As a result, Robert Mugabe's ZANU came to power, Mugabe being declared first president of the Republic of Zimbabwe, proclaimed on April 17 1980. The constitution in force provided for reserved white representation, but Mugabe skilfully manoeuvred the opposition until he could obtain the necessary two-thirds majority to change the constitution and make Zimbabwe a one-party state (1987).

Zimmermann Telegram The instructions from the German foreign minister, Arthur Zimmermann (1864–1940), to his ambassador in Washington that, in the event of America entering World War I, Mexico should be incited to attack it on the promise of restoration of the territories lost in the 1848 war. Intercepted and deciphered by British intelligence, the telegram was passed to President Wilson who released it to the press on 1 March 1917. It strongly influenced US public opinion against Germany and, combined with the outrage felt at unrestricted German submarine warfare, helped to bring America into the war on the Allied side (6 April 1917).

Zinoviev Letter The extracts from a letter from the chairman of the Comintern, Zinoviev (Grigori Evseyevich Apfelbaum, 1883–1936), urging members of the British Communist Party to sedition and revolution, which appeared in the British press on 25 October 1924. Although it was claimed that the letter was a forgery, publication was held responsible for the defeat of the Labour Party in the election held later that year.

Zionism A 19th-century Jewish cultural movement turned to political ends by Theodore Herzl, who called the first World Zionist Congress (1897) with the aim of creating a Jewish national state as a refuge against persecution. Feeling that such a state must be founded in Palestine, delegates at the 1905 Congress rejected the offer made by the British government of a national home in Uganda. Under Chaim Weizmann, advocates of Zionism obtained the Balfour Declaration from the British government (1917) and during the British mandate were able to promote Jewish settlement in Palestine from 1920 on a scale which was to rouse Palestinian fears and provoke the Arab revolt (1937). Since the formation of the state of Israel (1948), the World Zionist Congress has been seen as an international pressure group supporting the policies of the Israeli government. As such, it has been denounced by Arab governments, and Zionism itself has even been condemned in the general assembly of the UN as 'a form of racism and racial domination' (10 November 1975).